The South China Sea Dispute as International Law and Politics

Maritime Cooperation in East Asia

Series Editors

Seokwoo Lee (*Inha University Law School*)
Keyuan Zou (*University of Central Lancashire*)

VOLUME 13

The titles published in this series are listed at *brill.com/mcea*

The South China Sea Dispute as International Law and Politics

Discovering the Role of Law in Times of Power Shift

By

Youngmin Seo

BRILL | NIJHOFF

LEIDEN | BOSTON

Library of Congress Cataloging-in-Publication Data

Names: Seo, Youngmin, author.
Title: The South China Sea dispute as international law and politics : discovering the role of law in times of power shift / by Youngmin Seo.
Description: Boston, Massachusetts : Brill, [2024] | Series: Maritime cooperation in East Asia, 2405-934X ; volume 13 | Includes bibliographical references and index. | Contents: The facts and the formal law – The South China Sea dispute as law-fare – The South China Sea dispute from the perspective of international relations theories – What should international law do for the South China Sea dispute?
Identifiers: LCCN 2024004721 (print) | LCCN 2024004722 (ebook) | ISBN 9789004696341 (hardback : acid-free paper) | ISBN 9789004696358 (e-book)
Subjects: LCSH: South China Sea–International status. | South China Sea–Claims. | Law of the sea–South China Sea. | Dispute resolution (Law)–Southeast Asia. | China–Foreign relations–Southeast Asia. | Southeast Asia–Foreign relations–China.
Classification: LCC KZA1692 .S46 2024 (print) | LCC KZA1692 (ebook) | DDC 341.4/2–dc23/eng/20240209
LC record available at https://lccn.loc.gov/2024004721
LC ebook record available at https://lccn.loc.gov/2024004722

Typeface for the Latin, Greek, and Cyrillic scripts: "Brill". See and download: brill.com/brill-typeface.

ISSN 2405-934X
ISBN 978-90-04-69634-1 (hardback)
ISBN 978-90-04-69635-8 (e-book)
DOI 10.1163/9789004696358

This book is printed on acid-free paper and produced in a sustainable manner.

Contents

Preface

The South China Sea, a region steeped in history, geopolitics, and international law, has emerged as one of the most contentious and challenging arenas of our time. The territorial and maritime disputes that simmer beneath its azure waters have defied easy resolution, capturing the world's attention and evoking concerns about regional stability and the future of international relations.

In this book, "The South China Sea Dispute as International Law and Politics: Discovering the Role of Law in Times of Power Shift," I embark on a comprehensive examination of the legal resolution of the South China Sea dispute through the lens of international relations theories. While the international law of the sea is designed to regulate the behavior of states at sea, the enduring complexities of the South China Sea dispute persist despite the United Nations Convention on the Law of the Sea (UNCLOS) and the earnest efforts of international legal scholars to propose a peaceful resolution. This intractable conflict is further compounded by the growing rivalry between the United States and China in Indo-Pacific, making the prospects of a peaceful resolution increasingly uncertain. In light of the fact that international law operates within the context of international politics, any legal proposals must be evaluated against the backdrop of political scientists' analyses.

The book commences with an exploration of the formal legal frameworks governing territorial and maritime disputes in the South China Sea, followed by an examination of the differing legal perspectives between China and the Western world concerning the international legal system, the Law of the Sea regime, and the South China Sea dispute. I delve into the effectiveness of the UNCLOS system and the urgent need to clarify its core institutions. Additionally, this book investigates how political scientists view the South China Sea dispute through the theoretical lenses of realism, liberalism, and constructivism. The analyses and predictions derived from each of these theoretical approaches offer valuable insights for international lawyers. Realism highlights the need for international law to adapt to shifting power dynamics while proactively preventing potential hegemonic conflicts between China and the United States. In contrast, liberalism and constructivism advocate for collective efforts within international law to promote cooperation in the region. Both theories propose a well-designed regional maritime regime as an effective approach to managing and resolving territorial and maritime disputes in the South China Sea.

This book not only presents a theoretical framework but also offers practical suggestions for how the international law of the sea can play a role in mitigating the South China Sea dispute. These recommendations include recognizing the evolving power balance between China and the United States through bilateral agreements or amendments within the UNCLOS framework. Furthermore, it is proposed that the disputants and stakeholders consider establishing a soft law regime, akin to the Arctic Council for the Arctic Ocean conflict, which may be called the "South China Sea Council," to facilitate cooperation and dispute resolution.

It is essential to emphasize that this book does not claim to provide all-encompassing solutions to this intricate and pressing problem. Instead, it serves as a steppingstone for further discourse, debate, and policy considerations. It is my hope that the insights presented in these pages will contribute to the ongoing efforts of international lawyers, scholars, policymakers, and practitioners who are tirelessly seeking a peaceful and lawful resolution to the South China Sea dispute.

As I navigate the turbulent waters of international relations and international law, I am guided by the principles of cooperation, diplomacy, legitimacy, and a shared commitment to the peaceful resolution of disputes. While the South China Sea dispute poses a formidable challenge, it also offers an opportunity—an opportunity to underscore the enduring value of international law and the capacity of nations to collaborate for the common good.

This book is intended to serve as a compass for all those who are determined to chart a course towards a more stable and harmonious future in the South China Sea and beyond during these times of shifting power dynamics.

Acknowledgements

My journey toward this book, "The South China Sea Dispute as International Law and Politics," has been a voyage through diverse and enriching experiences. From my tenure at the Ministry of Foreign Affairs of the Republic of Korea to my role as a diplomat in Los Angeles and Bangladesh, and the valuable insights gathered from my engagement in multilateral and bilateral diplomatic processes, this journey has deeply enriched my understanding of international relations and the vital role of international law. In this process, I have benefited immensely from my time away from my role in the Korean Foreign Ministry, which allowed me to dedicate myself fully to this endeavor. I am profoundly grateful to the exceptional individuals who have contributed to my academic and professional development.

Foremost, I extend my heartfelt appreciation to my dissertation committee members at the University of California at Berkeley School of Law—Professor John C. Yoo, Professor Katerina Linos, and Professor Vinod K. Aggarwal. Their unwavering support, insightful guidance, and intellectual mentorship have been immeasurable throughout my research and writing journey. Each of them played a unique and indispensable role in shaping this work. Professor Yoo, as the principal supervisor for my JSD, demonstrated remarkable brevity in pinpointing research questions and providing guidance for further scholarly exploration. Professor Aggarwal's expertise in international relations theory has proven instrumental in my understanding how such theories can facilitate the legal resolution of international disputes. Professor Linos, an international lawyer, demonstrated how to leverage international politics in devising practical legal approaches to real-world conflicts.

At the heart of this academic endeavor, my wife, Eunhee Yoon, has been a steady source of inspiration and encouragement. Her unfailing support, especially during the trying times of the Covid-19 pandemic during which I conducted my JSD research, served as a driving force behind the completion of this book. Her belief in me has been a constant wellspring of strength.

I must also acknowledge my mentors, Professor Seok Hyun Kim, ITLOS Judge Zha Hyoung Rhee, Ambassador Sun Pyo Kim, and Ambassador Jong In Bae of the Korean Foreign Ministry. Their guidance, challenges, and continued support have been pivotal in shaping my academic and professional trajectory.

This book is a testament to the collective contributions of these exceptional individuals and the enduring spirit of international cooperation and diplomacy. My hope is that the insights shared within these pages will advance ongoing discourse and policy considerations related to the South China Sea dispute, ultimately guiding us toward a more stable and harmonious future.

Figures and Tables

Figures

Tables

Acronyms

UNCLOS	United Nations Convention on the Law of the Sea
CHAPTER	Likely referring to chapters in a legal document
US	United States
SCS	South China Sea
DOD	Department of Defense (U.S.)
ICJ	International Court of Justice
EEZ	Exclusive Economic Zone
PLA	People's Liberation Army (China)
UN	United Nations
CLCS	Continental Shelf Commission
ITLOS	International Tribunal for the Law of the Sea
ILC	International Law Commission
WTO	World Trade Organization
CE	May refer to a legal entity
ADIZ	Air Defense Identification Zone
CSIS	Center for Strategic and International Studies
OPNAVINST	Operational Navy Instructions (U.S. Navy)
RSIS	S. Rajaratnam School of International Studies
NDCP	National Defense College of the Philippines
MIT	Massachusetts Institute of Technology
NY	New York
ASIL	American Society of International Law
RCEP	Regional Comprehensive Economic Partnership
IRASEC	Research Institute on Contemporary Southeast Asia
CCTV	China Central Television
PHL	Philippines
CNBC	Consumer News and Business Channel
PRC	People's Republic of China
CUES	Code for Unplanned Encounters at Sea
MOU	Memorandum of Understanding
EO	Executive Order
CN	China
SAIS	School of Advanced International Studies
VA	Virginia
RAND	Rand Corporation (think tank)
UNTS	United Nations Treaty Series
USA	United States of America

CHAPTER 1

The Facts and the Formal Law

The South China Sea (SCS) (Map 1.1) is a semi-enclosed sea bordered on the west by Vietnam, on the east by the Philippines, Malaysia, and Brunei Darussalam, on the south by Indonesia and Malaysia, and on the north by China and Taiwan. The width of the SCS is approximately 550–650 nautical miles (nm), and its length is more than 1,200 nm. Many of these islands are partially submerged land masses unsuitable for habitation and are little more than shipping hazards. For example, the total land area of the Spratly Islands encompasses less than three square miles.[1]

The SCS dispute is one of the most complex territorial and maritime disputes in the world today. While the dispute involves China (including Taiwan), Vietnam, the Philippines, Malaysia, Indonesia, and Brunei, it has evolved within the context of a geopolitical rivalry between the United States (US) and an emergent China.[2] The SCS has fundamental and strategic value in terms of maritime security as major commercial shipping routes pass through this sea, which links the Western Pacific to the Indian Ocean and the Persian Gulf. An estimated $3.4 trillion worth of international shipping trade passes through the SCS each year.[3] The US Department of Defense (DOD) has stated that "the [SCS] plays an important role in security considerations across East Asia because Northeast Asia relies heavily on the flow of oil and commerce through [SCS] shipping lanes, including more than 80 percent of the crude oil to Japan, South Korea, and Taiwan."[4]

1 U.S. Energy Information Administration, South China Sea, at https://www.eia.gov/international/analysis/regions-of-interest/South_China_Sea.

2 Maximo Paulino T. Sison III, "Universalizing the Law of the Sea in the South China Sea Dispute," *Ocean Development and International Law*, 49, no. 2 (2018), p. 157. See also Yinhong Shi, Rising China: Political Leadership, Foreign Policy, and "Chineseness," in Vinod K. Aggarwal and Sara A. Newland (eds.), *Responding to China's Rise: US and EU Strategies* (Cham: Springer: 2015), p. 108.

3 CSIS, How Much Trade Transits the South China Sea?, *China Power*, at https://chinapower.csis.org/much-trade-transits-south-china-sea/.

4 Department of Defense, Annual Report to Congress [on] Military and Security Developments Involving the People's Republic of China 2017, May 15, 2017, p. 41. See also Clive Schofield, Dangerous Ground: A Geopolitical Overview of the South China Sea, in Sam Batemen and Ralf Emmers (eds), *Security and International Politics in the South China Sea* (2009), p. 18; Robert Beckman, "The UN Convention on the Law of the Sea," *American Journal of International Law*, 107 (2013), p. 143.

 | DOI: 10.1163/9789004696358_002

MAP 1.1 The South China Sea
SOURCE: THE SOUTH CHINA SEA ARBITRATION, AWARD, JULY 12, 2016, P. 9

The conspicuous nature of the SCS dispute pertains to the interpretation and application of the law. Namely, the dispute encompasses the legal status of maritime features and who has the sovereignty thereupon, island-building, overlapping national jurisdiction of littoral states, the exploitation and exploration of living and non-living resources, and freedom of navigation of military vessels within foreign ocean areas. As such, legal disparities among claimants have been a source of continuous conflicts.

Not surprisingly, there have been many suggestions for the resolution of the SCS dispute from both legal and political experts.[5] These proposals, however, have not been successfully adopted, and the rise of China further complicates the region. In order to find viable solutions to this dispute, international law and international relations should be considered concurrently, so that any legal proposals would prove their efficacy by being tested against international relations theories. In this context, this book is concerned mainly with answering questions about the role of and potential solutions under international law

5 See, e.g., (1) Valencia, Van Dyke, and Ludwig proposed the creation of a regional resource management body by putting the sovereignty issue aside. See Mark J. Valencia, John M. Van Dyke, and Noel Ludwig, *Sharing the Resources of the South China Sea* (The Hague: Kluwer Law International, 1997), (2) Hasjim Djalal suggested a so-called "doughnut formula," thereby a Joint Development Zones (JDZS) regime could be established from where an area of the High Seas left in the middle of the SCS as a result of delimitation. See Hasjim Djalal, "Indonesia and the SCS Initiative," *Ocean Development and International Law*, 32, No, 2 (2001), pp. 97–105, (3) Stein Tønnesson claimed the Sino-Vietnamese maritime boundary agreement and fishery agreement for the Tonking Gulf might serve as precedents for resolving the maritime dispute in the SCS. See Stein Tønnesson, The Tonkin Gulf Agreements: a model of conflict resolution?, in C.J. Jenner and Tran Troung Thuy (ed.), *The South China Sea: A Crucible of Regional Cooperation or Conflict-Making Sovereignty Claims?* (Cambridge: Cambridge University Press, 2016), pp. 151–170, (4) Havas Oegroseno claims that China and ASEAN could confer a "Coral Triangle Initiative" and the "Cooperative Mechanism of the Straits of Malacca and Singapore" on collaborations, modalities, mechanisms. See Arif Havas Oegroseno, "State Practices in Southeast Asia: Possible Collaboration amongst Claimants in the South China Sea Dispute," *The International Journal of Marine and Coastal Law*, 32 (2017), pp. 364–372, and (5) the Center for Strategic & International Studies (CSIS) Expert Working Group on the SCS proposed model agreements for the code of conduct, fisheries management, and resource production. See CSIS, Defusing the South China Sea Disputes: A Regional Blueprint, A Report of the CSIS Expert Working Group on the South China Sea, CSIS, October 2018. For the suggestions by political scientists, see, e.g., Min Gyo Ku, "Belling the Chinese Dragon at Sea: Western Theories and Asian Realities," *Ocean Development & International Law*, 47, no. 1 (2017); Hoang-Anh Nguyen & Hong-Van Tran, "A Neoliberal Institutionalist Approach to the Modern Vietnam-China Maritime Dispute," *Yonsei Journal of International Studies*, 6, no. 2 (Fall/Winter 2014); and Namrata Goswami, Power Shifts in East Asia: Balance of Power vs. Liberal Institutionalism, Perceptions, Volume XVIII, Number 1 (Spring 2013), pp. 3–31.

in light of analyses of international politics: what should international law do considering political scientists' predictions for the SCS dispute?

In terms of *lex lata*, the resolution of the legal dispute in the SCS revolves around three issues: First, whether there are islands or rocks in the SCS satisfying the United Nations Convention on the Law of the Sea (UNCLOS or the Convention)[6] that confer sovereignty to states; second, which state has valid title to maritime features based on general international law; third, whether China's assertive claims, such as historic claims with the nine-dash line or customary international law, can prevail over written rules, including UNCLOS.

1 The Facts and Recent Events

The Spratly Islands consist of more than 140 islets, rocks, reefs, shoals, and sandbanks spread over an area of more than 410,000 square kilometers (km2).[7] China, Taiwan, and Vietnam claim territorial titles over all the Spratlys, while the Philippines and Malaysia claim some of their features, and Brunei claims one feature within its exclusive maritime zone. The Paracel Islands, approximately halfway between Vietnam and China, consists of about 35 islets, shoals, sandbanks, and reefs with approximately 15,000 km2 of the ocean surface. China, Taiwan, and Vietnam claim sovereignty over them.[8] Scarborough Shoal (a coral reef), located approximately 118 nm from the Philippines and approximately 460 nm from China, is another disputed feature between the Philippines and China. Most of the reef is either completely submerged or above water only at low tide.[9] The "Pratas Islands" (which are located just over 200

6 United Nations Convention on the Law of the Sea, Montego Bay, opened for signature December 10, 1982, entered into force November 16, 1994, 1833 UNTS 397, available from DOALOS.

7 Robert Beckman, "The UN Convention on the Law of the Sea," *American Journal of International Law*, 107 (2013), p, 143. The British Captain Spratly named an island in the group "Spratly Island" and thereafter the group became called as the Spratly Islands. China calls them the Nansha Islands; Vietnam, the Truong Sa Islands; and the Philippines, the Kelayaan Islands. See Teh-Kuang Chang, "China's Claim of Sovereignty Over Spratly and Paracel Islands: A Historical and Legal Perspective," *Case Western Journal of International Law*, 23 (1991), p. 400.

8 Robert Beckman (2013), p. 144.

9 Department of Foreign Affairs, Philippine Position on Bajo de Masinloc (Scarborough Shoal) and the Waters Within Its Vicinity, Official Gazette of the Republic of the Philippines, Apr. 28, 2012, at http://www.gov.ph/2012/04/18/philippine-position-on-bajo-de-masinloc-and-the-waters-within-its-vicinity. This Shoal was named after the wrecked British ship upon it on September 12, 1748. See Bill Hayton, *The South China Sea: The Struggle for Power in Asia* (Yale University Press, 2014), p. 11, fn. 17.

nm southwest of Hong Kong) and "Macclesfield Bank" (which is south of the Pratas Islands) are claimed by China and Taiwan.

1.1 *History of the Dispute*

Regardless of what methodology or theory one may adopt in order to analyze the SCS dispute, understanding the historical background of the dispute should be a starting point to get a sense of why the disputants maintain their current claims. China argues that it has historic title to the Spratlys and Paracels and the water bodies thereof. States may possess a territory through an ancient and historical connection with it, which is one type of territorial acquisition in international law.[10] Vietnam and the Philippines base their territorial sovereignty on discovery and occupation. Other claimants seem to argue territorial title only, yet China appears to rely on historic rights to justify its maritime claim as well.

China/Taiwan claim both the Paracel and the Spratly Islands based on:

1. From 206 B.C.–220 A.D. The Paracels, the Spratlys, Macclesfield Bank, Scarborough Shoal, the Pratas were first discovered by the Chinese in the Han dynasty;[11]
2. From 220–280 A.D. During the Three Kingdom Period, General Kang Tai, famous ancient Chinese navigator of the East Wu State mentioned the Nansha Islands in his book entitled *"Funan Zhuan" (or Journeys to and from Phnom)* (the name of an ancient state in present-day Cambodia), stating "[i]n the [SCS], there are coral islands and reefs; below these islands and reefs are rocks upon which the corals were formed";[12]

10 Laurent Mayali and John Yoo, "Resolution of Territorial Disputes in East Asia: The Case of Dokdo," *Berkeley Journal of International Law*, 36, no. 3 (2018), p. 526.

11 Zhiguo Gao and Bingbing Jia, "The nine-dash line in the South China Sea: history, status, and implications," *American Journal of International Law*, 107, no. 1 (2013), p. 99; R. Haller-Trost, International Law and the History of the Claims to the Spratly Islands, p. 10 (South China Sea Conference, American Enterprise Institute, September 7–9, 1994), in Mark J. Valencia et al. (1997), p. 20, fn. 28. The oldest relics found on Itu Aba/Taiping reportedly were pottery shards made in China during the Han dynasty (206 BC–220 AD), indicating historic China was the earliest SCS discoverer. A long and complicated history took place between the earliest evidence of Chinese "discovery" and the present day occupation by the Taiwan Authority. See Myron H. Nordquist and William G. Phalen, Interpretation of UNCLOS Article 121 and Itu Aba (Taiping) in the South China Sea Arbitration Award, in Myron H. Nordquist et al. (2017), p. 62.

12 Ministry of Foreign Affairs of the People's Republic of China, "Historical Evidence To Support China's Sovereignty over Nansha Islands," November 11, 2017.

3. Fei Yuan of the Jin Dynasty (265–420 A.D.) wrote about the fishing and collecting of coral samples by Chinese fishermen on the SCS in his article Chronicles of Guangzhou;[13]
4. After Emperor Zhenyuan of the Tang Dynasty (785–805 A.D.) came to the throne, China included the Nansha Islands on its administrative map;[14]
5. From 618–906 A.D., Chinese awareness of the Spratlys grew when Chinese voyages increased in frequency and range during the T'ang Dynasty;
6. In 1292, Kublai Khan made a documented visit to Java, sailing through the Spratlys;[15]
7. In order to commemorate the reigns of the two Ming Emperors, Cheng-tsu (1403–1424 A.D.) and Hsuan-Tsung (1426–1435 A.D.), Yung-lo and Hsuan-the were attached to the Paracels' two sub-groups of islands, Amphitrite and Crescent;[16]
8. From the 12th through the 17th centuries, Chinese records made occasional reference to the islands and their "sandy banks," including maps displaying elevations;[17]
9. In 1724, 1755, 1767, and 1810, the Chinese Government marked the Nansha Islands on the authoritative maps and exercised administrative jurisdiction over these islands;[18]
10. In 1833, Germany carried out surveys on the Paracel and Spratly Islands, but these surveys ceased after the Ching government protested;[19]

---

13 *Ibid.*

14 *Ibid.*

15 Richard D. Beller, "Analyzing the Relationship between International Law and International Politics in China's and Vietnam's Territorial Dispute Over the Spratly Islands," *Texas International Law Journal*, 29, no. 2 (Spring 1994), p. 305.

16 Dieter Heizing, *Disputed Islands in the South China Sea: Paracels-Spratlys-Pratas-Macclesfield Bank* (Wiesbaden: O. Harrasowitz, 1976), p. 23.

17 Mark J. Valencia, John M. Van Dyke, and Noel Ludwig, *Sharing the Resources of the South China Sea* (The Hague: Kluwer Law International, 1997), p. 21.

18 The Nansha Islands were marked as Chinese territory in many maps drawn in the Qing Dynasty such as A Map of Administrative Divisions of the Whole China of the 1724 Map of Provinces of the Qing Dynasty, A Map of Administrative Divisions of the Whole China of the 1755 Map of Provinces of the Imperial Qing Dynasty, the 1767 Map of Unified China of the Great Qing for Ten Thousand Years, the 1810 Topographical Map of Unified China of the Great Qing for Ten Thousand Years and the 1817 Map of Unified China of the Great Qing for Ten Thousand Years. See Ministry of Foreign Affairs of the People's Republic of China, "Historical Evidence To Support China's Sovereignty over Nansha Islands," 11/17/2020, at https://www.fmprc.gov.cn/mfa_eng/topics_665678/3754_666060/t19231.shtml).

19 Chao, "South China Sea: Boundary Problems Relating to the Nansha and Hsisha Islands," *Chinese Yearbook of International Law and Affairs*, 9 (1989), pp. 76–77.

11. The 1868 Guide of the SCS has accounts of the activities of the Chinese fishermen in the Nansha Islands;[20]
12. In 1877, China's first ambassador to Britain, KUO Sung-Tao, made an official statement to express that the Paracel Islands "belong to China";[21]
13. In 1881–1884, China protested against Germany when Germany conducted a series of surveys around the Paracel Islands;[22]
14. In 1884–1885, China protested against France when France made an effort to incorporate Itu Aba/Taiping Dao into French Indochina during the Sino-French war;[23]
15. In the 1887 Sino-French "Convention Respecting the Delimitation of the Frontier between China and Tonkin," France recognized that the Paracel (and Spratly) Islands were part of China;[24]
16. In 1902, the Ching Dynasty's first official patrol to the Paracels was launched by three warships from its Canton fleet, led by Admiral Li Chun and Vice-Admiral WU Ching-yung. During their stay on the Paracels, they planted imperial flags and a stone tablet to commemorate the arrival of formal Chinese authority—this tablet was discovered in 1979 by China's People Liberation Army stationed on the North Island;[25]
17. In 1907, a Japanese businessman, Nishizawa Yoshiji, and his employees occupied Pratas Island, which ended in 1908 when China paid Nishizawa an indemnity of 130,000 silver dollars, and Japan formally recognized Chinese sovereignty over the Pratas group.[26] Afterward, in 1908, the Chinese Special Provincial Commission for the Management of the Area launched a second official patrol to perform an official reconnaissance of the islands and to establish sites for the construction of houses, roads,

20 Ministry of Foreign Affairs of the People's Republic of China, "Historical Evidence to Support China's Sovereignty over Nansha Islands," 11/17/2000.

21 Kuan-Hsiung Wang, Peaceful Settlement of Disputes in the South China Sea through Fisheries Resources Cooperation and Management, Maryland Series in Contemporary Asian Studies, November 3, 2015 (222), p. 6.

22 Some Chinese writers claim that a Chinese protest was issued, yet some commentators argue there appears to be a lack of proof by stating that Germany neither sought nor received permission from China for the surveys and the Chinese government did not seem to have noticed, let alone issued a protest. See Bill Hayton (2014), pp. 48–49.

23 Myron H. Nordquist et al., Interpretation of UNCLOS Article 121 and Itu Aba (Taiping) in the South China Sea Arbitration Award, in Myron H. Nordquist et al. (2017), p. 62 (citing Shicun Wu, *Solving Disputes for Regional Cooperation and Development in the South China: A Chinese Perspective* (Chandos Publishing, 2013)).

24 Hungdah Chiu and Choon-ho Park, "Legal Status of the Paracel and Spratly Islands," *Ocean Development and International Law*, 3 (1975), pp. 11–13.

25 Kuan-Hsiung Wang (2015), p. 7.

26 Marwyn S. Samuels, *Contest for the South China Sea* (Methuen: New York and London, 1982), p. 53.

a radio station, and phosphate processing plants. Upon their return from a one-month stay on the Paracels, the Commission submitted an Eight-Point-Program Report recommending, *inter alia*, the administrative absorption and economic development of the Paracel Island;[27]

18. In May 1909, Guangdong Governor Zhang despatched a boat to the Paracels and then two more the following month; afterward, a new map of Guandong was published showing the Paracel Islands as part of the province;[28]
19. From 1921–1932, the Republic of China issued five licenses for the exploitation of the Paracel Archipelago;[29]
20. In 1928, the Republic of China appointed a commission to investigate the Paracel Islands, and they sailed to the islands on a navy battleship on May 22, 1928;[30]
21. In 1930, China refused to settle a dispute with France after France first occupied and then claimed the Spratlys, and in 1933, Germany halted a survey of the islands after China protested;
22. Between 1932 and 1935, the Chinese Government set up a Committee for the Review of Maps of Lands and Waters of China;[31]
23. In 1933, a Chinese cartographer, Chen Duo, published his Newly-Made Chinese Atlas in which the Chinese sea border stretched down to 7° N, including the Spratly Islands;[32]
24. In 1935, the Commission of the Chinese Government for the Review of Maps of Land and Waters published *The Map of Islands in the South China Sea*;[33]
25. In December 1946, the then Chinese government sent senior officials to the Nansha Islands for their recovery. A take-over ceremony was held on

---

27 This report was later approved first by Governor-General Chang of Guangdong, then by Kwan-Hsu Emperor, and finally, carried out by the Chinese government in 1911 by incorporating the Paracels into Guangdong Province, to be administered by the Prefectural Authority of Hainan Island. See *ibid.*, pp. 53–54.

28 Bill Hayton (2014), p. 52, fn. 34, 36; According to Hayton, China seems to have regarded the Paracels as its southernmost territory not the Spratlys until 1933. *Ibid.*, pp. 54–55.

29 Steven K. T. Yu, "Who Owns the Paracels and Spratlys? – An Evaluation of the Nature and Legal Basis of the Conflicting Territorial Claims," *Chinese Yearbook of International Law and Affairs*, 9 (1989), p. 6.

30 Marwyn S. Samuels (1982), pp. 57–60.

31 Ministry of Foreign Affairs of the People's Republic of China, "Historical Evidence to Support China's Sovereignty over Nansha Islands," 11/17/2000.

32 Bill Hayton (2014), p. 45.

33 Position Paper of the Government of the People's Republic of China on the Matter of Jurisdiction in the South China Sea Arbitration by the Republic of the Philippines, December 7, 2014, para.20 (Position Paper).

the islands, a monument erected in commemoration of it, and troops were sent over on garrison duty;[34]

26. In 1947, China produced a map depicting a u-shaped line, the so-called "nine-dash line" that covers roughly 90 percent of the SCS;[35]
27. In 1951, Zhou En-lai, the Foreign Minister of the People's Republic of China, stated that the Spratlys were still a part of the PRC, regardless of a US-British draft treaty at the San Francisco Peace Conference when Japan renounced its claim to the islands.[36]

On September 4, 1958, China proclaimed that the Pratas Islands, the Paracel Islands, the Macclesfield Bank, and the Spratly Islands belonged to China in its Declaration on Territorial Sea. Chinese leaders maintain that China has "indisputable sovereignty" over all the islands in the SCS.[37]

China further argues that the Cairo and Potsdam Declarations corroborated its sovereignty over the SCS at the end of World War II.[38]

Vietnam claims that the Paracel and the Spratly Islands have been part of its territory from time immemorial. Vietnamese claims to sovereignty over the whole Spratly Islands are based on historical grounds, preoccupation, and effective occupation:

1. Court documents during the reign of King Le Thanh Tong (1460–1497) indicate that both the Spratlys and Parcel Archipelagoes were considered to be Vietnamese territory;[39]

34 Ministry of Foreign Affairs of the People's Republic of China, "Its Origin," November 17, 2000, at https://www.fmprc.gov.cn/mfa_eng/topics_665678/3754_666060/t19233.shtml.

35 Ronald O'Rourke, "Maritime Territorial and Exclusive Economic Zone (EEZ) Disputes Involving China: Issues for Congress," Congressional Research Service (R42784), May 24, 2018, p. 24. Scholarly accounts place the publication date from 1946 to 1948. See, e.g., M. Sheng-Ti Gau, "The U-Shaped Line and a Categorization of the Ocean Disputes in the South China Sea," *Ocean Development & International Law,* 43, no. 1 (2012), p. 58.

36 Richard D. Beller, "Analyzing the Relationship between International Law and International Politics in China's and Vietnam's Territorial Dispute Over the Spratly Islands," *Texas International Law Journal,* 29, no. 2 (Spring 1994), p. 308.

37 Collected Documents on the Foreign Relations of the People's Republic of China, 2 (Peking, 1961), p. 32, cited in Kuan-Hsiung Wang (2015), p. 9, fn. 30.

38 Anisa Heritage and Pak K. Lee, "The Sino-American confrontation in the South China Sea: insights from an international order perspective," *Cambridge Review of International Affairs,* 33, no. 1 (2020), p. 144. For the timeline of military events in the SCS since 1945, see Van Pham, "The Use or Threat of Force in the South China Sea Disputes Since 1945: A Timeline" in Enrico Fels and Truong-Minh Vu (eds.), *Power Politics in Asia's Contested Waters: Territorial Disputes in the South China Sea* (Cham: Springer International Publishing: 2016), pp. 523–539.

39 The Hoang Sa and Truong Sa Archipelagoes (Paracels and Spratly) II (Vietnem Courier, Hanoi, 1985), p. 74, cited in Mark J. Valencia et al. (1997), p. 30, fn. 112.

2. According to the 1630s' records: the Journal of Batavia reported that the Vietnamese had sovereignty over the Paracels, and Dutch merchant boats that ran aground were assisted by the Vietnamese;
3. Vietnamese maps of the 17th century show both groups of islands as part of Vietnamese territory and place them under the administration of the Bihn Son district of Quang Nghia prefecture;[40]
4. Foreign Minister Vuong Van Bac stated: "in 1802, Emperor Gia Long set up the Hoang Sa (the Paracel Islands) Company to exploit resources in the vicinity";[41]
5. In the 19th century, Vietnam produced maps and administrative records that supported its sovereignty over the Spratlys;
6. In 1884, the French established a protectorate over Vietnam and began to assert claims to the Paracel and Spratly Islands;
7. In 1932, the French Governor-General, Pierre Pasquier (who integrated the Paracels into the Thua Thien provincial administration), reaffirmed the 1802 statement by Vuong Van Bac, and in 1938, Emperor Bao Dai confirmed it once again;[42]
8. Between 1933 and 1939, France asserted physical control over nine of the Spratly islet and published formal notice of annexation in its own Official Journal on July 16, 1933;[43]
9. In 1951, Vietnam asserted its sovereignty over the Spratly Islands during the Peace Conference in San Francisco, and no one protested against its claim to sovereignty over the Spratlys at the conference;[44]
10. In 1961, South Vietnam's first president, Ngo Dinh Diem, adopted a decree on its claim;
11. Since 1973, Vietnam has occupied part of the Spratly archipelago and maintained garrisons on at least 22 features thereupon (nine of occupied

---

40 Socialist Republic of Vietnam Ministry of Foreign Affairs, The Hoang Sa and Truong Sa Archipelagoes and International Law (Hanoi, 1988), pp. 4, 19, 65, cited in Mark J. Valencia et al. (1997), p. 30, fn. 114.

41 Cable from US Mission to the United Nations to US State Department, Subj: Tests of GVN Letter, p. 3 (Jan. 18, 1974) (1974USUNN00175), in Kirsten Sellars, "Rocking the Boat: The Paracels, The Spratlys, and the South China Sea Arbitration," *Columbia Journal of Asian Law*, 30 (2017), p. 228, fn. 33.

42 *Ibid.*

43 Mark J. Valencia et al. (1997), p. 30.

44 See Liselotte Odgaard, *Maritime security between China and Southeast Asia: conflict and cooperation in the making of regional order* (Abingdon and New York: Routledge, 2016), p. 95. In regards to the 1951 San Francisco Peace Conference, Vietnam also argues that the rejection of the Soviet proposal to grant China sovereignty over the Spratly Islands is seen as proof that the islands are not Chinese.

features are naturally exposed at high-tide–Spratly Island, West London Reef, Amboyna Cay, Pearson Reef, Sin Cowe Island, Namyit Island, Sand Cay, Barque Canada Reef, and South Cay).

Vietnam allegedly has strong arguments per the above. Nevertheless, there is a serious weakness in its own historical records. For instance, a statement to the Chinese Charge d'Affaires by North Vietnam's Second Foreign Minister Ung Van Khiem on June 15, 1956, states that "According to Vietnamese data, the Sisha and Nansha Islands are historically part of Chinese territory." Also, when China claimed its territorial sea that included the Spratlys in 1958, the Vietnamese Workers Party newspaper placed the news onto its front page,[45] and North Vietnam's Premier Pham Van Dongs sent a brief letter to Chinese Premier Zhou Enlai:

> The Government of the Democratic Republic of Viet Nam recognizes and approves the declaration of the Government of the People's Republic of China on China's territorial sea made on September 4, 1958, regarding the decision taken with respect to China's territorial sea ... The Government of the Democratic Republic of Viet Nam respects this decision.[46]

Such Vietnamese confirmation of the damage to its own legal position lasted until 1974, when it pronounced its sovereignty over the Paracels and Spratlys.[47] In 1988, Vietnam justified that the statements were a pragmatic necessity for gaining the support of an ally during a militarily difficult time[48] as they were made "when Vietnam had to fight against the U.S. intervention and aggression" and when Vietnam and China had become "true allies in their common struggle against the U.S."[49] Subsequently, in 1979, 1982, and 1988, the Vietnamese government's White Papers asserted that the Spratly Islands were the Chang Sha Islands in Vietnamese's history, and the Vietnamese government had

45 Richard D. Beller, "Analyzing the Relationship between International Law and International Politics in China's and Vietnam's Territorial Dispute Over the Spratly Islands," *Texas International Law Journal*, 29, no. 2 (Spring 1994), p. 309.

46 Bill Hayton (2014), p. 96.

47 Chen Jie, "China's Spratly Policy: With Special Reference to the Philippines and Malaysia," *Asian Survey*, 34, no. 10 (October 1994), p. 901. Fact Sheet, No. 2/74, South Vietnamese Embassy, Washington, D.C., January 28, 1974, in Choon-Ho Park, *East Asia and the Law of the Sea* (Seoul: Seoul National University Press, 1983), p. 212.

48 Mark J. Valencia et al. (1997), p. 33.

49 The Ministry of Foreign Affairs, *The Hoang Sa and Truong Sa Archipelagoes and International Law* (Hanoi, 1988), pp. 21–23.

exercised jurisdiction over the Spratly Islands.[50] With regard to the mode of dispute settlement, Vietnam appears to have in mind the ICJ litigation[51] or UNCLOS compulsory dispute settlement mechanism to resolve the dispute.[52]

The Philippines occupies 8 features—Nanshan Island, Thitu Island (a runway established), Flat Island, West York Island, Northeast Cay (these 5 features since 1974), Liankiam Cay, Loaita Island, and Commodore Reef (these three features since 1978),[53] and its claim to sovereignty over the Spratly Islands (most of them, but not Spratly island itself) is basically based on occupation on *res nullius* or abandoned islets after World War II.[54] Less than three weeks after its independence from the US on July 4, 1946, the then Vice-President and Foreign Minister of the Philippines, Elpidio Quirino, claimed the Spratlys as essential to its security. On May 17, 1950, Quirino, as president, declared that the islands belonged to the Philippines. However, the Philippines did not press its claim at the San Francisco Peace Conference in 1951.[55]

The Philippines argues that the Spratly islands were *terra nullius* because the 1951 Peace Treaty confirms that Japan has renounced its rights to the islands, not specifying recipients of the abandoned title.[56] Interestingly, the Philippines' *res nullius* claim stems from private citizens' discovery and occupation of the Spratlys: Thomas Cloma, a Filipino businessman who took possession of some of the Spratlys on May 11, 1956.[57] Thomas Cloma and his employees raised the national flag of the Philippines on various islands, including Spratly Island, Taiping Island, Nam Yit Island, and Thitu Island. Cloma proclaimed these islands as the "Archipelago of Freedomland" (Kalayaan) a few

50 Nong Hong (2012), p. 17. Vietnam allegedly holds that the Spratlys do not generate EEZ and continental shelf, and any zones around these islands should be limited to territorial seas. See Interview with Nguyen Qui Binh, Legal Advisor to the Vietnamese Foreign Affairs, at the First Technical Working Group Meeting on Legal Matters in the South China Sea, Phuket, Thailand, July 5, 1995, cited in Mark J. Valencia et al. (1997), p. 31, fn. 133.

51 Mark J. Valencia et al. (1997), p. 33.

52 See Richard Javad Heydarian, "The Importance of Being China," January 12, 2020, *The National Interest*, at https://nationalinterest.org/feature/importance-being-china-112951. See also Experts Call for Vietnam to Sue China in International Court over South China Sea Incursions, October 9, 2019, *Radio Free Asia*, at https://www.rfa.org/english/news/vietnam/lawsuit-10092019152725.html/.

53 Bill Hayton (2014), p. 69.

54 See generally Haydee B. Yoroc, "The Philippine Claim to the Spratly Islands Group," *Philippine Law Journal*, 58, no. 2 (1983), pp. 42–63.

55 Bill Hayton (2014), pp. 58, 64–70. Treaty of Peace with Japan, signed at San Francisco, on September 8, 1951, 3 U.S.T. 3169, 136 U.N.T.S. 45.

56 Kuan-Hsiung Wang (2015), p. 12, fn. 45.

57 For the close relationship between Thomas Cloma and Carlos P. Garcia, the then Vice-President and Foreign Minister of the Philippines, *see* Bill Hayton (2014), pp. 66–67.

days later.[58] On July 6, 1956, he established a new state, the Free Territory of Freedomland, with a capital at Pag-asa Island, calling himself as "Chairman, Supreme Council of State."[59] In response to Cloma's proclamation, the Philippines denied that it had not officially claimed the islands, confirming Cloma had acted as an individual.[60]

Nevertheless, on July 10, 1971, the Philippine government officially claimed part of the Spratly Islands to be its territory in response to an incident in which a Taiwanese naval patrol unit fired upon a Filipino vessel operating in the Spratly Islands:

1. The Philippines has a legal title to the island group as a consequence of the occupation by Tomas Cloma;
2. The presence of the Chinese forces on Itu Aba (Taiping Island) constituted a serious threat to the security of the Philippines;
3. The Chinese occupation of some islands in the Spratly group constituted *de facto* trusteeship on behalf of the World War II allies, which precluded the garrisoning of the islands without the allies' consent;
4. The Spratly group is within the archipelagic territory claimed by the Philippines for two reasons.[61] First, on June 11, 1978, President Ferdinand E. Marcos declared Presidential Decree No. 1599, which enclosed an area constituting a distinct and separate municipality of the Province of Palawan, which was to be known as Kalayaan.[62] Second, on December 10, 1982, and on May 8, 1984, the Philippines signed and ratified UNCLOS, which placed an understanding that reads: "4. Such signing shall not in any manner impair or prejudice the sovereignty of the Republic of the Philippines over any territory over which it exercises sovereign authority, such as the Kalayaan Islands, and the waters appurtenant thereto."[63]

58 Marwyn S. Samuels (1982), pp. 81–82; President Marcos Ferdinand Marcos renamed Freedomland the Kalayaan Islands – *Kalayaan* being the Tagalog word for freedom – and in June 1978 issued Decree 1596 incorporating Kalayaan as a municipality of Palawan province. See Bill Hayton (2014), p. 70.

59 Marwyn S. Samuels (1982), p. 82.

60 Bill Hayton (2014), p. 11. Meanwhile, the Philippines also held a somewhat uncertain stance toward Cloma's proclamation. For instance, in December 1956, Filipino Vice President Garcia revealed the equivocal position of the Philippine government. See Marwyn S. Samuels (1982), pp. 82–83.

61 The Government of the Philippines, "Government States Position," New Philippines, July 10, 1971, p. 10.

62 See https://www.un.org/Depts/los/LEGISLATIONANDTREATIES/PDFFILES/PHL_1978_Decree.pdf.

63 United Nations Treaty Collection, United Nations Convention on the Law of the Sea, at https://treaties.un.org/Pages/ViewDetailsIII.aspx?src=TREATY&mtdsg_no=XXI-6&chapter=21&Temp=mtdsg3&clang=_en#EndDec.

In 2001, the Philippines became the first country to settle civilians on the Spratlys deliberately.[64]

Malaysia did not claim any section of the Spratly Islands until 1978, in which year a senior Malaysia official visited and claimed a number of islands in the southern region of the Spratlys, including Amboyna Cay, Commodore, and Swallow Reef.[65] Malaysia claims twelve islands and features of the SCS, six of which it occupies: Ardaier Reef (occupied since 1986 by about 20 soldiers), Dallas Reef (occupied since 1987), Louisa Reef (a navigation light and an accommodation module erected, although it is viewed not above water at high tide), Mariveles Reef (occupies since 1986), Royal Charlotte Reef, and Swallow Reef (occupies since 1983 and on which Malaysia built an airstrip in 1993), Erica Reef, Investigator Reef, Luconia Reef, Commodore Reef (occupied by the Philippines), and Amboyna Cay and Barque Canada Reef (occupied by Vietnam).

Initially, Malaysia based its claims to those islands on the natural prolongation of the continental shelf (the "continental shelf theory").[66] In 1979, the Malaysian government published "Map Showing the Territorial Waters and Continental Shelf Boundaries,"[67] which shows the continental shelf off the east coast of the Malaysian peninsula, Sarawak, and Sabah and the boundary enclosing the Amboyna Cay, Commodore Reef, and Swallow Reef.[68] Later, Malaysia added discovery and occupation of the islands based on the above official maps to its claim. Malaysia has maintained its troops on the Swallow Reef since 1983, and it occupied two more features (Mariveles Reef and Dallas Reef) in 1986.[69]

In 1983, Malaysia's Ministry of Foreign Affairs announced its official position that the Swallow Reef has always been part of the Malaysian territory and that Vietnam occupies its territory Amboyna Cay, demanding Vietnam to withdraw

64 According to official 2010 census, the Thitu/Pagasa Island has a population of 222 and around 60 live there at any one time. See Bill Hayton (2014), p. 105.

65 D. J. Dzurk, "Boundary and Resources Disputes in the South China Sea," *Ocean Yearbook*, 5 (1985), p. 260.

66 The wording of relevant provisions of UNCLOS and the 1966 Malaysia's Continental Act pertain to submerged features as Article 76 of UNCLOS stipulates: The continental shelf of a coastal State comprises the seabed and subsoil of the submarine areas that extend beyond its territorial sea throughout the natural prolongation of its land territory to the outer edge of the continental margin.

67 Map 44 of Map Atlas, Memorial of Malaysia, Vol. 4, *Case Concerning Sovereignty over Pedra Branca/Pulau Batu Puteh, Middle Rocks and South Ledge* (Malaysia/Singapoer), Judgment, *ICJ Reports 2008.*

68 Kuan-Hsiung Wang (2015), p. 11.

69 *Ibid.*

from the Cay.[70] In 1988, after the China-Vietnam conflict, Malaysia's Deputy Foreign Minister reiterated that the islets were within Malaysia's continental shelf areas and had been so since the publication of the 1979 map.[71]

Brunei currently claims two reefs: Louisa Reef (also claimed by Malaysia) and Rifleman Bank. Regarding Louisa Reef, Brunei bases its claim on the theory of equidistance points against Malaysia. For Rifleman Bank, Brunei argues that the Bank is located within the alleged continental shelf of Brunei, presenting a map published in 1988, which encompasses the Bank within its maritime area. Since Brunei is surrounded on three sides by Malaysia, the claims of both nations are often treated as the claims of one state.[72] Brunei claims a maritime zone based on the prolongation of its continental shelf, thereby protesting foreign marine scientific research in its claiming ocean.

The United States is not a direct disputant in the SCS dispute, yet it has paid great attention to this issue due to its bigger stake in the region. According to US policy on the SCS dispute from 1995 on,[73] the US demands a peaceful resolution of the issue by the claimants, opposes the threat or use of force to assert any claims, maintains neutrality on the merits of competing sovereignty claims, willing to help in the peaceful resolution of disputes,[74] and keeps lines of communication in the region, repudiating any excessive maritime claims.[75]

While not taking sides with a particular claimant, America questions the motive of China in posing territorial and maritime claims in the region. On April 26, 2019, Randall Schriver, then US Assistant Secretary of Defense for Indo-Pacific Security Affairs, stated, "[w]e do have some suspicion about China's motive ... [China is] not participant in upholding international law

70 Statement of the Malaysian Foreign Ministry, September 9, 1983, in Shicun Wu, *Solving Disputes for Regional Cooperation and Development in the South China: A Chinese Perspective* (Chandos Publishing, 2013), p. 141.

71 R. Haller-Trost, International Law and the History of the Claims to the Spratly Islands, p. 33 (South China Sea Conference, American Enterprise Institute, September 7–9, 1994), in Mark J. Valencia et al. (1997), p. 36, fn. 177.

72 Mark J. Valencia et al. (1997), p. 38.

73 M. Taylor Fravel, Policy Report: U.S. Policy Toward the Disputes in the South China Sea Since 1995, S. Rajaratnam School of International Studies (RSIS), March 2014.

74 On November 12, 2017, during a meeting with Vietnamese President Tran Dai Quang, former President Donald Trump of the US offered his services as a mediator or arbitrator, saying, "if I can help mediate or arbitrate, please let me know ... I'm a very good mediator and arbitrator." See Steve Holland and Mai Nguyen, "Trump offers to mediate on South China Sea," *Reuters*, November 12, 2017, at https://www.reuters.com/article/us-trump-asia-vietnam/trump-offers-to-mediate-on-south-china-sea-idUSKBN1DC04H.

75 Nehginpao Kipgen, *The Politics of South China Sea Disputes* (London & New York: Routledge, 2020), p. 90.

consistently … [America has] suspicion [about] what they seek in the code of conduct."[76] China perceives that the US is not a neutral party on the SCS dispute.[77]

Some scholars claim that the US recognized Chinese sovereignty over the Spratly and Paracel Islands during negotiations for the San Francisco Peace Treaty; however, the US changed its position after the consultations with the Philippines and the Republic of China in consideration of a communist China controlling the islands in the SCS.[78]

2 Recent Events

Recognizable conflicts in the SCS have taken place between China and the US concerning the different interpretations of UNCLOS. As "core interest," China increasingly adopts assertive actions, while America continues to enforce freedom of navigation as its "key national interest" since the early 20th century.[79] On the other hand, the Philippines filed a lawsuit against China in 2013, and the arbitral tribunal took sides with the Philippines in 2016. China refused and rejected the Arbitral process and the award, but have been building artificial islands since 2014.

2.1 *Naval Conflicts between the United States and China*

The US Freedom of Navigation (FON) Program was created in 1979 to preserve American national interests and demonstrate non-acquiescence to excessive maritime claims asserted by coastal states.[80] On some core UNCLOS

76 "US Suspicious of Beijing's Motive in South China Sea 'Code of Conduct'," *Radio Free Asia*, April 26, 2019, at https://www.rfa.org/english/news/china/malaysia-southchinasea-04262019163855.html.

77 WU Shicun, South China Sea: expect more instability in 2021 as the US encourages 'lawfare' and conflict, January 25, 2021, National Institute for South China Sea Studies, China, at http://en.nanhai.org.cn/index/research/paper_c/id/419.html.

78 Anisa Heritage and Pak K. Lee (2020), p. 141. As a result, Article 2(f) of the Peace Treaty ended up mentioning no the Paracels and Spratlys to avoid islands lying along the "Acheson Line" falling under the hands of Communist China. See Kimie Hara, "The San Francisco Peace Treaty and Frontier Problems in the Regional Order in East Asia: A Sixty Year Perspective," *The Asia-Pacific Journal*, 10, no. 17 (2012), p. 4.

79 Caitlin Campbell et al., *China's "Core Interest" and the East China Sea*, US-China Economic and Security Review Commission Self Research Backgrounder, May 10, 2013.

80 U.S. Department of Defense, "Freedom of Navigation Program Fact Sheet" (March 2015), at https://policy.defense.gov/Portals/11/Documents/gsa/cwmd/DoD%20FON%20Program%20--%20Fact%20Sheet% 20(March%202015).pdf.

institutions, China and the US have different interpretations. The US maintains that UNCLOS does not grant the authority of prohibiting military activities of a foreign state to coastal states, and warships enjoy innocent passage under Article 17 of the Convention. In contrast, China contends that coastal states can regulate a foreign state's economic affairs and military activities within their exclusive economic zones (EEZ), and naval vessels do not have the right of innocent passage.[81] This starkly opposing interpretation, along with the unclear language of UNCLOS, has provided confidence to each side to push back over the years continually.

In March 2001, September 2002, March, and May 2009, Chinese ships and aircraft confronted and harassed the US naval ships *Bowditch, Impeccable*, and *Victorious* conducting survey and ocean surveillance operations in China's EEZs. On April 1, 2001, a Chinese fighter collided with a US Navy EP-3 electronic surveillance aircraft flying in international airspace about 65 miles southeast of China's Hainan Island, which was forced to land on Hainan Island.[82]

On December 5, 2013, a Chinese navy ship put itself in the path of the US Navy cruiser *Cowpens* as it was operating 30 or more miles from China's aircraft carrier *Liaoning*, forcing the *Cowpens* to change course to avoid a collision. Again, on August 19, 2014, a Chinese fighter conducted an aggressive intercept of a US Navy P-8 maritime patrol aircraft flying about 135 miles east of Hainan Island.[83] On May 17, 2016, Chinese fighters flew unsafely within 50 feet of a Navy EP-3 electronic surveillance aircraft in the SCS.[84]

On September 30, 2018, an incident occurred between the US Navy destroyer *Decatur* (DDG-73) and a Chinese destroyer when the *Decatur* conducted a

81 There have been a series of military incidents between the U.S. and China within Chinese. For instance, on September 30, 2018 an incident occurred in the SCS between the U.S. Navy destroyer Decatur (DDG-73) and a Chinese destroyer, as the Decatur was conducting a Freedom of Navigation (FON) near Gaven Reef in the Spratly Islands. For a detailed description of the incident, see the Congressional Research Service, U.S.-China Strategic Competition in South and East China Seas: Background and Issues for Congress, R42784, September 24, 2019, p. 3.

82 For a description of some of these incidents and their connection to the issue of military operating rights in EEZs, see Raul Pedrozo, "Close Encounters at Sea, The USNS Impeccable Incident," *Naval War College Review*, Summer 2009.

83 Transcript of remarks by DOD Press Secretary Rear Admiral John Kirby at August 22, 2014, press briefing, at http://www.defense.gov/Transcripts/Transcript.aspx?TranscriptID=5493; Transcript of remarks by DOD Press Secretary Rear Admiral John Kirby at August 22, 2014, press briefing, at http://www.defense.gov/Transcripts/Transcript.aspx?TranscriptID=5493.

84 See, for example, Michael S. Schmidt, "Chinese Aircraft Fly Within 50 Feet of U.S. Plane Over South China Sea, Pentagon Says," *New York Times*, May 18, 2016.

FON operation near Gaven Reef in the Spratly Islands. In the incident, the Chinese destroyer overtook the US destroyer close to the US destroyer's port side, requiring the US destroyer to turn to the right to avoid the Chinese ship.[85] In this incident, the Chinese ship warned the US destroyer by radio, stating, "[i]f you don't change course, your [sic] will suffer consequences." US officials characterized the actions of the Chinese ship in the incident as "unsafe and unprofessional."[86] In July 2016, US Chief of Naval Operations Admiral John Richardson noted that "[t]he US Navy will continue to conduct routine and lawful operations around the world, including in the SCS, in order to protect the rights, freedoms and lawful uses of sea and airspace guaranteed to all. This will not change."[87]

As if to show that this is true, on March 24, 2023 Arleigh Burke-class guided-missile destroyer USS Milius (DDG 69) conducted FON operations near the Paracel Islands[88] and on December 21, a Chinese J-11 fighter jet flew within six meters (20 feet) of a US Air Force RC-135 aircraft over the South China Sea.[89]

In 2023, the U.S.-Philippine Bilateral Defense Guidelines acknowledged that armed attacks by third parties against Philippine forces in the SCS could trigger U.S. mutual defense obligations under the U.S.-Philippine Mutual Defense Treaty.[90] Thus, an armed conflict between Chinese and Philippine coast guards,

85 U.S. officials stated that at the point of closest approach between the two ships, the stern (i.e., back end) of the Chinese ship came within 45 yards (135 feet) of the bow (i.e., front end) of the Decatur.

86 John Power and Catherine Wong, "Exclusive Details and Footage Emerge of Near Collision Between Warships in South China Sea," *South China Morning Post*, November 4, 2018, at https://www.scmp.com/week-asia/geopolitics/article/2171596/exclusive-details-and-footage-emerge-near-collision-between. See also Jane Perlez and Steven Lee Myers, "'A Game of Chicken': U.S. and China Are Risking a Clash at Sea," *New York Times*, November 8, 2018, at https://www.nytimes.com/2018/11/08/world/asia/south-china-sea-risks.html.

87 Idrees Ali and Matt Spetalnick, "U.S. Warship Challenges China's Claims in South China Sea," Reuters, October 21, 2016, at https://www.reuters.com/article/us-southchinasea-usa-exclusive/u-s-warship-challenges-chinas-claims-in-south-china-sea-idUSKCN12L1O9.

88 U.S. 7th Fleet Public Affairs, 7th Fleet Destroyer conducts Freedom of Navigation Operation in South China Sea, March 23, 2023, at https://www.c7f.navy.mil/Media/News/Display/Article/3339703/7th-fleet-destroyer-conducts-freedom-of-navigation-operation-in-south-china-sea/#.ZBou-KOUaKU.twitter.

89 AL JAZEERA, China fighter jet flew within six metres of US surveillance plane, December 30, 2022, at https://www.aljazeera.com/news/2022/12/30/chinese-fighter-jet-flew-within-20-feet-of-american-plane-us-say.

90 Congressional Research Service, China Primer: South China Sea Disputes, In Focus, Updated August 21, 2023, at https://crsreports.congress.gov/product/pdf/IF/IF10607. In May 2023, U.S. Secretary of Defense Lloyd Austin reaffirmed U.S. defense commitments in the South China Sea under the U.S.-Philippines Mutual Defense Treaty. See Tomotaka Shoji, The Philippines' policy on the South China Sea under the Marcos administration: Recalibrating

aircraft, and public vessels could result in an armed engagement between the United States and China.[91]

2.2 *Arbitration between the Philippines and China*

Starting April 2012, the Philippines and China were locked in a standoff at Scarborough Shoal (Huangyan Dao in Chinese; Bajo de Masinloc or Panatag in Tagalog) after Philippine authorities intercepted and arrested Chinese fishermen who were found to harvest threatened or endangered species (e.g., coral, sea turtles, sharks, and giant clams) around the waters of the shoal.[92] The standoff lasted about two months, as the two sides could not agree on the terms of mutual withdrawal. The standoff ended in July 2012 when the Philippines withdrew its vessels under the assumption that it had reached an agreement with China on a mutual withdrawal of vessels.[93] However, China denied a mutual withdrawal agreement, establishing *de facto* control over the Scarborough Shoal through occupation by its vessels and by erecting a barrier across the lagoon of the shoal.[94]

As a result, on January 22, 2013, the Philippines submitted its SCS dispute with China to arbitration under the compulsory dispute settlement provisions of UNCLOS. On February 19, 2013, China rejected the arbitration rejecting the tribunal's jurisdiction by submitting its position paper.[95] However, the tribunal

---

its distance from the United States and China, International Information Network Analysis, The Sasakawa Peace Foundation, May 16, 2023, at https://www.spf.org/iina/en/articles/shoji_16.html.

91 It is observed that President Ferdinand Marcos Jr, who came to power in June 2022, takes a firmer stance against China than the previous administration, publicly denouncing and sharing footage of alleged Chinese aggression. See Rebecca Ratcliffe, Risk of miscalculation' rises in South China Sea as Beijing ramps up aggressive tactics, September 29, 2023, The Guardian, at https://www.theguardian.com/world/2023/sep/29/risk-of-miscalculation-rises-in-south-china-sea-as-beijing-ramps-up-aggressive-tactics.

92 Maximo Paulino T. Sison III, "Universalizing the Law of the Sea in the South China Sea Dispute," *Ocean Development and International Law*, 49, no. 2 (2018), p. 160.

93 During the standoff negotiations, China warned the Philippines not to "internationalize" the dispute by (1) referring it to international arbitration, (2) seeking the help of ASEAN, or (3) seeking the help of the U.S., which has an alliance with the Philippines under the 1951 Mutual Defense Treaty. *Ibid.*, p. 161.

94 For a timeline of the events in the 2012 Scarborough Standoff, see Francois-Xavier Bonnet, "Geopolitics of Scarborough Shoal," Research Institute on Contemporary Southeast Asia, (IRASEC) Discussion Paper No. 14 (November 2012), p. 5, at www.irasec.com/ouvrage34.

95 Position Paper of the Government of the People's Republic of China on the Matter of Jurisdiction in the South China Sea Arbitration Initiated by the Republic of the Philippines, December 7, 2014, at https://www.fmprc.gov.cn/nanhai/eng/snhwtlcwj_1/t1368895.htm.

found jurisdiction for the Filipino claims.[96] On July 12, 2016, the tribunal rendered a unanimous award, ruling that China's expansive maritime claims and related actions in the SCS are inconsistent with UNCLOS. As Article 11 of Annex VII (Arbitration) of UNCLOS sets out, the award is binding the Philippines and China.

Specifically, the award found the Chinese claim to historic rights unlawlful according to the nine-dash line in the SCS. As discussed in the following sections, China has never expressly clarified the nature or scope of its historic rights. Nor has it ever clarified its understanding of the meaning of the "nine-dash line."[97] Under the assumption that the nine-dash line is a claim to the living and nonliving resources within the maritime space it encompasses, the tribunal decided that Chinese claims to historic rights, or other sovereign rights or jurisdiction, in the areas encircled by the nine-dash line is contrary to UNCLOS, and thus, without lawful effect to the extent that the dashed line exceeds the geographic and substantive limits of China's maritime entitlements under the Convention.[98]

The award is also significant in interpreting the conditions that divide rocks and islands under Article 121(3). Upon extensive examination, the tribunal concluded that "none of the high-tide features in the Spratly Islands is capable of sustaining human habitation or economic life of their own" and therefore, "such features shall have no [EEZ] or continental shelf."[99]

The tribunal further found that China has, through the operation of its marine surveillance vessels, breached the Philippines' sovereign rights to the non-living resources of its continental shelf in the area of Reed Bank.[100] Also, the tribunal declared that China had breached the Philippines' sovereign rights over the living resources of its EEZ by promulgating its 2012 moratorium on fishing in the SCS, without exception for areas of the SCS falling within the EEZ of the Philippines and without limiting the moratorium to Chinese flagged vessels.[101] As for Scarborough Shoal, having confirmed it as a traditional fishing ground for fishermen of many nationalities, the tribunal ruled that the measure

96 See Award, Jurisdiction, para. 153; Award, Merits, para. 447. See also, Bernard H. Oxman, "The South China Sea Arbitration Award," *University of Miami International and Comparative Law Review*, 24 (2017), p. 235.

97 The South China Sea Award, Merits, para. 180.

98 *Ibid.*, paras. 207–211, 278.

99 Award, Merits, paras. 554–570, 626; Bernard H. Oxman, "The South China Sea Arbitration Award," *University of Miami International and Comparative Law Review*, 24 (2017), p. 255.

100 The South China Sea Award, Merits, para. 1203, B (8).

101 *Ibid.*, para. 1203, B (9).

in which China prevented Filipino fishermen from engaging in traditional fishing there from May 2012 onward was illegal.[102]

China rejected the ruling, saying that it "is null and void and has no binding force" and that China "neither accepts nor recognizes [the award]."[103] Shortly before the arbitral award, in June 2016, the Russian and Chinese governments issued the Declaration on the Promotion of International Law,[104] through which the two countries expressed their joint interpretation of the overarching framework of international law. It emphasized the principles of sovereign equality, non-intervention and that "all dispute settlement means and mechanisms [should be] based on consent."[105] China has explicitly expressed its view on the SCS dispute consistently and continuously, which will be discussed in the following Chapter.[106]

2.3 *Land Reclamation and Island-Building*

China currently occupies the entirety of Paracel Islands and some ocean features in the Spratlys.[107] China has built seven fortified islands throughout the Spratlys.[108] On Fiery Cross Reef, China built an airstrip more than 3000 meters

102 *Ibid.*, para. 1203, B (11).

103 China, "Statement of the Ministry of Foreign Affairs of the People's Republic of China on the Award of 12 July 2016 of the Arbitral Tribunal in the South China Sea Arbitration Established at the Request of the Republic of the Philippines," at https://www.fmprc.gov.cn/nanhai/eng/snhwtlcwj_1/t1379492.htm.

104 Ministry of Foreign Affairs of the Russian Federation (2016), The Declaration of the Russian Federation and the People's Republic of China on the Promotion of International Law, June 25, 2016, at http://www.mid.ru/en/foreign_policy/position_word_order/-/asset_publisher/6S4RuXfeYlKr/content/id/2331698.19.

105 Harriet Moynihan, *China's Evolving Approach to International Dispute Settlement*, March 2017, Chatham House the Royal Institute of International Affairs, p. 4.

106 According to Hayton, three months after the ruling, China allowed Philippine and Vietnamese boats to resume fishing at Scarborough Shoal and China avoided drilling for oil and gas on the wrong side of the invisible lines prescribed by UNCLOS. See Bill Hayton, "Beijing shifts strategy in South China Sea," *Nikkei Asian Review*, July 12, 2017, at https://asia.nikkei.com/Politics/Beijing-shifts-strategy-in-South-China-Sea2; see also Allen R. Carlson, "Why Chinese Nationalism Could Impact the East and South China Seas VERY Differently," *The National Interest*, September 24, 2015, at https://nationalinterest.org/feature/why-chinese-nationalism-could-impact-the-east-south-china-13922.

107 These include Cuarteron Reef, Gaven Reef, McKennan Reef, Hughes Reef, Johnson Reef, Fiery Cross Reef, Mischief Reef, and Subi Reef.

108 Asia Maritime Transparency Initiative, Center for Strategic and International Studies, at http://amti.csis.org/category/south-china-sea/. Kelly observes that China has taken a play from Japan's playbook when Tokyo built up the Okinotori reefs in the 1980s to bolster its own claim. See Michael J. Kelly, "United States Ratification of the Law of the Sea

long and a seaport capable of receiving major surface combatants.[109] China completed similar airstrips on two of the other fortified islands. At least three of the seven island-building projects are inside the Philippine EEZ. Also, China has built a military infrastructure on seven islands in the SCS via China's land reclamation projects. There are large-scale military installations on Fiery Cross Reef, Subi Reef, and Mischief Reef. Each of the three has a completed military airstrip, underground storage bunkers, military communication-sensor-radar arrays, hardened shelters for, what appears to be offensive missiles, and close-in-weapons defenses.[110]

The four smaller islands (Johnson South Reef, Cuarteron Reef, Gavan Reef, and Hughes Reef) hold anti-aircraft guns and likely have a close-in-weapons system to protect against cruise missile strikes.[111] China keeps enforcing its law against other disputants and opening new research stations on artificial reefs.[112]

From early 2018 to late 2019, China regularly utilized its Spratlys outposts to support naval and coast guard operations in the SCS.[113] Meanwhile, in 2019, China did not resume land reclamation or major military infrastructure construction at its seven Spratly Islands outposts.[114] US experts appraise that

Convention: Securing our Navigational Future While Managing China's Blue Water Ambitions," *Case Western Reserve Journal of International Law,* 45 (2012), p. 469.

109 CSIS's Asia Maritime Transparency Initiative: Fiery Cross Reef, at https://amti.csis.org/fiery-cross-reef/ (explaining that the airstrip is 3110 meters and a port facility is being constructed as well).

110 Asian Maritime Transparency Initiative, A Constructive Year for Chinese Base Building, December 14, 2017, at https://amti.csis.org/constructive-year-chinese-building/.

111 Asia Maritime Transparency Initiative, China's New Spratly Island Defenses, December 15, 2016, at https://amti.csis.org/chinas-new-spratly-island-defenses/; Amanda Macias, China Is Quietly Conducting Electronic Warfare Tests in the South China Sea, *CNBC*, July 5, 2018; Jesse Johnson, "In First, China Permanently Stations Search-and-Rescue Vessel in South China Sea's Spratly Chain," *Japan Times,* July 29, 2018.

112 Hannah Beech, "U.S. Warships Enter Disputed Waters of South China Sea as Tensions With China Escalate," New York Times, April 21, 2020, at https://www.nytimes.com/2020/04/21/world/asia/coronavirus-south-china-sea-warships.html.

113 Office of the Secretary of Defense, Military and Security Developments Involving the People's Republic of China 2020, Annual Report to Congress, p. 101.

114 China's outposts in the Spratly Islands can support military operations and have advanced weapon systems, according to the US appraisal. However, there is currently no significant evidence of air activity in the region. See Office of the Secretary of Defense, Military and Security Developments Involving the People's Republic of China 2020, Annual Report to Congress, p. 100. The US also assesses that China could launch an invasion of small Taiwan-occupied islands in the SCS, such as Pratas or Itu Aba. See *ibid.*, p. 114.

China's reclamation and militarization of features in the SCS have "subtly changed the situation without provoking a strong military response."[115]

After an absence of tense conflicts over hydrocarbons in 2022, experts predict that oil and gas development in the region could re-emerge as a primary flashpoint after 2023, as the disputants push ahead with new exploitation projects.[116]

3 International Law and the Resolution of the South China Sea Dispute

The conspicuous nature of the SCS dispute is concerned with rights and obligations under international law. The interpretation and application of relevant provisions of international treaties and legal principles are at the core of the dispute. Territorial sovereignty (a major source of the dispute) has to be settled under general international law. The rest of the dispute can be identified as ocean law issues. UNCLOS has some obscurity and room for interpretation in contents. The US has maintained that UNCLOS represents customary international law with which it is committed to observing;[117] and Taiwan has taken steps to bring its legislation into conformity with UNCLOS.[118]

3.1 *Territorial Sovereignty*

The disposal of territorial title over maritime geographic features is essential to dealing with maritime conflicts in the SCS. International law recognizes several ways to gain legal possession of territory. There is no authoritative international agreement or other positive law on this question. Instead, international case law, state practice, historic custom, and scholarly commentary have contributed to the definition of territorial acquisition under international law. The decentralized distribution of authority justifies changes in the international

115 Michael J. Mazarr et al. (2018), p. 95.

116 (ALMOST) EVERYONE IS DRILLING INSIDE THE NINE-DASH LINE, ASIA MARITIME TRANSPARENCY INITIATIVE, March 8, 2023, at https://amti.csis.org/almost-everyone-is-drilling-inside-the-nine-dash-line/.

117 "United States Oceans Policy," Statement of the President (10 March 1983), 19 Weekly Compilation of Presidential Documents, No. 10 (14 March 1984), p. 383.

118 For Taiwanese legislations and the difference from China, see Song Yann-Huei & Zou Keyuan, Maritime Legislation of Mainland China and Taiwan: Developments, Comparison, Implications, and Potential Challenges for the United States, *Ocean Development and International Law*, 31 (2000), pp. 310–312.

law of possession over time. Conquest or subjugation, for example, is no longer accepted as a legal mode of territorial acquisition.[119]

States can argue they have obtained a land territory based on historic title, contiguity, discovery and occupation, prescription, accretion, state secession (or *uti possidetis*), cession, and conquest (the mode of acquisition of territory).[120] The issue of territorial title[121] is often complex and involves the application of various legal principles to the facts, including principles deriving from the prohibition on the acquisition of territory by force and the invalidity of coerced treaties.[122]

First, by historic title (an ancient and historic connection with the land), a nation may claim possession of territory. The concept informs the principle of "immemorial possession" and relies upon the evidence of general repute or opinion as to matters of historical fact. As Crawford points out, particularly in Asia, traditional boundaries play a significant role.[123] This type of title has been supported by international adjudication.[124] In the *Minquiers and Echrehos* case, both France and the United Kingdom contend that they have an ancient or original title to Echreos and the Minquiers.[125]

Second, a nation may acquire unclaimed territory that is geographically proximate to land that it already possesses: contiguity.[126] Considerations of contiguity and geographical unity come to the fore when the disputed territory is uninhabited, barren, or uncharted. Thus, in the *Land, Maritime and Frontier Dispute* case, the Chamber held that the island of Meanguerita was a dependency of the larger island of Meanguera due to its small size, its proximity, and the fact that the claimants to the dispute treated the two as a single unit.[127]

119 Laurent Mayali and John Yoo, "Resolution of Territorial Disputes in East Asia: The Case of Dokdo," *Berkeley Journal of International Law*, 36, no. 3 (2018), p. 525.

120 For a detailed explanation, see *ibid.*, pp. 526–533.

121 The name of "title" is preferred now because the "mode of acquisition of territory" is not being able to embrace all the different ways by which territorial sovereignty is established. See Marcelo G. Kohen and Mahadou Hebie, Territory, Acquisition, *The Max Planck Encyclopedia of Public International Law* (Oxford University Press, 2012), IX, pp. 887–900.

122 James Crawford, *Brownlie's Principles of Public international law*, 8th ed. (Oxford: Oxford University Press, 2012), p. 221.

123 *Ibid.*

124 The *Minquiers and Ecrehos* Case (France v. UK), Judgment, ICJ Reports 1953, para. 47; El Salvador/Honduras, ICJ Reports 1992, para. 351.

125 The *Minquiers and Ecrehos* Case (France v. the U.K.), Judgment, ICJ Report 1953, para. 53.

126 Laurent Mayali and John Yoo (2018), p. 526.

127 *Land, Island and Maritime Frontier Dispute* (El Salvador/Honduras: Nicaragua intervening), Judgement, 11 September 1992, ICJ Reports 1992, p. 570.

Contiguity is little more than a technique in the application of the normal principles of effective occupation; thus, this notion *per se* is not helpful.[128] In the *Island of Palmas* arbitration of 1925,[129] Judge Huber mentions that "the alleged principle itself is by its very nature so uncertain and contested that even government of the same State on different occasions maintained contradictory opinions as to its soundness."[130] In addition, the contiguity argument was rejected in the *Clipperton* case and was not a factor considered in the *Minquiers and Ecrehos* case.[131] Malaysia, the Philippines, and Vietnam claim that they are entitled to some or all of the Spratly Islands based on their proximity to these features, a claim to which China thoroughly objects.[132]

Third, discovery and occupation are major modes of territorial acquisition. A nation may discover land that is unclaimed by any other organized political unit. Such land is considered *terra nullius*. To maintain title, a state must maintain the effective occupation, also named "*effectivités*"[133] of the discovered land. By discovery, a mere "inchoate" title to sovereignty arises, which is to be reinforced by effective occupation.[134] International tribunals define effective occupation as acts required to show an intention to occupy and display government authority in a continuous and uncontested fashion.[135]

A wide range of acts may constitute manifestations of the exercise of state sovereignty, which includes the three traditional powers of a state: legislative, executive, and judicial power. In the *Minquiers and Ecrehos* case, ICJ declared that "[t]his legislative Act [a British Treasury Warrant of 1375] was a clear

128 James Crawford (2012), pp. 237–8.

129 This arbitration is between the Netherland and the US regarding the Island Palmas located between the Philippines and Indonesia. See *Island of Palmas* (1928) 2 RIAA.

130 *Island of Palmas* (1928) 2 RIAA, p. 854.

131 Mark J. Valencia et al. (1997), p. 40.

132 Ji Guoxing, The Spratlys Disputes and Prospects for Settlement, ISIS, Malaysia, 1992, p. 18.

133 Doctrine and case law use the French term *effectivités* to refer to acts undertaken in the exercise of State authority through which a State manifests its intention to act as the sovereign over a territory. Conditions for valid *effectivités* related both to the entity performing them, and the specific nature of the acts performed.

134 *Island of Palmas* (1928) 2 RIAA, p. 869 (Judge Huber concluded that "An inchoate title however cannot prevail over a definite title founded on continuous and peaceful display of sovereignty").

135 Therefore, an act performed by a trustee under the system enshrined in Chapter XII of the UN Charter, or acts performed by a belligerent occupant are not performed *à titre de souverain*. They cannot be taken into account in a territorial dispute as having probative value for the establishment of a title of sovereignty. See Marcelo G. Kohen and Mahadou Hebie, Territory, Acquisition, *The Max Planck Encyclopedia of Public International Law*, (Oxford University Press, 2012), IX, p. 894. See sldo PCIJ, Legal Status of Eastern Greenland, Judgement, April 5, 1933, pp. 27–28.

manifestation of British sovereignty over the Ecrehos at a time when a dispute as to such sovereignty had not yet arisen."[136] In the *Ligitan/Sipadan* case, Malaysian sovereignty was declared by ICJ based on its legislation regulating turtle egg fishing. The court opined that "both the measures taken to regulate and control the collecting of turtle eggs and the establishment of a bird reserve must be seen as regulatory and administrative assertions of authority over territory which is specified by name."[137]

Administrative and judicial acts have also been taken into account in the *Minquiers and Ecrehos* case. ICJ considered that the tribunal of Jersey had exercised jurisdiction over the Ecrehos for more than 100 years. The construction of navigational aids can be legally relevant for very small islands as acts *à titre de souverain,*[138] although they do not constitute *per se* an act manifesting the exercise of sovereignty.[139] Military activities and police surveillance were considered to be *effectivités*, but official publications, depending on their context, may or may not constitute evidence of *effectivités*.

Fourth, by prescription, states can acquire territory that is possessed by other states if discovery in good faith and effective control over the territory is proved.[140] In practice, distinguishing effective occupation and prescription is difficult; neither *Island of Palmas* nor *Eastern Greenland* employs the categories.[141] Prescription resembles the common law doctrine of adverse possession and the civil law doctrine of acquisitive prescription, or Roman law's usucapio.[142]

Fifth, a nation may increase its territory due to natural changes in land features (accretion). For instance, deposits on a sea coast may result in an extension of sovereignty. A more drastic example is the emergence of an island within the territorial sea of Iwo Jima due to volcanic activity in 1986; in such a case, no formal acts of appropriation are required.[143]

136 The *Minquiers and Ecrehos* Case (France v. the U.K.), Judgment, *ICJ Report 1953*, p. 66.

137 *Sovereignty over Pulau Ligitan and Pulau Sipadan* (IndonesialMalaysia), Judgment, *ICJ Reports 2002*, para. 145.

138 *Maritime Delimitation and Territorial Questions between Qatar and Bahrain*, Merits, Judgment, *ICJ Reports 2001*, para. 197.

139 The *Minquiers and Ecrehos* Case (France v. the U.K.), Judgment, *ICJ Report 1953*, p 70–71.

140 Laurent Mayali and John Yoo (2018), p. 526.

141 James Crawford (2012), p. 222.

142 Roger O'Keefe, "Legal Title versus Effectivités: Prescription and the Promise and Problems of Private Law Analogies," *International Community Law Review*, 13, 2011, pp. 147–188; Laurent Mayali and John Yoo (2018), p. 526.

143 James Crawford (2012), p. 240. Sometimes dramatic increase in state territory, such as the creation of new islands as a result of volcanic activity is called as avulsion. See Martin Dixon (2017), p. 169.

Sixth, state secession or *uti possidetis* is claimed by new states that come into existence from the dissolution of an empire or larger nation to maintain previous colonial borders.[144]

Seventh, cession refers to the transfer of territorial possession to other nations by treaty or agreements. This may be for financial gain, as occurred with the transfer of Alaska from the Soviet Union to the US, or it may be in the settlement of a border dispute or as part of a more general arrangement.[145] Cession can also occur at the end of the war when the defeated nation gives up territory as part of a peace settlement.[146] In the *Island of Palmas* case, the US based its title on cession from Spain under the Treaty of Paris 1989, by which Spain had ceded the Philippines to the America that believed the *Island of Palmas* to be included.

Eighth, conquest was a historic means of acquiring territory. The use of force was lawful before 1945, or perhaps 1928 (the date of the Kellogg-Briand Pact), and the acquisition of territory through conquest was common. With the UN Charter that renders using force illegal, conquest disappeared as a mode of territorial acquisition. Similarly, a treaty of cession imposed by the use of force is to be void. For example, Iraq could not obtain title to Kuwait's territory by way of force.[147]

In addition to the above, we should survey other legal principles, such as the intertemporal principle, the critical date, and the effect of maps. To begin with, Judge Max Huber confirmed the "intertemporal principle" in *Island of Palmas* by opining that one must assess the facts in light of the international law at the "relevant time," not the law at the time the issue falls to be decided.[148] Thus, Huber examined whether the mere Spanish discovery of the 2.4 sq km island was sufficient in the early 16th century to give it a good title at that time.[149] It would seem incongruous if title were required to be maintained at every moment of time, thereby threatening many titles.[150]

Next, every dispute should designate a certain date (critical date) on which the contentious facts are to be found and assessed. All matters arising after that date should not be taken into account in deciding title to territory because the circumstances existing at that date are important.[151] In general, international

144 Laurent Mayali and John Yoo (2018), p. 527.
145 Martin Dixon (2017), p. 167.
146 Laurent Mayali and John Yoo (2018), p. 527.
147 Martin Dixon (2017), p. 168.
148 *Island of Palmas* (1928) 2 RIAA, p. 831.
149 Anthony Aust, *Handbook of International Law* (Cambridge University Press, 2010), p. 35.
150 James Crawford (2012), p. 218.
151 Martin Dixon (2017), p. 164.

courts or tribunals will choose the critical date for a particular case with reference to the law applicable to the facts and the necessity of confining the dossier to the more relevant facts before the existence of a dispute.[152] In *Island of Palmas,* it was the date of the Treaty between Spain and the US (1898) at which the latter's claim first arose. In *Pulau Ligitan and Pulau Sipadan*, it was the year 1969 at which the competing claims of Indonesia and Malaysia to the islands advanced.[153]

The effect of maps also should be kept in mind regarding territorial title. In *Island of Palmas*, Judge Huber stressed that "[a]ny maps which do not precisely indicate the political distribution of territories ... clearly marked as such, must be rejected forthwith."[154] In *Honduras Borders*, the tribunal noted that descriptive materials, such as maps, are of "slight value," especially "when it relates to territory of which little or nothing was known and in which it does not appear that any administrative control was actually exercised."[155] Along the same line, ICJ observed, in *Burkina Faso v. Republic of Mali,* that maps "merely constitute information which varies in accuracy from case to case ... [and] cannot constitute a territorial title" as being "only extrinsic evidence of varying reliability or unreliability."[156]

That being said, maps are still considered relevant proof because they reflect a government's intention to claim the land within its territory.[157] Meanwhile, failure to include an island within its territorial boundaries, even only on a map, would reflect a government's belief that it had no claim to possession.[158] It is useful to review the attributes of old maps by European cartographers. European cartographers relied in large part on two sources of information: First, eyewitness reports filed by Christian missionaries who had provided new information. Second, the general description of the territories is more

152 James Crawford (2012), p. 219.

153 Martin Dixon (2017), p. 164.

154 *Island of Palmas* (1928) 2 RIAA, p. 852.

155 *Honduras Borders* (Guatemala v. Honduras), 2 R.I.A.A. (1933), p. 1325.

156 *Frontier Dispute* (Burkina Faso v. Mali), 22 December 1986, Judgment, *ICJ Reports 1986*, p. 582.

157 *Ibid.* Similarly, in *Territorial and Maritime Dispute between Nicaragua and Honduras in the Caribbean Sea*, ICJ stated that "the submission of cartographic material by the Parties essentially serves the purpose of buttressing their respective claims and of confirming their arguments. The Court finds that it can derive little of legal significance from the official maps submitted and the maps of geographical institutions cited; these maps will be treated with a certain reserve." See *Territorial and Maritime Dispute between Nicaragua and Honduras in the Caribbean Sea* (Nicaragua v. Honduras), 8 October 2007, Judgment, *ICJ Reports 2007*, para. 217.

158 Laurent Mayali and John Yoo (2018), p. 517.

important than "[h]istorical details and geographical accuracy" especially for "distant lands inhabited by strange people with bizarre customs and a colorful way of life."[159]

On the whole, the question of who owns the maritime feature in the Paracel and Spratly Islands generally favors China and Taiwan.[160] China may have visited the Paracel and Spratly Islands for more than six centuries before any other nations claiming them. China may have accumulated data concerning protests of violations of its claim of right. According to Chinese claimed records, China appears to have a better basis of the claim (the inchoate title) than does Vietnam and the Philippines. If Chinese history materials, books, and maps are correct, it seems that China discovered the Spratly Islands from 206 B.C. to 220 A.D. Also, a better-documented visit to the Spratlys was a 1292 expedition by Kublai Khan to Java that sailed through these islands and briefly described them. Based on these data, China may claim that an inchoate title was established.[161]

However, as Judge Huber indicated, "[a]n inchoate title ... cannot prevail over a definite title founded on continuous and peaceful display of sovereignty."[162] In this sense, Vietnam may contend that an inchoate Chinese title was not perfected before Vietnamese claims began; if this is true, the territory was *res nullius* (owned by no state) until the 20th century. Vietnam may argue that its claim began earlier than 1930, with a French ship planting flags and marking the islands. China is urged to prove that the acts of fisherman who visited the Paracels and Spratlys were not merely private acts.[163]

Some publicists suspect the reliability of Chinese history materials as evidence.[164] Hayton doubts that China has archaeological evidence, amounting to proof of occupation, that any Chinese ships made voyages across the SCS until the 10th century CE.[165] Hayton argues that the first meaningful, legal act

---

159 *Ibid.*, p. 518.

160 For a similar analysis, see Richard D. Beller, "Analyzing the Relationship between International Law and International Politics in China's and Vietnam's Territorial Dispute Over the Spratly Islands," *Texas International Law Journal*, 29, no. 2 (Spring 1994), p. 310.

161 *Ibid.*, p. 305.

162 *Island of Palmas* (1928) 2 RIAA, p. 869.

163 In *Clipperton* Island, those of the American guano hunters were not mere private persons. See Richard D. Beller (1994), p. 305.

164 In contrast, some view that Chinese claims are stronger than those of other claimants. See, e.g., Anthony Carty, The South China Sea Disputes Are Not Yet Justiciable, in Shicun WU and Keyuan Zou (2016), p. 50.

165 Bill Hayton (2014), pp. 11, 97–98. For a detailed analysis on this argument, see Bill Hayton, "When Good Lawyers Write Bad History: Unreliable Evidence and the South China Sea Territorial Dispute," *Ocean Development & International Law*, 48, no. 1 (2017), pp. 17–34.

of sovereignty occurred on December 12, 1946, when two Chinese (Taiwanese) Navy ships arrived at Itu Aba.[166] Similarly, Liselotte Odgaard examines that China did not exercise jurisdiction, military or otherwise, over the Spratlys before 1988.[167]

China needs to prove that it has obtained the inchoate title and conducted and displayed sovereignty over the Spratly and Paracel Islands over time. In territorial dispute resolution, what is critical is not whether one has absolute evidence but a relatively provable one that has relative superiority in the decision of territorial title.[168] In *Gulf of Fonseca*, ICJ awarded Meanguera and Meanguerita to El Salvador after reviewing the relevant manifestation of sovereignty.[169] That means that it will be sufficient for China to produce evidence of "an intentional display of power and authority over the territory, by the exercise of jurisdiction and state functions, on a continuous and peaceful basis"[170] with the minimally better claim. In other words, China does not have to present all evidence about what it argues, such as its records of General Kang Tai of the East Wu State of the Three Kingdoms Period (220–280 AD).

Meanwhile, Vietnam's positions should be surveyed through the lens of the principle of estoppel (a state that has taken a particular position may be under an obligation to act consistently with it on another occasion).[171] As ICJ opined in *the Preah Vihear Temple* case, a rival claimant may be estopped by its previous conduct.[172] In many situations, acquiescence and express admissions are part of the evidence of sovereignty.[173] Despite the Vietnamese justification of its previous statements favoring Chinese title to the Spratlys, its previous position will hound Vietnam continually.

---

166 Bill Hayton (2014), p. 95.

167 The concept of effective occupation did not exist in the Confucian legal system. See Liselotte Odgaard, *Maritime security between China and Southeast Asia: conflict and cooperation in the making of regional order* (Abingdon and New York: Routledge, 2016), pp. 92–93.

168 Garth Abraham, "Paradise Claimed: Disputed Sovereignty over the Chagos Archipelago," *South African Law Journal*, 128, no. 1 (2011), pp. 98–99.

169 *Land, Island and Maritime Frontier Dispute* (El Salvador/Honduras: Nicaragua intervening), ICJ Report 1992, pp. 570–579.

170 *Eritrea/Yemen – Sovereignty and Maritime Delimitation in the Red Sea*, Award of the Arbitral Tribunal in the First Stage – Territorial Sovereignty and Scope of the Dispute, Judgment, October 9, 1998, PCA, para. 239.

171 When a state has acted to its detriment in relying on a formal declaration by another state, the latter may be estopped from denying its responsibility for any adverse consequences. See Anthony Aust, *Handbook of International Law* (Cambridge: Cambridge University Press, 2010), p. 8. For a similar view on Vietnam's weakness on estoppel, see Bill Hayton (2014), p. 96.

172 Anthony Aust (2010), p. 38; *Temple of Preah Vihear* (Cambodia/Thailand), *ICJ Reports 1962*.

173 James Crawford (2012), p. 234.

The Philippine legal arguments look weak as well. Its claims are largely based on the assumption that the Spratly Islands were abandoned by the 1951 San Francisco Peace Treaty[174]—it obtained sovereignty over them by the 1956 Cloma's occupation on the Spratlys. However, Cloma's activities cannot be attributed to the Philippines because Cloma was not a Filipino official. Also, the 1951 Peace Treaty did not leave the Spratly islands as *res nullius*, nor attempted to attribute disputed islands titles to other states beyond removing Japanese legal rights.[175] As ICJ confirms, in *Pedra Branca*, the "abandonment of sovereignty over part of its territory" must be "manifested clearly and without doubt by that conduct and the relevant facts."[176] Under Article 2(f),[177] Japan no longer had a legal claim to the Spratlys and Paracels;[178] thus, the legal rights of the disputants remain unchanged by the Peace Treaty. The resolution of the territorial title falls under general international law.[179]

Parenthetically, China debunks Philippine territorial claims over the Spratlys by pointing out that territorial boundary treaties in the late 19th or early 20th centuries do not contain the Spratlys as the Philippines' territory: for instance, the 1989 Treaty of Paris, the 1900 Treaty of Washington between the US and Spain, and the 1930 treaty between the UK and the US did not include islands in the SCS as the Philippines' territory.[180]

3.2 *Freedom of the Seas*

The history of international law has been full of territorial temptation since the Peace of Westphalia.[181] However, the law of the sea has been a kind of

174 The Philippines also claims that the Spratlys were "de facto under the trusteeship of the Allied Powers." As a result, the status of the islands as "trusts" nullified any previous ownership of them, and justified its occupation of the features. See Mark J. Valencia et al. (1997), p. 34.

175 American policymakers deliberately left unresolved territorial disputes between Japan and its neighbors in order to reach a quick peace. See Thomas Schwartz and John Yoo, "Asian Territorial Disputes and the 1951 San Francisco Peace Treaty: The Case of Dokdo," *Chinese Journal of International Law*, 18 (2019), p. 536.

176 *Sovereignty over Pedra Brance/Pulau Batu Phteh, Middle Rocks and South Ledge* (Malaysia/Singapore), *ICJ Reports 2008*, para. 122.

177 Article 2(f) stipulates that "Japan renounces all right, title and claim to the Spratly Islands and to the Paracel Islands."

178 Thomas Schwartz and John Yoo (2019), p. 544.

179 *Ibid.*, p. 538.

180 Chinese Society of International Law, "The South China Sea Arbitration Awards: A Critical Study," *Chinese Journal of International Law*, 17 (2018), p. 252.

181 Bernard H. Oxman, "The Territorial Temptation: a Siren Song at Sea," *American Journal of International Law*, 100, no. 4 (2006), p. 830.

exception; Grotius's thesis of *mare liberum* (the "Free Sea" or "Open Sea") gained popularity over John Selden's *Mare Clausum* (the "Closed Sea")—freedom of the seas became the rule of the game.[182]

UNCLOS contains provisions of navigation and the right and obligation of coastal states and foreign states; yet, due to its indeterminacy of some institutions, the US and China interpret the same treaty text differently in terms of lawful activities in the SCS.[183] The disparities in the interpretation of freedom of the seas (often referred to as freedom of navigation) lie in, *inter alia*, the innocent passage of military vessels in foreign territorial seas and military activities in foreign EEZs. Article 17 of UNCLOS stipulates that "Subject to this Convention, ships of all States, whether coastal or land-locked, enjoy the right of innocent passage through the territorial sea." In accordance with Articles 58 and 87, freedoms of the high seas are applied to EEZs, which include freedom of navigation, freedom of overflight, and other internationally lawful uses of the sea related to these freedoms.

The US and most Western states hold that coastal states have the right to regulate economic activities (e.g., fishing and oil exploration) but not to regulate foreign military activities within their EEZs. UNCLOS does not expressly authorize military activities in foreign EEZs without the consent of the foreign nation. That being said, the US maintains that military activities are justified as traditional freedom of the sea, falling under "other internationally lawful uses of the sea" in Article 58 of UNCLOS.[184] On state practice, the US adduces that only 27 states retain restrictions that limit the exercise of high seas freedoms by foreign navies beyond 12 nm from the baselines.[185]

For the US, the freedom of the seas means that its navy can operate in about 30.4 percent of the world's oceans (which is the size of EEZs).[186] This position

182 For the debate and historical background of *Mare Liberum* and *Mare Clausum* between Hugo Grotius (the Latinised Version of Huig de Groot) and John Selden, see Bill Hayton (2014), pp. 38–47.

183 *Ibid.*, p. 40.

184 James W. Houck and Nicole M. Anderson, "The United States, China, and Freedom of Navigation in the South China Sea," *Washington University Global Studies Law Review*, 13 (2014), pp. 443–444.

185 These states include Bangladesh, Brazil, Burma, Cambodia, Cape Verde, China, Egypt, Haiti, India, Iran, Kenya, Malaysia, Maldives, Mauritius, North Korea, Pakistan, Portugal, Saudi Arabia, Somalia, Sri Lanka, Sudan, Syria, Thailand, United Arab Emirates, Uruguay, Venezuela, and Vietnam. Meanwhile, Ecuador and Peru claim an extension of their territorial sea beyond 12 nm. See Ronald O'Rourke, Maritime Territorial and Exclusive Economic Zone (EEZ) Disputes Involving China: Issues for Congress, Congressional Research Service (R42784), May 24, 2018, pp. 8–9, fn. 23.

186 For a comparative size of the various maritime zones, see https://www.gc.noaa.gov/gcil_maritime.html.

is repeatedly confirmed by US officials. For instance, in December 2018, then President Trump signed into law the Asia Reassurance Initiative Act, which authorized the spending of US$1.5 billion a year for 2019–2023 to enhance the US presence in the Indo-Pacific, including the enforcement of Freedom of Navigation (FON).[187]

By contrast, China understands UNCLOS giving coastal states the right to regulate foreign economic and military activities in their EEZs. For China, "freedom of navigation" is defined in a narrow manner to pertain to commercial vessels' navigation only.[188] China perceives "peaceful uses of the seas" under Articles 88[189] and 301[190] of UNCLOS as banning military activities in foreign EEZs.[191] Further, China holds that FON by warships is a Western colonial practice, facilitating the European colonization of Asian states.[192] On April 22, 2019, Shen Jinlong, commander of the Chinese People's Liberation Army (PLA) Navy, stressed that "[f]reedom of navigation ... should not be used as an excuse to infringe upon the legitimate rights and interests of littoral states."[193]

Interestingly, in 2013, China acknowledged that it conducted surveillance and marine data collection in EEZ of foreign states, including the US EEZ.[194] Also, some US lawyers criticize that China has frequently interfered

187 Reuters, US Destroyer Sails in Disputed South China Sea Amid Trade Talks, January 7, 2019, at https://www.reuters.com/article/us-usa-trade-china-southchinasea/u-s-navyship-sails-in-disputed-south-china-sea-amid-trade-talks-with-beijing-idUSKCN1P10DS.

188 Mark J. Valencia, "The US-China Maritime Surveillance Debate," The Diplomat, August 4, 2017; Ronald O'Rourke, "Maritime Territorial and Exclusive Economic Zone (EEZ) Disputes Involving China: Issues for Congress," Congressional Research Service (R42784), May 24, 2018, p. 33.

189 Article 88 of UNCLOS.

190 Article 30 of UNCLOS.

191 Zhang Haiwen, "Is it Safeguarding the Freedom of Navigation or Maritime Hegemony of the US?" *Chinese Journal of International Law*, 9 (2010), pp. 44–45.

192 Haiwen Zhang, "Is it safeguading the freedom of navigation or maritime hegemony of the United States? – Comments on Raul (Pete) Pedrozo's article on military acitivities in the EEZ," *Chinese Journal of International Law*, 9, no. 1 (2010), p. 37.

193 VOA News, China Navy Chief Takes Dig at US Freedom of Navigation Patrols, April 23, 2019, at https://www.voanews.com/east-asia-pacific/china-navy-chief-takes-dig-us-freedom-navigation-patrols#:~:text=QINGDAO%2C%20CHINA%20%2D%20Freedom%20of%20navigation,disputed%20South%20China%20Sea%20islets.

194 Kimverly Hsu and Craig Murray, *China's Expanding Military operations in Foreign Exclusive Economic Zones*, US-China Economic and Security Review Commission Staff Research Backgrounder, June 19, 2013, at https://www.uscc.gov/sites/default/files/Research/Staff%20Backgrounder_China%20in%20Foreign%20EEZs.pdf. See also James W. Houck and Nicole M. Anderson, "The United States, China, and Freedom of Navigation in the South China Sea," *Washington University Global Studies Law Review*, 13 (2014), p. 446.

with non-Chinese commercial fishing operations, which ignores freedom of navigation.[195]

What does formal international law say? China appears to believe that what is not clearly authorized in UNCLOS is not permitted. In principle, general international law proscribes that what is not prohibited is allowed. ICJ confirmed this "lotus principle" ("restrictions upon the independence of States cannot therefore be presumed")[196] in its advisory opinion on *Legality of the Threat or Use of Nuclear Weapons,* that "States are free to threaten or use nuclear weapons unless it can be shown that they are bound not to do so by reference to a prohibition in either treaty law or customary international law."[197]

According to the traditional interpretation, military activities consistent with the principles of international law contained in the UN Charter are understood to be lawful under UNCLOS.[198] Further, the UNCLOS III negotiations were neither tasked with regulating military activities or the use of weapons nor prepared to stem such negotiations. In this sense, it would seem incongruous to consider the terms of Article 301 as constituting a general limitation on military activities at sea.[199]

That being said, an interpretative trend may change in conjunction with a shift in subsequent state practice. Because international law is based on what states say and what states do, it is true that apparent abrogation from its rules can result in the evolution of new rules.[200] This issue will be discussed in detail in the following Chapters.

3.3 *The Legal Status of Geographic Features*

The Spratly and Paracel Islands consist of multiple maritime features of different shapes. Although none of the claimants in the SCS have clarified their legal views on geographic features, identifying the legal status of geographic features is a starting point of negotiations. As the maxim of "the land dominates

195 Ronald O'Rourke (2018), p. 31.

196 *S.S. Lotus* (France v. Turkey), PCIJ, Series A, No. 10, September 7, 1927, p. 18.

197 *Legality of the Threat or Use of Nuclear Weapons*, Advisory Opinion, *ICJ Report 1996*, p. 238, para. 21.

198 Robin R. Churcill and Alan V. Lowe, *The International Law of the Sea,* 3rd edition (Manchester: Manchester University Press, 1999), pp. 430–1.

199 Alexander Proelss (ed.), *United Nations Convention on the Law of the Sea: A Commentary* (Oxford: Hart Publishing, 2017), p. 1944.

200 Lindsay Moir, *Reappraising the Resort to Force* (Oxford: Hart Publishing, 2010), pp. 114–5. See also TJ Farer, "The Prospect for International Law and Order in the Wake of Iraq," *American Journal of International Law*, Vol 97 (2003), p. 623.

the sea" indicates, maritime zones are generated only from the land territory.[201] In other words, some features are entitled to have maritime zones of national jurisdiction, but others are not bestowed on any sea areas.

In the UNCLOS system, geographic features are divided into (1) islands, (2) rocks, (3) low-tide elevations, (4) artificial islands, installations, and structures, and (5) submerged features according to its geological and sociological formation. First, on islands and rocks, Article 121(1) of UNCLOS defines an island as "a naturally formed area of land, surrounded by water, which is above water at high tide." Among islands that satisfy this condition, features that cannot sustain human habitation or economic life of their own are to be subcategorized as rocks (Article 121(3)). Rocks confer no EEZ or continental shelf. Since its entry into force of UNCLOS, Article 121 has been one of the most debated legal institutions.

Second, on low-tide elevations, Article 13 of UNCLOS sets out that "[a] low-tide elevation is a naturally formed area of land which is surrounded by and above water at low tide but submerged at high tide." Low-tide elevations are not islands, thereby confers no maritime zones of their own. In practice, a coastal state can use low-tide elevations within 12 nm of any land territory to be part of the baseline from which the breadth of the territorial sea is measured.[202]

Third, on artificial islands, installations, and structures, Article 60(1) stipulates that "the coastal State shall have the exclusive right to construct and to authorize and regulate the construction, operation and use of: (a) artificial islands; (b) installations and structures for the purposes provided for in Article 56 and other economic purposes; and (c) installations and structures which may interfere with the exercise of the rights of the coastal State in the zone."[203] These features are not entitled to any maritime zones of their own.[204] Regardless, coastal states have found many benefits from constructing artificial structures at sea. The SCS claimants have built installations and structures on low-tide elevations or submerged features within 200 nm of other claimants.[205] Of note, one observer argues that there are no islets that are entitled to

201 This maxim was approved by international courts and tribunals: for instance, by *Territorial and Maritime Dispute* (Nicaragua v. Colombia), ICJ Reports 2012, para. 140.

202 Article 13(2) of UNCLOS.

203 Moreover, a coastal state that constructs such artificial features is expected to establish "safety zones" around artificial islands, installations and structures up to 500 meters around them.

204 Article 60(8) of UNCLOS.

205 Robert Beckman, "The UN Convention on the Law of the Sea," *American Journal of International Law*, 107 (2013), p. 151.

any territorial seas at all in the Spratlys.[206] Again, none of the claimants have identified the legal status of disputed geographic features or maritime zones stemming from such features.

In the meantime, an authoritative opinion on maritime features involving Article 121, for the first time, was delivered by the Philippines-China arbitral tribunal in 2016. Above all, the tribunal clarifies a criterion that "human habitation" or "economic life" must be based on the natural condition of the feature itself without external or artificial modifications. For instance, "human habitation" is defined as where the inhabitants are "the natural population of the feature, for whose benefit the resources of the exclusive economic zone were seen to merit protection."[207] Upon examining the history of UNCLOS, the Tribunal emphasized that the purpose of creating the EEZ regime was "to preserve the resources of those waters for the benefit of the population of the coastal State."[208] In short, the SCS tribunal contributes to the interpretation of Article 121 to some degree.[209]

---

206 Summary of Proceedings of First Technical Working Group Meeting Working Group Meeting on Legal Matters in the South China Sea, Phuket, Thailand, July 2–5, 1995, p. 10, in Mark J. Valencia et al. (1997), p. 48, fn. 237.

207 The South China Sea Award, para. 542.

208 The South China Sea Award, para. 513.

209 The gist of tribunal's interpretation of Article 121 includes: 1. The term "rock" is not limited to features composed of solid rock. Thus, the geological and geomorphological characteristics of a high-tide feature are not relevant to its classification as a "rock"; 2. The "status of a feature is to be determined on the basis of its natural capacity, without external additions or modifications intended to increase its capacity to sustain human habitation or economic life of its own"; 3. The "critical factor" for the qualification of "human habitation" is the "non-transient character of the inhabitation, such that the inhabitants can fairly be said to constitute the natural population of the feature, for whose benefit the resources of the exclusive economic zone were seen to merit protection"; 4. The qualification of "economic life of their own" "will ordinarily be the life and livelihoods of the human population inhabiting and making its home on a maritime feature or group of features." Thus, "economic life ... must be oriented around the feature itself and not focused solely on the waters or seabed of the surrounding territorial sea"; 5. Under Article 121(3) of UNCLOS, "the ability to sustain either human habitation or an economic life of its own would suffice to entitle a high-tide feature to an exclusive economic zone and continental shelf"; 6. The capacity of a feature under Article 121(3) is an objective criterion based on the feature itself. It is "concerned with the capacity of a maritime feature to sustain human habitation or an economic life of its own, not with whether the feature is presently, or has been, inhabited or home to economic life"; 7. "The capacity of a feature to sustain human habitation or an economic life of its own must be assessed on a case-by-case basis"; 8. The "capacity of a feature should be assessed with due regard to the potential for a group of small island features to collectively sustain human habitation and economic life"; 9. In the application of Article 121(3), while evidence of the objective physical conditions on a particular feature is relevant, the historical use of the feature is also reliable evidence

This active clarification by an international tribunal did not come without criticism. Nordquist and Phalen note that "imperfect wording with deliberate ambiguities" of Article 121 was a product "following years of intense and unsuccessful negotiations," and in this sense, the SCS tribunal has "misjudged the positive impact the Award would otherwise engender."[210] They further urge the international community not to accept or comply with the tribunal's interpretation of Article 121 in the hope that "future dispute settlement efforts will treat the Article 121 interpretation in the Award as a misguided precedent."[211]

All things considered, it would seem correct reasoning that a few features, such as Itu Aba, can be regarded as islands, and some as rocks in the Paracels and Spratlys based on its socio-geophysical configuration.[212]

3.4 *Maritime Zones*

Upon deciding the territorial title, the disputants will decide or delimitate, if necessary, maritime zones that arise from land features. UNCLOS enumerates rules of territorial seas (up to 12 nm), contiguous zone (up to 24 nm), archipelagic waters for archipelagic states, exclusive economic zones (up to 200 nm), continental shelf (up to 350 nm), and the high seas. Here, we start with rules for coastal baselines, from which the seaward limits of maritime zones are measured.

First, UNCLOS acknowledges normal and straight coastal baselines. Coastal states should identify coastal lines (usually lower-water lines) on a sea chart by way of drawing figures in the first place. The normal baseline (the low-water line along the coast, as marked on large-scale official charts) is the rule (Article 5), and the straight baseline is the exception to the rule. Under Article 7, coastal

---

in determining its capacity to sustain human habitation or an economic life of its own. See Maximo Paulino T. Sison III (2018), pp. 165–166. See also The South China Sea Award, paras. 539–551.

210 Myron H. Nordquist and William G. Phalen, Interpretation of UNCLOS Article 121 and Itu Aba (Taiping) in the South China Sea Arbitration Award, in Myron H. Nordquist et al. (2017), pp. 76–77.

211 *Ibid.*, pp. 77–78.

212 Nordquist and Phalen argue that Itu Aba objectively meets all reasonably conceivable requirements for the definition of an "island" in accordance with Article 121(3) of UNCLOS, thereby criticizing the SCS award as "factually flawed in its holding that the island of [Itu Aba] is merely a 'rock.'" See *ibid.*, p. 66. See also Robert Beckman and Clive Schofield, "Defining EEZ claims from islands: A potential South China Sea change," *International Journal of Marine and Coastal Law*, 29 (2014), pp. 210–211. For the nature and attributes of Itu Aba, see the South China Sea Award, paras. 466–467, 580–584. On the other hand, some argue that there are no islets eligible for any territorial seas at all in the Spratlys. See Mark J. Valencia et al. (1997), p. 48, fn. 237.

states may employ straight baselines in "localities where the coastline is deeply indented and cut into, or if there is a fringe of islands along the coast in its immediate vicinity."[213] Waters on the landward side of the baseline become the internal waters of the coastal state in which coastal states enjoy sovereignty (Article 2(1)); consequently, the passage of foreign vessels is not allowed therein—no innocent passage is bestowed with the exception of areas which had not previously been considered as internal waters.[214] Interestingly, no disputants have challenged others' straight baselines in the SCS.[215] Certainly, the US government and some American lawyers denounce straight baselines in the region as illegal.[216]

Second, Part II of UNCLOS provides for the rules governing the territorial sea up to 12 nm from the baselines in which the coastal state exercises sovereignty.[217] The Convention safeguards the passage of foreign ships in the territorial sea without coastal states' intervention in the name of "innocent passage."[218] Innocent passage means navigation traversing continuously and expeditiously without entering internal waters and not prejudicial to the peace, good order, or security of the coastal state (Articles 18 and 19). Within the contiguous zone, extending beyond the territorial sea to a maximum of 24 nm from the baselines, the coastal state may exercise the control necessary to prevent and punish infringement of its customs, fiscal, immigration, or sanitary laws and regulations within its territory or territorial sea (Article 33).

Third, UNCLOS acknowledges archipelagic water for the benefit of "archipelagic states" that are "constituted wholly by one or more archipelagos and may include other islands."[219] Archipelagic states (e.g., Indonesia[220] and the Philippines) may apply different rules to draw straight archipelagic baselines under Article 47. Archipelagic states measure the breadth of the territorial sea,

---

213 Article 7(1) of UNCLOS.
214 Article 8 of UNCLOS.
215 Robert Beckman (2013), p. 146.
216 For example, Bureau of Intelligence & Research, US Department of State, Limits in the Seas No. 33, Straight Baselines: the Philippines (1973); Robert Beckman (2013), p. 146.
217 Article 2(1) of UNCLOS.
218 Article 17 of UNCLOS.
219 Article 46(b) of UNCLOS.
220 As of 2013, Indonesia is the only State that has designated archipelagic sea lanes in accordance with the Convention and submitted a chart with such lanes to the International Maritime Organization for adoption. See Nong Hong, Jianwei Li, and Pingping Chen, "The Concept of Archipelagic State and the South China Sea: UNCLOS, State Practice and Implication," *China Oceans Law Review*, 2013, no. 1, p. 217.

EEZ, and continental shelf from the archipelagic baseline;[221] thereby, the sovereignty of an archipelagic state can extend to the waters enclosed by such archipelagic baselines.[222]

Fourth, Part V of UNCLOS regulates the EEZ regime, which may extend to a maximum of 200 nm from the baselines. EEZ (a *sui generis* maritime zone created by UNCLOS) is a concept of recent origin.[223] Within the EEZ, coastal states have "sovereign rights for the purpose of exploring and exploiting, conserving and managing the natural resources" and jurisdiction over "the establishment and use of artificial islands, installations and structures," "marine scientific research," and "the protection and preservation of the marine environment" (Article 56). Under 58, all states enjoy the freedoms of navigation, overflight, laying and maintenance of submarine cables, and other uses related to these freedoms.

Fifth, Part VI of the Convention sets forth provisions concerning the continental shelf, which extends to the outer edge of the continental margin or to a distance of 200 nm from the baselines (Article 76). Coastal states exercise sovereign rights to explore the continental shelf and exploit its natural resources; these rights are "exclusive" and "do not depend on occupation, effective or notional, or on any express proclamation" (Article 77).

Sixth, all parts of the ocean that are not included in the above zones (the territorial sea, contiguous zones, the archipelagic waters, and EEZ) are the high seas (Article 86). No state may validly purport to subject any part of the high seas to its sovereignty (Article 89); the high seas are open to all states and freedom of the high seas (such as freedom of navigation, overflight, fishing and scientific research, and freedom to lay submarine cables and pipelines, and construct artificial islands and other installations) can be exercised by all states (Article 87).

3.5 *Maritime Boundaries*

If the breadth between (the X island of) state A and (the Y island of) state B is over 400 nm apart, both states can undertake their economic activities

221 Article 48 of UNCLOS.

222 Article 49(1) of UNCLOS.

223 While EEZ's historical roots lie in the trend since 1945 to extend the limits of coastal state jurisdiction ever seawards (such as the Truman Proclamations and the resource-oriented claims of Latin American and African states), its more direct and immediate origins lie in the preparations for UNCLOS III Conference. See R.R. Churchill and A.V. Lowe (1999), p. 160.

within their own EEZ without the hindrance of another. However, the need for maritime delimitation arises when the breadth between (the X island of) state A and (the Y island of) state B is less than 400 nm—given the contour and configuration of maritime features in the SCS, maritime zones of national jurisdiction overlap, necessitating maritime delimitation.

UNCLOS contains rules governing boundary delimitation between opposite or adjacent coastal states: Article 15 for the territorial sea and Articles 74 and 83 for EEZ and continental shelf. The median line is the rule for the territorial sea delimitation; if there are historic titles or other special circumstances, the median line can be adjusted (Article 15). This is in substance identical with Article 12 of the 1958 Territorial Sea Convention and consistent with the pattern of state practice.[224]

For the continental shelf delimitation, the 1958 Convention on the Continental Shelf adopted the "equidistance principle."[225] Under this unequivocal principle, an overlapping area could be divided along the equidistance line. However, due to a lack of consensus during UNCLOS III negotiations, relevant UNCLOS provisions (Articles 74 and 83) ended up taking an equivocal standard, "an equitable solution."

In the absence of specific criteria or methods by which negotiating states can reach "equity," states have been bound to diverge in the concept of "equitable." There is no single maritime boundary line in the SCS except for the Gulf of Tonkin.[226] China with a long coastline prefers special circumstance EEZ delimitation and the doctrine of natural prolongation for continental shelf. In contrast, archipelagic Indonesia and the Philippines advocate the method of equidistance.

As Map 1.2 shows, there will be many trijunction points in the SCS. Under the assumption that Itu Aba is a rock, the maritime zone of the disputants still considerably overlap;[227] multiple claimants should sit at the same negotiation table for maritime delimitation.[228]

---

224 Convention on the Territorial Sea and the Contiguous Zone, Geneva, April 29, 1958.

225 Article 6(2) of the Convention on the Continental Self: In the absence of agreement, and unless another boundary line is justified by special circumstances, the boundary shall be determined by application of the principle of equidistance.

226 China and Vietnam signed an agreement on the delimitation of the Tonkin Gulf (Beibu Gulf in Chinese and Bac Bo in Vietnamese) on December 25, 2000. See Zou Keyuan, "Sino-Vietnamese Agreement on the Maritime Boundary Delimitation in the Gulf of Tonkin," *Ocean Development of International Law*, 36 (2005), pp. 13–24.

227 Myron H. Nordquist and William G. Phalen, Interpretation of UNCLOS Article 121 and Itu Aba (Taiping) in the South China Sea Arbitration Award, in Myron H. Nordquist et al. (2017), p. 76.

228 Sam Bateman, Maritime Boundary Delimitation, Excessive Claims and Effective Regime Building in the South China Sea, in Yann-huei Song and Keyuan Zou (2014), p. 135.

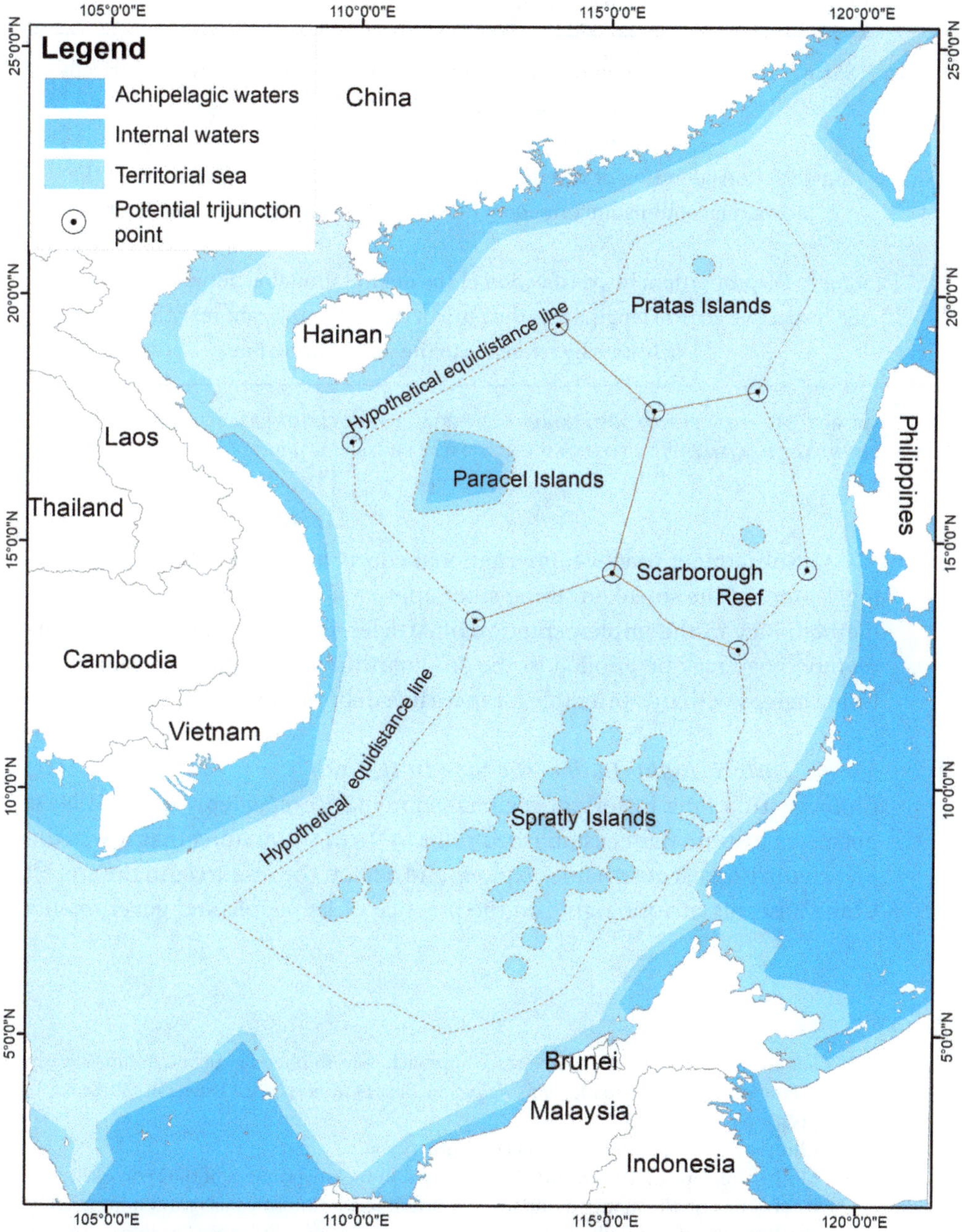

MAP 1.2 Notional equidistance lines in the South China Sea, including the Islands
SOURCE: REPRODUCED BY THE AUTHOR FROM: SAM BATEMAN, MARITIME BOUNDARY DELIMITATION, EXCESSIVE CLAIMS AND EFFECTIVE REGIME BUILDING IN THE SOUTH CHINA SEA, IN YANN-HUEI SONG AND KEYUAN ZOU (EDS.), *MAJOR LAW AND POLICY ISSUES IN THE SOUTH CHINA SEA: EUROPEAN AND AMERICAN PERSPECTIVES* (LONDON AND NEW YORK: ROUTLEDGE, 2014), P. 125

TABLE 1.1 The three-stage maritime delimitation approach

(*Stage 1*) The establishment of a provisional delimitation line using geometrically objective methods

↓

(*Stage 2*) Consideration of whether factors are calling for the adjustment of the provisional equidistance/median line to achieve an equidistance result

↓

(*Stage 3*) Disproportionality verification of the delimitation line between the ratio of the respective coastal lengths and the ratio between the relevant maritime area of each state by reference to the delimitation line

SOURCE: STEPHEN FIETTA AND ROBIN CLEVERLY, *A PRACTITIONER'S GUIDE TO MARITIME BOUNDARY DELIMITATION* (OXFORD UNIVERSITY PRESS 2016), P. 54

As a subsequent practice, international courts and tribunals have increasingly adopted the so-called "three-stage approach" as a standard delimitation methodology in the implementation of Articles 74 and 83 (Table 1.1).[229] This methodology may be applied to the SCS maritime delimitation inasmuch as China agrees with this principle for maritime delimitation.[230]

3.6 *Historic Rights Claim (The Nine-Dash Line)*

China (with a long history of regional supremacy) repeatedly claims that it possesses historic rights established prior to UNCLOS, arguing that it was the first country to discover, name, explore, and exploit the resources in the SCS.[231] China bases its historic rights on the practice of its people and governments

229 For an explanation of the "three-stage approach," see Stephen Fietta and Robin Cleverly, *A Practitioner's Guide to Maritime Boundary Delimitation* (Oxford University Press 2016), pp. 52–95.

230 Chinese Society of International Law (2018), p. 309.

231 Ministry of Foreign Affairs, PRC, Position Paper of the Government of the People's Republic of China on the matter of jurisdiction in the South China Sea arbitration initiated by the Republic of the Philippines, December 7, 2014, para 4, at https://www.fmprc.gov.cn/nanhai/eng/snhwtlcwj_1/t1368895.htm. China alleges that its historic rights should be considered an integral part of territorial title and maritime delimitation. See Chinese Society of International Law, "The South China Sea Arbitration Awards: A Critical Study," *Chinese Journal of International Law*, 17 (2018), pp. 421–2.

throughout the long course of history.[232] Further, China holds that it has historic rights to internal waters, territorial sea, contiguous zone, EEZ, and continental shelf of the region.[233]

The Chinese theory on historic rights is three-fold: (1) the formation and nature of historic rights are governed by general international law, not UNCLOS;[234] (2) UNCLOS shows respect for historic rights in Articles 10, 15, 51, and 298; and (3) UNCLOS has not superseded historic rights, leaving a relationship between historic rights and the EEZ/continental shelf regimes open.[235]

The question that arises is whether a history-based argument can conform with the UNCLOS system. A map plays an important role in Chinese claims to the SCS: the "nine-dash line." A map depicting a u-shaped line shows nine line segments of the SCS that, if connected, would enclose an area covering roughly 90 percent of the SCS.[236] An official map of the SCS was believed to have been published using 11 lines to indicate the boundary of the islands, islets, reefs, banks, and adjacent waters over which China exercised sovereignty in 1947, but an official account of the map is missing. (Map 1.3)[237] Two of these lines in the Tonkin Gulf area were later omitted, thereby appearing as "nine-interrupted lines" or "nine-dash line." (Map 1.4)

In a 2009 diplomatic note (protesting Vietnam and Malaysia's joint submission) to the UN Commission on the Limits of the Continental Shelf (CLCS), China included the nine-dash line map (Map 1.4).[238] The nine-dash line

232 Ministry of Foreign Affairs, PRC, Statement of the Government of the People's Republic of China on China's territorial sovereignty and maritime rights and interests in the South China Sea, July 12, 2016, at https://www.fmprc.gov.cn/nanhai/eng/snhwtlcwj_1/t1379493.htm.

233 Chinese Society of International Law (2018), p. 475.

234 *Ibid.*, p. 437 (arguing that, during UNCLOS III, the negotiating states did not have the intention to address the specific regimes of historic rights including historic bay and historic title).

235 *Ibid.*, p. 442.

236 Ronald O'Rourke (2018), p. 24.

237 The "nine-dash line" was allegedly included in a map named "New China Construction Atlas" in 1936 by then one of China's most eminent geographers, Bai Meichu. Between 1936 and 1945 versions of the line were published on 26 other maps. See Bill Hayton (2014), p. 56). Other Scholarly accounts place the publication date in 1946 to 1948. See, e.g., M. Sheng-Ti Gau, "The U-Shaped Line and a Categorization of the Ocean Disputes in the South China Sea," *Ocean Development & International Law*, 43, no. 1 (2012), p. 58.

238 China, Note Verbale No. CML/17/2009, May 7, 2009), at www.un.org/depts/los/clcs_new/submissions_files/mysvnm33_09/chn_2009re_mys_vnm_e.pdf. China has not published geographic coordinates specifying the location of the dashes. Furthermore, a geographic description of China's dashed line is complicated by inconsistencies between China's 2009 map and other Chinese map, such as the 1947 map.

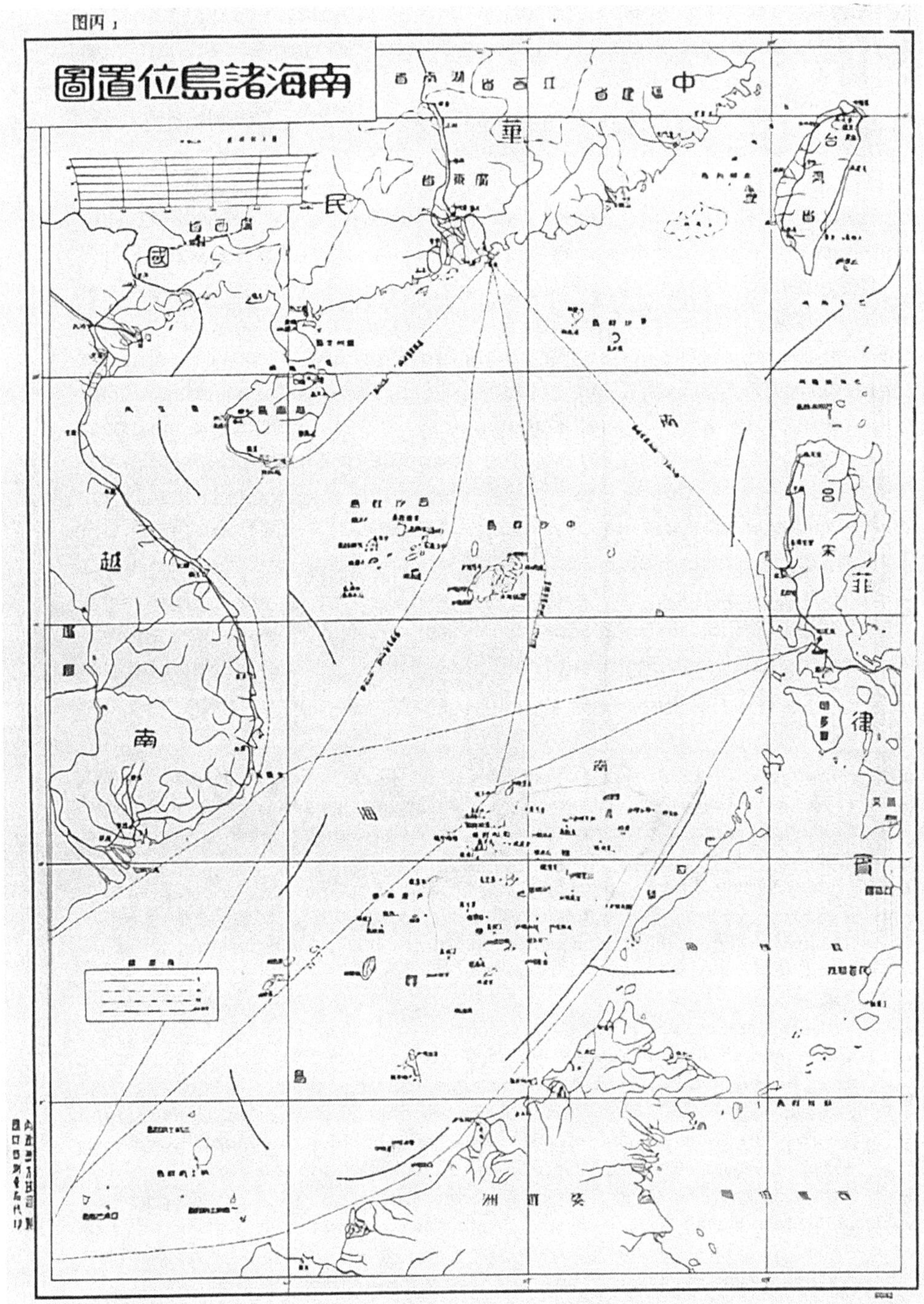

MAP 1.3 China's (Kuomingtang) 11-dash line map of 1947 entitled "Map of South China Sea Islands"
SOURCE: LIMITS IN THE SEAS, NO. 143, MARITIME CLAIMS IN THE SCS, US DEPARTMENT OF STATE, DECEMBER 5, 2014, P. 3

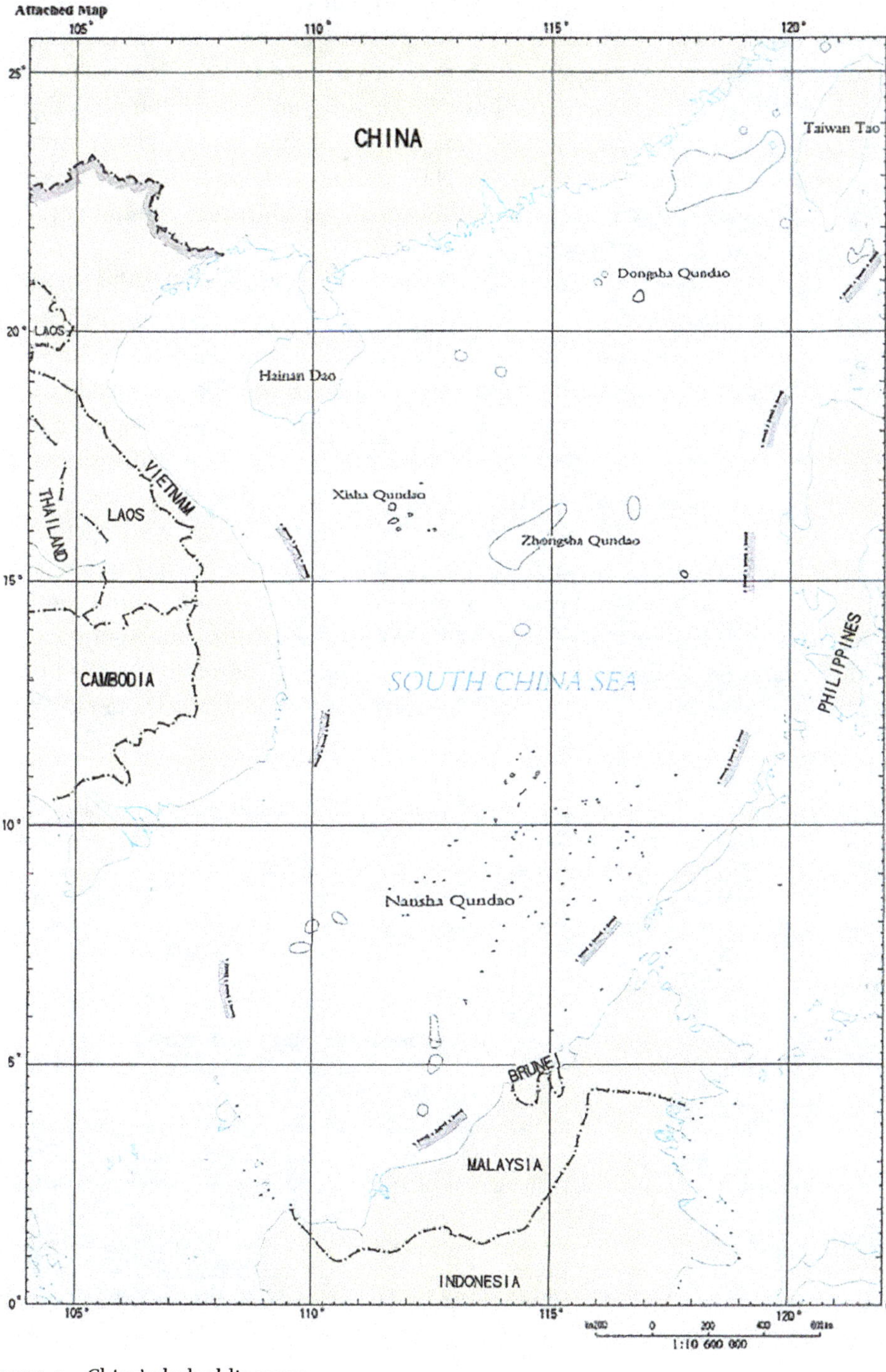

MAP 1.4 China's dashed-line map
SOURCE: CHINA'S NOTES VERBALES OF 2009

encompasses approximately 2,000,000 km^2 of maritime space, equal to about 22 percent of China's land area.[239] The legal nature of the claim with this map remains a mystery. Some experts claim that the purpose of these lines is simply to claim the islets enclosed in the lines.[240] Zhiguo Gao, former Chinese judge at ITLOS (2008–2020), argues that China "claims all the islands and surrounding near-shore waters that belong to China" along with some historic rights (e.g., traditional fishing rights), but without claiming "the water column or the airspace above the [SCS] as something internal."[241]

Under international law, three possible hypotheses are conceivable regarding the nine-dash line: (1) a claim to the territorial title over maritime features, (2) a claim to a national boundary, and (3) a claim to historic rights of the sea.[242] First, if China claims territorial sovereignty over maritime features inside the line, the map can be useful within the ambit of international law. Maps can be relevant proof, reflecting a government's intention to claim the land within its territory. In fact, in its 2009 note verbale, China used different legal terms in the same way as UNCLOS divides:[243] "sovereignty" for territorial sea (Article 2), "sovereign rights," and "jurisdiction" for EEZ and continental shelf (Articles 56, 77, 79, and 81), and "relevant waters" or "seabed and subsoil" for EEZ and continental shelf.[244] For example, Shicun Wu, President of the National Institute of South China Sea Studies, explains that "the nine-dash-line should be the line of the ownership over all the features inside the line and adjacent waters."[245]

---

239 The nine-dash line overlaps with the entitlements of all the neighboring coastal states covering 80 percent of the Philippines' EEZ, 80 percent of Malaysia's EEZ, 50 percent of Vietnam's EEZ, 90 percent of Brunei's total EEZ, and 30 percent of Indonesia's EEZ in the SCS. See Antonio Carpio, *The South China Sea Dispute: Philippine Sovereign Rights and Jurisdiction in the West Philippine Sea* (2017), p. 30, at https://www.imoa.ph/downloads/.

240 See Kuan-Ming Sun, Policy of the Republic of China Toward the South China Sea, *Marine Policy*, 19, 1995, pp. 401, 405.

241 Myron H. Nordquist et al. (2009), p. 300 (Q&A: Panel III).

242 For a detailed analysis of characteristic of nine-dashed line, see Bureau of Oceans and International Environmental and Scientific Affairs, US Department of State, Limits in the Seas, China: Maritime Claims in the South China Sea, No. 143, pp. 11–24.

243 The Chinese statement in the 2009 note verbale can be interpreted in this light: "China has indisputable sovereignty over the islands in the South China Sea and the adjacent waters, and enjoys sovereign rights and jurisdiction over the relevant waters as well as the seabed and subsoil thereof (see attached map)."

244 According to one U.S. government study, support for this interpretation can be found in China's laws and statements, such as Article 2 of China's 1992 territorial sea law claims a 12-nm territorial sea around the "Dongsha [Pratas] Islands, Xisha [Paracel] Islands, Nansha (Spratly) Islands and other islands that belong to the People's Republic of China" (Law on the Territorial Sea and the Contiguous Zone of 25 February 1992).

245 Dr. Wu also argues that China has never claimed the whole SCS inside the line as its historic waters. See Bill Hayton (2014), p. 250). See also Jiangyu Wang, "Legitimacy,

Second, if China claims the nine-dash line as a national boundary line, it would run counter to international law. This is simply because a national boundary line cannot be drawn unilaterally by submitting a map containing a national boundary line to the UN. Of course, China must understand the necessity to agree on national boundaries with its neighbors based on its own experience.[246] The disputants should negotiate to draw maritime boundary delimitation in accordance with Articles 74 and 83 of UNCLOS. The Chinese Society of International Law affirms that the nine-dash line indicates a national boundary and thus "the waters within the line may partake of a sovereignty nature."[247] On the other hand, Jia Yu, then Deputy Director of the China Institute for Marine Affairs, expounds that China "has never defined the dashed line as a 'national boundary' between China and its neighboring states, and never viewed the ocean space [therein] as China's internal waters or territorial waters, and never exercised sovereignty [therein] as it does for China's land territories. The practice of all Chinese governments in the past has also never treated the dashed line as a national boundary and exercised [sovereignty] accordingly."[248]

Third, if China suggests the nine-dash line as bespeaking historic waters, it may only be validated within the maritime delimitation context as "relevant circumstances" in drawing the delimitation lines at best; otherwise, the use of the map will unlikely be validated in general international law. Article 14 of China's 1998 EEZ and continental shelf law sets out that "[t]he provisions of this Act shall not affect the historical rights of the [PRC]."[249] Gao and Jia argue

---

Jurisdiction and Merits in the South China Sea Arbitration: Chinese Perspectives and International Law," Journal of Chinese Political Science, 22, no. 2 (2017), p. 202 (noting that "China's position on land claims is clear: all lands within the nine-dash line are thus claimed to be part of Chinese territory"); Katherine Morton, "China's ambition in the South China Sea: is a legitimate maritime order possible?" *International Affairs*, 92, no. 4 (2016), p. 919 (arguing that "[t]he original purpose of the map was to locate islands rather than to define maritime jurisdiction over natural resources and waters").

246 China has a land boundary of 22,457 km, bordering 14 neighboring countries: Afghanistan 91 km, Bhutan 477 km, Burma 2129 km, India 2659 km, Kazakhstan 1765 km, North Korea 1352 km, Kyrgyzstan 1063 km, Laos 475 km, Mongolia 4630 km, Nepal 1389 km, Pakistan 438 km, Russia (northeast) 4133 km, Russia (northwest) 46 km, Tajikistan 477 km, Vietnam 1297 km. See Central Intelligence Agency, The World Factbook, at https://www.cia.gov/library/publications/the-world-factbook/geos/ch.html).

247 Chinese Society of International Law (2018), p. 324.

248 Jia Yu, "Zhongguo Zai Nanhai de Lishixing Quanli" (China's historic rights in South China Sea), Chinese Legal Science, 3 (2015), p. 198, cited in Jiangyu Wang, "Legitimacy, Jurisdiction and Merits in the South China Sea Arbitration: Chinese Perspectives and International Law," *Journal of Chinese Political Science*, 22, no. 2 (2017), p. 202.

249 See https://www.un.org/Depts/los/LEGISLATIONANDTREATIES/PDFFILES/chn_1998_eez_act.pdf.

that "the nine-dash line represents China's claims over all the lands within the line, plus "historic rights within the nine-dash line—under Article 14 of its 1998 law on the EEZ and the continental shelf—in respect of fishing, navigation, and exploration and exploitation of resources."[250]

Based on this claim, the US regards China's dash-line map as illegal.[251] However, Chinese claims can be explained in the context of future maritime delimitation. Similarly, Chinese scholars perceive historic rights associated with the nine-dash line as having zonal implications: thus, they argue that historic rights should be taken into consideration in territorial and maritime delimitation negotiations as an integral part of the dispute.[252] Unless China asserts its right to the entire water body of the SCS by the nine-dash line, it would seem incongruous to conclude that the nine-dash line is inconsistent with UNCLOS.

Admittedly, the concept of "historic bays" or "historic waters" over which a nation exercises sovereign authority has been accepted under international law in limited situations. Article 10(6) of UNCLOS acknowledges the existence of historic bays. Also, Article 15 provides that the general rule governing delimitation of overlapping territorial seas does not apply in instances of "historic title or other special circumstances." These provisions are substantially identical to Articles 7 and 12 of the 1958 Convention on the Territorial Sea and the Contiguous Zone.

International adjudication has dealt with historic bays or titles. In the *1951 Fisheries* Case (the U.K. v. Norway), ICJ acknowledged the idea of a historic claim.[253] In the 1982 *Continental Shelf* (Tunisia v. Libyan Arab Jamahiriya), ICJ observes that "[h]istoric titles must enjoy respect and be preserved as they have always been by long usage ... [Historic bays or historic titles] are governed by general international law which does not provide for a *single* 'régime' for [them], but only for a particular régime for each of the concrete, recognized cases of 'historic waters' or 'historic bays.'"[254] Also, in the 1992 *Gulf of Fonseca* case, ICJ accepted the Gulf of Fonseca as a historic bay and its waters as historic waters while acknowledging a shared ocean resource among nations as

250 Z. Gao and B.B. Jia, "The Nine-Dash Line in the South China Sea: History, Status, and Implications," *American Journal of International Law*, 107 (2013), pp. 108–110.

251 Bureau of Oceans and International Environmental and Scientific Affairs, US Department of State, Limits in the Seas, "China: Maritime Claims in the South China Sea," No. 143, p. 19.

252 Chinese Society of International Law (2018), p, 421–3.

253 *Fisheries* Case (U.K. v. Norway), *ICJ Reports 1951*, p. 130.

254 *Continental Shelf Case* (Tunisia/Libyan Arab Jamahiriya), Judgment, *ICJ Reports 1982*, para. 100.

"condominium" ownership (co-owned historic waters) over the waters and resources of the Gulf of Fonseca.[255]

In the meantime, the legality of alleged Chinese claims to historic rights was dealt with in the 2016 SCS arbitration. Upon reviewing the legal nature of the nine-dash line,[256] the tribunal concluded that the nine-dash line is a claim to the living and nonliving resources within the maritime space it encompasses.[257] Under this assumption, the tribunal found that China had never acquired or enjoyed historic rights in the SCS before or since the entry into force of UNCLOS[258] and thus repudiated any historic rights under the UNCLOS system.[259] Chinese scholars criticize this tribunal's finding for jumping to a conclusion without inquiring into the intent of the state parties to UNCLOS.[260]

Admittedly, the UN Secretariat prepared a study entitled "Juridical Regime of Historic Waters, Including Historic Bays" in 1962.[261] This Study emphasized the following three factors in terms of historic title to the maritime area: (1) the authority exercised over the area by the state claiming it as "historic waters"; (2) the continuity of such exercise of authority; and (3) the attitude of foreign states.[262] If the conclusion of this Study can function as the standard work of reference in the SCS, China is obligated to adduce that its claim satisfies these three elements.[263] The Chinese Society of International Law concurs with this

255 *Land, Island and Maritime Frontier Dispute* (El Salvador/Honduras; Nicaragua intervening), *ICJ Reports 1992*, paras. 383–4, 418.

256 The tribunal analyzed materials: (1) the June 2012 Chinese Offshore Oil Corporation notice of open blocks for petroleum exploration adjacent to the western edge of the "nine-dash line"; (2) Summer Ban on Marine Fishing in the South China Sea Maritime Space issued on May 2012 that appears to claim fishing rights in the SCS (Award, para. 210); and (3) China's statements proclaiming its respect for freedom of navigation and overflight in the SCS, such as China's Vice Foreign Minister statement on October 27, 2015. See the South China Sea Award, paras. 210–2.

257 The South China Sea Award, July 12, 2016, para. 214.

258 *Ibid.*, paras. 263–275.

259 *Ibid.*, para. 262 (stating that "upon China's accession to the Convention and its entry into force, any historic rights that China may have had to the living and nonliving resources within the 'nine-dash line' were superseded"). See also ibid para. 1203(B)(2) (declaring that the nine-dash line is unlawful, and UNCLOS "superseded any historic rights, other sovereign rights or jurisdiction, in excess of the limits imposed therein").

260 Chinese Society of International Law (2018), p. 434.

261 Juridical regime of historic waters, including historic bays – Study Prepared by the Secretariat, A/CN.4/143 (1962), originally printed in Yearbook of the International Law Commission, Vol. II (1962).

262 *Ibid.*, para. 185.

263 Chinese scholars point out that this 1962 UN Study can be applied to historic rights in general, including the SCS. See Chinese Society of International Law (2018), p. 448.

assessment, saying that "[t]he legal status of a State's historic waters should be determined on a case-by-case basis, with a focus on the jurisdiction exercised by the State" inasmuch as "[t]here are no one-size-fits-all rules regulating the nature, content and scope of historic rights in international law."[264]

To this end, China should overcome the denial by Vietnam and the Philippines of Chinese historic rights in the SCS in the first place, and the fact that China publicly manifested the nine-dash line claim to the outside world only in 2009. Equally important to note is that the Republic of China (Taiwan), the 1947 map's original publisher, allegedly changed its position. In 1993, Taiwan promulgated that "[t]he SCS area within the historic water limit is the maritime area under the jurisdiction of [Taiwan], where [it] possesses all rights and interests."[265] However, subsequent Taiwanese maritime legislation and its public statements suggest that this view may no longer be officially held by Taiwan.[266]

3.7 *Submerged Landmass and Island-Building*

Almost all the disputants in the region have built certain artificial structures on the occupying maritime features, many of which are low-tide elevations. In general, states have "freedom to construct artificial islands and other installations" on the high seas (Article 87(1)(d)) under the condition that artificial islands cannot generate an EEZ or a continental shelf (Article 60(8)).[267] The SCS tribunal holds that Subi Reef (Zhubi Jiao), Gaven Reef (South), Hughes Reef (Dongmen Jiao), Mischief Reef (Meiji Jiao), and Second Thomas Shoal (Ren'ai Jiao) are low-tide elevations incapable of appropriation, nor generating any maritime zones.[268]

Recently, the Chinese Society of International Law advances an interesting argument that "[t]he question whether or not a low-tide elevation can

264 Chinese Society of International Law (2018), p. 447.

265 On 13 April 1993, the Republic of China Executive Yuan approved the Policy Guidelines for the South China Sea in which it approves historic rights by the nine-dash line. See Kuan-Hsiung Wang, "The ROC's Maritime Claims and Practices with Special Reference to the South China Sea," *Ocean Development & International Law*, 41, no. 3 (2010), p. 245.

266 US Department of State, Limits in the Seas No. 127, Taiwan's Maritime Claims, November 15, 2005, at https://2009 2017.state.gov/documents/organization/57674.pdf.

267 Article 60(8): Artificial islands, installations and structures do not possess the status of islands. They have no territorial sea of their own, and their presence does not affect the delimitation of the territorial sea, the exclusive economic zone or the continental shelf.

268 The South China Sea Award, para. 1203(B)(3)-(7).

MAP 1.5 The 2023 China standard map

SOURCE: HTTPS://CN.CHINADAILY.COM.CN/A/202308/28/WS64EC4CEBA3109D7585E4B1E1.HTML

be appropriated as territory is in itself an issue of territorial sovereignty."[269] Chinese scholars repudiate the above tribunal's finding as having "detrimental effect on China's sovereignty over and maritime rights and entitlements based on the archipelago"[270] in the sense that its sovereignty over the Paracels or Spratlys archipelagos can extend even to low-tide elevations.[271] By extension, Chinese scholars argue, under some circumstances (where low-tide elevations can be used as base points), "low-tide elevations are land territory"[272] as having a "significant effect on maritime delimitations."[273] In 2023, China released the 2023 edition of the Standard Map of China. This map includes the SCS, which encompasses the submerged landmass. (Map 1.5)

It remains to be seen how the Chinese government officially clarifies its position on island-building over submerged landmass in the region. However, it seems clear that Article 60(8) is designed to "discourage nations from building up submerged reefs and low-tide elevations in order to generate extended maritime zones where none had existed previously."[274]

3.8 Dispute Settlement Mechanism

Since all the coastal disputants of the dispute are state parties to UNCLOS, the dispute settlement mechanism of the Convention can be utilized by them any time they wish. Namely, ocean-related legal disputes can utilize judicial bodies, such as ICJ and the International Tribunal for the Law of the Sea (ITLOS), or arbitral tribunals established by dispute parties' agreement. Under UNCLOS, dispute settlement options regarding the interpretation and application of the Convention can be divided into two groups: "non-binding or diplomatic processes" and "arbitration or judicial settlement procedures." Though UNCLOS encourages parties to use non-binding peaceful means (e.g., negotiation and conciliation), disputants often fail to resolve their disputes through this mechanism. This is where compulsory procedures entailing binding decisions come to the fore.[275]

269 Chinese Society of International Law (2018), p. 265.
270 *Ibid.*, p. 510.
271 *Ibid.*, p. 513.
272 *Ibid.*, p. 519.
273 *Ibid.*, p. 520.
274 Mark J. Valencia et al., (1997), p. 46.
275 MD. Saiful Karim, Litigating law of the sea dispute using the UNCLOS dispute settlement system, in Natalie Klein (eds), *Litigating International Law Disputes* (Cambridge: Cambridge University Press, 2014), p. 266.

Any dispute concerning the interpretation or application of UNCLOS that is not settled by other means may be submitted by any party to the dispute to a binding settlement (Article 286). Section 2 of Part XV of UNCLOS contains the range of tribunals to be used under the "compulsory" settlement procedures: ITLOS, ICJ, an arbitral tribunal constituted by Annex VII, and a special arbitral tribunal constituted in accordance with Annex VIII (Article 287).[276] For some categories of disputes (e.g., boundary delimitations, disputes on historic bays or titles, or territorial disputes), states can be excluded from the "compulsory mechanism" (Article 298).[277] China invoked this opt-out manual in 2006 and declared it would not accept all the allowable dispute categories.[278]

The Chinese position on dispute settlement through international courts is that an "explicit consent of the parties is the prerequisite for international arbitration";[279] if states give no consent, there are no international legal rights and obligations that can be imposed upon a sovereign state against its will, except for the very limited exceptions of *jus cogens* or peremptory norms.[280] Indeed, China acknowledges the existence of territorial and maritime disputes with other claimants. However, China asserts that the tribunal "had no jurisdiction over any of the Philippines' submissions and that the awards were made ultra

276 R.R. Churchill and A.V. Lowe, *The Law of the Sea* (Manchester: Manchester University Press, 1999), pp. 453–454 (noting that Section 2 of Part XV is the "essence of the Convention's dispute settlement procedures").

277 Article 298: 1. When signing, ratifying or acceding to this Convention or at any time thereafter, a State may ... declare in writing that it does not accept any one or more of the procedures provided for in section 2 with respect to one or more of the following categories of disputes: (a)(i) disputes concerning the interpretation or application of articles 15, 74 and 83 relating to sea boundary delimitations, or those involving historic bays or titles, provided that a State having made such a declaration shall, when such a dispute arises subsequent to the entry into force of this Convention and where no agreement within a reasonable period of time is reached in negotiations between the parties, at the request of any party to the dispute, accept submission of the matter to conciliation under Annex V, section 2; and provided further that any dispute that necessarily involves the concurrent consideration of any unsettled dispute concerning sovereignty or other rights over continental or insular land territory shall be excluded from such submission.

278 China's declaration of August 25, 2006, made after its ratification of UNCLOS, at http://www.un.org/Depts/los/convention_agreements/convention_declarations.htm#China%20after%20ratification.

279 Letter from the Ambassador of the People's Republic of China to the Kingdom of the Netherlands to the individual members of the Tribunal, February 6, 2015. See also Chinese Society of International Law, "The South China Sea Arbitration Awards: A Critical Study," *Chinese Journal of International Law*, 17 (2018), p. 250 (noting that "[the arbitral tribunal does] violence to the principle of consent").

280 Congyan Cai, *The Rise of China and International Law: Taking Chinese Exceptionalism Seriously* (New York: Oxford University Press, 2019), p. 31.

vires, and are not well-founded in fact or law, thus null and void"[281] because the SCS litigation is all about the territorial title and maritime delimitation, over which the tribunal has no jurisdiction *ab initio* due to its 2006 opt-out declaration.[282]

As shown in the SCS dispute, international disputes inevitably involve political and legal dimensions. Some lawyers examine that courts (as legal institutions) have no authority to decide political questions; therefore, if the question at issue cannot be resolved by applying legal criteria, it must decline to adjudicate insofar as the normal function of a court is to apply the law.[283] Others note that international judicial review can be conducive to resolving politically sensitive cases, including the SCS dispute.[284] Parenthetically, political scientists perceive the SCS disputes as purely geopolitical matters which should fall within power politics or diplomacy.[285]

Nordquist and Phalen assess the SCS arbitration as not comporting with "the compromise text found in Article 298, which exempts a few highly political categories of disputes from compulsory third party adjudication."[286] According to Kristen Boon, consent of the parties, the ability of parties to persuade their people into understanding arbitration, and the arbitral tribunal's ability to tactically manage consent are prerequisites for the success of arbitration.[287] The SCS arbitration leaves considerable room for debate on the issue

281 Chinese Society of International Law, "The South China Sea Arbitration Awards: A Critical Study," *Chinese Journal of International Law*, 17 (2018), p. 218.

282 Chinese Society of International Law, "The South China Sea Arbitration Awards: A Critical Study," Chinese Journal of International Law, 17 (2018), p. 353. See also ibid., p. 250 (arguing that "[i]t is an indisputable fact that there exists a complex issue between China and the Philippines over territorial sovereignty and maritime delimitation [which is] beyond the Tribunal's jurisdiction").

283 J. G. Merrills, *International Dispute Settlement*, 5th ed. (Cambridge University Press, 2011), pp. 152–156.

284 K.E. Boon, "International arbitration in highly political situations: the South China Sea dispute and international law," *Washington University Global Studies Law Review*, 13 (2014), pp. 487–492.

285 See e.g., R.D. Kaplan, *Asia's cauldron: the South China Sea and the end of a stable Pacific* (New York: Random House, 2014).

286 Myron H. Nordquist and William G. Phalen, Interpretation of UNCLOS Article 121 and Itu Aba (Taiping) in the South China Sea Arbitration Award, in Myron H. Nordquist, John Norton Moore, and Ronán Long, International Marine Economy: Law and Policy (Brill Nijoff, 2017), pp. 76–77.

287 Kirsten E. Boon, "International arbitration in highly political situations: the South China Sea dispute and international law," *Washington University Global Studies Law Review*, 13, no. 487 (2014), p. 490.

of non-participation and non-compliance in light of consent to a third-party dispute settlement in the UNCLOS system.[288]

4 Structure of the Book

The subsequent Chapters concentrate on exploring feasible legal resolutions for the SCS conflict based on international relations theories. The administration and resolution of the SCS conflict do not entirely rely on formal law, which was comprehensively analyzed in the previous chapter. This paper conducts an interdisciplinary study of political topics like power's role in international relations and law, regimes' utility and advantage in settling maritime disputes, and China's rise and how it affects the international legal system.

Chapter 2 presents a summary of legal discrepancies between China and the West. Fundamentally, China and the West hold different perceptions of the international legal system, the law of the regime, and the South China Sea (SCS) dispute. International lawyers, including those specializing in the law of the sea, frequently find themselves in disagreement when combating lawfare on interpretations of the formal law. This assessment explores the practicality and effectiveness of the law of the sea system and stresses the crucial need to clarify UNCLOS institutions.

Chapter 3 evaluates international relations theories on the rise of China and the Sino-American conflict in the South China Sea. Chapter 3 evaluates international relations theories on the rise of China and the Sino-American conflict in the South China Sea. Chapter 3 evaluates international relations theories on the rise of China and the Sino-American conflict in the South China Sea. Realism, liberalism, and constructivism analyze these issues differently. Realism prioritizes power, interest, anarchy, and security, while power transition theory and the inevitability of war are explored in terms of the power shift in the region. Meanwhile, liberalism emphasizes the conditions under which cooperation arises. The chapter examines the influence of economic interdependence, international institutions (regimes), and globalization on the South China Sea conflict. Constructivism emphasizes the influence of ideational factors such as

288 Kirsten E. Boon, "International arbitration in highly political situations: the South China Sea dispute and international law," Washington University Global Studies Law Review, 13 (2014), p. 490 (arguing that "[c]onsent is important because the states involved need to make a commitment to submit themselves to a third party. Parties often get to arbitration after negotiations fail ... [S]tates must be willing to acknowledge that the arbitral tribunal can change legal entitlements").

culture, norms, identity, and epistemic communities over purely materialistic views. In the context of the SCS dispute, this paper presents a potential constructivist approach and examines the role of the epistemic community.

Chapter 4 argues for the importance of international law in resolving the SCS dispute, drawing on analyses from various theories in international relations. The examination of power's role in international law and its significance during times of power shifts informs suggested bilateral and multilateral approaches for reflecting such shifts in the law of the sea between China and the US. Additionally, the creation of a regime for the SCS is deemed necessary and beneficial, with recommendations for the advantages of a soft-law regime.

CHAPTER 2

The South China Sea Dispute as Law-Fare

This Chapter examines the disparities in legal perspectives between China and the West. Sino-American legal warfare (*falu zhanzheng* or *falu zhan;* lawfare) is now in full swing in terms of interpreting and applying the law of the sea against the SCS region.[1] Lawfare involves "arguing that one's own side is obeying the law, criticizing the other side for violating the law [weifa], and making arguments for one's own side in cases where there are also violations of the law."[2] China perceives legal warfare as a "form of combat," along with public opinion warfare and psychological warfare,[3] and in turn, the US as "a method of warfare where law is used as a means of realizing a military objective."[4] In order to get a good sense of the Sino-American lawfare underway today, Chinese and Western views on international law, the UNCLOS sea system, and the SCS dispute are analyzed, with some recommendations for the law of the sea regime.

1 The Chinese Legal View

In China, political power has been maintained, in large part, by cultural means, such as the teachings of imperial Confucianism, which contributed to legitimizing or sanctioning the ruling authority as the underlying classical philosophy

1 The term "lawfare" originally coined by former deputy judge advocate general of the US Air Force Charles Dunlap. See Edmund J. Burke, Astrid Stuth Cevallos, *In Line or Out of Order? China's Approach to ADIZ in Theory and Practice* (RAND Corporation, 2017), p. 11.

2 Han Yanrong, "Legal Warfare: Military Legal Work's High Ground: An Interview with Chinese Politics and Law University Military Legal Research Center Special Researcher Xun Dandong," Legal Daily (PRC), February 12, 2006, cited in Dean Cheng, Winning Without Fighting: Chinese Legal Warfare, Heritage Foundation, Backgrounder, No. 2692 (May 18, 2012), p. 2.

3 Dean Cheng, Winning Without Fighting: Chinese Legal Warfare, Heritage Foundation, Backgrounder, No. 2692 (May 18, 2012), p. 2. For an account of the "three warfare" (san zhan) of China, see Dean Cheng, Winning Without Fighting: Chinese Legal Warfare, Heritage Foundation, Backgrounder, No. 2692 (May 18, 2012), pp. 1–2 (adding that "China is approaching lawfare as an "offensive weapon capable of hamstringing opponents and seizing the political initiative").

4 Charles J. Dunlap, Jr., Law and Military Interventions: Preserving Humanitarian Values in 21st Century Conflicts, Harvard University Kennedy School of Government, Carr Center for Human Rights Working Paper, November 29, 2001, p. 8.

 | DOI: 10.1163/9789004696358_003

of social order.[5] Further, a traditional concept "*tianxia*" (天下; world order under heaven) that predates Confucianism has influenced the Chinese view of law and society (normative and political dimensions).[6] History and collective memories thereon have real influence over the Chinese people's view of international law, not least the law of the sea.

1.1 *The Chinese View on the International Legal System*

There were rules and practices within Chinese civilization in ancient China similar to Western international law and practice, albeit not international in the modern sense.[7] In this traditional system, the "Middle Kingdom" of China (*zhongguo*) and subordinated states under the suzerainty system coexisted,[8] cultural subordination, symbolic tributes, and economic exchanges underlying social basis.[9]

China's perception of international law was influenced mainly by three traditional schools of thought, which were developed some three thousand years ago: Daoism, Confucianism, and Legalism. First, "Daoism" (道教), based on the work of Lao Zhou (老子), puts forward a "system of natural laws"[10] that emphasizes "inaction" as the primary legal principle, which entails the rejection of human-made law and the modern notion of the rule of law.[11] The Daoist emphasis on "harmony" is understood to have influenced the non-interference principle in Chinese diplomacy.[12]

5 John K. Fairbank, The Early Treaty System in The Chinese World Order, in John K. Fairbank (ed.), *The Chinese World Order* (Cambridge: Harvard University Press, 1968), p. 273.

6 David A. Bell, Realizing Tianxia: Traditional Values and China's Foreign Policy, in Ban Wang (ed.), Chinese Visions of World Order: Tianxia, Culture, and World Politics (Durham and London: Duke University Press, 2017), p. 131.

7 Zhiguo Gao, China and the Law of the Sea, in Myron H. Nordquist et al. (2009), p. 267.

8 Zhao Tingyang, "A Political World Philosophy in Terms of All-under-heaven (Tian-xia)," *Sage Journal*, 56, no. 5 (2009).

9 Anlei Zuo, "China's Approaches to the Western-dominated International Law: A Historical Perspective from the Opium War to the South China Sea Arbitration Case," *University of Baltimore Journal of International Law*, 6, no. 1 (2018), pp. 27–28.

10 Hu Shih, The Natural Law in the Chinese Tradition, Natural Law Institute Proceedings, pp. 127–129.

11 Daoism favors simplicity over bureaucratic systems, such as courts, laws, and punishment. See Weng Li, "Philosophical Influences on Contemporary Chinese Law," *Indiana International & Comparative Law Review*, 6 (1996), p. 327. See also Zhipeng He and Lu Sun, *A Chinese Theory of International Law* (Law Press China and Springer, 2020), p. 109 (explaining that Daoist thought "emphasizes the obedience to the natural order, adopted a more negative attitude toward the law, and opposed human intervention, struggle, resistance, and regulation").

12 Dvir Aviam Ezra, China's Perspective of International Courts and Tribunals, Student Paper of Hebrew University, p. 6.

Second, "Confucianism" (*Li*; 儒家) highlights personal connection, moral values, local rituals, and traditions over institutions. The doctrine of absolute sovereignty and the "courts are a taboo" mindset pertain to these ideas.[13] Also, the Confucianist hierarchical concept of relationships was a central tenet to sustaining a civil society built on five natural relationships (father and son, ruler and subject, husband and wife, elder and younger brother, and the relationship between friends) that are the foundation of the tribute system.[14] Under Confucianism, natural law as moral rules to regulate individual behavior functions to encourage people to behave in a socially proper way; in this context, if a body of international law is perceived as inconsistent with the principle of Confucian ideas, the Chinese people may obliviously harbor an animus against such rules.[15]

Third, "Legalism" (*Fa*; 法家) teaches that enforceable and strict rules are necessary to construct a harmonious society under the assumption that human nature is bad (Confucians and Daoists see human nature as good).[16] Legalism has some bearing on legal positivism; in this sense, it may explain China's increasing acceptance of binding international law. Sometimes, the Communist Party uses the Legalist tradition in an attempt to justify party discipline or procedure.

The Chinese people perceive Confucianism and Legalism as the two most important and mutually complementary belief systems (though *Fa* inconsistent with *Li* can never be a real law) regarding social order and peace and stability, a perception which invariably constitutes the Chinese view on the application of international law to the world order.[17] Nevertheless, Chinese society has long not cultivated any belief, trust, and confidence toward the law; rather, China's traditional culture has a negative and distrustful attitude toward the law.[18]

---

13 *Ibid.*, p. 8; Junwu Pan, "Chinese Philosophy and International Law," *Asian Journal of International Law*, Vol 1 (2011), pp. 5–6. See also Zhipeng He and Lu Sun, *A Chinese Theory of International Law* (Law Press China and Springer, 2020), p. 107 (noting that in the Confucian thought system, the objective existence and subjective emphasis of social classes was the foundation and core of social structure, which partakes of family and social identity as differentiable standards).

14 Junwu Pan (2011), p. 235 (explaining that *Li* advances the hierarchical structure in a civil society that is built on five natural relationships: father and son; ruler and subject; husband and wife; elder and younger brother; and the relationship between friends).

15 *Ibid.*, pp. 234, 238.

16 R Eno, Legalism and Huang-Lao Thought, Indiana University, Early Chinese Thought [B/E/P374] (2010), p. 10, at http://www.indiana.edu/~p374/Legalism.pdf.

17 Junwu Pan (2011), pp. 234–6.

18 Zhipeng He and Lu Sun (2020), pp. 107, 110. Buddhism also has contributed to Chinese people's legal perception; however, the Buddhism's emphasis on enduring the present

The traditional Chinese international legal system was predicated upon the subordinated states' recognition of China's superiority.[19] Thus, when China met Western powers that operated within the Westphalian system, China perceived itself as a superior "central kingdom" to all other states; China did not realize what international law was due to the lack of understanding of the "*ius gentium*" concept, which was foreign to the traditional tribute system in Asia.[20] Despite some events that taught the utility of international law to China,[21] China did not understand the importance of international law.

In the meantime, from the First Opium War (1839) on, the "Century of Humiliation" (*bainian guochi;* 百年国耻) wreaked havoc on China until the Chinese Communist Party (CCP) triumphed in the Chinese Civil War in 1949. The memory of the Century of Humiliation hurts the mindset and approach of the Chinese people toward international law and the concept of the rule of law.[22] By extension, opposition to the Western-dominated international law defined the Chinese worldview of an international legal order,[23] thereby generating the idea that international law was "the accomplice of political oppression and economic exploitation as a language of power and interests."[24]

---

suffering and putting hopes in the future does not necessitate the weaponization of the law. Esp., p. 110.

19 Anlei Zuo (2018), p. 27.

20 Suzanne Ogden, "Sovereignty and International Law: the Perspective of the People's Republic of China," *New York University Journal of International Law and Politics*, 7, no. 1 (1974), pp. 2–3 (noting that China lacked an awareness of itself as a political state, rather considered itself instead as a cultural entity in the nineteenth century).

21 For instance, in 1864, China successfully defended its territorial waters (inner oceans) and demanded compensation ($1,500) after Prussia seized three Danish merchant ships as war prize in violation of China's neutrality through reference to international law. See Immanuel C. Y. Hsü, *China's Entrance into the Family of Nations: The Diplomatic Phase, 1858–1880* (Cambridge: Harvard University Press, 1960), pp. 132–4.

22 In the "Century of Humiliation," China's control over its territory shrank by a third, its traditional imperial system collapsed, and the country was riven by internal uprisings, invasion, and civil war. See, Alison Adcock Kaufman, "The 'Century of Humiliation,' Then and Now: Chinese Perceptions of the International Order," *Pacific Focus*, 25, no. 1 (2010), p. 2. See also S. S. Kim, "Sovereignty in the Chinese Image of World order", in Ronald St. John Macdonald (ed.), *Essays in Honour of Wang Tieya* (Dordrecht: Martinus Nijhoff Publishers, 1994), pp. 428–429 (explaining China's persistent stance on the primacy of state sovereignty has its deep roots in this miserable experience).

23 Daniel J. Hoffheimer, "China and the International Legal Order: An Historical Introduction," *Case Western Journal of International Law*, 11 (1979), p. 255.

24 Anlei Zuo (2018), p. 31. See also David Kennedy, The Mystery of Global Governance, in Jeffrey L. Dunoff & Joel P. Trachtman (eds.), *Ruling the World?: Constitutionalism, International Law, and Global Governance* (Cambridge: Cambridge University Press, 2009), p. 51 (noting that international rule of law was also perceived in China as the rule of

Thus, even today, China views the existing international legal system as having inherited much from "colonialism, imperialism, hegemonism, etc. in a close and continuing historical relevance of the past."[25]

Meanwhile, China has its Sinicized understanding of "sovereignty" and "sovereign equality." To begin with, "sovereignty" can be translated into three Chinese words: 主权 (*zhuquan*) as sovereignty or authority; 统治权 (*tong zhiquan*) as dominion or governance; and 至高统治权 (*zhigao tong zhiquan*) as supreme power or sovereignty.[26] From these translations, we grasp that sovereignty is equal to the right of lordship, dominion and governance, and control of state symbols as supreme authority and power, which implies social hierarchy.[27] According to K'ung Meng, sovereignty is defined as:

> [A]ny nation ... should in no way be deprived of its right to the claim of international entity. [Social and governmental systems] are internal problems and outside the jurisdiction of the law of nations and do not affect its right to the claim of international entity. To deny the sovereignty of any state under any pretext [such as social system] is illegal.[28]

China holds fast to an absolute version of sovereignty and the non-interference principle that takes precedence over other values as a corollary.[29] This explains why China strongly repudiates "foreign interference" in the interest of the

Western-dominated international law for Western-dominated global governance paradigms).

25 Anlei Zuo (2018), pp. 34, 49. China's distrust of international law as an accomplice of colonialism, international oppression, and exploitation was reinforced by the history of Japan encroaching on Chinese sovereignty, which supported by the West. See Seth P. Tillman, *Anglo-American Relations at the Paris Peace Conference of 1919* (Princeton and New Jersey: Princeton University Press, 2015), pp. 333–34 (explaining how Japan fortified its demands at the Peace Conference by valid international legal engagements, which eventually contributed to the Chinese communist movement).

26 See https://www.mdbg.net/chindict/chindict.php?page=cedict; https://dictionary.cambridge.org/dictionary/english-chinese-simplified/sovereignty.

27 Gary Lilienthal & Nehaluddin Ahmad, The South China Sea Islands Arbitration: Making China's Position Visible in Hostile Waters, *Asian-Pacific Law & Policy Journal*, 18, no.2 (2017), p. 94 (adding that China strives to avoid "the alienation of sovereignty or any form of outside national influence on the empire-society").

28 Suzanne Ogden (1974), p. 17, fn. 71.

29 Alison Adcock Kaufman (2010), p. 11. Russia takes the same position on Sovereignty: The Russian Constitutional Court has upheld this absolutist vision of national sovereignty in decisions limiting assertions of sovereignty by regional entities within Russia. See Mikhail Antonov, Theoretical Issues of Sovereignty in Russia and Russian Law, *Review of Central and East European Law*, 37, Issue 1 (2012), pp. 104–105.

preservation of the regime, political security, and the protection from threats to its territorial integrity and sticks to narrowly consent-based views of sources of rights and obligation in international law.[30]

The experience of the Century of Humiliation also instigates China's adherence to the principle of sovereign equality in international affairs.[31] As a Chinese lawyer affirmed in 1963, China began perceiving any propositions beyond the concept of the universality of international law, such as world law or supranational law, as impairing state sovereignty.[32] Avery Goldstein expounds:

> History, especially the interpretation of history, affects every country's contemporary interaction with the outside world. History not only bequeaths some of the substantive issues on the foreign policy agenda ... It also affects foreign policy decision-making when leaders draw lessons from past experience or invoke analogical reasoning that compares the country's current circumstances to those it faced before.[33]

In fact, Former Chinese Premier Wen Jiabao stated in 2008 that "respect for sovereignty and non-interference in the internal affairs of other countries is the prerequisite for sound State-to-State relations. China is firm in upholding its hard-won-sovereignty and territorial integrity and will never tolerate any external interference."[34] This attitude is also confirmed by Chinese scholars having held many conferences on "sovereignty" or "non-interference." For example, from 2001 to 2009, the Chinese Society of International Law held four conferences under topics related to sovereignty.[35]

---

30 Jacques deLisle, "China's Approach to International Law: A Historical Perspective," *American Society of International Law Proceedings*, 2000, p. 272.

31 Xue Hanqin, *Chinese Contemporary Perspectives on International Law: History, Culture, and International Law* (Maubeuge: All-Pocket, 2012), p. 28.

32 Suzanne Ogden (1974), p. 10, fn. 34.

33 Avery Goldstein, Parsing China's Rise: International Circumstances and National Attributes, in Robert. S. Ross and Feng Zhu (eds.), *China's Ascent: Power, Security, and the Future of International Politics* (Ithaca and London: Cornell University Press, 2008), pp. 74–5.

34 Statement by Premier of the State Council of the People's republic of China, "A China Committed to reform and opening-up and Peaceful Development", at the General Debate of the 63rd Session of the United Nations General Assembly on September 24, 2008, cited in See Xue Hanqin (2012), pp. 71–72.

35 Specific topics run thus: "humanitarian intervention and the principle of sovereignty" (2001); "the establishment of the International Criminal Court and its impact on State sovereignty" (2001); "international order and the principle of sovereignty" (2004); "responsibility to protect and its relation with the principle of sovereignty" (2005); "State sovereignty and international protection of human rights" (2008). See Xue Hanqin (2012), p. 71, fn. 137.

According to one famous Chinese definition of international law, "if [international law] is disadvantageous to these causes, to the socialist cause, or to the cause of peace of the people of the world, we will not use it and should create a new instrument to replace it."[36] This definition predicates that a few Western powers monopolized the creation and manipulation of, and the interpretation and application of, "single common" international law to suit their interests, forcing non-Western States to obey it.[37] This is what the Chinese government still holds for international law, as illustrated in the SCS arbitration.[38] Further, some Chinese publicists assert that the goal of China's rejuvenation can be achieved by "confrontation against the existing Western-dominated world order."[39]

As a socialist state, socialist legal thinking and Communist theory inform Chinese perspectives on international law. International law was often regarded as a means of plundering weaker countries and compelling a capitalist world order.[40] A key principle of Communist theory is that the state superstructure, including all laws, reflects society's economic base and serves the ruling class's

---

36 ZHU Liru, "Refuting Chen Tiqiang's Absurd Theory of International Law," Renmin Ribao [People's Daily] (September 18, 1957), cited in Junwu Pan, "Chinese Philosophy and International Law," *Asian Journal of International Law*, 1 (2011), p. 239, fn. 18; Hungdah Chiu, "Communist China's Attitude toward International Law," *American Journal of International Law*, 60, p. 247 (noting that "Communist China used to perceive law as 'an instrument of the state, undergoing successive adaptations to make it conform to Communist-party-dictated policies'"). Another famous definition of international law by a Chinese scholar is that "[i]nternational law is a body of rules of conduct including principles, rules and institutions which are binding on the states in their international relations. They are formed in the process of conducting international relations and recognized by all nations, and express the volition of the governing classes of the states." See Geng-Sheng Zhou, International Law (Beijing: Commercial Press, 1983), 1, p. 3, cited in Paul C. Yuan, "China's Challenge to Traditional International Law: An Exposition and Analysis of Chinese Views and Behavior in International Law and Politics," Dalhousie Law Journal, 10, no. 3 (1987), p. 23.

37 Congyan Cai, *The Rise of China and International Law: Taking Chinese Exceptionalism Seriously* (New York, NY: Oxford University Press, 2019), p. 18; Phil C. W. Chan, "China's Approaches to International Law since the Opium War," *Leiden Journal of International Law*, 27 (2014), p. 891.

38 China views Western-dominated international law as "the mouthpiece of hegemonism, imperialism, international oppression and exploitation toward non-Western countries due to its low inclusiveness." See CCTV, China calls arbitral court "mouthpiece" for certain groups, July 5, 2016 at http://english.cctv.com/2016/07/05/VIDEVHUV2clDFs3O5QGWR-mad160705.shtml.

39 Anlei Zuo (2018), p. 36.

40 Hsin Wu, "A Criticism of Bourgeois International Law on the Question of State Territory," *People's China and International Law*, 1 (1974), p. 323.

interests.[41] Chinese scholars argue that contemporary international law is to be understood as "an indispensable means to realize socialist modernization and construction"[42] and that Western lawyers use a vassal state theory to manifest bourgeois international law to bind civilized nations.[43] If some Chinese elites still perceive international law through the lens of class analysis, they will unlikely accept those rules that appear to serve the interests of powerful (capitalist) states.[44]

The Marxist theory of law suggests that the law (domestic and international) is a tool for legitimizing the ruling class or nation; thus, the law is no more than an effective weapon for legitimizing an unjust status quo rather than a revolutionary weapon for establishing a new order.[45] Under a similar worldview, China and Russia (the former Soviet Union) regard the law as an outcome of reality and an instrument of state policy, a servant of policy.[46] In 1996, then President Jiang Zemin claimed law to be an instrument of state policy and international law as a foreign policy instrument.[47]

---

41 Hungdah Chiu, "Communist China's Attitude toward International Law," *American Journal of International Law*, 60, p. 251.

42 LIU Fengming, Xiandai Guoji Fa Gangyao [Essentials of Modern International Law] (Beijing: Mass Press, 1982), p. 5, cited in Junwu Pan (2011), p. 239, fn. 21.

43 Ying Tao, Recognize the True Face of Bourgeois International Law from a Few Basic Concepts, 1 KUO-CHI WEN-T'I YEN-CHIU [hereinafter KCWTYC] (Studies in International Problems) 42, 42, 44 (1960), cited in Gary Lilienthal & Nehaluddin Ahmad, The South China Sea Islands Arbitration: Making China's Position Visible in Hostile Waters, *Asian-Pacific Law & Policy Journal*, 18, no. 2 (2017), p. 101, fn. 141.

44 Chen Tiqiang, "The People's Republic of China and Public International Law," *Dalhousie Law journal*, 8 (1984), pp. 16–17 (arguing that China must keep international law through Marxism-Leninism, and noting that two Marxist-Leninist ideas (use of class analysis and the application of proletarian internationalism) are found in Chinese international law thinking).

45 Samuel S. Kim, "The People's Republic of China and the Charter-Based International Legal Order," *American Journal of International Law*, 72 (1978), pp. 325–326 (noting that "the basic rules of [multilateral treaties] may be perceived as still following closely the traditional international law formulated by Western bourgeois nations"). China has built its own stance on the law based on the Marxist legal theory. See Xue Hanqin (2012), p. 25.

46 YU Xingzhong, "Legal Pragmatism in the People's Republic of China" in Perry Keller (ed.), *Chinese Law and Legal Theory* (Aldershot, Hampshire: Ashgate Publishing Limited, 2001), pp. 71–2. China and Russia share a similar position on the global order and a similar historical experience; China and Russia argue that they have been discriminated against by the West for a long time. See Jinghan Zeng, Yuefan Xiao, and Shaun Breslin, "Securing China's core interests: the state of the debate in China," *International Affairs*, 91, no. 2 (2015), p. 265, fn. 95.

47 Jonathan G. Odom, "A China in the Bull Shop? Comparing the Rhetoric of A Rising China with the Reality of the International Law of the Sea," *Ocean and Coastal Law Journal*, 17 (2012), pp. 222–223. Chou Fu-lun asserts that "[i]nternational law ... is also, just as any law,

As for customary international law, China does not have much motivation to abide by some customary rules of the class nature that it considers as discriminatory inasmuch as the West developed some customary rules in the absence of a role of a "non-civilized" China.[48] Concerning international agreements, China categorized treaties into two groups: equal and unequal.[49] The unequal treaties have been refuted not to be a source of international law as illegal and void[50] because unequal treaties "undermine the most fundamental principles of international law, [sovereignty]."[51] China today seems to recognize treaties and customs as principal sources of international law.[52]

China denies the sources of international law of general principles of law and the decisions of international counts unless general principles and international decisions are recognized in treaties or as customs.[53] Notably, China does not trust international judicial mechanisms because the process

---

a political instrument." See Hungdah Chiu, "Communist China's Attitude toward International Law," *American Journal of International Law*, 60, p. 248, fn. 14.

48 Junwu Pan (2011), p. 241; Paul C. Yuan (1984), p. 425. In history, China was not treated as a fully sovereign State as a non-civilized nation by the Western powers. See Lassa Oppenheim, International Law: A Treatise (1905), pp. 108–109 (arguing that "[s]tatehood alone does not include membership of the Family of Nations ... [T]here are States in existence, although their number decreases gradually, which are not, or not fully, members of that family because their civilization, if any, does not enable them and their subjects to act in conformity with the principles of International Law"). See also Zhipeng He and Lu Sun, *A Chinese Theory of International Law* (Law Press China and Springer, 2020), p. 103; Suzanne Ogden (1974), pp. 6–7.

49 Details of how China concluded a series of "unequal treaties" are that: "Through the leading of the Opium War, the Second Opium War, the Sino-French War, the Sino-Japanese War of 1894–1895, and the armed conflict of the Eight-Power Allied Forces in Beijing, the exchanges between China and the international legal system were initially reflected in the series of treaties that the strong powers had asked China to sign. Although these treaties were ostensibly signed equally by both parties, the treaties signed by China under the powers' using or threatening to use force are clearly unequal treaties." See Zhipeng He and Lu Sun, *A Chinese Theory of International Law* (Law Press China and Springer, 2020), p. 102.

50 Paul C. Yuan (1984), p. 424.

51 Junwu Pan (2011), p. 243.

52 Zhao Yue, A Preliminary Criticism of Bourgeois International Law, *Journal of International Studies*, 3 (1959), p. 8 (arguing that "In many important treaties concluded with ... other countries, our country proposed a series of democratic principles which have produced great influence and become commonly observed principles among various countries"); Hungdah Chiu, "Communist China's Attitude toward International Law," American Journal of International Law, 60 (1966), p. 258, fn. 52 (noting that "[t]reaties are an important source of international law and an important form of expressing international law").

53 Phil C. W. Chan, "China's Approaches to International Law since the Opium War," *Leiden Journal of International Law*, 27 (2014), p. 880.

is "foreign-made" and does not offer a level playing field.[54] Similarly, China negatively perceives international organizations, holding that international organizations should not exist above State sovereign rights because their rights begin where State sovereign rights end.[55]

What is the rule of law of the international community? China often stresses that "[China] will make greater contribution to the maintenance and promotion of international rule of law."[56] Further, in October 2014, at the 4th Plenum of the CPC, China placed the "rule of law" (*fazhi*; 法治 or 法制), at the top of its agenda, calling for the Chinese government to take a more significant role in shaping the norms that underpin the international legal order.[57] However, at its core, *fazhi* differs fundamentally from the rule of law in a way that the international community understands. Chinese lawyers must commit to the belief that law is subject to the Party's leadership and acknowledge the fundamental principles of the Chinese rule of law to maintain the rule of the Party: the Party's will is the law, and the Party can never violate the law.[58]

It is instructive to review the "Five Principles of Peaceful Coexistence" by which China has articulated the Chinese notion of sovereignty in modern terms.[59] China perceives the "Five Principles" as the "the core [or main]

54 Harriet Moynihan (2017), p. 3.

55 Suzanne Ogden (1974), p. 21. China insists that international organizations are not subjects of international law; if they are allowed to be international entities it will detract from the absolute national sovereignty. *Ibid.*, p. 16.

56 Yi Wang, "China: a Staunch Defender and Builder of the International Rule of Law," *Chinese Journal of International Law,* 13 (2014), p. 637. See also Jielong Duan, "Statement on the Rule of Law at the National and International Levels," *Chinese Journal of International Law*, 6 (2007), p. 186 (insisting that China "great importance to the rule of international law and puts it into actual practice").

57 Harriet Moynihan (2017), p. 2.

58 Eugene Gregory, Ronald Alcala, and Shane Reeves, "Chinese Fazhi and the International Order," *Harvard International Review*, 39 (Fall 2018), pp. 2–4 (explaining that "[r]ather than promote basic principles [such as the supremacy of law and judicial independence], *fazhi* is instead used as a rhetorical tool to legitimize the Party's rule").

59 The Five Principles are (1) Mutual respect for each other's territorial integrity and sovereignty; (2) Mutual nonaggression; (3) Mutual noninterference in each other's internal affairs; (4) Equality and mutual benefit; and (5) Peaceful coexistence. This "Five Principles" was coined by then-Premiere Zhou Enlai in 1953, included in the Sino-Indian treaty of 1954 in its preamble, advanced at the first Asian-African Conference held in Bandung in 1955 as the basis of Chinese foreign policy, and subsequently enshrined in China's constitution in 1982. See Alison Adcock Kaufman, "The 'Century of Humiliation,' Then and Now: Chinese Perceptions of the International Order," *Pacific Focus*, 25, no. 1 (2010), p. 27;

part of the fundamental principles of international law" as substantive and anti-hegemonic, which became entrenched in the Chinese legal philosophy opposing Western-dominated international law.[60] If treaties and customs meet the just and equitable requirements of its Five Principles, China recognizes them as the source of international law;[61] meanwhile, some Chinese writers affirm that the growing number of such treaties has already transformed these principles into customs.[62] On May 27, 2014, then Vice Minister of Foreign Affairs of China, LIU Zhenmin, claimed that the Five Principles had been accepted as a general practice of fundamental principles accepted as law among states.[63] Under this logic, China will continue to maintain its foreign relations with all states on the basis of the Five Principles.[64]

China's legal power is precipitously on the rise. It remains to be seen how the Five Principles contribute to (or hamper) the maintenance of the international legal system, specifically, the resolution of the SCS dispute. One certain thing is that China will likely adhere to the peaceful settlement of its boundary disputes under the Five Principles.[65]

Ministry of Foreign Affairs of the PRC, The Five Principles of Peaceful Coexistence - The time-tested guideline of China's policy with neighbors, July 30, 2014; JIA Guide, New China and International Law: Practice and Contribution in 70 Years, *Chinese Journal of International Law*, 18, no. 4 (2019), p. 730.

60 Wang Tieya, "International Law in China: Historical and Contemporary Perspectives," *Recueil des Cours* (1990–II), p. 276; Anlei Zuo (2018), pp. 35–6.

61 Gary Lilienthal & Nehaluddin Ahmad, "The South China Sea Islands Arbitration: Making China's Position Visible in Hostile Waters," *Asian-Pacific Law & Policy Journal*, 18, no. 2 (2017), pp. 101–102.

62 Hungdah Chiu, "Communist China's Attitude toward International Law," *American Journal of International Law*, 60 (1986), p. 258.

63 This speech was delivered at a colloquium to celebrate the 60th anniversary of the "Five Principles." See Zhenmin Liu "Following the Five Principles of Peaceful Coexistence and Jointly Building a Community of Common Destiny," *Chinese Journal of International Law*, 13 (2014), pp. 477–480, esp., p. 478. Also, in 2006, then Director-General of the Treaty and Law Department of China, Duan Jielong, asserted the Five Principles have become a "basic principle guiding the relations among states in the international community." See Jielong Duan, "Statement on the Rule of Law at the National and International Levels," *Chinese Journal of International Law*, 6 (2007), p. 186.

64 Le Yucheng, "Achievements and Experiences: 60 Years of China's Diplomacy," in Zhao Jinjun (eds.), China's Diplomacy, 1949–2009 (in Chinese), Peking University Press, 2010, p. 1, cited in Xue Hanqin (2012), p. 96, fn. 193.

65 Xue Hanqin (2012), p. 63; Michael D. Swaine, "Chinese Views on the South China Sea Arbitration Case between the People's Republic of China and the Philippines," *China Leadership Monitor*, No. 51, p. 9 (assessing that "Chinese sources suggest that, despite the furor

1.2 *The Chinese View on the International Law of the Sea System*

China's dissatisfaction with the current law of the sea order, to a large extent, derives from its relatively low international status during UNCLOS I (1958), II (1960), and III (1973–1982) negotiations. It was only 1971 when the People's Republic of China (China or PRC) was allowed to join the UN, meaning that there were no seats for the PRC at UNCLOS I and II negotiations.[66] China ended up with a negative view toward the four 1958 Conventions.[67] China perceives that a few big naval powers manipulated the 1958 Conference, and the four Conventions were the product of the colonial era serving big powers' own interests.[68] In other words, the four 1958 conventions, in China's view, did not reflect the interests of many developing states, including China.[69] In this sense, China demanded, "a fair and reasonable new law of the sea" to satisfy changed circumstances and to meet contemporary needs.[70]

The Chinese position on maritime legal issues was first presented in UNCLOS III; for instance, China adduced its position on the territorial sea that the breadth thereupon that coastal states should decide it unilaterally based on sovereignty.[71] Further, China "firmly took side with the Third World countries"

and extremism resulting from the arbitration issue, Beijing will continue to support the use of peaceful, negotiated methods in addressing the SCS disputes").

66 UNCLOS I took place in Geneva from February 24 to April 29, 1958 and UNCLOS II took place in Geneva from March 17 to April 27, 1960. For an historical account of the UNCLOS I and II, see, e.g., James Harrison, *Making the Law of the Sea* (Cambridge: Cambridge University Press, 2011), pp. 31–37.

67 On April 29, 1958, as recorded in the Final Act (A/CONF.13/L.58, 1958, UNCLOS, Off. Rec. vol. 2, 146), the United Nations Conference on the Law of the Sea opened for signature four conventions and an optional protocol: the Convention on the Territorial Sea and the Contiguous Zone (CTS); the Convention on the High Seas (CHS); the Convention on Fishing and Conservation of the Living Resources of the High Seas (CFCLR); the Convention on the Continental Shelf (CCS); and the Optional Protocol of Signature concerning the Compulsory Settlement of Disputes (OPSD).

68 Zhiguo Gao, China and the Law of the Sea, in Myron H. Nordquist et al. (2009), pp. 269–270.

69 *Ibid.*

70 Samuel S. Kim (1979), p. 3.

71 UN Doc A/AC.138/SC.II/SR.55 (1973); A/AC.138/SC.II/L.34 China: Working Paper on sea area within the limits of national jurisdiction (July 16, 1973). In 1930, when the first attempt to codify international law was made at the first Conference on the Progressive Codification of International Law held at the Hague, then the Republic of China officially asserted, for the fist time, a three-mile territorial sea measured from the low water mark along the coast. See Zhiguo Gao, China and the Law of the Sea, in Myron H. Nordquist, Tommy T.B. Koh, and John Norton Moore (eds), Freedom of Seas, Passage Rights and the 1982 Law of the Sea Convention (Leiden and Boston: Nijhoff , 2009), p. 268.

in UNCLOS III.[72] China supported the fight of developing countries against hegemonism and the establishment of a new international economic order.[73] In this view, China formed a united front to fight against naval powers under the assumption that the law of the sea treaty is a "political declaration against maritime hegemony, rather than as an international legal document on the regime of the oceans."[74]

When UNCLOS III was concluded with a convention, China praised its adoption as a "victory of the long-term struggle of the Third World countries for equal maritime right and against the superpowers' maritime hegemony."[75] Despite this achievement, China was not satisfied with some of the important clauses in UNCLOS, thereby expressing a commitment to continuing its struggle against superpower maritime hegemony to establish a new order on the oceans.[76] Why did China ratify UNCLOS? According to the 1996 explanation by the Chinese Foreign Ministry, China believed that "UNCLOS as a whole was consistent with the PRC position" and beneficial to Chinese maritime rights and jurisdiction and long-term interests.[77]

Instead of or parallel with UNCLOS, China maintains the "*mare-clausum* interpretation" of the core provisions of UNCLOS, in which its restrictive approach spans across all topics of the Convention: "innocent passage," "freedom of navigation," "boundary delimitation," "the international seabed regime," "marine scientific research," and so forth.[78] The overarching assumption of Chinese *mare-clausum* lies in the notion that "freedom of the seas"

---

72 Mincai Yu, "China Being a Maritime Power under the UNCLOS: Issues and Way Ahead," *Journal of East Asia and International Law*, 7 (2014), p. 315. The US and the USSR belong to the First World, and the majority of the Asian, African, and Latin American countries are the Third World. Those between the two are developed countries of the Second World. See Paul C. Yuan, "The United Nations Convention on the Law of the Sea from Chinese perspective," *Texas International Law Journal*, 19, no. 2 (1984), p. 423.

73 At the 1974 UNCLOS III session, Chinese Representative Shen Wei-liang strongly criticized the four 1958 Conventions as being "outmoded and in the interest of the superpowers in pursuing maritime hegemony," and insisted that the four freedoms of the high seas are nothing but freedoms of superpower aggression, threat and plunder against other countries, particularly the developing countries. See Chinese Representative Speaks at Subcommittee of UN Seabed Committee, Xinhua Zhoubao, April 9, 1973, pp 17–18, cited in Paul C. Yuan (1984), p. 427, fn. 50.

74 Paul C. Yuan (1984), p. 417.

75 Renmin Ribao (People's Daily, in Chinese), May 4, 1982, cited in Zhiguo Gao, China and the Law of the Sea, in Myron H. Nordquist et al. (2009), p. 276, fn. 44.

76 Renmin Ribao (People's Daily), May 4, 1982, p. 7, cited in Paul C. Yuan (1984), p. 419, fn. 15.

77 Nong Hong (2012), pp. 115–117.

78 Zhiguo Gao, China and the Law of the Sea, in Myron H. Nordquist et al. (2009), p. 277.

under UNCLOS is enjoyed by a few strong maritime powers and designed to protect freedom of the seas at the expense of coastal states.[79]

As for the warships' innocent passage through foreign territorial seas, as stipulated in the 1958 "Declaration on the Territorial Sea"[80] and maintained throughout UNCLOS III,[81] China perceives that "[t]he provisions of [UNCLOS] concerning innocent passage through the territorial sea shall not prejudice the right of a coastal State to request … a foreign State to obtain advance approval from or give prior notification to the coastal State for the passage of its warships through the territorial sea of the coastal State."[82]

Chinese scholars point out that the right of innocent passage of foreign warships through the territorial sea has never been generally recognized over the past 100 years.[83] For example, the International Law Commission (ILC) confirmed in 1955 that "[t]he coastal State may make the passage of warships through the territorial sea subject to previous authorization or notification. Normally it shall grant innocent passage."[84] Eventually, the 1958 Convention on

---

79 Speech given by Chiao Kuanhua (Vice Foreign Minister), at 28th UN General Assembly, October 1973, Peking Review, No 40, 5 October 1973, pp. 15–16, cited in Zhiguo Gao, China and the Law of the Sea, in Myron H. Nordquist et al. (2009), p. 270, fn. 14.

80 By this Declaration, foreign warships and aircrafts, without permission, should not pass over Chinese territorial sea and territorial airspace. See Anh Duc Ton, "Innocent Passage of Warships International Law and the Practice of East Asian Littoral States," *Asia-Pacific Journal of Ocean Law and Policy*, 1 (2016), p. 237; Zou Keyuan (2005), p. 59. In 1963 alone, China issued 15 "serious warnings" to the US for the alleged intrusions of its warships into China's territorial sea. *Ibid.*, p. 81.

81 The Chinese delegate argued that the regime of passage in the territorial sea has vital importance to the sovereignty and security of the coastal state, so that all relevant provisions shall ensure to protect the sovereignty of the coastal state against any encroachment and threat. From this perspective, China denied innocent passage for military vessels. China presented a joint proposal to seek prior approval of coastal states before foreign military vessels navigating the territorial sea, which was not adopted due to US and Soviet rejection. See Zou Keyuan (2008), p. 71.

82 *Ibid.*, p. 72, fn. 24.

83 See, e.g., Shao Jin, "The question of innocent passage of warships after UNCLOS III," *Marine Policy*, 13, No 1 (January 1989), p. 67.

84 In its Commentary, ILC stated that "because 'a number of States do require previous notification or authorization,' it could not "dispute the right of the States to take such a measure." See Report of the International Law Commission to the General Assembly," in Yearbook of the International Law Commission, Vol. 2 (New York, 1956), pp. 276–277. However, in its 1954 version, ILC drafted the text as "save in exceptional circumstances, warships shall have the right of innocent passage through the territorial sea without previous authorization or notification." See Report of the International Law Commission to the General Assembly, in Yearbook of the International Law Commission, Vol. 2 (New York, 1954), p. 161.

the Territorial Sea and the Contiguous Zone was silent on the passage of warships; thus, China claims that state practice did not support innocent passage of foreign warships in the territorial sea. JIA Guide rebukes the US for sending its warships to territorial seas, which is coercion states to "accept the US' unilateral interpretation of the rules" as a hegemonic act.[85]

As of 1996, it was reported that 26 nations demanded either prior authorization or consent or prior notification for innocent passage of foreign warships in their territorial seas.[86] US Commander's Handbook on the Law of Naval Operations listed 27 states that require prior permission for passage through the territorial sea and 12 states that require prior notification.[87] Interestingly, China is reported to have rarely implemented this restriction on foreign vessels.[88] Further, Zhiguo Gao (former Chinese ITLOS judge, 2008–2020) views demanding prior consent for the passage of foreign warships in the territorial sea as inconsistent with UNCLOS.[89]

On the nature of EEZ, China maintains that UNCLOS distinguishes EEZ from the high seas, and thus, "freedom of navigation and overflight" in and over the EEZ is no longer tantamount to the freedom of the high seas.[90] Under this logic, China argues that foreign military activities and maritime reconnaissance do not fall under the "freedom of navigation and overflight" in and over

85 JIA Guide, New China and International Law: Practice and Contribution in 70 Years, *Chinese Journal of International Law*, 18, no. 4 (2019), p. 740.

86 The 1996 UN Secretary-General Report indicates that states demanding prior authorization or consent include Algeria, Antigua-Barbuda, Bangladesh, Barbados, China, Grenada, Iran, Maldives, Myanmar, Pakistan, Romania, Saint Vincent and the Grenadines, Somalia, Sri Lanka, Syria, United Arab Emirates, and Yemen and Countries requiring prior notification include Denmark, Estonia, Guyana, India, Malta, Mauritius, Republic of Korea, Seychelles and Sweden. See Report of the Secretary General, U.N. Doc., A/51/645, November 1, 1996, p. 78, fn. 35.

87 Cited in Ivan Shearer, "Military Activities in the Exclusive Economic Zone: The Case of Aerial Surveillance," *Ocean Yearbook*, 17, 2003, p. 552.

88 Zou Keyuan (2008), p. 72.

89 Zhiguo Gao, China and the Law of the Sea, in Myron H. Nordquist et al. (2009), pp. 271, 284–5 (examining that adhering to the position of requiring prior consent for the passage of warships in the territorial sea "poses a major problem for China if it wishes to stay within the framework of the Convention").

90 At UNCLOS III, China supported the majority of developing States which claimed a 200-mile EEZ, suggesting EEZ should not be regarded as part of the high seas. See UN Doc A/AC.138/SC.II/L.34 (China: Working Paper on sea area within the limits of national jurisdiction, 1973). See also Ren Xiaofeng and Cheng Xizhong, "A Chinese Perspective," *Marine Policy*, 29 (2005), p. 140 (noting that for China, EEZ is an "area beyond and adjacent to the territorial waters of the coastal State, where the coastal State enjoys sovereign rights and exclusive jurisdiction for specific matters").

the EEZ, but rather should comply with the laws and regulations adopted by the coastal States under Article 58(1) and (3). As mentioned in Chapter 1, China bases its position on UNCLOS provisions associated with "peaceful uses" and "peaceful purposes."[91] On one side, the term peaceful purpose does not rule out military activities in general; on another side, the use of maritime space only for peaceful purposes must mean complete non-militarization, ruling out all military activities, such as in the Antarctic Treaty; based on the latter, China sticks to the concept that military activities (not having a direct bearing on passage by foreign warships) are encroachments on the national security of coastal states as a threat to use force (not a 'peaceful use' of the sea.)[92]

Zou Keyuan explains that it would seem incongruous to conclude that states can conduct military activities freely without engagement with the coastal state, while marine scientific research (MSR) in foreign EEZ is subject to the coastal state's jurisdiction; further emphasizing that "[s]ome kind of check-and-balance mechanism for foreign military activities in the EEZ seems reasonable."[93] In reality, China hardly enforced its law until 2001; however, it seems that China has changed its benign stance since then, into more active engagement and enforcement, as the EP-3 incident shows.[94]

It is worth paying attention to a middle-ground position regarding military activities in foreign EEZs proposed by Sienho Yee, editor-in-chief of the Chinese Journal of International Law. Based on a deep analysis of Articles 58 and 59 in light of the text, object, purpose, structure, context, and the drafting history thereof, Yee argues that UNCLOS is not completely silent on the topic.[95] In his view, it is reasonable to infer that "the existence of the balancing mechanism

91 The term "peaceful uses" or "peaceful purposes" is used in the Preamble and Articles 88, 141, 143(1), 147(2)(d), 155(2), 240(a), 246(3), and 301 in UNCLOS. There appears to be no substantial difference in the purpose of these two terms. See M. Nordquist (ed.), *United Nations Convention on the Law of the Sea 1982: A Commentary* (M. Nijhoff, 1995), Vol. III, p. 90.

92 Ren Xiaofeng and Cheng Xizhong (2005), pp. 142–3.

93 Zou Keyuan (2008), p. 76.

94 Robert T. Kline, "The Pen and the Sword: the People's Republic of China's Effort to Redefine the Exclusive Economic Zone through Maritime Lawfare and Military Enforcement," *Military Law Review*, 216 (2013), p. 123 (explaining that at the time of the EP-3 incident, she was conducting a standard mission that had been performed in one form or another by the US Navy for several years in similar oceans).

95 Sienho Yee (2010), pp. 2–3 (advancing questions, such as 1) whether or not the military activities in EEZ constitute "freedom of navigation or other lawful uses of the seas"; 2) whether as such military activities respect peaceful purposes; 3) whether "due regard" of the flag States of warships includes the security interest of coastal States; 4) whether "residual rights" under Article 59 have a role to play; and 5) whether military activities fall under the scope of maritime scientific research).

regarding 'residual rights' in Article 59 seems to favor the view that, in addition to resource rights, some other rights are envisioned."[96]

Yee expounds that despite the Singaporean proposal to delete draft Article 59 in UNCLOS III, negotiating states sustained Article 58 in the Convention for the benefit of coastal States, which supports the interpretation that this framework militates in favor of security concerns the coastal state in its EEZ: "[i]n our high-tech age, one man's survey may be another's war preparation."[97] Some Western scholars concur with this assessment of Article 59.[98]

In a similar vein, China argues that foreign "(military) hydrographic surveys" and "intelligence gathering activities" in and over EEZ should fall under the broad category of MSR, which is subject to the consent of coastal states.[99] China worries that these military activities are military and battlefield preparation in nature, and thus, constitutes a threat of force against the coastal state, not to mention the violation of the principle of peaceful use of the sea in UNCLOS.[100] Further, China perceives that foreign states can collect the MSR data under the veneer of military surveys to avoid coastal states' consent. With this understanding, China denounces the US as abusing freedom of navigation to conduct "intelligence-gathering operations" that prejudices the security of China,[101] as shown in the 2009 *Impeccable* incident.[102]

---

96 *Ibid.*, p. 4. Residual rights refer to the rights or jurisdiction with respect to a matter in the EEZ in cases where the Convention does not specifically attribute them to either the coastal State or other States. See Moritaka Hayashi, "Military and Intelligence Gathering Activities in the EEZ: Definition of Key Terms," *Marine Policy*, 29 (2005), p. 126.

97 Sienho Yee (2010), pp. 3–4 (additionally arguing that "the framework ... seems to contain the wherewithal to deal with such an interest and militate in favor of the coastal State, because of the importance of security interest in the light of the proximity of the zone of activities to the coastal State").

98 For instance, Klein advances, by implication, that "it seems that some naval activities, those that do not interfere with coastal state rights, are permissible." See Natalie Klein (2011), p. 53.

99 Zhiguo Gao, China and the Law of the Sea, in Myron H. Nordquist et al. (2009), pp. 293–4.

100 *Ibid.*, pp. 293–4. See also the Regime of Exclusive Economic Zone: Issues and Responses, A Report of the Tokyo Meeting, 19–20 February 2003, Ship and Ocean Foundation and the East-West Center, 2003, p. 31, at https://www.eastwestcenter.org/system/tdf/private/EEZTokyoMeeting.pdf?file=1&type=node&id=31954.

101 Zhang Haiwen, "The Conflict between Jurisdiction of Coastal States on MSR in EEZ and Military Survey," in Myron H. Nordquist et al (2006), pp. 317–31. Valencia claims that American operations are testing China's ability to detect foreign vessels and aircraft by "tickling" their radar stations, interfering with ship to shore communications and attempting to detect how Chinese submarines enter and leave their bases. See Mark J. Valencia, "The South China Sea Brouhaha: Separating Substance from Atmospherics," *Policy Forum* 10–044, August 10, 2010.

102 Sam Bateman (2005), 163–74 (noting that it is unlikely that the *Impeccable*'s survey could be considered as an infringement on China's coastal state economic rights. Nor does

It is argued that, in practice, no difference exists between regular MSR vessels' and information gathering vessels' equipment and between marine data collected by both vessels.[103] In this view, China argues that all marine data collecting activities should fall under the MSR category, especially out of regard for modern ocean technology and equipment.[104]

Lastly, China suggests that the law of the sea system should reflect the developments that have occurred since the adoption of UNCLOS.[105] In this regard, it is worth paying attention to the fact that China has experience with invoking the doctrine of *rebus sic standibus*[106] to revise treaties, even before the Vienna Convention on the law of the Treaties incorporated the doctrine.[107]

1.3 *The Chinese View on the South China Sea Dispute*

China has explicitly expressed its view on the SCS dispute continually by, *inter alia*, the Position Paper by the PRC Government (Position Paper),[108] the Statement of the Chinese Society of International Law,[109] and several statements by

---

the US seek commercial gain from the data collected). For a detailed description of the *Impeccable* incident, see Jonathan G. Odom, "The true 'lies' of the Impeccable Incident: What Really Happened, Who Disregarded International Law, and Why Every Nation (outside of China) Should be Concerned," *Michigan State Journal of International Law*, 18, no. 3 (2010), pp. 1–42; Raul Pedrozo, "Close Encounters at Sea, The USNS Impeccable Incident," *Naval War College Review* (Summer 2009).

103 Zhang Haiwen, "Is It Safeguarding the Freedom of Navigation or Maritime Hegemony of the United States? Comments on Raul (Pete) Pedrozo's Article on Military Activities in the EEZ," *Chinese Journal of International Law*, 9 (2010), p. 31.

104 *Ibid.*

105 Zhiguo Gao, China and the Law of the Sea, in Myron H. Nordquist et al. (2009), p. 293 (mentioning as development the Post-Cold War context and the September 11, 2001 terrorist attacks).

106 *Fisheries Jurisdiction* Case (Federal Republic of Germany v. Iceland), Judgment, *ICJ Report 1973*, p. 63 (opining that "[i]nternational law admits that a fundamental change in the circumstances which determined the parties to accept a treaty, if it has resulted in a radical transformation of the extent of the obligations imposed by it, may … afford the party affected a ground for invoking the termination or suspension of the treaty [which has been] embodied in Article 62 of the Vienna Convention on the Law of Treaties").

107 Tiqiang Chen, "The People's Republic of China and Public International Law," *Dalhousie Law Journal*, 8 (1984), p. 22.

108 Ministry of Foreign Affairs, China, "Position Paper of the Government of the People's Republic of China on the Matter of Jurisdiction in the South China Sea Arbitration Initiated by the Republic of the Philippines," December 7, 2014, at http://www.fmprc.gov.cn/mfa_eng/zxxx_662805/t1217147.shtml.

109 Chinese Society of International Law (2018), pp. 207–748.

the Ministry of Foreign Affairs and its Ministers of the PRC.[110] This Section surveys the Chinese view on the SCS dispute with reference to "A Critical Study" of the Chinese Society of International Law (the "Society"; 中国国际法学会), which was published in 2018 (Critical Study or Study).[111] This Study has been conducted for over a year by more than 60 Chinese experts on law, politics, history, and geography.[112]

> China has sovereignty over Nanhai Zhudao (the SCS Islands), consisting of Dongsha Qundao (the Pratas Islands), Xisha Qundao (the Paracel Islands), Zhongsha Qundao (the Macclesfield Bank) and Nansha Qundao (the Spratly Island Group). China has internal waters, territorial sea, contiguous zone, exclusive economic zone and continental shelf based on Nanhai Zhudao. Furthermore, China has historic rights in the South China Sea ... China has territorial sovereignty over Nansha Qundao (the Spratly Island Group) and Zhongsha Qundao (the Macclesfield Bank) and has enjoyed maritime entitlements based upon the two archipelagos each as a unit.[113]

In most cases, states with *de facto* control over a disputed territory refute the existence of the territorial dispute.[114] However, China acknowledges that disputes exist over territorial sovereignty and maritime delimitation in the SCS.[115] In China's view, the heart of the SCS dispute lies in the territorial issue over

110 See e.g., Statement of the Chinese Foreign Ministry on the Award of 12 July 2016 of the SCS Tribunal established at the Request of the Republic of the Philippines, July 12, 2016, at http://www.fmprc.gov.cn/mfa_eng/zxxx_662805/t1379492.shtml; "Remarks by Chinese Foreign Minister Wang Yi on the Award of the So-called Arbitral Tribunal in the South China Sea Arbitration," July 12, 2016, at http://www.fmprc.gov.cn/mfa_eng/zxxx_662805/t1380003.shtml; and "Veil of the Arbitral Tribunal Must be Tore Down – Vice Foreign Minister Liu Zhenmin Answers Journalists' Questions on the So-called Binding Force of the Award Rendered by the Arbitral Tribunal of the South China Sea Arbitration Case," PRC Ministry of Foreign Affairs, July 16, 2016, at http://www.fmprc.gov.cn/mfa_eng/wjbxw/t1381879.shtml.

111 Chinese Society of International Law (2018), pp. 207–748.

112 *Ibid.*, p. 218. Considering the allegedly indiscrete relationship between the Society and the Chinese government, the view expressed in "Critical Study" can be viewed as (quasi) official, consistent with that of the Chinese government.

113 *Ibid*, p. 475

114 Reinhard Drifte, "Territorial conflicts in the East China Sea – From Missed Opportunities to Negotiation Stalemate," *The Asia-Pacific Journal*, 22, no. 3 (2009), p. 3.

115 Chinese Society of International Law (2018), p. 250.

certain component features, not in the status of and maritime entitlements generated by the individual maritime features.[116]

In this understanding, China criticizes the Philippines formulating a case in 2013 for fragmenting the dispute into various discrete pieces and camouflaging its submissions with mere issues of maritime entitlements of relevant features;[117] China points out that the question of maritime entitlement of a feature can only be decided after territorial title over the feature is attributed to a particular state.[118] Further, China argues that the legal status and maritime entitlements of insular features must be considered in the process of maritime delimitation, not in the international adjudication regarding the interpretation and application of UNCLOS.[119]

Since China perceives that the principle of sovereign equality sustains the international system and that international dispute settlement should be predicated on sovereign states' consent,[120] it levels the lack of consent against the SCS tribunal.[121] Chinese scholars emphasize that states have the right to decide how to settle a dispute, especially those disputes involving sovereignty and territorial integrity.[122] In fact, the SCS dispute is all about sovereignty, territorial integrity, and regime stability.[123]

Also, China criticizes the SCS arbitration for twists of legal logic. In *Maritime Delimitation and Territorial Questions* between Qatar and Bahrain, ICJ states that "maritime rights derive from the coastal State's sovereignty over the land, a principle which can be summarized as 'the land dominates the sea.'"[124] Following this logic, China argues that "no international court or tribunal had ever determined [features'] maritime entitlements without having decided on sovereignty over [such maritime features]" on the basis that determination of

116 *Ibid.*, pp. 254, 259, 353.

117 *Ibid.*, pp. 257, 271.

118 *Ibid.*, pp. 257, 265.

119 *Ibid.*, p. 257.

120 *Ibid.*, p. 246.

121 Letter from the Ambassador of the People's Republic of China to the Kingdom of the Netherlands to the individual members of the Tribunal, February 6, 2015.

122 Jinghan Zeng, Yuefan Xiao, and Shaun Breslin, "Securing China's core interests: the state of the debate in China," *International Affairs*, 91, no. 2 (2015), pp. 245–66.

123 Jeffrey W. Legro, "What China Will Want: The Future Intentions of a Rising Power," *Perspectives on Politics*, 5, no. 3 (September 2007), p. 518.

124 *Maritime Delimitation and Territorial Questions between Qatar and Bahrain*, Merits, Judgment, *ICJ Reports 2001*, p. 40, para.185, citing *North Sea Continental Shelf* (Federal Republic of Germany/Denmark; Federal Republic of Germany/Netherlands), Judgment, *ICJ Reports 1969*, para. 96.

territorial title over an island is the prerequisite for what maritime zones such a feature may generate.[125]

Based on the above, Chinese scholars denounce the 2016 SCS tribunal as a "law-abusing tribunal," arbitration as "judicial activism," and the award as "ill-founded" stood on "an erroneous approach."[126] Similarly, on July 13, 2016, Liu Zhenmin, then Chinese Vice Foreign Minister, raised a question over the legitimacy, saying the tribunal was the result of political manipulation, lacking representativeness and fairness (Eurocentric), and the arbitrators were impartial: "these five judges … are doing it for a profit, [providing] paid services."[127]

On historic rights, China holds that: 1) general international law (not UNCLOS) is the governing rule for the formation of historic rights; 2) the negotiation history,[128] structure,[129] and contents of UNCLOS indicate that the Convention shows respect for historic rights; and 3) UNCLOS does not supersede historic rights, leaving the relationship between historic rights and EEZ and continental shelf open.[130] In addition, China interprets the preamble of UNCLOS ("matters not regulated by this Convention continue to be governed by the rules and principles of general international law") to cover historic

125 Chinese Society of International Law (2018), p. 264. See also the Position Paper, para. 14 (arguing that "[a] maritime feature not subjected to a State's sovereignty does not grant any maritime rights or entitlements … Only the State with sovereignty over the maritime feature might claim the maritime rights in respect of that feature … If the sovereignty of a maritime feature was undetermined, there could not be any dispute for arbitration").

126 Chinese Society of International Law (2018), pp. 340, 541 See also Xinhua News Agency, Law-abusing Tribunal Issues Ill-founded Award on South China Sea Arbitration, July 12, 2016, at http://news.xinhuanet.com/english/2016-07/12/c_135507651.htm; People's Daily, OP-ED: South China Sea Arbitration Abuses International Law, Threatens World Order, June 29, 2016, at http://en.people.cn/n3/2016/0629/c90000-9078797.html.

127 Ministry of Foreign Affairs of the PRC, Veil of the Arbitral Tribunal Must Be Tore Down: Vice Foreign Minister Liu Zhenmin Answers Journalists' Questions on the So-called Binding Force of the Award Rendered by the Arbitral Tribunal of the South China Sea Arbitration Case, July 13, 2016, at https://www.fmprc.gov.cn/mfa_eng/wjbxw/t1381879.shtml. Four of the five arbitrators of the tribunal were from Germany, France, the Netherlands, and Poland. See Jiangyu Wang, "Legitimacy, Jurisdiction and Merits in the South China Sea Arbitration: Chinese Perspectives and International Law," *Journal of Chinese Political Science*, 22, no. 2 (2017) p. 200.

128 China views that UNCLOS III indicate that the negotiators did not have the intention to address the regime of historic rights (historic bay or historic title), and did not intend to settle the relationship between historic rights and the regimes of EEZ and continental shelf. See Chinese Society of International Law (2018), pp. 437, 439.

129 *Ibid.*, p. 436 (arguing that UNCLOS provides no rules on the constituent elements and nature of historic rights. Relevant Articles (10(6), 15, 51(1) and 298(1)) refer to historic rights differently, which structure indicates that "it is meant to maintain historic rights").

130 *Ibid.*, p. 442.

rights.[131] Historic rights under general international law, as the argument goes, are diverse in character; hence, there is no single regime for such rights, each regime being *sui generis.*[132]

China claims that historic rights—drawing on zonal implications[133]—are generally "regarded as a relevant circumstance which should be taken into account in maritime delimitation," constituting a relevant circumstance of delimitation.[134] Further, it argues that "international courts or tribunals have never addressed the issue of historic rights in isolation from the issue of maritime delimitation" where maritime delimitation is necessary.[135] More importantly, China affirms that "the emergence and development of China's historic rights" in the SCS is closely linked with the establishment of China's sovereignty over the SCS Islands; thus, historic rights and sovereignty cannot be viewed separately.[136]

At the same time, China claims that the Spratly Islands have all the characteristics of an archipelago, which have been understood as one economic and political entity for exploration, exploitation, and administration.[137] Under this logic, China contends that the Spratlys are fully qualified as an archipelago as "widely acknowledged and recognized in the international community."[138]

Article 46(b) of UNCLOS defines archipelago as "a group of islands, including parts of islands, interconnecting waters and other natural features which are so closely interrelated that such islands, waters, and other natural features form an intrinsic geographical, economic and political entity, or which historically have been regarded as such." Archipelagic states can adopt the archipelagic straight baseline system (Article 46(a)).[139] Not being an archipelagic state under Article 46, China cannot invoke the archipelagic straight baseline for the Spratly and Paracel Islands. Nevertheless, China adduces that the regime of continental states' outlying archipelago has been established by state practice instead of, or parallel with UNCLOS under customary international law.[140]

131 *Ibid.*, p. 337.
132 *Ibid.*, p. 436.
133 *Ibid.*, p. 423.
134 *Ibid.*, p. 326 (arguing that "[i]nternational jurisprudence also confirms that historic rights constitute a relevant circumstance to be taken into account in maritime delimitation").
135 *Ibid.*, p. 422.
136 *Ibid.*, p. 422.
137 *Ibid.*, p. 499.
138 *Ibid.*, p. 500.
139 Article 46(a): 'archipelagic State' means a State constituted wholly by one or more archipelagos and may include other islands.
140 Chinese Society of International Law (2018), p. 479.

During UNCLOS III negotiations, many proposals favoring the outlying archipelagos of continental states were presented; however, in the end, the regime of the archipelagic straight baseline system was allowed only for archipelagic states. China interprets this history in that the issue of continental states' outlying archipelagos was shelved at UNCLOS III, and has not dissipated, being left in the hands of customary international law as a matter not regulated by the Convention.[141] History tells, in China's view, that "continental States have effectively preserved the regime of the outlying archipelago as a unit during the negotiation."[142]

Under this premise, China claims that the definition of archipelago in Article 46(b) can be applied to continental (Chinese) outlying archipelagos, enabling China to employ straight baselines in the Spratlys down the road.[143] Further, China argues that a state's sovereignty over an archipelago extends to the whole archipelago regardless of whether it be "high-tide features" or "low-tide elevations."[144] In connection with low-tide elevation, China believes that the question of whether or not a low-tide elevation can be appropriated as territory is an issue of territorial sovereignty.[145]

Chinese lawyers widely support the idea of outlying archipelagos.[146] For example, Jiang and Zhang grumble that if China cannot employ straight

141 *Ibid.*, p. 484. At UNCLOS III, many proposals was made and such proposals included all kinds of archipelagos without distinguishing between island States' archipelagos and continental States' outlying archipelagos. See Working paper co-sponsored by Canada, Chile, Iceland, India, Indonesia, Mauritius, Mexico, New Zealand and Norway, A/CONF.62/L.4, UNCLOS III Official Records, Vol. III, pp. 82–83.

142 Chinese Society of International Law (2018), p. 486. There seem to be some 20 continental states possessing outlying archipelagos, and 17 of them have treated their outlying archipelagos as units, adopting the method of straight baselines in drawing baselines and treating them as units in their legislation with some exceptions, such as the US (Hawaiian Islands, Aleutian archipelago, Florida Keys, Midway Islands, Virgin Islands), New Zealand (Cook Islands), and Russia (Franz Josef Land). Ibid., p. 494.

143 Chinese Society of International Law (2018), pp. 498, 507.

144 *Ibid.*, p. 513. Therefore, China argues its territorial sovereignty over the Spratly Islands is possibly extended to low-tide elevations, such as Mischief Reef and Second Thomas Shoal. See *Ibid.*, p. 520.

145 In this sense, China denounces the SCS Arbitral Tribunal as having addressed this issue without having jurisdiction territorial sovereignty. See Chinese Society of International Law (2018), p. 265.

146 J. Ashley Roach explains that at least there are 9 scholars (8 of whom are mainland Chinese) support China's right to draw straight baselines enclosing the Spratly (Nansha) Islands. See J. Ashley Roach, "Offshore Archipelagos Enclosed by Straight Baselines: An Excessive Claim?" *Ocean Development & International Law*, 49, no. 2 (2018), pp. 183–187 (devaluing that "these nine papers arguing in favor of enclosing offshore archipelagos with straight baselines are neither well documented nor persuasive").

baselines for the Spratly Islands due to its non-archipelagic state status, it will be a "*de facto* punishment on a group of States," which is no more than treating China as "second class" sovereign land.[147] Equally worrying is the argument that the SCS is "archipelagic waters" and islands therein are "distant archipelagos," which enables China to gain "real interest" by using the "wider drying reefs to delineate its territorial sea baselines" to enjoy "longer baselines, and (archipelagic) water areas larger than its internal waters."[148] It remains to be seen whether China takes such a controversial step of proclaiming the archipelagic status over the Spratlys and Paracels. One view holds that the Chinese decision will be as a response to or in consideration of the region's political developments.[149]

Lastly, the recent development in the SCS, including the arbitration, is reminiscent of the past "unhappy memories of the Western-dominated international law for China as the Western-dominated international law has come with humiliation, exploitation and oppression."[150] China complains that "Western-dominated international law has not always been part of the solution, but rather part of the problem."[151] This is the sentiment behind Chinese elites who encouraged the Chinese government to neither acknowledge nor respect the SCS Arbitration in the hope that this obstinacy would improve the "international rule of law in a way that benefits China."[152]

---

147 Jiang Li and Zhang Jie, A Preliminary Analysis of the Application of Archipelagic Regime and the Delimitation of the South China Sea, *China Oceans Law Review*, no. 1, 2010, p. 158 (in Chinese), cited in Nong Hong et al. (2013), p. 222, fn. 61.

148 Kuen-chen Fu, Freedom of Navigation and the Chinese Straight Baselines in the South China Sea, in M. H. Nordquist et al. (2015), pp. 190–196.

149 Nong Hong et al. (2013), p. 238–9.

150 K. J. Noh, Making a Mockery of International Law: the Arbitral Tribunal on the South China Sea Prepares the Way for War, (July 19, 2016), at http://www.counterpunch.org/2016/07/19/making-a-mockery-of-international-law-the-arbitral-tribunalon-the-south-china-sea-prepares-the-way-for-war/.

151 Anlei Zuo (2018), p. 45.

152 Huang Wei, "Expert evaluates the tribunal: An opportunity to promote the establishment of our maritime laws and rules in a way that benefits China" (专家评南海仲裁:中国推动利我国际海洋法规则建立的契机), *People's Daily*, July 14, 2016, at http://www.people.com.cn/n1/2016/0714/c32306-28553189.html, cited in Michael D. Swaine, "Chinese Views on the South China Sea Arbitration Case between the People's Republic of China and the Philippines," *China Leadership Monitor*, no. 51, p. 7. More generally, some Chinese scholars propose that China can, in the longer run, "take part in amending and framing the international rules of the game" or even, "eventually become a framer of international rules," creating and leading a new international system superior to the current one. See Li Nan, "'Zhongguo de guoji zeren guan' yanjiuhui zongshu" [Summary of Seminar on "The Concept of China's International Responsibility"], Dangdai Yatai 2008–06 (November/

2 The Western Legal View

The Western legal view stands in stark contrast to that of Chinese international lawyers. In the West, sovereignty is a law-based concept defined and constructed through international law. In addition, the concept of *mare liberum* is at the core of Western legal philosophy in viewing maritime legal institutions. The SCS arbitral award categorically pronounces what the West views the SCS dispute.

2.1 *The Western View on the International Legal System*

The concept of sovereignty is an underpinning principle of international law. It underlies almost any other principle and institution of international law.[153] In Western intellectual history, the meaning of sovereignty has changed across historical and political contexts and, as such, has undergone a profound process of debate at any given time and space.[154] The modern Western notion of sovereignty has its root in the 1648 Treaty of Westphalia, by which the principle of the equality of States, territorial delimitation of State authority, and the principle of non-intervention were formally initiated.[155] Vattel defined sovereignty that "[s]ince men are naturally equal, and a perfect equality prevails in their rights and obligations ... [N]ations ... are naturally equal, and inherit from nature the same obligations and rights. Power or weakness does not in this respect produce any difference."[156]

The West perceives sovereignty as freedom from subjection (independence): law's liberation from the bondage of political power.[157] Sovereignty (a

---

December 2008), pp. 154–5, cited in Alison Adcock Kaufman, "The 'Century of Humiliation,' Then and Now: Chinese Perceptions of the International Order," *Pacific Focus*, 25, no. 1 (2010), p. 23, n.63.

153 Samantha Besson, Sovereignty, Wolfrum, Rüdiger (ed.), *Max Planck Encyclopedias of International Law* (Oxford: Oxford University Press, 2012), Vol. IX, p. 387.

154 *Ibid.*, p. 367.

155 Samantha Besson, Sovereignty, Wolfrum, Rüdiger (2012), Vol. IX, p. 368. See also Rainer Grote, Westphalian System, *Max Planck Encyclopedias of International Law* (Oxford: Oxford University Press, 2012), Vol. X, p. 871 (noting that the main legal principles stemming from the Westphalian system are the equality of states, state sovereignty based on exclusive territorial jurisdiction, the principle of non-intervention, and state consent as the only valid source of international legal obligation).

156 Vattel, *Le Droit des gens* (1758) I.Prelim. §18, cited in James R. Crawford (2012), p. 12 (assimilating a small republic to a dwarf who is as much a man as a giant).

157 Gary Lilienthal & Nehaluddin Ahmad, The South China Sea Islands Arbitration: Making China's Position Visible in Hostile Waters, *Asian-Pacific Law & Policy Journal*, 18, no. 2 (2017), p. 94.

general principle of international law and a principle about international law) involves a monopoly of governing authority.[158] In the meantime, the concept of state sovereignty (in its internal and external dimensions) has developed to the extent to which sovereignty is perceived to be bound by international law, sometimes without states' consent, if not frequently.[159] It is argued that international law has entered the next level in which an argument that international law is entirely dependent on state consent (express or implied) would make little sense.[160] In fact, many Western scholars assert that sovereignty can be limited as a corollary to sovereignty's modern configuration: sovereignty is law-based, defined, and constructed through international law.[161]

International law was developed by political entities that had emerged as independent political entities equal in law, similar in form to manage their external relations.[162] Being European in origin, international law was expanded, with the colonizers, to the Americas, Asia, Africa, and eventually to Oceania.[163] Today many Western lawyers agree that international law exists for the sake of a people. In other words, the West views that "[s]tates are recognized by international law as trustees for the people committed to their care," which has become the axiom of most norms of international law. If accepted without limits, the *raison d'être* of international law falls within the well-being of human individuals instead of the freedom or autonomy of states.[164] That is, international law is perceived to no longer bind "only by self-limitation of the sovereign, but on the contrary by reference to the people whose autonomy is at stake."[165]

For a long time, Western writers have believed that the function of international law is to provide a framework within which international politics

158 Samantha Besson, Sovereignty, Wolfrum, Rüdiger (2012), Vol. IX, p. 378.

159 *Ibid.*, p. 376

160 James R. Crawford (2012), p. 5.

161 Samantha Besson, Sovereignty, Wolfrum, Rüdiger (2012), Vol. IX, p. 387.

162 James R. Crawford (2012), p. 9. ICJ defines, in an avisory opinion, states as "political entities equal in law, similar in form ... the direct subjects of international law." See *Reparation for Injuries Suffered in the Service of the United Nations*, Advisory Opinion, *ICJ Reports 1949*, pp. 177–8.

163 James R. Crawford (2012), p. 4. The nature of international law as the governing medium of international relations was confirmed by PCIJ in 1927 in the *Lotus* case that "International law governs relations between independent States. The rules of law binding upon States therefore emanate from their own free will as expressed in conventions or by usages generally accepted as expressing principles of law and established in order to regulate the relations between these co-existing independent communities or with a view to the achievement of common aims." See *ibid.*, p. 18.

164 Samantha Besson, Sovereignty, Wolfrum, Rüdiger (2012), Vol. IX, p. 379.

165 *Ibid.*, p. 388.

works,[166] which is, in principle, for the benefit of the orderly management of international relations.[167] The West understands that the Westphalian system has sustained a stable structure for foreign relations.[168] Also, Western international lawyers regard the law as an "objective body of authoritative rules which can be understood and relied upon by the people."[169] Seen in this way, the law-making process of these rules depends on political processes, but the application of such rules should be delinked from political consideration, about which the Chinese commentators label "rightist heresy."[170]

On the sources of international law, Western lawyers agree that Article 38 of the Statute of ICJ stipulates the sources: international conventions, international custom, the general principles of law recognized by civilized nations, and judicial decisions while accepting the teachings of the most highly qualified publicists of the various nations as subsidiary means for the determination of rules of law. Meanwhile, Western lawyers understand international organizations and individuals, in addition to states, as subjects of the law of nations under certain (limited) conditions.[171]

For the West, the rule of law (albeit its protean concept over time) has three components that are (1) a government of laws (the power of the state may not be exercised arbitrarily), (2) the supremacy of the law (the law must be applied to the sovereign and instruments of the state, and (3) equality before the law (the law must be applied to all persons equally, offering equal protection without prejudicial discrimination).[172] A "government of laws" may mean non-arbitrariness in the exercise of state power in their international relations; the "supremacy of the law" may be understood that weak or middle powers and great powers, including the hegemon, must abide by international law; and "equality before the law" may require more general and consistent application of international law to states and other entities.[173]

In the West, it had been believed that once China entered the international scene, it would not destroy or remake international law; rather, it would play the game out of regard for existing rules, thereby increasing its respect for

166 Louis Henkin, *How Nations Behave* (New York: Columbia University Press, 1979), p. 18.

167 Philip C. Jessup, A *Modern Law of Nations* (New York: Macmillan, 1948), p. 16.

168 R. H. Jackson, The evolution of International Society, in J. Baylis and S. Smith (eds.), *The Globalization of World Politics* (Oxford: Oxford University Press, 2001), p. 44.

169 Hungdah Chiu (1986), p. 247.

170 *Ibid.*

171 Philip C. Jessup (1948), pp. 16–17.

172 Simon Chesterman, Rule of Law, in Rudiger Wolfrum (2012), Vol. VIII, p. 1014.

173 Chesterman takes a similar view with the exception that, in his view, "supremacy of the law is less applicable to the international legal system." See Simon Chesterman, Rule of Law, in Rudiger Wolfrum (2012), Vol. VIII, pp. 1020–1.

agreed law of nations.[174] However, with time, the West realized their anticipation was ill-advised. For example, the 2017 US Trade Representative Report complains:

> After its accession to [WTO] in 2001, China was supposed to revise hundreds of laws, regulations and other measures to bring them into conformity with its WTO obligations, as required by the terms set forth in its Protocol of Accession. [US] hoped that the terms set forth in [the Protocol] would dismantle existing state-led policies and practices … incompatible with an international trading system … based on open, market-oriented policies and rooted in the principles of nondiscrimination, market access, reciprocity, fairness and transparency. But those hopes were disappointed … China has used [WTO] to become a dominant player in international trade.[175]

By the same token, some Western lawyers worry that China will never respect the current international legal system if such rules do not support China's interests; under this assumption, they predict that China will use its ability to remake a new international law discourse for its benefit at the expense of the existing international legal order.[176] In contrast, other lawyers in the West assess that China will remain in the existing international legal system because it is conducive to advancing Chinese interests. Burke-White, for instance, claims that "rising powers are not attempting to wholly destroy the edifice of international law nor even rejecting international law *per se*,"[177] which is what history suggests: "[n]ew powers have embraced the system … because it

174 Louis Henkin (1979), pp. 109–110.

175 United States Trade Representative, 2017 Report to Congress on China's WTO Compliance, January 2018, p. 2. China's 2001 accession to the WTO led China to agree to a host of regulations on imports and exports, intellectual property, and trade remedies. See Vinod K. Aggarwal and Sara A. Newland, Introduction, in Vinod K. Aggarwal and Sara A. Newland (2015), p. 6.

176 For instance, Kinzelbach parses that China tries to change the discourse of human rights law and the political reality of China's ascendancy "undoubtedly increases China's ability to shape the international human rights discourse." See Katrin Kinzelbach, "Will China's Rise Lead to a New Normative Order? An Analysis of China's Statements on Human Rights at the United Nations (2000–2010)," *Netherlands Quarterly of Human Rights*, 30 (2012), p. 81.

177 William W. Burke-White, "Power Shifts in International Law: Structural Realignment and Substantive Pluralism," *Harvard International Law Journal*, 56 (2015), p. 3.

furthers their interests. They are using their newfound power to adapt it from within."[178]

Whether China respects or resists the existing international legal system remains to be seen. However, one certainty is that change in international legal order seems inevitable for better or worse, to the extent necessary for reflecting the systemic change of international relations.

2.2 *The Western View on the International Law of the Sea System*

Western efforts to keep the core principles of the law of the sea (i.e., freedom of the seas) from going astray have been led by the US (a major maritime power) in the form of protests and naval operations. As a norm entrepreneur (borrowing concepts from political scientists) America actively took part in the UNCLOS III negotiation: for instance, about 150 accredited members of the US delegation participated in the 1974 session, engaging in every meeting.[179] Since the adoption of UNCLOS, the US has proactively objected to and protested against cases that the US deemed unlawful[180] because a stable legal regime assuring *mare liberum* is at the core of US national security.[181]

Indeed, the US has upheld freedom of navigation from day one of its founding (long before the establishment of the PRC in 1949), and consistently through the establishment of the UNCLOS system.[182] As such, for America, freedom of the seas has been a "vital interest" while wielding enormous sea power to contribute to global stability and mutual security.[183]

---

178 *Ibid.*, p. 76.

179 Myron H. Nordquist and William G. Phalen, Interpretation of UNCLOS Article 121 and Itu Aba (Taiping) in the South China Sea Arbitration Award, in Myron H. Nordquist et al. (2017), p. 10.

180 For the chronicles of US effort to maintain *mare liberum* after the adoption of UNCLOS, see J. Ashley Roach and Robert W. Smith (2012). See also Sophia Kopela, *Dependent Archipelagos in the Law of the Sea* (Leiden: Martinus Nijhoff Publishers, 2013), p. 176 (explaining that "[a]part from the USA, few other states have protested against straight baseline systems in outlying archipelagos").

181 J. Ashley Roach and Robert W. Smith (2012), pp. 4–6.

182 Jonathan G. Odom, "A China in the Bull Shop? Comparing the Rhetoric of A Rising China with the Reality of the International Law of the Sea," *Ocean and Coastal Law Journal*, 17 (2012), pp. 225–226.

183 See The White House, the National Security Strategy of the United States, August 1991, p. 15, at https://nssarchive.us/wp-content/uploads/2020/04/1991.pdf (noting that "[US] has long supported international agreements designed to promote openness and freedom of navigation on the high seas ... As a maritime nation, with our dependence on the sea to preserve legitimate security and commercial ties, freedom of the seas is and will remain a vital interest. ... American sea power ... makes a strong contribution to global stability and mutual security").

UNCLOS is an outcome of a careful balance of coastal and maritime States interests as a compromise between *mare liberum* and *mare clausum*. However, the West perceives that *mare liberum* should outweigh *mare clausum*, given the fact that, before 1982, most of the oceans were free for use by all states, and in UNCLOS III, coastal states yield free navigation of others (naval powers) through their offshore oceans in return for maritime powers yielding the economic control of adjacent offshore areas to coastal states.[184]

In terms of warships' innocent passage through foreign territorial seas, despite developing states' attempts to add a provision requiring prior notification or authorization during UNCLOS III, no consensus was made, leaving no provision for allowing or denying warships a right of innocent passage in the Convention.[185] Thus, the US advocates that warships enjoy the right of innocent passage in the territorial seas of coastal states.[186] Tommy Koh, the Chairperson of the concluding session of UNCLOS III, supports this position, stating that "[w]arships do … have a right of innocent passage through the territorial sea, and there is no need for warships to acquire the prior consent or even notification of the coastal State."[187]

However, some Western scholars point out that state practice and customary rules on innocent passage of warships in the territorial sea hitherto the conclusion of UNCLOS were not in favor of the Western assertion; rather, their argument supports the opposite. Erik Franckx, for example, argues that in the 1930s, the US suggested that warships should get coastal states' authorization before navigating their territorial seas,[188] as is the case with the 1930 Hague Codification Conference.[189]

In the meantime, with its naval power growing exponentially after World War II, the US changed its attitude toward allowing warships to enjoy innocent

184 J. Ashley Roach and Robert W. Smith (2012), pp. 3–4.

185 Bernard H. Oxman (1981), p. 235.

186 This position has been recurrently ascertained in the 2004 and 2007 resolutions of advice and consent to accession to UNCLOS recommended by the Senate Executive Reports. See J. Ashley Roach and Robert W. Smith (2012), Appendix Nine, pp. 775–814.

187 Bernard H. Oxman (1984), p. 854, fn. 159.

188 League of Nations Doc. C.74.M.39.1929.V (L.N. Pub. No.1929.V.2), 66 and 73, cited in Erik Franckx (1990), p. 485.

189 In this Conference, the US delegate stated that innocent passage as a matter of right did not extend to warships, although it was ordinarily granted as a matter of usage and comity. See Sixth Meeting of the Second Committee on Territorial Waters of the Conference for the Codification of International Law, League of Nations Doc.C.351(b).1930.V (L.N. Pub. No.1930.V.16), p. 59.

passage through territorial seas. In 1983, the USSR still prohibited warship navigation from passing through its territorial sea, allowing warships' passage only in the Baltic, the Sea of Okhotsk, and the Sea of Japan (the East Sea).[190] US and USSR navies conflicted involving the right of innocent passage of foreign warships in 1986, 1988, but as a result of bilateral consultation, they adopted the 1989 "Joint Statement on Uniform Interpretation of Rules of International Law Governing Innocent Passage." This Joint Statement ascertained the right of warships to innocent passage in the territorial seas of coastal States,[191] which influenced other states to allow foreign warships' innocent passage through their territorial seas.[192]

On the nature EEZ and the availability of foreign military activities therein, the West maintains that the very nature of the exclusive "economic" zone is exclusively concerned with protecting or utilizing the natural resource in EEZ, not with security concerns.[193] In this interpretation, the West asserts that coastal states cannot limit foreign military activities in their EEZ.[194] Illustrative

---

190 Article 12 of the Rules for Navigation and Sojourn of Foreign Warships in the Territorial and Internal Waters and Ports of the USSR, ratified by the Council of Ministers Decree No. 384 of April 25, 1983, cited in J. Ashley Roach and Robert W. Smith (2012), p. 233.

191 Article 2 contains that "All ships, including warships, regardless of cargo, armament or means of propulsion, enjoy the right of innocent passage through the territorial sea in accordance with international law, for which neither prior notification nor authorization is required." See 1989 USA-USSR Joint Statement on the Uniform Interpretation of Rules of International Law Governing Innocent Passage, Adopted in Wyoming, USA on September 23, 1989, at https://cil.nus.edu.sg/wp-content/uploads/formidable/18/1989-USA-USSR-Joint-Statement-with-Attached-Uniform-Interpretation-of-Rues-of-International-Law-Governing-Innocent-Passage.doc.

192 Zou Keyuan (2008), p. 73 (arguing that this history indicates a gap or deficiency in the UNCLOS system, which necessitates amendment filling in the gap in the future).

193 Erik Franckx (2011), p. 200; Peter Dutton, "Three disputes and three objectives: China and the South China Sea," *Naval War College Review*, 64, no. 4 (2011), pp. 49–50 (noting that "the EEZ is *sui generis* and the coastal states' jurisdiction is confined to the exploration and exploitation of living and non-living resources within [EEZ]. Jurisdiction is not equivalent to sovereignty").

194 George V. Galdorisi and Alan V. Kaufman, "Military Activities in the Exclusive Economic Zone: Preventing Uncertainty and Defusing Conflict," *California Western International Law Journal*, 32 (2002), p. 262; Natalie Klein (2011), p. 46 (comparing coastal States' right to regulate acts that prejudice their peace, good order, or security in the territorial sea with what is not in EEZ). Meanwhile, Pirtle divides military activities into "movement rights" and "operational rights." See Charles E. Pirtle, "Military Uses of Ocean Space and the Law of the Sea in the New Millennium," *Ocean Development and International Law*, 31 (2000), p. 8.

of this position is US commentary of UNCLOS: "[m]ilitary activities ... are recognized historic high seas uses that are preserved by article 58. [The right to conduct military activities may be under] the obligation to have due regard to coastal State resource and other rights ... [However it] is the duty of the flag State, not the right of the coastal State, to enforce this 'due regard' obligation."[195]

To support this conclusion, many Western international lawyers adduce that the general understanding of negotiators at UNCLOS III was that EEZ would be part of the high seas, over which coastal states had acquired "certain strictly-defined competencies,"[196] thereby permitting foreign military activities in EEZ.[197] Despite some efforts to insert an enforceable "security interest" into the EEZ regime at UNCLOS III, the majority of states rejected those proposals.[198] They add that military activities consistent with the UN Charter should be allowed in EEZ[199] and that military activities in EEZ appear to be not prohibited in light of the structure of Article 58, at the very least.[200]

Of course, some Western writers put forward a moderate approach to accommodate both sides' concerns regarding military activities in EEZ. For instance, Klein argues that coastal states do have economic concerns in their EEZ over the conduct of foreign military activities that may interfere with their economic activities therein, though acknowledging freedom of navigating, including military activities, under the 1958 High Seas Convention and UNCLOS.[201] Hence, Klein claims that there can be certain restrictions on military activities in foreign EEZs with due regard to the rights and duties of the coastal

195 US Commentary—The 1982 United Nations Convention on the Law of the Sea and the Agreement on Implementation of Par XI, cited in J. Ashley Roach and Robert W. Smith (2012), Appendix Eight, p. 694.

196 Bernard H. Oxman, An analysis of the Exclusive Economic Zone as formulated in the Informal Composite Negotiating Text, in Thomas A. Clingan (Jr.) (ed.), *Law of the Sea: State practice in zones of special jurisdiction* (Law of the Sea Institute, 1982), pp. 57–78. Interestingly, Zou also acknowledges that notwithstanding no provisions of military uses of the high seas, historically military activities have been allowed under customary international law: "it is difficult to infer that the establishment of the EEZ was intended to limit foreign military operations." See Zou Keyuan (2008), p. 75.

197 Jon M. Van Dyke, Consensus and Confrontation: The United States and the Law of the Sea Convention: a Workshop of the Law of the Sea Institute, January 9–13, 1984, Honolulu, Hawaii, Law of the Sea Institute, University of Hawaii, 1985, pp. 302–03.

198 M. Nordquist (1995), Vol. II, pp. 558–560.

199 M. Nordquist (1995), Vol. V, pp. 154–5.

200 Yoshifumi Tanaka, *The international law of the sea* (Cambridge: Cambridge University Press, 2015), p. 396.

201 Natalie Klein (2011), pp. 45, 7. See also Jon M. Van Dyke (2004), p. 31.

state.[202] Also, Schmitt adduces that if military activities considerably interfere in coastal states' fishing activities or cause pollution contrary to coastal states' regulations, they are not allowable,[203] and Hayashi advances that naval exercises of unreasonable scale with the use of weapons are not permitted.[204]

Do "peaceful uses" impose hindrance to the conduct of naval activities in the foreign EEZ?[205] Admittedly, the US (along with the USSR) intentionally avoided specific discussion of the restriction of naval activities in EEZ at UNCLOS III.[206] States understood the proposed provision of Article 301[207] as none other than applying to settings that would violate Article 2(4) of the UN Charter.[208] It has been argued that UNCLOS was not designed to deal with security concerns; the legality of the conduct of naval activities in terms of Articles 88 and 301 cannot be decided under UNCLOS.[209] In this view, Hayashi argues that "Articles 88 and 301 do not prohibit all military activities on the high seas and in EEZs as long as such activities conform to the UN Charter."[210]

202 Natalie Klein (2011), pp. 47–8.

203 John Astley III and Michael N. Schmitt, "The Law of the Sea and Naval Operations," *Air Force Law Review*, 42 (1997), p. 119.

204 Moritaka Hayashi, "Military and Intelligence Gathering Activities in the EEZ: Definition of Key Terms," *Marine Policy*, 29 (2005), p. 129.

205 Articles 88 and 301 contain peaceful uses of the seas. The origin of Article 88 ("[t]he high seas shall be reserved for peaceful purposes") dates back to 1973 when Ecuador, Panama, and Peru proposed that "[t]he international seas shall be open to all States ... and their use shall be reserved for peaceful purposes." See M. Nordquist (1995), Vol. III, p. 88.

206 B. Boczek, "Peaceful purposes provisions of the United Nations Convention on the Law of the Sea," *Ocean Development and International Law*, 20 (1989), p. 368.

207 In 1980, ten developing nations suggested a proposal (which became Article 301) as an additional sentence to Article 88 but failed to obtain necessary support ("All States shall refrain from any threat or use of force against the sovereignty, territorial integrity or political independence of any State, or in any other manner inconsistent with the purpose of the United Nations and the principles of international law"). Subsequently, the proposal was separated to appear in the later part applicable to all zones of ocean space. See M. Nordquist (1995), Vol. III, p. 89.

208 Article 2(4) of the UN Charter: All Members shall refrain in their international relations from the threat or use of force against the territorial integrity or political independence of any state, or in any other manner inconsistent with the Purposes of the [UN]. See also Myron H. Nordquist et al. (2009), Q&A: Panel III, p. 303.

209 S. Kaye, Freedom of Navigation in a Post 9/11 World: Security and Creeping Jurisdiction, in David Freestone et al. (2006), pp. 347–364.

210 Moritaka Hayashi, "Military and Intelligence Gathering Activities in the EEZ: Definition of Key Terms," *Marine Policy*, 29 (2005), p. 125.

On MSR, the US advocates that "military survey,"[211] "hydrographic survey,"[212] and "operational oceanography"[213] are not MSR because MSR means oceanography, marine chemistry, marine biology, scientific ocean drilling and coring, geological/geophysical research, as well as other activities with a scientific purpose.[214] In the US view, these non-MSR activities (albeit as marine data collection)[215] can be conducted in the foreign EEZs without the consent of coastal States. Specifically, state practice and some scholarly observations seem to allow hydrographic surveying in the absence of coastal states' consent. Due to the silence on surveys in the four 1958 Conventions,[216] states freely conducted marine surveys in most of the oceans seaward of the narrow territorial sea.[217] Also, the 2010 UN guide on MSR depicts hydrographic surveying distinct from MSR.[218] In reality, hydrographic surveying is conducted distinctly from

211 Military survey refers to activities undertaken in territorial seas, archipelagic waters, straits for navigation, EEZ, high seas, and on the continental shelf involving marine data collection (whether or not classified) for military purposes. Military surveys can include oceanographic, hydrographic, marine geological, geophysical, acoustic, and related data. See Department of the Navy, Office of the Chief of Operations, OPNAVINST 3128.9F, July 1, 2014, para. 4.b.

212 Hydrographic survey refers to marine data collection activities undertaken in the territorial seas, archipelagic waters, straits for navigation, EEZ, high seas, and on the continental shelf for the production of nautical charts and similar products to support safety of navigation. See Department of the Navy, Office of the Chief of Operations, OPNAVINST 3128.9F (July 1, 2014), para. 4.c.

213 Operational oceanography is the routine collection of ocean observations, such as temperature, pressure, current, salinity and wind, in all maritime zones for the purpose of monitoring and forecasting the weather (meteorology), climate, and ocean state (e.g., surface currents and waves). See J. Ashley Roach and Robert W. Smith (2012), p. 417.

214 J. Ashley Roach and Robert W. Smith (2012), p. 414.

215 The US categorizes "marine data collection" into: (1) MSR; (2) hydrographic surveys and military surveys; (3) operational oceanography (ocean state estimation, weather forecasting, climate prediction); and (4) exploration and exploitation of natural resources and underwater cultural heritage (shipwrecks). Each concept of "marine data collection" refers to discrete activities. *Ibid.*, pp. 413–4.

216 The 1958 Geneva Conventions consist of the Continental Shelf Convention, the High Seas Convention, the Territorial Sea Convention, and the Fishing Convention.

217 J. Ashley Roach and Robert W. Smith (2012), p. 419.

218 Marine Scientific Research: A revised guide to the implementation of the relevant provisions of the United Nations Convention on the Law of the Sea, Division for Ocean Affairs and the Law of the Sea, Office of Legal Affairs, United Nations, UN Publication Sales No. E.10.V.12, 2010, p. 16, para. 56 (noting that the freedom envisioned in Article 87 is not limited to MSR but also extends to hydrographic surveys).

MSR; thus, states may perceive hydrographic survey as a technical activity for the safety of navigation, not MSR.[219]

In the West, there is widespread criticism of the Chinese revisionist interpretation of UNCLOS (which were the outcome of a package deal and consensus) that China was apparently silent on issues like hydrographic survey and military activities in foreign EEZs and voluntarily ratified UNCLOS in 1996 despite its dissatisfaction with some maritime institutions.[220] Shortly thereafter, China deliberately began to disregard the negotiation history, ignoring that China voluntarily ratified the Convention with few written declarations, none of which interpreted in the manner China seeks to now.[221]

Overall, the West worries that China picks and chooses certain UNCLOS rules that it deems helpful to China while repudiating others that do not serve Chinese interests.[222] Indeed, China perceives UNCLOS as the "first step toward the establishment of a new international legal order for the oceans,"[223] thereby adhering to its interpretation and practice (e.g., on historic rights) to develop (new) international maritime norms palatable to China.[224] The West is further concerned about the likelihood that other states will follow in the footsteps of Chinese gaining from its selective compliance,[225] about which China pronounces its leadership.[226]

219 Sam Bateman (2004), pp. 79, 81 (explaining that "hydrographic surveying is a clear and distinct activity that, as evident in the low altitude of the aircraft, its repetitive flight pattern, and the typically relatively shallow waters of the area being surveyed, is not easily confused with other marine scientific research"). See also Alfred Soons, *Marine Scientific Research and the Law of the Sea* (Springer, 1982), pp. 125, 157 (noting that "hydrographic surveying can be conducted in foreign EEZs without [coastal states' consent]. Articles 19, 21, and 40 pertain to "hydrographic surveying" not MSR).

220 Zhiguo Gao, China and the Law of the Sea, in Myron H. Nordquist et al. (2009), p. 278.

221 Jonathan G. Odom (2012), pp. 243–4 (adding that many of Chinese proposals were dismissed, whereas the majority view prevailed at UNCLOS III). See also Michael Carr, "China and the Law of the Sea Convention," *Australian Journal of Chinese Affairs*, 9 (1983), p. 40.

222 Jonathan G. Odom (2012), pp. 219–220, 244.

223 Zhiguo Gao, China and the law of the sea, in Myron H. Nordquist et al. (2009), pp. 294–5.

224 Jinming Li and Dexia Li, "The dotted line on the Chinese map of the South China Sea: a note," *Ocean Development & International Law*, 34, no.3–4 (2003), pp. 287–295; Keyuan Zou (2001), pp. 149–168.

225 Jonathan G. Odom (2012), p. 245 (noting that China does "selective compliance in the name of imperfections, drawbacks, or shortcomings").

226 For example, Kuen-chen Fu anticipates, regarding the issue of outlying archipelagos, that if China adopts a special straight baseline regime for the Spratly and Paracel Islands, "some other non-archipelagic States might follow the precedent created by China, and apply the same principle and allow Chinese vessels and aircrafts to sail through or overfly their own distant archipelagic waters in other parts of the world." See Kuen-chen Fu,

2.3 *The Western View on the South China Sea Dispute*

The West understands that China shows a profound disrespect for international law in the SCS, which disrupts regional maritime order. The Western position on the SCS dispute rests on, at its core, three diktats that China should: (1) align its maritime claims with international law as reflected in UNCLOS; (2) abide by the 2016 SCS award, and; (3) restrain from provocation in the region.[227] As is the case with other campaigns against China, the US leads the legal campaign (qualitative and quantitative) to contend with Chinese interpretation. Meanwhile, the 2016 SCS arbitral award is believed to contain an agreeable view of the Western lawyers, though criticism of the arbitration is slowing increasing in the West.[228]

In support of the SCS Arbitral award, the Western nations have urged China to comply with the award. For example, in April 2017, the Joint Communiqué of the G7 Foreign Ministers' Meeting multilaterally regarded the award as "a useful basis for further efforts to peacefully resolve disputes in the [SCS]."[229] States, such as America and Australia, also individually called for China to

---

Freedom of Navigation and the Chinese Straight Baselines in the South China Sea, in M. H. Nordquist et al. (2015), pp. 190–196.

227 See, e.g., Michael D. Swaine, "Chinese Views on the South China Sea Arbitration Case between the People's Republic of China and the Philippines," *China Leadership Monitor*, no. 51, pp. 8–9 (noting that "[n]o external entity exists to enforce the ruling, and while Beijing may eventually come to accept aspects of it, this will most likely only occur over the long term, and as a result of growing awareness in Beijing that its stance on the issue is having a serious negative impact on the PRC's prestige and influence in the global order, on important inter-state relationships, and on China's international image as a peace-oriented, law-abiding citizen of the global community"). See also Radio Free Asia, U.S. Sends Note to UN Rebuking China's Claims in South China Sea, June 3, 2020; Dean Cheng, China's War against International law in the South China Sea, *National Interest*, May 19, 2015, at http://nationalinterest.org/feature/chinas-war-against-international-law-the-south-china-sea-12913?page=show.

228 For example, Nordquist and Phalen fulminate against the SCS arbitration in light of the tribunal's interpretation and application of Article 121. See Myron H. Nordquist and William G. Phalen, Interpretation of UNCLOS Article 121 and Itu Aba (Taiping) in the South China Sea Arbitration Award, in Myron H. Nordquist et al. (2017), pp. 76–78 (arguing that "[t]he Award … falters when it diverts from adherence to the text of the Convention … the Tribunal misjudges the positive impact the Award would otherwise engender. Confusion not clarity was the general result for Article 121(3)" and hence anticipating that "future dispute settlement efforts will treat the Article 121 interpretation in the Award as a misguided precedent and that the dispute settlement provisions in the Convention will hereafter be honored as originally agreed … future tribunals are likely to interpret Article 121 in accordance with the Convention text where jurisdictional pressures surrounding a dispute do not lead to over-reaching political determinations for procedural reasons").

229 G7 Foreign Ministers' Meeting Joint Communiqué, Lucca, April 10–11, 2017, at www.esteri.it/mae/resource/doc/2017/04/g7_-_joint_communiqu_final.pdf.

abide by the award.[230] Notably, the US has repeatedly issued statements,[231] diplomatically protested against China, or supported the ASEAN States;[232] further, America has taken actions over the past four decades to uphold the law of the sea in the SCS region.[233] Since 2014, the US priority has been moved to protect freedom of navigation through Freedom of Navigation Operation (FON) in the region.[234] In July 2020, Pompeo, then the Secretary of State, reiterated that:

> Beijing uses intimidation to undermine the sovereign rights of [other claimants in the SCS] … assert[ing] unilateral dominion, and replac[ing] international law with "might makes right." … Beijing has offered no coherent legal basis for its "Nine-Dashed Line" claim … In line with the Tribunal's legally binding decision, [China] has no lawful territorial or maritime claim to Mischief Reef or Second Thomas Shoal … nor does Beijing have any territorial or maritime claims generated from these features.[235]

US naval operations are understood as responsible for why freedom of navigation remains in the regions.[236] In January 2021, Lloyd Austin, US Secretary

230 US Department of State, Decision in the Philippines-China Arbitration, Press Statement, July 12, 2016, at https://2009-2017.state.gov/r/pa/prs/ps/2016/07/259587.htm; Australian Department of Foreign Affairs and Trade, Australia Supports Peaceful Dispute Resolution in the South China Sea, July 12, 2016, at https://www.dfat.gov.au/news/news/Pages/australia-supports-peaceful-dispute-resolution-in-the-south-china-sea. See also M. Taylor Fravel et. al., What Is the Future of the South China Sea? *Foreign Policy*, July 12, 2016, at https://foreignpolicy.com/2016/07/12/what-is-the-future-of-the-south-china-sea/.

231 For instance, in November 2019, US Department of State states that "PRC maritime claims in the [SCS], exemplified by the preposterous 'nine-dash line,' are unfounded, unlawful, and unreasonable. These claims, which are without legal, historic, or geographic merit, impose real costs on other countries." See, A Free and Open Indo-Pacific, Advancing a Shared Vision, November 4, 2019, p. 23.

232 Following Hillary Clinton's speech in 2012, 11 other countries commented on the Sea disputes. This was the first time they had been raised at a meeting of AFF: American forthrightness had given ASEAN members and other countries the political cover they needed to speak up. See Bill Hayton (2014), p. 191.

233 Jonathan G. Odom (2012), p. 227.

234 Anisa Heritage and Pak K. Lee, "The Sino-American confrontation in the South China Sea: insights from an international order perspective," *Cambridge Review of International Affairs*, 33, no. 1 (2020), p. 148.

235 Michael R. Pompeo, US Position on Maritime Claims in the South China Sea, Press Statement, July 13, 2020, at https://2017-2021.state.gov/u-s-position-on-maritime-claims-in-the-south-china-sea/index.html.

236 Jonathan G. Odom (2012), pp. 228–9 (citing remarks of Robert M. Gates, Secretary of Defense at Vietnam National University on October 11, 2010).

of Defense, described China as "a regional hegemon."[237] All in all, the US will increase its reaction (e.g., FON) to China's assertions in the SCS. This is particularly so given that preventing the emergence of a regional hegemon has been a long-standing goal of US grand strategy.[238]

Western international lawyers expect the current UNCLOS system to address the SCS dispute by serving the primary, if not sole, authority on legal matters, against which China denies a positive role of UNCLOS to play in territorial and maritime disputes in the region.[239] Rather, the phenomenon that China's effort to shape regional maritime norms to give China freedom of action is gaining traction concerns the West.[240] Of course, a few Western writers foresee that "China will succumb to international pressure and eventually abide by the [SCS] ruling," which enables the UNCLOS system another strength.[241]

Since the 2016 SCS arbitration award was rendered, China has increasingly advocated the necessity of employing a special straight baselines system for the Spratly Islands area as archipelagic waters.[242] The preliminary Western view on this issue was revealed in the SCS award. The SCS tribunal repudiates the possibility that China would enclose the Spratly Islands following the system of archipelagic or straight baselines to render the group of islands a single unit.[243] The tribunal points out that (1) China is a continental state incapable

---

237 Congressional Research Service (2021), p. 14. Admittedly, whether China has become or when China might achieve (regional) hegemony is one of the academic debates among political scientists. See, e.g., Jinghan Zeng et al., "Securing China's core interests: the state of the debate in China," *International Affairs*, 91, no. 2 (2015), p. 245; Yuen Foong Khong, "Primacy or world order? The United States and China's rise: a review essay," *International Security*, 38, no. 3 (Winter 2013–14), p. 154; Joseph S. Nye, "Is the American Century Over?" *Political Science Quarterly*, 130, no. 3 (2015), pp. 393–400.

238 Congressional Research Service (2021), p. 14.

239 Michael D. Swaine, "Chinese Views on the South China Sea Arbitration Case between the People's Republic of China and the Philippines," *China Leadership Monitor*, no. 51, p. 9.

240 James Manicom (2014), p. 357; Peter Dutton, Cracks in the Global Foundation: International Law and Instability in the South China Sea, in Patrick Cronin (ed.), *Cooperation from Strength: The United States, China and the South China Sea* (Washington DC: Center for a New American Security 2012), p. 74.

241 Mico A Galang (2016), p. 3.

242 There were some preliminary claims to the Spratlys as outlying archipelagic status, without specifically mentioning it, before the arbitration. For instance, in its 2014 Position Paper, China mentioned an idea of what we see "outlying archipelagos" in that "[t]he Nansha Islands comprises many maritime features. China has always enjoyed sovereignty over the Nansha Islands in its entirety, not just over some features thereof … It is plain that, in order to determine China's maritime entitlements based on the Nansha Islands under the Convention, all maritime features comprising the Nansha Islands must be taken into account." See China's Position Paper, paras. 20–21 (emphasis added). http://www.fmprc.gov.cn/mfa_eng/zxxx_662805/t1217147.shtml.

243 The South China Sea Award, July 12, 2016, p. 236.

of being qualified as an archipelagic state under UNCLOS, (2) the Spratlys do not meet the mathematical formula (a water-to-land ratio requirement) contained in Article 47, (3) the legal status of the Spratlys as an offshore archipelago does not fit into the category of Article 7, and (4) no customary rules exist to govern outlying archipelagos that take precedence over the provisions of the Convention.[244]

Western international lawyers affirm that the claim to outlying archipelagic states was not included on UNCLOS simply due to the lack of consensus at UNCLOS III.[245] Further, they point out that in the case of archipelagic states, UNCLOS adopted a reasonableness test for the utilized enclosure following a water-to-land ratio rule: the baseline segments cannot be longer than 100 nm, and the ratio of water to land enclosed by the baselines cannot exceed 9 to 1.[246] Under this logic, "outlying archipelagos," if any, should also meet this requirement. The basic principle will be that archipelagic waters should be limited in scope enclosing "relatively compact oceanic groups" with the lines of a general configuration of the archipelago under Article 47(3), thereby excluding some small features that are too peripheral.[247]

According to a US simulation, if China employs straight baselines for the Spratly Islands as an "outlying archipelago of continental states," China might enclose about 230,769 km2 of the ocean within baselines that contain every feature it considers part of the Spratly Islands, which produces a water-to-land ratio of 13,339:1 (not 9:1). If China employs above-water features and nearby low-tide elevations, China would enclose about 122,345 km2 of the ocean (a water-to-land ratio of 6,494:1) or, at the least way, if it uses closely-grouped high-tide features within baselines, a water-to-land ratio will be 275:1[248] Under

244 *Ibid.*, pp. 236–7.

245 J. Ashley Roach, "Offshore Archipelagos Enclosed by Straight Baselines: An Excessive Claim?" *Ocean Development & International Law* 49, no. 2 (2018), pp. 178, 190 (criticizing Chinese claim as baseless because of the lack of the basis of the existing regime of archipelagic waters, but also of customary rules that are elusive and hard to discover). See also Sophia Kopela (2013), p. 38 (noting that "the Conference abandoned the issue of dependent archipelagos and adopted the regime, which had already attained consensus among the participating states").

246 Alexander Proelss (2017), Part I, p. 359.

247 *Ibid.*, pp. 359, 361 (adducing a practical role of the percentage formula that "island States comprised of relatively small very dispersed islands in its group, such as Kiribati, would not qualify; nor with Micronesia and others, at least in one single unitary baseline system" esp. p. 359).

248 The others would be Union Banks with 494.63 square kilometers of water and 0.37 square kilometers of land (1,338 to 1), Tizard Bank with 818.31 square kilometers of water and 0.69 square kilometers of land (1,187 to 1), London Reefs with 292.67 square kilometers of water and 0.33 square kilometers of land (888 to 1), and North Danger Reef with 28.09 square kilometers of water and 0.31 square kilometers of land (92 to 1). See Asia Maritime

any scenario, it seems evident that if China takes any step toward proclaiming outlying archipelagic to the Spratly or Paracel Islands, tensions will escalate in the region.

It remains to be seen whether China will become respectful for maritime legal order or the SCS arbitration. It is reasonable to infer that China will not be submissive to *mare liberum* maritime order because the order, in China's view, disproportionately contributes to American interests.

3 An Analysis of the South China Sea Lawfare

This Section analyzes the Sino-Western (American) lawfare surrounding the law of the sea and the SCS dispute. Western and Chinese international lawyers perceive the role of the law of the sea and the nature of the SCS, including the SCS arbitration, differently through the prism of their location and identity.[249] The indeterminacy of core UNCLOS provisions is another culprit responsible for the disparities in interpretation. Eventually, the need for clarifying the law of the sea regime is revisited.

3.1 *Is the International Law of the Sea International?*

As international law is of universal character, international law of the sea is of universal character by nature. However, as is the case with general international law, the law of the sea is not identically interpreted and applied among international lawyers.[250] The fact that international law was used to abet powerful states to legitimize their exploitation of the Third World may have fashioned negative images of the "international" law of the sea in those nations that share colonial memory. Both Chinese and Western lawyers hold that international law has served the narrow interests of great powers[251] since

Transparency Initiative, Reading Between the Lines: the Next Spratly Legal Dispute, March 21, 2019, at https://amti.csis.org/reading-between-lines-next-spratly-dispute/.

249 Anthea Roberts (2017), pp. 10–11 (adding that the divergent approaches between Chinese and Western international lawyers reflect differences in their processes of socialization, including in how each government or media portrays the arbitration and the cases underlying merits. *Ibid.*, p. 7).

250 Xue Hanqin (2012), p. 16.

251 Nico Krisch (2005), pp. 381–407; R. P. Anand (1986), p. 190 (noting that traditional international law is historically described as "the law of the strong" in which system "the principle of equality had no place but was persistently invoked by the small States to satisfy their vanity or sometimes appeal to the good conscience of the big powers who were seldom, if ever, persuaded by the idealistic doctrine").

great powers have promoted norms conducive to their interests and have limited rules harming their interests.[252]

In other words, powerful states (re)make international law of the sea to maintain the *mare liberum* system lawfully benefiting naval powers' prerogatives by using a "position of preeminence or dominance by virtue of their superior power."[253] Simpson depicts this phenomenon as "legalized hegemony."[254] As such, a maritime system congenial to naval powers—not necessarily inimical to the rest of the world—was formulated, maintained, and exported to small and middle powers by the medium of some of their (dominant) interpretation in the name of "international" law of the sea.[255]

In fact, different memories and identities are responsible for the deep divergence of international law of the sea between the West and China. Memory significantly impacts international institutions, laws, and norms; in return, the legal norms and systems have fostered collective memory in many countries.[256] Notably, collective memories ingrained in the West and China affect them to

252 See generally Helen Keller and Daniela Thurnherr, *Taking International Law Seriously* (Berne: Staempfli Publishers Ltd., 2005). Take China for example, Britain and the other Western empires relied upon an originally Eurocentric discourse of civilization, sovereignty, and universalism to claim extraterritoriality and natural-law rights in the interest of trade, travel, and proselytizing, without allowing China the same rights and privileges. See Li Chen, Universalism and Equal Sovereignty as Contested Myths of International Law in the Sino-Western Encounter, *Journal of the History of International Law*, 13 (2011), p. 77.

253 Gerry Simpson (2004), pp. x, 67. See Oscar Schachter (1982), p. 32.

254 Gerry Simpson (2004), pp. 62–88. The phenomenon of "legalized hegemony," according to Simpson, is defined as "the existence within an international society of a powerful elite of states whose superior status is recognized by minor powers as a political fact giving rise to the existence of certain constitutional privileges, rights and duties and whose relations with each other are defined by adherence to a rough principle of sovereign equality." See *Ibid.*, 68.

255 Anthea Roberts (2017), p. 9. Roberts analyzes the editorial boards of many international law journals and shows that many of such journals are dominated by Western international law academics, thereby entailing the "normalization of certain Western perspective. *Ibid*, p. 110. Law of the sea journals are not an exception to this phenomenon. For instance, as of November 2021, the editor-in-chief of the International Journal of Marine and Coastal Law is David Freestone (The George Washington University Law School), the editor-in-chief, Emeritus Editor, and assistant to the co-editors-in-chief of Ocean Development & International Law are, in a sequence, Karen N. Scott (University of Canterbury), Ted L. McDorman (University of Victoria), and Rosemary Garton (University of Victoria), and the editor-in-chief of Marine Policy is Dr. Q. Hanich (Australian National Centre for Ocean Resources and Security).

256 Eric Langenbacher, Collective Memory as a Factor in Political Culture and International Relations, in Eric Langenbacher and Yossi Shain (eds.), *Power and the Past: Collective Memory and International Relations* (Washington DC: Georgetown University Press,

perceive the law of the sea from different viewpoints. Collective memory is "intersubjectively shared interpretations of a poignant common past with a high degree of effect," providing a sense of communal identity for a group as a predominant way that history comes to life to affect the present's political culture.[257] The law of the sea system is viewed, processed, interpreted, and exported differently according to which collective memories a particular state entertains.[258]

Different theories and purposes influence states to interpret international law of the sea differently as well. Chinese ICJ judge Xue Hanqin claims that a particular national context (culture or history) compels states to interpret international law in a certain way.[259] Similarly, Chen argues that some international rules are binding, "[y]et there is still room for varying interpretation and application … Every state interprets the law (considered binding upon itself) and applies it according to its own interpretation."[260] Further, China tries to develop a new approach toward the interpretation and justification of international rules with Chinese characteristics with a view to revealing biased interpretation and application of Western-dominated international law.[261]

Chinese scholars have confidence that if China develops a new theory with Chinese characteristics, international law will subsequently develop in a more balanced and healthy way, thereby enabling the majority of developing states to have more opportunities to "effectively safeguard their legitimate rights

---

2010), pp. 19–20 (noting that the League of Nations and the UN were set up in response to historical upheavals and as means to prevent such traumas from occurring again).

257 Eric Langenbacher, Collective Memory as a Factor in Political Culture and International Relations, in Eric Langenbacher and Yossi Shain (eds.), *Power and the Past: Collective Memory and International Relations* (Washington DC: Georgetown University Press, 2010), pp. 26–27. Collective memories are delivered and maintained through communications (textbooks, political rhetoric), symbols (flags, national anthems), and symbolic interactions (commemorative ceremonies). See Thomas U Berger, The Power of Memory and Memories of Power: The Cultural Parameters of German Foreign Policy-Making since 1945, in Jan-Werner Müller (ed.), *Memory and Power in Post-War Europe: Studies in the Presence of the Past* (Cambridge: Cambridge University Press, 2002), p. 80.

258 Thomas U Berger, The Power of Memory and Memories of Power: The Cultural Parameters of German Foreign Policy-Making since 1945, in Jan-Werner Müller (ed.) (2002), p. 80 (adding that political leaders who seek to mobilize societal resources for some common goal tend to invoke collective memories to explain and legitimize their policies).

259 Xue Hanqin (2012), pp. 16–17. Professor Schachter also emphasizes the necessity of considering socio-historical dimension, which affects the structure and process of international law, to comprehend how international law is understood in states. See O. Schachter (1982), pp. 22–23.

260 Tiqiang Chen (1984), p. 19.

261 Zhipeng He and Lu Sun (2020), p. 61.

and interests in the international legal mechanisms."[262] Of course, a primary goal of developing Chinese international law theories is to "safeguard China's interests."[263]

As a matter of fact, developing new international law theories to back "legalized hegemony" up is not a new phenomenon; quite the contrary. In preparation for the Opium Wars, Western international lawyers and writers developed new theories that would justify compelling China to change its policy without abandoning the universalistic claims of modern international law: they reconceptualized the doctrine of sovereignty of a non-Christian nation in the 19th century.[264] Vattel eloquently defended, in 1758, that "each nation remains at liberty to consider whether it be convenient for her to encourage or permit commerce ... [I]f one nation ... thinks foreign commerce dangerous to the state, she may renounce and prohibit it."[265] However, in 1836, British trader James Matheson (1796–1878) rejected Vattel's proposition, rather offered his international law theory that China had "surrendered such rights, and [was] no longer in a position to enforce them [against the UK]" as China had accepted English law terms; as a result, Chinese obligation to continue the trade was complete and binding.[266] In brief, the Western merchants, lawyers, and diplomats developed a theory that "China's refusal to recognize the extraterritorial or universal sovereignty of the Western empires constituted a just cause of war."[267]

More significantly, China considers that international law becomes binding not only because of states' acceptance (consent) but also because of their acknowledgment that the binding nature of such rules is in the interest of states, which engenders an expectation that others will also behave the same way.[268] Seen in this way, states do not have to comply with a particular rule that is not in their interest despite states' acceptance of a rule being expressed in ratifying a treaty.

---

262 *Ibid.*

263 *Ibid.*, p. 52.

264 Li Chen, Universalism and Equal Sovereignty as Contested Myths of International Law in the Sino-Western Encounter, *Journal of the History of International Law*, 13 (2011), p. 102.

265 Emmerich de Vattel, *The Law of Nations; Or, Principles of the Law of Nature, Applied to the Conduct and Affairs of Nations and Sovereigns*, trans. by Joseph Chitty (London: Stevens & Sons, 1834 [1758]), pp. 39–40, cited in Li Chen (2011), p. 105.

266 Meanwhile, John Quincy Adams (1767–1848) attempted to change the principles of then international lawyers to better suit the new balance of power between the aspiring Euro-american empires and those targeted countries, and justified the Opium War as Britian having "the righteous cause." See Li Chen (2011), pp. 106–9.

267 *Ibid.*, p. 111.

268 Tiqiang Chen (1984), p. 19.

China and the West see the same treaty text but envisage a different picture: "sleeping in the same bed but dreaming different dreams."[269] Therefore, each side contends that the opposite side's interpretation of UNCLOS institutions (such as warships innocent passage and military activities in foreign EEZ) is an excessive claim, having "the potential to destabilize the legal order at sea if followed by other state parties to the UNCLOS."[270] In the face of Western bias, China grumbles that "as long as China expresses its own independent views or holds different views from America, it will be considered assertive."[271]

The 2016 SCS arbitration epitomizes the non-international law of the sea. Chinese and Western international lawyers reveal different historical narratives, dissimilar imaginations of global governance, and separate ideas of world order between the two worlds. China criticizes the arbitration for disclosing "the ignorance and struggles that 'the Rest' have endured from the West in terms of the structural biases and systemic violence of Eurocentrism in international law and international legal scholarship."[272] Although it is not that there is no Western scholar who supports China (directly or indirectly),[273] Western international lawyers try to gain support from other states by advancing illegal or illegitimate Chinese interpretation of the law of the sea. Speaking of how many states support either the West or China, some 40 countries stand by Chinese positions.[274]

---

269 Hungdah Chiu (1986), p. 253.

270 Yann-huei Song, "Declarations and Statements with Respect to the 1982 UNCLOS: Potential Legal Disputes between the United States and China after U.S. Accession to the Convention," *Ocean Development & International Law,* 36 (2005), p. 268; Zou Keyuan (2008), p. 77.

271 Wang Fan and Ling Shengli, 'Zhongguo de waijiao zhengce bian qiangying le ma? Ruhe lijie zhongguo de xin waijiao' [Did China's foreign policy become more assertive? How to understand China's new diplomacy], Dangdai shijie [Contemporary world], no. 3, 2013, p. 23, cited in Jinghan Zeng, Yuefan Xiao, and Shaun Breslin, "Securing China's core interests: the state of the debate in China," *International Affairs*, 91, no. 2 (2015), p. 249, fn. 18.

272 Anlei Zuo (2018), p. 48 (arguing that "China's approaches to international law are based firstly on its traditional worldview and culture and secondly on its historical experiences with the Western dominated international law").

273 Kirsten E. Boon, "International arbitration in highly political situations: the South China Sea dispute and international law," *Washington University Global Studies Law Review*, 13 (2014), pp. 490–2 (arguing the consent is dispositive for international adjudication: "no consent, no resolution of the problem").

274 Megha Rajagopalan and Nick Macfie, China Says More Than 40 Countries Support Its Stance on South China Sea, *Reuters,* May 20, 2016, at https://www.reuters.com/article/us-southchinasea-china-idUSKCN0YB1EO. For example, Sreenivasa Rao Pemmaraju, former Chairman of International Law Commission, criticizes the arbitration by saying that the SCS dispute "can be assessed only by examining the nature of acts and functions of

Borrowing from Buzan's analysis, Chinese international lawyers appear to have the "postcolonial view" rather than a "globalization view." That is, Chinese lawyers and scholars may perceive "international society as an uneven core-periphery structure in which the West still has a privileged, but partly contested, hegemonic role, and non-Western regions are in varying degrees subordinate to Western power and values."[275] In this epistemic frame, China (as a regional hub) will likely keep producing a divergent view on the Western-dominated law of the sea to draw more states to its preferred interpretation of UNCLOS.[276] Its defeat at an arbitral tribunal has expedited China to adopt the hub and spoke approach to expand its interpretative influence on the spoke states.[277] The lack of an authoritative body or process to reconcile fragmented and divergent interpretations in international society is another reason why the Sino-American lawfare is ineluctable.[278]

On the whole, the law of the sea is sometimes not international. Zuo observes that the process of "sinicization" of international law of the sea is under way;[279] upon completion, China continues to proselytize the rest of the

---

sovereignty that China claims to have performed from times immemorial or through history. See Sreenivasa Rao Pemmaraju, "The South China Sea Arbitration (The Philippines v. China): Assessment of the Award on Jurisdiction and Admissibility," *Chinese Journal of International Law*, 15 (2016), para. 52. Of course, many nations generally accepted the ruling of the SCS arbitration and called on China to respect it. See Find Out Which Countries are Taking Sides in the South China Sea, Asia Maritime Transparency Initiative (2016), at https://amti.csis.org/sides-in-south-china-sea/.

275 Barry Buzan, "China in International Society: Is 'Peaceful Rise' Possible?" *The Chinese Journal of International Politics*, 3 (2010), pp. 29–30 (adding the "globalization view" as seeing "international society as fairly evenly, if thinly, spread at the global level" assuming that "the global level will tend to get stronger in relation to the regional one, and international society become more homogenized as a result of the operation of global economic, cultural and political forces (aka capitalism). This view sees either a triumph of liberal Western hegemony, or a kind of compromise in which some non-Western elements are woven into the Western framing").

276 William W. Burke-White, "Power Shifts in International Law: Structural Realignment and Substantive Pluralism," *Harvard International Law Journal*, 56, no. 1 (2015), p. 44.

277 Doug Bandow, Look Out, Asia: China's Peaceful Rise Is Over, *National Interest*, 18 July 2016, at https://nationalinterest.org/blog/the-skeptics/look-out-asia-chinas-peaceful-rise-over-17026. For an account of how China criticizes the tribunal for its composition, see Chinese Society of International Law, "The South China Sea Arbitration Awards: A Critical Study," *Chinese Journal of International Law*, 17 (2018), pp. 626–7.

278 William W. Burke-White (2015), p. 44.

279 Jinghan Zeng et al. (2015), p. 246–7 (stating that "[d]omestically, when new concepts are put forward (often by China's leaders), they are not always clearly defined; frequently, the process of filling the concept with real meaning occurs subsequently and incrementally").

world to make them understand China properly and achieve a (China-led) regional legal order.[280]

3.2 *The Utility and Fertility of* UNCLOS

UNCLOS is the result of political compromises among various groups of competing interests against the backdrop of the Cold War, during which negotiations, a full discussion on some complex issues were hard to pan out.[281] This is why UNCLOS lacks a clear definition of some core regimes, rather blurred by vague and ambiguous language subject to multiple interpretations, thereby engendering controversy and contention among nations of all persuasions.[282]

Therefore, since the adoption of UNCLOS, weak coastal states gradually began interpreting maritime institutions with the territorialized notion of the ocean in mind;[283] further, they have developed the exclusive concept of "not in my backyard,"[284] sounding the death knell of *mare liberum*. Logue depicts this process as the "revenge of John Selden."[285] At the heart of this interpretative commotion is EEZ (a "zone of tension").[286] Purportedly, negotiators at UNCLOS III intended some of the UNCLOS institutions to admit different interpretations.[287] That is, naval powers and coastal states strategically reached a consensus on silence over controversial issues (e.g., military activities in foreign

280 Anlei Zuo (2018), p. 39. See also Zhipeng He and Lu Sun (2020), p. 59 (explaining that a goal of the Chinese program of interpreting international rules is to shift the state of a western monopoly of international law theories).

281 Ren Xiaofeng and Cheng Xizhong (2005), p. 145.

282 Paul C. Yuan (1984), p. 417. Not long after the adoption of UNCLOS, international lawyers worried about the vagueness of maritime institutions, such as the status of EEZ and the scope and scale of MSR. *Ibid.*, p. 418.

283 For an account of a trend in expanding territorialized notion of the ocean by coastal states, see Bernard H. Oxman (2006), pp. 830–851.

284 Jo Inge Bekkevold and Geoffrey Till, Conclusion: International Order at Sea in the Twenty-First Century, in Jo Inge Bekkevold and Geoffrey Till (2016), p. 313.

285 John Logue, "The Revenge of John Selden: The Draft Convention on the Law of the Sea in Light of Hugo Grotius's Mare Liberum," *Grotiana*, 3 (1982), pp. 27–56.

286 Ren Xiaofeng and Cheng Xizhong (2005), p. 139. See also G. V. Galdorisi and A.G. Kaufman, "Military Activities in the Exclusive Economic Zone: Preventing Uncertainty and Defusing Conflict," *Californian Western International Law Journal*, 32 (2002), p. 257; Sam Bateman, Hydrographic Surveying in Exclusive Economic Zones – Is it Marine Scientific Research?, in Myron H. Nordquist et al. (2009), p. 117; Manjula R. Shyam, "The U.N. Convention on the Law of the Sea and Military Interests in the Indian Ocean," *Ocean Development & International Law*, 15:2 (1985), p. 167.

287 Natalie Klein (2011), p. 44.

EEZ), thereby leaving ample room for differences of opinion on UNCLOS among international lawyers.[288]

UNCLOS is an outcome of a "package deal"[289] through the consensus approach, in which selective application of UNCLOS provisions is not allowed.[290] It seems that the framers of UNCLOS regarded these compromises as the strengths.[291] Of course, political compromises do not necessarily prohibit the meaning of institutions from being discovered. In principle, a treaty shall be interpreted in accordance with "ordinary meaning" in light of their "context" and "object and purpose."[292] Hence, international lawyers can adopt this standard as a point of departure to discover the envisaged meaning and scope of the UNCLOS regimes.

The urgent necessity of determining the meaning of UNCLOS emerges surrounding, *inter alia*, the concept of freedom of the seas, such as warships' innocent passage through territorial seas, military activities, and military surveying distinct from MSR in EEZs. It is understandable why coastal states are sensitive to warships' passage through their territorial waters.[293] Warships, by nature, represent the military power of the flag state; their mere passage through the territorial sea makes an impression of a "benign show of force" even in the absence of tension or conflict between the States concerned.[294] ICJ, in the 1949 *Corfu Channel* case, reviewed the activities undertaken by the warship to

288 Manjula R. Shyam, "The U.N. Convention on the Law of the Sea and Military Interests in the Indian Ocean," *Ocean Development & International Law*, 15, no. 2 (1985), p. 149.

289 In this approach, all the main parts of UNCLOS should be dealt with as an entity, as a single negotiated package, where the laws of give and take presumably had struck a reasonable balance between participating states considered as a whole. See Evensen's keynote address at XXVII, cited in James Harrison, *Making the Law of the Sea* (Cambridge: Cambridge University Press, 2011), p. 45, fn. 96. Article 309 ("[n]o reservations or exceptions may be made to this Convention unless expressly permitted by other articles of this Convention").

290 Before signing UNCLOS, many delegates shared the view that although not all their aspirations were satisfied, they would accept the package in a spirit of compromise. See Xuexia Liao, "The LOSC as a Package Deal and Its Implications for Determination of Customary International Law," *The International Journal of Marine and Coastal Law*, 35 (2020), p. 11.

291 Tommy Koh assessed that "these compromises are the strengths, not weaknesses, of the Convention." See Ambassador Tommy T.B. Koh, President, Third U.N. Conference on the Law of the Sea, A Constitution for the Oceans (December 1982), at http://www.un.org/depts/los/convention_agreements/texts/koh_english.pdf.

292 Article 31 of Vienna Convention on the Law of Treaties of 1969.

293 As of 2012, 43 states were reported to restrict foreign warships' innocent passage through their territorial sea. See J. Ashley Roach and Robert W. Smith (2012), pp. 239–262; Anh Duc Ton (2016), p. 230.

294 Natalie Klein (2011), p. 30.

determine the legality of the passage, insinuating warships innocent passage through territorial seas being lawful.[295]

The context of UNCLOS provisions as well seems to allow warships' innocent passage through the territorial sea. The passage is innocent so long as it is not prejudicial to the coastal states' peace, good order, or security (Article 19(1)). If a warship's passage is prejudicial to the peace, good order, or security of coastal states by engaging "any threat or use of force," "any exercise or practice or practice with weapons," or "the launching, landing or taking on board of any aircraft," such passage renders illegal (Article19(2)). The importance lies not in the physical presence of warships but in the activities undertaken by warships during their passage.[296] Further, military submarines enjoy innocent passage once they navigate on the surface, showing their flag (Article 20), and foreign unclear-powered ships (normally military vessels)[297] enjoy innocent passage under certain conditions (Article 23).[298] Logically, "warships," "submarines," and "nuclear-empowered vessels" are treated equally in terms of innocent passage through the territorial seas under particular conditions.[299]

Is the context of UNCLOS provisions clear enough to determine the legality of military activities in foreign EEZs? The EEZ is a "*sui generis*" or "*tertium genus*" area in the sense of being neither part of the high seas nor territorial waters.[300] In fact, the topic of military activities in EEZs was not duly discussed at UNCLOS III;[301] thus, relevant state practice on and scholarly interpretation were divergent even right after the adoption of and before entry into force of UNCLOS.[302]

295 Albania argued that foreign ships had no right to pass through its territorial waters without prior notification to, and the permission of, Albania. The UK rejected this claim and sent the warships to the territorial sea of Albania, on those ships Albania fired in the North Corfu Channel. See *Corfu Channel* (UK v. Albania), ICJ Reports 1949, pp. 22, 30.

296 For a contrary view, see Natalie Klein (2011), pp. 30–31.

297 Alexander Proelss (2017), p. 215.

298 Despite this provision, many states have domestic laws requiring the flag states of nuclear-empowered ships prior notification or consent, rendering this issue a serious point of contention. See Alexander Proelss (2017), Part I, p. 215.

299 If warships engage in harmful activities provided for in Article 19, submarines navigate underwater, not showing the national flag, and nuclear-empowered ships navigate without necessary documents, and fail to observe precautionary measures taken by international agreements, their passage will not be seen innocent.

300 Maria Gavouneli, *Functional Jurisdiction in the Law of the Sea* (Leiden: Brill, 2007), p. 66; F.V. García Amador, The Latin American contribution to the development of the law of the sea, *American Journal of International Law*, 68 (1974), pp. 33–50.

301 Manjula R. Shyam (1985), pp. 162–3.

302 Sam Bateman, Hydrographic Surveying in Exclusive Economic Zones – Is it Marine Scientific Research?, in Myron H. Nordquist et al. (2009), p. 117–8; Manjula R. Shyam (1985), p. 149.

Coastal states often perceive foreign naval operations in their EEZs as threatening or imposing.[303] This is why many coastal states (such as China, India, Brazil, and Malaysia) object to foreign military activities in their EEZs.[304] As discussed above, the opponents of military activities in EEZs hold that such activities do not fall under the general rights of navigation, hampering resource exploitation of coastal states in the form of marine or military surveys,[305] on which a growing number of actors appear to agree, including some Western lawyers.[306]

The US, among others, assertively maintains a *mare liberum* approach in interpreting UNCLOS at its most extreme.[307] Maritime powers defended freedom of military activities in EEZs, conceding the right to economic activities to coastal states during UNCLOS III.[308] It would seem correct to assume that if UNCLOS had envisaged the denial of naval activities in foreign EEZs, maritime powers (such as US, USSR, UK) would not have agreed to the EEZ regime in the absence of painstaking negotiation and detail.[309]

---

303 Manjula R. Shyam (1985), p. 164.

304 J. Ashley Roach and Robert W. Smith (2012), pp. 380–386; Katherine Morton, "China's ambition in the South China Sea: is a legitimate maritime order possible?" *International Affairs*, 92, no. 4 (2016), p. 926. For their respective statements, see United Nations, Division for Ocean Affairs and the Law of the Sea, Office of Legal Affairs, *The Law of the Sea: National Legislation on the Exclusive Economic Zone* (New York: UN, 1993).

305 Manjula R. Shyam (1985), p. 163.

306 John Astley III and Michael N. Schmitt, "The Law of the Sea and Naval Operations," *Air Force Law Review*, 42 (1997), p. 137 (noting that military activities cannot be conducted if they significantly interfere with economic activities or pollute the ocean of the coastal state); E.D. Brown, *International Law of the Sea* (Dartmouth: Aldershot, 1994), Vol. I, p. 242 (noting that military exercises with the use of explosives are prohibited); Bernard Oxman (1984), p. 838 (arguing that weapon testing that significantly damages natural resources in EEZ is not allowed); B. Boczek (1998), p. 412 (stating that naval operations interfering with the peaceful use of the sea by, *inter alia*, limiting traditional or commercial fishing is illegal); G. Galdorisi and A. Kaufman (2002), p. 282 (noting that operations harming the interests of the coastal state is prohibited).

307 On January 18, 2007, the US responded to China regarding the *Bowditch* incidents in March 2000 and September 2002, "customary international law requires coastal states to exercise their limited, resource-related rights in their EEZs with 'due regard' for the rights of other states ... [UNCLOS] does not purport in any manner to restrict the military activities of a state in the EEZ [beyond the territorial sea]." See J. Ashley Roach and Robert W. Smith (2012), pp. 384–5.

308 D.P. O'Connell, The Influence of Law on Sea Power (1975), p. 3, cited in Sienho Yee (2010), p. 5, fn. 10 (noting that "[n]avies alone afford governments the means of exerting pressures more vigorous than diplomacy and less dangerous and unpredictable in its results than other forms of force, because the freedom of the seas makes them locally available while leaving them uncommitted").

309 Bernard Oxman (1984), pp. 831–832.

As discussed above, the Western international lawyers support military activities in foreign EEZs permissible as high seas freedom;[310] some proposals to restrict military activities in the EEZ were refuted at UNCLOS III, thereby entailing "other internationally lawful uses of sea" of all the states (Article 58(1)) to include military activities in EEZs.[311] In contrast, Chinese writers adopt limited interpretations on this issue.[312] Ren and Cheng argue that the freedom of states in foreign EEZs should be subject to "sovereign rights and the exclusive jurisdiction of the coastal States" that is considered as having indisputable superiority when conflicts arise between the right of coastal states and third states.[313]

Under the UNCLOS system, the resolution of the lawfulness of military activities in foreign EEZs revolves around three elements: (1) the meaning of "other internationally lawful uses of the sea related to [high seas] freedoms" (Article 58(1)); (2) the scope of obligation under "due regard" to the rights and duties of the coastal state (Article 58(3)); and (3) the applicability of "residual rights" for military activities in EEZs in light of "equity," "all the relevant circumstances" and "the interests involved to the parties and the international community" (Article 59).[314]

First, it is logical that "other internationally lawful uses of the sea" come with limits, such as naval exercises of reasonable scale without the use of weapons.[315] Second, at UNCLOS III, the proposal of developing countries to put "due regard to the security interests of the coastal State" in the text was rejected.[316] For China, "due regard" means foreign states to refrain from any

---

310 See, e.g., Moritaka Hayashi (2005), p. 128; G. Galdorisi and A. Kaufman (2002), p. 272; Barbara Kwiatkowska (1989), pp. 211–2; Bernard Oxman (1984), p. 838.

311 James Kraska, Maritime Power and the Law of the Sea: Expeditionary Operations in World Politcs (New York: Oxford University Press, 2011), pp. 269–270; Boleslaw A. Boczek, "Peaceful Purposes Provisions of the United Nations Convention of the Law of the Sea," Ocean Development and International Law, Vol. 20 (1989), p. 376.

312 B. Vukas, Peaceful uses of the sea, denuclearization and disarmament, in R.J. Dupuy and D. Vignes (eds.), *A Handbook on the New Law of the Sea* (Dordrecht: M. Nijhoff, 1991), p. 1253; R. Churchill, A.V. Lowe (1999), p. 427; T. Scovazzi (2000), p. 167.

313 Ren Xiaofeng and Cheng Xizhong (2005), p. 145.

314 Article 59: In cases where this Convention does not attribute rights or jurisdiction to the coastal State or to other States within the exclusive economic zone, and a conflict arises between the interests of the coastal State and any other State or States, the conflict should be resolved on the basis of equity and in the light of all the relevant circumstances, taking into account the respective importance of the interests involved to the parties as well as to the international community as a whole.

315 R.R. Churchill and A.V. Lowe (1999), pp. 527–8 (noting that limited military activities are only allowable in foreign EEZs that is a common scholarly view).

316 Moritaka Hayashi (2005), p. 133.

activities "which endanger the sovereignty, security and national interests of the coastal countries."[317] By contrast, for the US, due regard is left in the hands of the flag state in conducting military activities.[318] Third, it seems certain that coastal states' economic and safety interests are understood bigger than naval powers' interests in military activities in foreign EEZs by most states.[319] Fast-changing technology and its resultant impact on the military weapon system (such as robotic technology, combined with GPS and sensors) have a significant implication for military activities in foreign EEZs.[320] This would arguably lead to the conclusion that "the interests involved to the parties and the international community" in light of "equity" and "all the relevant circumstances" will likely permit coastal states to restrict military activities in their EEZs to some degree.[321]

MSR is also a serious point of contention within the UNCLOS regime. The UNCLOS negotiators neither devoted much attention nor reached an agreement on the definition of MSR.[322] Although UNCLOS contains the concepts of MSR, hydrographic surveying, and survey, it does not mean these activities are different institutions[323] given that the way that institutions were drafted and

---

317 *Ibid.*

318 US Commentary of UNCLOS, in Appendix Eight of J. Ashley Roach and Robert W. Smith (2012), p. 694.

319 Manjula R. Shyam (1985), p. 167.

320 For instance, "unmanned naval systems" (the drones of the sea) are being adopted by maritime powers for naval activities, and "unmanned naval vessels" could be used in armed or unarmed missions, including surveillance, intelligence, and reconnaissance, in foreign EEZs. See John Yoo (2017), pp. 112, 142; U.S. Navy, The Navy Unmanned Surface Vehicle (USV) Master Plan (2007), at http://www.navy.mil/navydata/technology/usvmppr.pdf.

321 Florian H.Th. Wegelein (2005), p. 98; TM Franck, *Recourse to Force: State Action Against Threats and Armed Attacks* (Cambridge, Cambridge University Press, 2002), p. 98 (noting that "[c]ommon sense, rather than textual literalism, is often the best guide to the interpretation of international legal norms").

322 Maria Gavouneli (2007), p. 64. In the 1976 Informal Single Negotiating Text defined MSR as "'marine scientific research' means any study or related experimental work designed to increase mankind's knowledge of the marine environment." See UN, Marine Scientific Research A revised guide to the implementation of the relevant provisions of the United Nations Convention on the Law of the Sea, Division for Ocean Affairs and the Law of the Sea Office of Legal Affairs, 2010, p. 6. Meanwhile, the US understands MSR as "those activities undertaken in the ocean and coastal waters to expand scientific knowledge of the marine environment and its processes." See J. Ashley Roach and Robert W. Smith (2012), p. 414.

323 Sam Bateman (2009), p. 110. In contrast, some scholars (mostly from the United States) argue that the term "MSR" was intentionally chosen to differentiate it from hydrographic surveys, marine surveys, and operational oceanography. See James Kraska, Maritime Power and the Law of the Sea: Expeditionary Operations in World Politics (New York: Oxford

combined at UNCLOS III.[324] Is hydrographic surveying different from MSR? There are three approaches: (1) seeing it as internationally lawful use of the sea under Article 58(1) (US and UK); (2) seeking prior permission (Australia and Canada);[325] and (3) regarding it as MSR (China).[326]

In practice, hydrographers generally view their surveying activities as part of MSR because non-hydrographic data is also elicited in operation;[327] similarly, the International Hydrographic Organization (IHO) regards hydrographic surveying as part of MSR.[328] This is why coastal states have trouble discerning survey ships from MSR vessels.[329] Further, some scientific information (e.g., hydrographic data) about foreign EEZs influences economic aspects (commercial exploitation and national development) of the coastal state.[330]

Nonetheless, if hydrographic surveying qualified as a non-MSR activity, the international community would need a legal regime to govern it.[331] Otherwise, the interpretation of the UNCLOS regime for MSR has to comport with most state practice, which deems hydrographic surveying part of MSR.[332]

University Press, 2011), pp. 272–277 (adding that "[MSR] may be used to describe activities undertaken ... to expand scientific knowledge of the marine environment and its processes" *ibid.*, p. 274).

324 Myron H. Nordquist and William G. Phalen, Interpretation of UNCLOS Article 121 and Itu Aba (Taiping) in the South China Sea Arbitration Award, in Myron H. Nordquist et al. (2017), pp. 8–9 (explaining that separate "informal working groups" with limited delegate participants presented, and later combined and adopted by consensus through the package deal approach).

325 Sam Bateman (2005), p. 170; Jon M. Van Dyke (2004), p. 32.

326 Zou Keyuan (2005), pp. 280–283.

327 Sam Bateman, Hydrographic Surveying in Exclusive Economic Zones – Is it Marine Scientific Research?, in Myron H. Nordquist et al. (2009), p. 112. For an account of how contemporary hydrographic surveying is undertaken in what process, see *ibid.*, pp. 105–132.

328 International Hydrographic Organization, The Need for a Hydrographic Service, IHO Publication M2 (June 2018).

329 Natalie Klein (2011), pp. 216–7.

330 International Hydrographic Organization (2018), p. 17; Moritaka Hayashi (2005), p. 131; Sam Bateman (2004), p. 79.

331 Keyuan Zou (2016), p. 174.

332 Bateman argues that (military) hydrographic surveying should be subject to coastal state consent as part of MSR on the grounds of the growth of state practice, developments in technology, and increasingly converging opinions among expert bodies. See Sam Bateman, Hydrographic Surveying in Exclusive Economic Zones – Is it Marine Scientific Research?, in Myron H. Nordquist et al. (2009), pp. 119–124 (adding that hydrographic surveys are also necessary to determine the features that constitute territorial sea baselines or basepoints and their geographical positions). Meanwhile, a UN survey indicates that national legislations do not normally distinguish MSR from hydrographic surveying. See UN, Office for Ocean Affairs and the Law of the Sea, *The Law of the Sea: National*

As we have seen above, the utility of UNCLOS sometimes proves its real worth, but sometimes not, where the futility of the Convention inevitably stands out. In this sense, it should come as no surprise that a growing number of states and international lawyers call on the process of interpreting and applying UNCLOS to reflect increasing state practice that purports to demand the reinstatement of the legitimate security interests of the coastal state over hitherto automatic overriding naval supremacy of maritime powers.[333]

3.3 *The Growing Need to Clarify Core UNCLOS Regimes*

Against the background of the Cold War rivalry, the negotiators devoted more attention to "open trade" and "navigation" than the major challenge of today (e.g., resources exploitation and security) at UNCLOS III.[334] Indeed, UNCLOS falls far short of addressing contemporary maritime issues arising from a changing global environment,[335] let alone containing applicable text language enough to determine the scope and limit of state behavior about core maritime institutions.

The conflictual situations in the SCS region involving the UNCLOS provisions will unlikely subside spontaneously. The 1969 Vienna Convention on the Law of Treaties (VCLT) stipulates that "subsequent practice" shall be considered in the interpretation of treaties.[336] As "specially affected nations," both the US and China will continue to assert, behave, enforce, and protest in line with each interpretation of UNCLOS.[337] Also, China and the US will try to confirm the legality of their treaty interpretation by concluding bilateral,

Legislation, Regulations and Supplementary Documents on Marine Scientific Research in Areas under National Jurisdiction (New York: UN, 1989), pp. 143–154.

333 Manjula R. Shyam (1985), pp. 148–9.

334 Bill Hayton (2014), p. 112 (explaining that UNCLOS III was a venue for Cold War arguments between capitalists and communists).

335 Katherine Morton (2016), p. 913.

336 Article 31 of VCLT: 1. A treaty shall be interpreted in good faith in accordance with the ordinary meaning to be given to the terms of the treaty in their context and in the light of its object and purpose ... 3. There shall be taken into account, together with the context: ... (b) Any subsequent practice in the application of the treaty which establishes the agreement of the parties regarding its interpretation [...]. Under Articles 31–2, the general steps to interpret treat articles are: (1) interpreting, in good faith, the "ordinary meaning" of the terms of treaty in light of their "context" and its "object and purpose"; (2) out of regard not only for provisions, but also for preamble and annexes of the treaty, any agreement, and instrument in terms of discovering the context; (4) making allowance for any "subsequent agreement, practice, and rules"; and (4) reviewing the "preparatory work" and "the circumstance of its conclusion" as supplementary means of interpretation.

337 Myron H. Nordquist and William G. Phalen, Interpretation of UNCLOS Article 121 and Itu Aba (Taiping) in the South China Sea Arbitration Award, in Myron H. Nordquist et al.

minilateral, or multilateral declarations or agreements to pull on state practice to their benefits with treaty evolution in mind.[338]

However, it is hard to expect that the international judicial system will defuse this lawfare. If, arguendo, international courts are engaged in interpreting controversial UNCLOS provisions, neither party will prevail due to the lack of consensus on the implementation of specific institutions or convergent expert opinions thereof.[339]

As a corollary to the above, the rule of law at sea will be damaged, the legitimacy of the UNCLOS regime will be exponentially diluted, and eventually, the UNCLO system will decay, causing disorder, costs, and risks.[340] On the other hand, it is possible that China or the US establishes each law of the sea portals instead of or parallel with UNCLOS, which, in turn, decreases the effectiveness and legitimacy of the current maritime system.[341]

Law and economics scholars distinguish between two different types of norms in regulatory systems: rules and standards.[342] Rules are clear and easy to apply, thus reducing costs to the legal system (in deciding compliance/non-compliance) and creating greater predictability. Rules, however, involve higher error rates because future decision-makers have less leeway to consider "totality of the circumstances."[343] In contrast, standards are relatively unclear

---

(2017), p. 35; P. Weil, "Toward Relative Normativity in International Law?" *American Journal of International Law*, 76 (1983), p. 434.

338 Georg Nolte, Report 3: Subsequent Agreements and Subsequent Practice of States Outside of Judicial or Quasi-judicial Proceedings, reprinted in Georg Nolte (2013), p. 346 (noting that "[i]f such interpretations are sufficiently coherent and widespread among the several bilateral, plurilateral or regional agreements, a subsequent practice establishing the agreed interpretation on the respective multilateral treaty provision can be identified").

339 Although the West or China asserts the existence of an agreement, the other party will dispute the existence of such an agreement. See Anthea Roberts, Subsequent Agreements and Practice: The Battle over Interpretive Power, in Georg Nolte (ed.) (2013), p. 97 (adding that "the treaty parties have wide discretion to define and redefine their treaty obligations through subsequent agreements and practices, even when these agreements constitute *de facto* amendments of the treaty" *Ibid.*, p. 98).

340 Anlei Zuo (2018), p. 51 (emphasizing that "international institutions and rules should constantly evolve to response to the changing needs in this world society where sovereign states are still the principle actors"); Jonathan G. Odom (2012), p. 250.

341 Anlei Zuo (2018), p. 53.

342 See, e.g., Colin S. Diver, "The Optimal Precision of Administrative Rules," *Yale Law Journal*, 93 (1983), p. 65; Louis Kaplow, "Rules versus Standards: An Economic Analysis," *Duke Law Journal*, 42 (1992), p. 557.

343 John Yoo, *Point of Attack: Preventive War, International Law, and Global Warfare* (New York: Oxford University Press, 2014), pp. 93–4.

and hard to apply. Standards render high decision costs, but ultimately lower error costs since decision-makers have some latitude in applying the norm to all the facts.[344] In short, "[t]he more complicated the legal rule, the greater the likelihood that these administrative costs, including error costs, will be high."[345]

UNCLOS indeed adopts the rule approach for some institutions[346] and the standard attitude for other regimes.[347] It is reasonable to infer that the negotiators at UNCLOS III (lawyers and diplomats) must have tried to regulate as much as they could while still reaching a consensus among ego-centric sovereign states.[348] However, significantly procrastinated sessions and the accompanying costs of the negotiators must have had a strong influence on states agreeing upon vague institutions in a consensus and package deal.[349] This is how some core provisions of UNCLOS ended up in the form of standards. Additionally, the negotiators had simply not foreseen some developments, such as climate change, marine degradation by massive land-based sources, and technological developments.

For such UNCLOS institutions couched in the standard approach, contemporary decision-makers (foreign ministries, international courts, and international lawyers) are perceived to be more qualified to develop subsequent measures to improve the regulatory function of UNCLOS.[350] This is because

---

344 Youngmin Seo, "The Marine Environmental Turn in the Law of the Sea and Fukushima Wastewater," *Fordham International Law Journal*, 45, no. 1 (2021), p. 69.

345 Richard A. Epstein, *Simple Rules for a Complex World* (Harvard University Press, 1995), p. 31.

346 See, e.g., Article 15 (delimitation of the territorial sea: the median line out of regard for special circumstances), Article 19 (meaning of innocent passage), Article 47 (archipelagic baselines: the specific water-to-land ratio requirement and the maximum length of baselines up to 100 nm), and Part XI (The Area) and Agreement relating to the Implementation of Part XI of UNCLOS.

347 See, e.g., Part V (EEZ) (permissibility of certain activities and methods of maritime boundary delimitation), and Part VIII (Regime of Islands) (drawing a line between islands and rocks), and Part XIII (MSR) (the inclusiveness of MSR in relation to certain marine data collection activities).

348 Youngmin Seo (2021), p. 70.

349 Approaching the end of UNCLOS III, delegates were getting tired of negotiating and being criticized in their capitals for the excessive length of the negotiations with high per diem rates "[t]he working premise at the end for largely exhausted delegates at the Third Conference was that imperfect solutions were better than no solutions at all." See Myron H. Nordquist and William G. Phalen, Interpretation of UNCLOS Article 121 and Itu Aba (Taiping) in the South China Sea Arbitration Award, in Myron H. Nordquist et al. (2017), pp. 27, 77.

350 Youngmin Seo (2021), p. 71.

current national authorities have access to superior information, which was unavailable to the framers, and are equipped with more data (international jurisprudence), experience (state practice), and better technical qualifications.[351] Understanding the achievement and limitation of UNCLOS III, States today can supplement, reinforce, and implement the maritime regimes that draw on "standards." To this end, bilateral, regional, minilateral, or multilateral declarations and agreements can be utilized.

A rule needs to explain previous state behavior: "[i]f a rule diverges sharply from state practice, it may be too impractical to govern international affairs, or it may identify aspirational, quixotic goals."[352] A sharp division between the law of the sea and state practice places nations in a bind.[353] Indeed, international norms shape a country, and the country, in return, shapes the international legal system.[354] In this sense, state practice is essential to clarify treaty provisions that draw on standards in that international law is nothing but what countries say and do.[355] In fact, the current legal conflicts between the West and China surrounding the SCS do not seem to fall within a clear division of violation or compliance. Rather, in a legal sense, legitimate interpretation of UNCLOS is bound to comport with what the majority of states say and do and whether other nations agree or disagree.[356]

International lawyers have requested a modus vivendi for undetermined UNCLOS institutions. UNCLOS is perceived as "the beginning of a long and arduous process of adjusting and readjusting the multiple interests of different political groups through various forms of conciliation and arbitration."[357] China and the US will be the key players in the making of modus vivendi.[358]

---

351 John Yoo (2014), pp. 94–6.

352 *Ibid.*, p. 98.

353 *Ibid.*, p. 23.

354 Zhipeng He and Lu Sun (2020), p. 139.

355 Lindsay Moir, *Reappraising the Resort to Force* (Oxford: Hart Publishing, 2010), pp. 114–5.

356 TJ Farer, "The Prospect for International Law and Order in the Wake of Iraq," *American Journal of International Law*, 97 (2003), p 623 (noting that "[b]ecause every action by a consequential state for which it claims legitimacy will produce prescriptive implications beyond its peculiar facts, it will generate a modification of the principal norm if other consequential states follow suit (or even declare a readiness to) when the appropriate occasion arises").

357 Paul C. Yuan (1984), p. 433.

358 Ren Xiaofeng and Cheng Xizhong (2005), p. 146 (stating that a bilateral mechanism between China and the US is better inasmuch as the disputes originate bilaterally). In this sense, Gao, former Chinese ITLOS judge states that "China is also looking forward

This Chapter has reviewed the conflicting legal views of the West and China and thus, demonstrated the need for the UNCLOS regimes to be clarified to avoid severe conflicts in the SCS. The next Chapter will switch gears and look at what lessons international law could derive from political scientists' discussions.

---

to dialogues with its counterpart(s) with a view to clarifying each other's positions and agreeing upon some possible conflict avoidance mechanisms. See Zhiguo Gao, China and the Law of the Sea, in Myron H. Nordquist et al. (2009), p. 295.

CHAPTER 3

The South China Sea Dispute from the Perspective of International Relations Theories

International law cannot exist in the absence of international relations; likewise, legal solutions to international disputes cannot exist without regard for political realities.[1] The resolution of the SCS dispute invariably revolves around international cooperation.[2] International relations theories have generated insight into states' behavioral motivation. Some scholars suspect that Western political theories rooted in European experience have little usage in making sense of Asian regionalism.[3] However, the core concepts of Western political theories (e.g., the distribution of power) seem relevant and useful within an Asian context.[4] In other words, balance of power of realism, liberal theories of interdependence and cooperation, and collective norms and social identities in constructivism help when examining the propriety of international law approaches to the SCS.[5]

1 Zhipeng He and Lu Sun (2020), p. 54 (noting that "international law is a system of rules for adjusting international relations, which cannot be separated from international relations for a moment").

2 Helen Milner conceptualizes cooperation as "goal-directed behavior that entails mutual policy adjustments so that all sides end up better off than they would otherwise be." See Helen Milner, "International Theories of Cooperation among Nations: Strengths and Weaknesses," *World Politics*, 44 (1992), p. 468.

3 Peter J. Katzenstein, Introduction: Asian Regionalism in Comparative Perspective, Peter J. Katzenstein and Takashi Shiraishi (eds.), *Network Power: Japan and Asia* (Ithaca, NY: Cornell University Press, 1997), p. 5.

4 G. John Ikenberry and Michael Mastanduno, The United States and Stability in East Asia, in G. John Ikenberry and Michael Mastanduno (eds.), *Interactional Relations Theory and the Asia-Pacific* (New York: Columbia University Press, 2003), pp. 421–22; Amitav Acharya, Thinking Theoretically about Asian IR, in David Shambaugh and Michael Yahunda (eds.), *International Relations of Asia*, 2nd ed. (Lanham: Rowman & Lifflefield Publisher, 2014), p. 60.

5 Zhipeng He and Lu Sun (2020), p. 54 (noting that these international relations theories would provide international law with theorization).

 | DOI: 10.1163/9789004696358_004

1 Research Programs in International Politics

International politics specialists perceive the world in a way that international lawyers rarely see; moreover, legal scholars and political scientists adopt different research methods. Legal scholarship, in most cases, focuses on determining what the law is, whereas political scientists elucidate the motives behind state behavior. International law is not familiar with theorizing and hypotheses, whereas political research is conducted through the lens of theories. Legal analysis is mostly descriptive and expositive, while much of political analysis relies on mathematical modeling and advanced statistical analysis using "large N" data sets.[6] With this in mind, realism, liberalism, and constructivism are introduced below.

1.1 *Realism*

The principal lexicon of realism includes anarchy, national interest, security competition, and war and power. The intellectual tradition of realist thinking dates back centuries, and even millennia, to include the philosophies of Thucydides, Machiavelli, and Hobbes. The most fundamental element of realism is the anarchic structure of the international system, which is believed to cause states to keep seeking security through self-help mechanisms (e.g., war). Realism assumes that ego-centric states struggle for power relative to other players; thus, conflict is pervasive, and cooperation is rare and superficial.[7] From a realist perspective, the most powerful states (hegemons) in the system tend to seek to remake the world in their own image, following their own values.[8] In other

6 Adam Irish, Charlotte Ku, and Paul F. Diehl, "Bridging the International Law-International Relations Divide: Talking Stock of Progress," *Georgia journal of International and Comparative Law*, 41 (2013), pp. 362–363.

7 Robert S. Ross and Zhu Feng, Introduction, in Robert S. Ross and Zhu Feng (eds.), *China's Ascent Power, Security, and the Future of International Politics* (Ithaca and London: Cornell University Press, 2008), pp. 2–3; Amitav Acharya, "Thinking Theoretically about Asian IR," in David Shambaugh and Michael Yahunda (2014), p. 62 (explaining that in realist thinking "international institutions operate on the margins of great power whims and caprice"); Stephen M. Walt, "International Relations: One World, Many Theories," *Foreign Policy*, no. 110 (Spring 1998), p. 31.

8 Robert Jervis, "Unipolarity: A Structural Perspective." *World Politics*, 61, no. 1 (2009), pp. 188–213; Michael Mastanduno, "Realism and Asia" in Saadia M. Pekkanen et al. (eds.), *Oxford Handbook of the International Relations of Asia* (Oxford: Oxford University Press, 2014), p. 28 (noting that states would balance power both internally by improving military capacity and externally by arranging alliances).

words, great powers seek to increase their external influence; to that end, they do anything they can.[9]

Realists are pessimists. Their gloomy view of world politics is predicated upon three core beliefs: (1) states (great powers) are the principal actors in world politics; (2) motives for state behavior are bound up with anarchy (the absence of governing authority over the great powers);[10] and, (3) power calculation (power distribution) dictates state thinking, entailing endless power competition.[11] States are obsessed with how power is distributed among them while pursuing maximizing their share of world power.[12]

At some risk of oversimplifying, there are three theoretical offshoots of this political theory.[13] First, classical realism (human nature realism), supported by Hans Morgenthau,[14] dominated the study of international relations from the late 1940s until the 1970s. Morgenthau argued that the distribution of state power and the character of individual states (revolutionary or status quo) are the key to understanding the nature of the international system. Classical realism assumes that states consistently search for opportunities to dominate others due to their "will to power" (entrenched in humans at birth), entailing a "limitless lust for power."[15]

Second, in response to Morgenthau's emphasis on human nature, Waltz proposed, in *Theory of International Politics*,[16] that international relations focuses on the effects of the international system, not human nature. Structural realism (or defensive realism), supported by Robert Jervis and Jack Snyder, assume that states merely aim to survive in a world of anarchy by focusing on security.

---

9 Scholars use "realism" differently: Rose discusses around 13 versions of realism. See Gideon Rose, "Review: Neoclassical Realism and Theories of Foreign Policy," *World Politics*, 51, no. 1 (1998), pp. 144–172.

10 Milner observes that anarchy has two meanings: a lack of order, which implies chaos or disorder, and the lack of government. See Helen Milner, "The Assumption of Anarchy in International Relations Theory: A Critique," *Review of International Studies*, 17, no. 1 (January 1991), pp. 69–74. Meanwhile, Yoo adduces the lawyer's definition of anarchy: "no world authority can enforce international rules in the same way that domestic governments maintain law and order. The world is composed of independent sovereign states with no higher sovereign above them." See John Yoo, "Embracing the Machines: Rationalist War and New Weapons Technologies," *California Law Review*, 105 (2017), p. 128.

11 John J. Mearsheimer, *The Tragedy of Great Power Politics* (Norton, 2014), pp. 17–18.

12 *Ibid.*, pp. 12, 33, 44.

13 Tudor Onea, "Putting the 'Classical' in Neoclassical Realism: Neoclassical Realist Theories and US Expansion in the Post–Cold War." *International Relations*, 26, no. 2 (2012), p. 156.

14 Hans Morgenthau, *Politics Among Nations: The Struggle for Power and Peace*, 5th ed. (New Work: Knopf, 1973).

15 John J. Mearsheimer (2014), p. 19.

16 Kenneth Waltz, *Theory of International Politics* (Reading, MA: Addison-Wesley, 1979).

In this view, states compete for power because power is the best means of survival; however, states care about maintaining the balance of power and are generally satisfied with the status quo unless their own security is challenged (hence, "defensive realism).[17] From this perspective, "excessive strength" is dangerous because if a state strengthens its power excessively, great powers are likely to cause other states to join forces against the expanding state.[18]

Third, offensive realists (such as Mearsheimer, Liberman, and Labs) challenged defensive realism based in part on: (1) there have been predatory revisionist states (e.g., Adolf Hitler's Germany), (2) conquest, in some cases, has had more benefits than costs; and (3) states do not know how much power is enough, thereby maximize relative power, not absolute power.[19] Offensive realists argue that states perceive power as the key to survival due to the absence of higher agency over great powers.[20]

"Security" is the most powerful motivation of state in anarchy for both offensive and defensive realists, but offensive and defensive realists adduce different prescriptions to attend to it.[21] Defensive realists understand the international structure to push states to maintain the existing balance of power[22] and constrain states from adopting offensive policies.[23] For defensive realists, the concept of the "offense-defense balance" is important. Conflicts occur when offense has the advantage; on the contrary, peace and cooperation persist

---

17 Amitav Acharya, Thinking Theoretically about Asian IR, in David Shambaugh and Michael Yahunda (2014), p. 64.

18 John J. Mearsheimer (2014), p. 20. Defensive realists posit that states have little intrinsic interest in military conquest; the costs of expansion generally outweigh the benefits. See Stephen M. Walt, "International Relations: One World, Many Theories," *Foreign Policy*, no. 110 (Spring 1998), p. 37.

19 Stephen M. Walt (Spring 1998), p. 37.

20 John J. Mearsheimer (2014), p. 21. Mearsheimer adds that the structure of the international system (the absence of a central authority, offensive military capacity of states, and the lack of confidence (fear) about other states' intention) compels states to act aggressively toward each other. See *Ibid.*, p. 3.

21 Jack L. Snyder, *Myths of Empire: Domestic Politics and International Ambition* (Ithaca, NY: Cornell University Press, 1991), pp. 11–12). Tang argues that offensive realist states seek security by intentionally harming others, but defensive realist states do not seek security by harming others on purpose. See Shiping Tang, *A Theory of Security Strategies for Our Time: Defensive Realism* (New York: Palgrave Macmillan, 2010), p. 31.

22 Eric J. Hamilton & Brian C. Rathbun, "Scarce Differences: Toward a Material and Systemic Foundation for Offensive and Defensive Realism," *Security Studies*, 22, no. 3 (2013), p. 443.

23 Jack Snyder and Stephen Van Evera, Myths of Empire: *Domestic Politics and International Ambition* (Ithaca, NY: Cornell University Press, 1991), p. 1 (adding that "[m]anageable economic or security problems were invariably made worse by militant, expansionist policies that provoked sharp international resistance." Ibid., pp. 307–8).

when defense has the lead.[24] If great powers are happy with the existing balance of power, they will not change it by force.

In contrast, offensive realists perceive the international system as creating powerful incentives for states to gain more power to achieve hegemony at the expense of their rivals.[25] Despite their differences, defensive and offensive realism are viewed as the same as neorealism or structural realism. In neorealism's view, states behave aggressively not because of a "will to power" but out of a desire to seek more chances of survival.[26]

Parenthetically, political scientists categorize the world into unipolar (with a single superpower controlling the system), bipolar (with two great powers), or multipolar (with three or more) per different levels of defined and measured power.[27] Also, the concept of the security dilemma stands out in realism. States that worry about their security are driven to acquire more power to escape from others' dominance, which endangers others' security, making them prepare for the worst; subsequently, the vicious circle of (in)security and power accumulation continues.[28]

Realists deny any effective role of international law in international politics (legal nihilism). In realists' view, it is dangerous for states to rely on the law (ignoring dominant states' power position and interest), which they label "utopian" or "idealist."[29] Realism assesses that international law is created and applied by a handful of great powers with a disproportionate role. Further, hegemonic states can abrogate existing rules, prevent adopting rules that they oppose, and monopolize the right to interpret the law; in short, economic and military power (not law) is the most crucial factor in foreign relations.[30]

---

24 Sean M. Lynn-Jones, "Offense-Defense Theory and Its Critics," *Security Studies*, 4, no. 4 (1995), p. 661.

25 Jack Snyder and Stephen Van Evera (1991), p. 1.

26 Sean M. Lynn-Jones (1995), p. 661. On one view the pendulum in states' motivation swings back and forth between offensive and defensive realist intention, although offensive realism is more likely to end up being defensive realism. See Klaus Heinrich Raditio, *Understanding China's Behavior in the South China Sea: A Defensive Realist Perspective* (Singapore: Palgrave Macmillan, 2019), pp. 29, 34.

27 John J. Mearsheimer (2014), p. 12.

28 John H. Herz, "Idealist Internationalism and the Security Dilemma," *World Politics*, 2, no. 2 (January 1950), p. 157. Meanwhile, Raditio argues that security dilemma cannot operate in a world where states adopt offensive realism because one or more states hold malign intentions as default value. See Klaus Heinrich Raditio (2019), p. 28.

29 Alexander Orakhelashvili, International law, international politics and ideology, in Alexander Orakhelashvili (2011), p. 333.

30 Robert O. Keohane and Joshep S. Nye, Jr., *Power and Interdependence* (Pearson, 2012), p. 37; Detlev F. Vagts, "Hegemonic International Law," *American Journal of International Law*, 95 (2001), p. 846, fn. 20 (naming the role of powerful states in interpring rules as

Morgenthau describes international law as a "primitive type of law resembling the kind of law that prevails in certain preliterate societies … because it is almost completely decentralized law" and emphasizes that that "[w]here there is neither community of interest nor balance of power, there is no international law" because international law is based on "[convergent] interests of [states]" and "the distribution of power."[31]

For realists, the reflection of the distribution of power is essential to the international legal system. If power distribution shifts, the law should change.[32] Also, they suggest that international rules work well to the extent that states agree on common interests and define the mechanism to achieve the same goals; otherwise, international law becomes ineffective.[33] In addition, realists expect that international law plays a role in solving distributional conflicts (who gets what and how much they get). In other words, great powers (rule-makers) find efficacy in international law as long as their privilege is maintained through self-enforcing equilibria therein; put differently, without paying attention to distributional consequences, market failures are rarely resolved.[34] Lastly, in this view, compliance with international adjudication is only guaranteed by balance of power and a hegemon.[35]

---

decisionism); Congyan Cai, *The Rise of China and International Law: Taking Chinese Exceptionalism Seriously* (New York, NY: Oxford University Press, 2019), p. 13; G. John Ikenberry, A New Order of Things?: China, America, and the Struggle over World Order, in Asle Toje (ed.), *Will China's Rise Be Peaceful? Security, Stability, and Legitimacy* (New York: Oxford University Press, 2018), p. 40.

31 Hans Morgenthau (1973), pp. 273–4. For many political scientists, international law is an oxymoron due to the lack of high legal authority. See Stephen D. Krasner, "Realist Views of International Law," Proceedings of the Annual Meeting (American Society of International Law), 96 (March 13–16, 2002), p. 265.

32 Stephen D. Krasner (2002), p. 266.

33 Bernhard Zangl et al., "Between Law and Politics: Explaining International Dispute Settlement Behavior" *European Journal of International Relations*, 18, no. 2 (2011), pp. 369–401. Oppenheim, leading international lawyer in the 1900s, concurred with realists in that the balance of power counts for much as "an indispensable condition of the very existence of international law." See Lassa Oppenheim, *International Law: A Treaties* (London: Longmans, Green and Company, 1912), Vol. 1, p. 193; Hans Morgenthau (1973), p. 274.

34 Stephen D. Krasner (2002), p. 266.

35 Robert O. Keohane, "The Theory of Hegemonic Stability and Changes in International Economic Regimes" in Ole R. Holsti et al. (1980), pp. 131–162; Eric A. Posner and John C. Yoo (2005), pp. 1–74 (arguing that "if the states believe that the tribunal is neutral, their interests remain constant, and the distribution of power between the states has not shifted, then they have roughly the same incentive to comply with the judgment of the tribunal as they did when they made the original agreement to establish the tribunal" *ibid.*, p. 17).

1.2 *Liberalism*

Whereas realism is obsessed with shifts in the distribution of power and war (a causal theory of war), liberalism focuses on the conditions under which cooperation emerges (a causal theory of peace),[36] whose philosophical background dates back to John Locke, Hugo Grotius, and Immanuel Kant.[37] Liberalists assert that international cooperation is possible because mutual gains outweigh conflicts in pursuit of dominance. Rational states prioritize cooperation, harmony, and peaceful co-existence, despite their ego-centrism. In the same context, states create and join international organizations because they find the benefits.[38] The liberal approach to international politics is fluid and bottom-up, based on a cost-benefit analysis, in which the foreign policy interests of states are changing.[39]

Liberalist thought shares three core beliefs: (1) States are the main actors in international politics; (2) there are "good" or "bad" states based on a nation's domestic arrangement (e.g., democracy or dictatorship); and (3) political and economic calculations matter more than a power calculation.[40] Most liberal theorists believe that it is possible to reduce the scourge of war substantially through (1) economic interdependence (commercial liberalism), (2) the spread of democracy (democratic liberalism), and (3) international institutions (institutional liberalism).[41]

First, commercial liberalists assume that creating and maintaining a liberal economic order will allow free economic exchange among states, which enables states to avoid war in the interest of accumulating wealth arising from

---

36 Stephan Haggard, The Liberal View of the International Relations of Asia, in Saadia M. Pekkanen et al. (2014), pp. 47, 58; Amitav Acharya, Thinking Theoretically about Asian IR, in David Shambaugh and Michael Yahunda (2014), p. 72.

37 Kant offers three constraints to making decisions with the potential of disrupting peace: democracy, international trade and international organization. See Immanuel Kant, "Perpetual Peace: A Philosophical Sketch" In Hans Reiss, *Kant's Political Writings* (Cambridge: Cambridge University Press, 1970), pp. 93–115.

38 Richard Ned Lebow, Classical Realism, in Tim Dunne, Milja Kurki and Steve Smith (eds.), *International Relations Theories: Discipline and Diversity* (Oxford: Oxford University Press, 2013), pp. 59–76.

39 Stephan Haggard, The Liberal View of the International Relations of Asia, in Saadia M. Pekkanen et al. (2014), pp. 45–6, 58 (noitng that liberalism criticizes realism for not providing a convincing theory of actors' preferences or intentions).

40 John J. Mearsheimer (2014), pp. 15–16.

41 Stephen M. Walt (Spring 1998), p. 32 (noting that "[a]ll liberal theories imply that cooperation is more pervasive than what [defensive realism] allows, while each view offers a different recipe for arriving at cooperation"); Amitav Acharya, Thinking Theoretically about Asian IR, in David Shambaugh and Michael Yahunda (2014), pp. 68–69.

the high level of economic interdependence.[42] Second, democratic liberalists argue that democracies are inherently more peaceful than autocratic states; logically, the more democratic states exist in the system, the less war breaks out (democratic peace theory).[43] Third, institutional liberalists stress the constructive role of international institutions in enhancing the prospects for cooperation among states, thereby reducing the likelihood of war. International organizations and/or international norms are perceived as fundamentally changing state behavior.[44]

Following World War II, neoliberal institutionalists focused on formal international organizations, and by the 1970s, turned their attention to the international regime, arguing that regimes are central in facilitating international cooperation and constraining state behavior.[45] For international lawyers, regimes are viewed as international law by another name.[46] Aggarwal defines regimes as "arrangements that regulate the imposition of unilateral controls and negotiation of bilateral accords; hence national actions are examined as a third type of governance structure."[47]

---

42 Stephen M. Walt (Spring 1998), p. 39.

43 Michael Doyle, "Liberalism and World Politics," *American Political Science Review*, 80, no. 4 (December 1986), pp. 1151–1169. However, with regard to the correlation of democracy with war, scholars acknowledge that once in an ongoing war, democracies go through a high level of intensity and longer duration due to higher "audience costs" (the political pressures on the leaders when they back down in the face of the challenge from other states), and if a state is in transition to democracy, international and civil wars are more likely due to weak political institutions. See Min Gyo Koo, *Island Disputes and Maritime Regime Building in East Asia: Between a Rock and a Hard Place* (Springer, 2009) p. 35; Jack Snyder (2004), pp. 57–59.

44 Katerina Linos and Tom Pegram, "What Works in Human Rights Institutions?," *American Journal of International Law*, 111, no. 3 (2017) (arguing that the UN and its institutional effort to promote national human rights institutions have worked in enhancing human rights even in authoritarian and transitional regimes); Stephen M. Walt (Spring 1998), pp. 39–40; Jack Snyder (November/December 2004), p. 58 (stressing that although international institutions cannot force states to behave in ways that are contrary to the states' own selfish interests, international institutions can help coordinate outcomes that are in the long-term mutual interest of both the hegemon and the weaker states).

45 Anu Bradford, Regime Theory, in Rudiger Wolfrum (2012), Vol. VIII, pp. 737, 740.

46 Anne-Marie Slaughter Burley, "International Law and International Relations Theory: A Dual Agenda," *American Journal of International Law*, 87 (1993), p. 206.

47 Vinod K. Aggarwal, "Building International Institutions in Asia-Pacific," *Asian Survey*, 33, no. 11 (November, 1993), p. 1030. Meanwhile, Krasner defines regimes as "sets of implicit or explicit principles, norms, rules, and decision-making procedures around which actors' expectations converge in a given area of international relations. Principles are beliefs of fact, causation, and rectitude. Norms are standards of behavior defined in terms of rights and obligations. Rules are specific prescriptions or proscription for action.

For regime theorists, regimes are essential to mitigate anarchy and facilitate cooperation among states and other potential actors,[48] given that state interests are not necessarily conflictual as international politics is a non-zero-sum game.[49] Also, regime theorists affirm that regimes can defuse the dilemmas of collective goods that arise from the self-interest of states.[50] The optimal provision of collective goods (e.g., the environment and collective security) can only be assured if a state eschews independent decision-making, which otherwise makes them "free riders."[51]

Not only is regime theory closely linked to international law, but liberalism, in general, is also germane to international rules. Liberalism puts forward the position that compliance with international law provides a good reputation to the state and the credibility of the international legal system to all the players.[52] Similarly, in regards to international adjudication, liberalists argue that the accumulation of opportunity costs would provide states with the motivation to abide by international adjudication; in brief, liberalists claim that the

---

Decision-making procedures are prevailing practices for making and implementing collective choice." See Stephen D. Krasner, "Structural Causes and Regime Consequences: Regimes as Intervening Variables," *International Organization*, 36, no. 2, International Regimes (Spring 1982), p. 186. Also, regimes are defined as "sets of mutual expectations, generally agreed-to rules, regulations, and plans, in accordance with which organizational energies and financial commitments are allocated" or "social institutions composed of agreed-upon principles, norms, rules, and decision-making procedures that govern the interactions of actors in specific issue area." See John Gerard Ruggie, "International Response to Technology: Concepts and Trends," *International Organization* 29 (Summer 1975), p. 569; Gail Osherenko and Oran R. Young, The Formation of International Regimes: Hypotheses and Cases, in Oran R. Young and Gail Osherenko (eds), *Polar Politics: Creating International Environmental Regimes* (Ithaca: Cornell University Press, 1993), p. 1.

48 Mark J. Valencia, *A Maritime Regime: For North-East Asia* (Oxford University Press, 1996), p. 18.

49 Anu Bradford, Regime Theory, in Rudiger Wolfrum (2012), Vol. VIII, pp. 737–8.

50 The theory of collective goods offers that the danger of the international community is a superfluity of would-be free riders, expecting others to take the burden. Although the situation calls for collective action and cooperation, self-interested states will decide not to contribute to obtaining the collective goods that will be enjoyed by all the states regardless of the contribution. See Robert O. Keohane (1985), p. 38, 69; Anu Bradford, Regime Theory, in Rudiger Wolfrum (2012), Vol. VIII, p. 740.

51 Mark J. Valencia, *A Maritime Regime: For North-East Asia* (Oxford University Press, 1996), p. 18.

52 Andrew T. Guzman, *How International Law Works: A Rational Choice Theory* (Oxford: Oxford University Press, 2008); Bruce Cronin, "The Paradox of Hegemony: America's Ambiguous Relationship with the United Nations," *European Journal of International Relations*, 7, no. 1 (2001), pp. 103–130.

reputational costs of ignoring international rulings and the care of the credibility of the international legal order lead states to comply with it.[53]

1.3 *Constructivism*

Constructivism as a theory of international relations appeared in the 1980s and 1990s as a critique of realism and liberalism,[54] rooted in constructivist social theory, of which the principal premise is that "people act toward objects, including other actors, on the basis of the meanings that the objects have for them."[55] Constructivists expound that social reality is created by debating values, ideas, knowledge, identity, and interests. Compared to realism's obsession with the power structure and liberalism's focus on the power of process (international trade, democratization, and regime), constructivism's emphasis lies in the power of debates about ideas (the fundamental building blocks of international life).[56] Adler defines constructivism as "[t]he view that the manner in which the material world shapes and is shaped by human action and interaction depends on dynamic normative and epistemic interpretations of the material world."[57]

For constructivists, the prevailing discourse in society is important because it reflects and shapes beliefs, interests, identities, and accepted norms of behavior of states; thus, states are demanded to monitor how ideas and identities are created and evolved closely.[58] Unlike realism and liberalism that posit the existence of an anarchic structure and the self-help system thereof, constructivists postulate that state interests and identities are not pre-ordained or given but (collectively) emerge and change through a process of mutual interactions and socialization.[59]

---

53 Beth A. Simmons, "Capacity, Commitment, and Compliance: International Institutions and Territorial Disputes," *Journal of Conflict Resolution*, 46, no. 6 (2002), pp. 829–856.

54 Scholars began to peer into events and changes in international politics through the lenses of this cognitive theory to counter the rationalist arguments of liberals and realists. See David Leheny, Constructivism and International Relations in Asia, in Saadia M. Pekkanen et al. (2014), p. 64. See generally Alexander Wendt (1999).

55 Alexander Wendt, "Anarchy is what states make of it: the social construction of power politics," *International Organization*, 46, no. 2 (Spring 1992), pp. 396–7. See also Emanuel Adler, "Seizing the Middle Ground: Constructivism in World Politics," *European Journal of International Relations*, 3, no. 3 (1997), p. 323.

56 Alexander Wendt (1992), pp. 391–2; Jack Snyder (2004), p. 60; Emanuel Adler (1997), pp. 321–2.

57 Emanuel Adler (1997), p. 322.

58 Stephen M. Walt (Spring 1998), p. 41.

59 Alexander Wendt (1992), p. 392 (adding that "[e]ach person has many identities linked to institutional roles ... [E]ach identity is an inherently social definition of the actor

In this view, constructivists understand that states find themselves in security dilemmas; however, security dilemmas have no bearing on anarchy. The concept of anarchy does not explain why conflict occurs between states, and thus, the real issue is how states understand anarchy.[60] What is important in constructivism is state practice ("changing the practices will change the intersubjective knowledge that constitutes the system")[61] and social structure through shared knowledge (anarchy of friends is different from that of enemies).[62] Thus, theoretically, if collective security identity is high in anarchy, a relatively weak predatory state can be defeated by the international community in the name of collective security.[63]

The concept of national interests is also of a protean nature for constructivists. National interests change in accordance with the flow of the work of intellectual entrepreneurs who promote new ideas in the process of naming and shaming actors in violation of accepted standards.[64] In this view, the role of expert consensus and the interplay of norm entrepreneurs and epistemic communities are emphasized.[65] For instance, if the supply of consensual

---

grounded in the theories which actors collectively hold about themselves and one another and which constitute the structure of the social world" ibid., pp. 397–8); Amitav Acharya, "Thinking Theoretically about Asian IR," in David Shambaugh and Michael Yahunda (2014), p. 73.

60 Alexander Wendt (1992), p. 394–5 (arguing that the current self-help world and power politics, which are socially constructed under anarchy, can be attributable to process, not structure). In this sense, constructivism is a neutral theory between conflict and cooperation. See Emanuel Adler (1997), p. 326.

61 Alexander Wendt (1992), p. 407.

62 Alexander Wendt, "Constructing international Politics," *International Security,* 20, no. 1 (Summer 1995), pp. 77–78.

63 Alexander Wendt (1992), p. 408.

64 This is why constructivism often studies the work of the transnational activist network. See Jack Snyder (2004), p. 60. See also Emanuel Adler (1997), p. 327 (explaining that in Constructivist idea, "national interests" are "facts whose 'objectivity' relies on human agreement and the collective assignment of meaning and function to physical objects").

65 By definition, an "epistemic community" is a network of professionals with recognized expertise and competence in a particular domain and an authoritative claim to policy-relevant knowledge within that domain or issue-area. See Peter M. Haas, Introduction: epistemic communities and international policy coordination, in Peter M. Haas (ed.), Knowledge, Power and International Policy Coordination, *International Organization*, 46 (Special Issue, 1992), pp. 3, 31–32. Haas explains that an epistemic community may have: (1) a shared set of normative and principled beliefs, which provide a value-based rationale for the social action of community members; (2) shared causal beliefs, which are derived from their analysis of practices contributing to a central set of problems in their domain, and which then serve as the basis for elucidating the multiple linkages between possible policy actions and desired outcomes; (3) shared notions of validity—that is,

knowledge evolves and interest group pressure on politicians increases, regime shift (regime building and management) occurs. Indeed, epistemic communities contribute to the transformation of state identities, interests, and practices by diffusing new normative views, which encourages states to act in a way that is compatible with the new constitutive norms.[66]

Although there is no fixed stylized approach to studying constructivism,[67] there seem to be four different groups based on methodological disagreement within the study of constructivism: (1) using standard methods alongside interpretive methods; (2) using insights from international law and jurisprudence (rule-guided behavior); (3) emphasizing narrative knowing; and (4) using techniques developed by post-modernism.[68]

Constructivism views that international law as a manifestation of shared expectations (as a consensus understanding of the system) about actors' appropriate or legitimate behavior.[69] In this view, international law is structured identities and interests that often result in formal rules and norms codified. As a cognitive entity that "[does] not exist apart from actors' ideas about how the world works," international law is observed through socialization and participation in collective knowledge.[70]

Moreover, international lawyers and constructivists use the same analytical enterprise; the former looks at *opinion juris* as evidence of a belief that some rules are law, which the latter regards as methods for establishing the existence of a norm.[71] Constructivists also discuss normative conflict and change with a view to ascertaining what makes a normative claim persuasive.[72] In short, constructivism is concerned with how international law evolves and constrains state behavior.[73]

---

intersubjective, internally defined criteria for weighing and validating knowledge in the domain of their expertise; and (4) a common policy enterprise—a set of common practices associated with a set of problems to which their professional competence is directed, presumably out of the conviction that human welfare will be enhanced as a consequence. *Ibid.*, p. 2, fn. 5.

66 Emanuel Adler (1997), pp. 343–4.

67 David Leheny, Constructivism and International Relations in Asia, in Saadia M. Pekkanen et al. (2014), p. 65.

68 Emanuel Adler (1997), pp. 335–6.

69 Jong Kun Choi and Yong-Soo Eun (2018), p. 152; Martha Finnemore (1996), p. 139.

70 Alexander Wendt (1992), p. 399.

71 Martha Finnemore (1996), p. 140.

72 *Ibid.*, p. 141.

73 Ronald L. Jepperson et al., Norms, Identity, and Culture in National Security, in Peter J. Katzenstein (ed.), *The Culture of National Security* (New York: Columbia University Press, 1996), pp. 33–75.

In this respect, international lawyers can perceive that constructivism supports the regulatory power of international law in the absence of enforcement because constructivists argue that some rules shape state behavior in ways that are not simply epiphenomenal of interests.[74]

2 China's Intentions—China's Goals and the South China Sea

China is the largest economy in the world when measured in gross domestic product based on purchasing power parity, and China continues to grow. In the past, when the potential hegemon found its growing power relative to the existing hegemon, the rising state invariably challenged the hegemon, which is the rule of the game.[75] What is China's intention in the SCS, and what Chinese approaches make sense to China? It is argued that China abandoned the "keeping a low profile" strategy in 2009 and adopted a more proactive stance to protect its interests.[76] China has not revealed its real intention or legal position for the SCS (dispute): "no specification of claims, no multilateral negotiations, and no internalization of the issue."[77] Below, Chinese possible intentions regarding the SCS are examined.

2.1 *Oil and Gas*

Some writers adduce oil and gas as the Chinese prime motive on the SCS issues.[78] According to the US Energy Information Agency, the estimate is that there is approximately 190 trillion cubic feet of natural gas and 11 billion barrels of oil in proved and probable reserves. A 2012 US Geological Survey estimated

74 Martha Finnemore (1996), p. 142 (noting that questions about why some rules exist and are complied with by states are not central to international legal scholarship, but to constructivists).

75 Michael Tkacik, "Understanding China's goals and strategy in the South China Sea: bringing context to a revisionist systemic challenge-intentions and impact," *Defense & Security Analysis*, 34, no. 4 (2018), p. 322.

76 Jinghan Zeng et al., "Securing China's core interests: the state of the debate in China," *International Affairs*, 91, no. 2 (2015), p. 258.

77 Mark J. Valencia et al. (1997), p. 77.

78 Leszek Buszynski, "Southeast Asia in the Post-Cold War Era," *Asian Survey*, 32, no. 9 (September 1992), p. 835. Hayton notes that much of oil and gas in the region is contained outside of the nine dash line. See Bill Hayton (2014), p. 147. Meanwhile, Owena and Schofield argue that the recovery factor of the SCS oil is reported to be lower (10%) than the conventional rate (35%), while the recovery factor for gas is reported to be about 75%. See Nick A. Owena and Clive H. Schofield, "Disputed South China Sea hydrocarbons in perspective," *Marine Policy*, 36 (2012), p. 813.

that there could be 160 trillion cubic feet of natural gas and 12 billion barrels of oil undiscovered in the SCS.[79]

China consumes a huge amount of oil and gas and depends heavily on imported oil due to its spectacular economic growth. China is reported to reach an oil consumption peak of 720 million tons by 2025[80] and is forecasted to import 75% of its oil from abroad by 2030.[81] The demand for imported oil will increase inasmuch as industrialization will continue by tenfold in future years.[82] Regarding energy security, China must keep considering the availability of supplies, and the reliability, and the affordability of available, reliable energy resources.[83]

History supports that China has the ambition to possess SCS natural resources exclusively. The motive of the 1974 armed conflict between China and South Vietnam in the Paracel Islands was noted as stemming from the "spiraling interest in the oil potential of the region."[84] Later, in 1979 (in the face of the second oil crisis), China launched its offshore oil exploration program in the SCS, signing contracts with 48 foreign oil companies to conduct maritime surveys far beyond China's coast.[85]

According to lateral pressure theory, if a state experiences high population growth rates and technological development, the state is pressured to increase

79 Defusing the South China Sea Disputes: A Regional Blueprint – A Report of the CSIS Expert Working Group on the South China Sea, *Center for Strategic & International Studies*, October 2018, p. 12.

80 Liu Zhihua, Report: China's oil consumption to peak by 2025, *China Daily*, October 17, 2019, at https://www.chinadaily.com.cn/a/201910/17/WS5da81492a310cf3e35571149.html). Beijing's estimates for hydrocarbon resources under the sea are considerably higher but still modest in relation to China's overall demand. See https://www.ceicdata.com/en/indicator/china/oil-consumption.

81 China Increasingly Reliant on Oil Imports—IEA, *China Daily*, November 19, 2008, at http://www.china.org.cn/environment/news/2008-11/19/content_16790574.htm.

Beijing's reliance on offshore petroleum and natural gas reserves makes their defense a national security issue, and clearly a concern for the People Liberation Army Navy (PLAN). See Bernard D. Cole, *China's quest for great power: ships, oil, and foreign policy* (Naval Institute Press, 2016), p. 140.

82 Bernard D. Cole, *China's quest for great power: ships, oil, and foreign policy* (Naval Institute Press, 2016), p. 136.

83 *Ibid.*, p. 132.

84 US diplomatic cable mentioned also "a concern that the communist Vietnamese might affirm Vietnam's claim" and "the long-term strategic potential of the islands." See U.S. Consulate General Hong Kong to US State Department, Subj: Peking's Calculations in the Paracels War, pp. 1–2 (Jan. 30, 1974) (1974HONGK01036), cited in Kirsten Sellars, "Rocking the Boat: The Paracels, The Spratlys, and the South China Sea Arbitration," *Columbia Journal of Asian Law*, 30 (2017), p. 225, fn. 17.

85 Min Gyo Koo (2009) p. 152.

stocks of resources to fuel further economic growth; as a result, the state is under "lateral pressure" to expand its external activities for, *inter alia,* raw materials, and markets.[86] Lateral pressure establishes extraterritorial national interests in exploration, commerce, or investment.[87] Due to its rapid economic development,[88] China may have encroached on the SCS due to the major lateral pressure coming from its elites or populace.

2.2 *Recovering Historical Regional Dominance*

Some observers argue that China's ambition in the SCS is driven by a historic mission to achieve its rightful status as a maritime nation.[89] This analysis advances that historically great powers gained their domination by controlling the seas adjacent to their territory;[90] China today tries to control its claimed areas ("greater China") and regain its historical role as the dominant power in Asia.[91] In the Chinese national psyche, in this view, the Spratly Islands have been its 'backyard' as part of the motherland's territory since ancient times; thus, the Chinese do not see themselves as joining the claim to the Spratlys at the end of the Cold War.

---

86 For a general account of the theory of lateral pressure, see Nazli Choucri and Robert Carver North, *Nations in conflict: national growth and international violence* (San Francisco: W.H. Freeman, 1975). See also Stephen Van Evera, *Causes of War: Power and the Roots of Conflict* (Ithaca, NY: Cornell University Press, 1999) (arguing that "expansionist activities are most likely to be associated with relatively high-capacity countries … with growth in population and advances in technology, p. 28); Randall Schweller, "Managing the Rise of Great Powers: History and Theory" in Alastain Iain Johnston and Robert S. Ross (eds.), *Engaging China: The Management of an Emerging Power* (London: Routledge, 1999), pp. 1–31.

87 Randall Schweller, "Managing the Rise of Great Powers: History and Theory" in Alastain Iain Johnston and Robert S. Ross (1999), p. 3.

88 According to World Bank, China's GDP growth (annual %) was 14% in 2007, 10% 2010, 7% in 2015, and 5.95% in 2019. See https://data.worldbank.org/indicator/NY.GDP.MKTP.KD.ZG?locations=CN.

89 Katherine Morton (2016), p. 911.

90 Klaus Heinrich Raditio (2019), p. 78 (noting that the US has done it over the Caribbean, Italy over the Mediterranean, and Greece over the Aegean).

91 Some argue that the Chinese claim to the SCS arises from the desire to consolidate the national border in the modern era, and promote the integration of Hong Kong and Taiwan with the mainland. See Leszek Buszynski, "Southeast Asia in the Post-Cold War Era," *Asian Survey*, 32, no. 9 (September 1992), p. 835; Mark J. Valencia et al. (1997), p. 84. Friedberg observes that China tries to establish a sphere of influence or zone of control to prevent the "century of humiliation" from happening again. See Aaron L. Friedberg (2005), p. 21.

This argument affects the legitimacy of the Chinese Communist Party. If the Party loses its territory to regional nations now (similar to losing its sovereign integrity to Western powers a century ago), the Chinese people will question the legitimacy of the Party.[92] The recovery of lost territory has been a national project in modern Chinese history, from which the Party has derived its legitimacy.[93] In this sense, Glaser argues, by implication, that China's main driver in the SCS dispute is "irredentism" rather than seeking a sphere of influence.[94]

However, many publicists suggest that China wants to establish a protective sphere in its surroundings. Tkacik claims that despite Chinese leaders' repeated assurances that it pursues no expansionist and hegemonic intention, there is ample room to believe that China seeks regional hegemony, followed by global hegemony.[95] Interestingly, regional players may agree that historically, East Asia has been an area of influence for China to some degree.[96] Regional actors perceive China as a *de facto* co-hegemon (along with the US), which comes at the cost of their territorial integrity.[97]

Admittedly, "control and exclusivity" are the essential features of a sphere of influence; China may hope to enjoy that privilege to serve China's economic and security interests outside of its recognized borders.[98] China's naval modernization comports with "China's rightful status in the world" that can be achieved by denying the US access to the Western Pacific.[99] Military control of the SCS is the critical step toward regional hegemony.[100]

---

92 Chen Jie (1994), pp. 893–894, 900.

93 Denny Roy, "Assertive China: Irredentism or Expansionism?" *Survival*, 61, no. 1 (2019), p. 55–7.

94 Charles Glaser, "Will China's Rise Lead to War?' *Foreign Affairs*, 90, no. 2 (March/April 2011); Denny Roy (2019), pp. 57–8 (stating that "if the presumed motivation of China in the SCS is irredentism, Chinese behavior in the region is less threatening").

95 Michael Tkacik (2018), p. 336. According to Mearsheimer, achieving global hegemony is unrealistic in the sense that (1) hegemony means domination of the entire world, yet (2) it is difficult of a state to project power across the world's oceans onto the territory of a rival great power. See John J. Mearsheimer (2014), pp. 40–41.

96 Leszek Buszynski, "Southeast Asia in the Post-Cold War Era," *Asian Survey*, 32, no. 9 (September 1992), p. 834.

97 R. J. Heydarian, Asia: All Eyes on the Obama–Xi Summit, *Asia Maritime Transparency Initiative*, September 25, 2015, at https://amti.csis.org/asia-all-eyes-on-the-obama-xi-summit.

98 Denny Roy (2019), p. 56.

99 Michael Tkacik (2018), p. 335; Katherine Morton (2016), p. 933.

100 Cui Liru, former president of the Chinese State Security Ministry, notes that "[i]n the Asia-Pacific, the dominant role of the US in a political and military sense will have to be

2.3 *Fear of Containment*

Some commentators estimate that without its control over the SCS, China may be more vulnerable to the US blockade.[101] Why does China worry about containment? As realism blatantly advances, US command of the sea in the Asia Pacific can be maintained by destroying Chinese navies in battle, blockading China in their ports, or denying its vessels access to critical sea lanes.[102] Suppose that China challenges the US-led (maritime) order in East Asia by expanding its influence, threatening the US military position; America would consider the option of containing China with available military assets, blocking China from accessing the global market.

Once a US-led blockade severely disrupts seaborne trade, China may be compelled into surrendering because a cash-strapped economy could no longer sustain the fight:[103] "[i]f China stepped out of line, America could simply close the gate and choke its growth. China therefore had a simple choice: accept American primacy and grow, or challenge it and stagnate."[104]

The SCS is the most advantageous geopolitical location at which China can challenge American supremacy, thanks to its proximity to China; thus, China has developed the so-called anti-access/area denial (A2/D2) capabilities in the region.[105] America worries about China's hidden intentions to challenge free trade and the supremacy of the US Pacific Fleet, whereas China fears a possible US strategy to isolate China within its immediate neighborhood by cutting it off from vital sea lines of communication, which would endanger

readjusted … It does not mean US interests must be sacrificed. But if the US insists on a dominant role forever, that's a problem. See Jane Perlez, Xi Jinping Extends Power, China Braces for a New Cold War, *New York Times*, February 27, 2018, at https://www.nytimes.com/2018/02/27/world/asia/xi-jinping-china-new-cold-war.html.

101 Terrence K. Kelly et al. (2013), p. 8 (claiming that since there are very capable missiles on the world market, it is possible to deny China maritime freedom of action by blocking critical maritime chokepoints using land-based ASMs).

102 John Mearsheimer (2001), pp. 84, 87.

103 *Ibid.*, p. 89. However, others argue that the US is unable to contain China because China is too big economically to persuade other nations to join force to counter China.

104 Hugh White (2012), p. 25.

105 Michael Tkacik (2018), p. 326. China has taken the "offshore defense strategy" centered on A2/D2 assets in sufficient quantity and quality to deny non-submerged US access to areas near its coast (the SCS and the Taiwan Strait), while increasingly retaining the ability to project power regionally. See Stephen Biddle and Ivan Oelrich, "Future Warfare in the Western Pacific: Chinese Antiaccess/Area Denial, U.S. Air Sea Battle, and Command of the Commons in East Asia," *International Security*, 41, no. 1 (Summer 2016), pp. 7–48; Katherine Morton (2016), p. 933.

China's energy security in the first place.[106] The SCS will provide China with a maritime buffer to offset the possible realization of encirclement by a US-led alliance.[107]

2.4 *Security Seeking Purpose*

Some writers claim that China's behavior is "security seeking," like other states seeking to minimize vulnerability to coercion. Control over the SCS would allow Beijing to better protect its access to energy in terms of both transportation and access to hydrocarbons, not to mention fishery resources; if successful, China could make any US blockade less feasible. Of course, China's security seeking in this manner denies security to other states (the security dilemma).[108] China may pursue expansion across the SCS to create secure maritime frontiers or buffer zones to head off US attacks on its homeland.[109]

In approaching the SCS, China takes advantage of the long-distance from America, which is reachable only by ship.[110] If China can gain command of the air and sea by securing land bases and militarizing artificial islands in the SCS, China with land-based air forces, can enhance its security against America capable only of air-based air forces.[111]

---

106 For example, Zhang argues that, in exercise of its seapower, China can control over shipping and resource exploitation in the East and South China Seaa, and the Yellow Sea. See Zhang Wenmu, "Sea Power and China's Strategic Choices," *China Security*, 2, no. 2 (2006), p. 25. See also Katherine Morton (2016), pp. 928–929, 932.

107 M. Taylor Fravel (2010), p. 517 (noting that wealthy states are very much interested in consolidating defensible frontiers or buffers as they have more to protect and defend). In this respect, when the US took the rebalancing strategy, the Chinese people regarded it as proof of power balancing to threat China. This is hardly surprising because the pivot inherently aims at targeting China by repositioning US naval assets from Atlantic to the Asia Pacific with a projected 40/60 ratio favoring the latter, enhancing the US alliances, and developing the "Air-Sea Battle" concept to counter A2/AD. See Mico A Galang (2016), p. 2.

108 Michael Tkacik (2018), pp. 334–335 (arguing that it can be "anti-status quo seeking" rather than "security seeking" because China denies other disputants' or US access to the SCS).

109 M. Taylor Fravel (2010), p. 517 (noting that "[t]erritorial expansion in pursuit of security results from fear and the perception of vulnerability to attack by the other great powers").

110 John Mearsheimer (2001), pp. 84, 87 (noting that great powers dominate the region in which they are located or adjacent regions that can be reached over land).

111 Hu stresses that "China should develop a powerful military defence system in order to protect its core interests." See Hu Jian, 'Cong taoguangyanghui dao jiji zuowei: zhongguo waijiao siwen, zhanlue yu ceyue de zhuanbian zoulun' [From taoguang yanghui to 'active conduct': the transformation of China's diplomatic thinking, strategy and tactics], Lilun

2.5 *Nationalism and Domestic Politics*

Chinese behavior in the SCS is also viewed as due to a rising tide of nationalism, which is often used to replace socialism as the new preferred societal glue.[112] This theory explains that Beijing's confusing actions may be attributable to domestic politics; Beijing may listen to the diverse voice of the increasingly assertive provinces to establish legitimacy.[113] Also, China makes the most of nationalism by using the Chinese media to build the regime's legitimacy.[114] The Tiananmen suppression in June 1989 and the worldwide collapse of communist regimes seem to have forced China to rely on nationalistic appeals to shore up legitimacy from its populace.[115]

Manipulating, making use of, or backfiring from nationalism in domestic politics in China's dealing with the SCS dispute may have a bearing on Chinese Confucianist ideals. In this philosophy, the people have the right to remonstrate with the throne regarding poor conduct and, by extension, rebel against an improper government.[116] Out of fear of losing public support, the Party may have instigated nationalism regarding the SCS dispute. Some scholars

daokan [Theoretical guide], no. 4 (2012), pp. 107–109, in Jinghan Zeng et al., "Securing China's core interests: the state of the debate in China," *International Affairs*, 91, no. 2 (2015), p. 258, fn. 60.

112 Jin Kai, Is China's 'Assertiveness' in the South China Sea All About Nationalism? The narrative of a nationalistic China obscures the real dynamics in the South China Sea, *The Diplomat*, April 11, 2016, at https://thediplomat.com/2016/04/is-chinas-assertiveness-in-the-south-china-sea-all-about-nationalism/; Allen R. Carlson, Why Chinese Nationalism Could Impact the East and South China Seas VERY Differently, *The National Interest*, September 24, 2015, at https://nationalinterest.org/feature/why-chinese-nationalism-could-impact-the-east-south-china-13922.

113 In contrast, some argue that domestic obstacles in China (e.g., social, demographic, and economic challenges) may derail any challenge to U.S. hegemony in the context of the SCS. See Michael Tkacik (2018), p. 323.

114 Bill Hayton (2014), p. 176 (noting that "Beijing would prefer the appearance of public pressure without the threat of public disorder. Aggressive online punditry is more easily turned off once its usefulness is exhausted"). See also John Mearsheimer (2001), p. 401 (explaining that "[a]fter Mao's passing ... communism lost much of its legitimacy with the Chinese public. In response, China's leaders have come to rely much more heavily on nationalism to maintain public support for the regime").

115 Chen Jie, "China's Spratly Policy: With Special Reference to the Philippines and Malaysia," *Asian Survey*, 34, no. 10 (October 1994), p. 897; Jeffrey W. Legro, "What China Will Want: The Future Intentions of a Rising Power," *Perspectives on Politics*, 5, no. 3 (September 2007), p. 517 (discussing that "China has a special sensitivity in [US dominance, Taiwan, and external pressure to democratize] due to the link between its colonial past, subsequent independence, and the legitimacy of the Communist regime").

116 Suzanne Ogden (1974), p. 3.

worry that if China's GDP growth becomes stagnant, the Party's incitement to nationalism against the SCS dispute may skyrocket because another necessary underpinning of securing the legitimacy of the Party would no longer exist.[117]

2.6 *Conclusion*

Reasonable researchers may agree that China has behaved in accordance with a combination of strategic (regional integration), military (enhancing security), economic (resource control), domestic (nationalism or domestic politics), opportunistic, bureaucratic, and individualistic (e.g., President Xi's) intentions.[118] The question is, why the SCS, and why now?

China seems to believe that the SCS is ideal for challenging America in the Pacific with its growing strengths (such as counter-intervention capabilities). China may further view that the short-term risk is outweighed by the benefits of long-term control over the SCS in achieving "regional hegemony" or "regional restructuring."[119] In other words, China willingly bears disputes with and criticism by its neighbors in the short term to strengthen its strategic power in any conflict with the US in the long term.[120]

Indeed, China is not ready to fight against the US militarily on a global scale; however, it seems exponentially difficult (expensive) for the US to intervene inside the First Island Chain (from southern Japan to the Philippines) and to conduct naval operation inside the Second Island Chain (from northern Japan via Guam to Indonesia) due to Chinese control over the SCS.[121]

---

117 Bill Hayton (2014), pp. 176–177 (noting that the Party seeks two kinds of legitimacy: material and psychological. The Party needs to produce rising living standards to their populations and also demonstrate their moral fitness (legitimacy) to rule).

118 For example, China's strategies on island-building and negotiations may have military, perceptual, or economic drivers. See Peter Dutton, "Three Disputes and Three Objectives—China and the South China Sea," *Naval War College Review*, 64, no. 4 (2011), p. 42; Michael Tkacik (2018), pp. 326–327.

119 Michael Tkacik (2018), pp. 333–335 (noting that China's recurrent pronouncement that it has no hegemonic intention notwithstanding, "Being number one implies hegemonic influence"). See also Mico A Galang (2016), p. 4 (noting that China perceives that the control of the SCS is a crucial factor for it to exercise dominance in its sphere of influence).

120 Michael Tkacik, pp. 333, 336.

121 In 1982, the PLA Navy (PLAN) developed a strategy which called for China to control of the First Island Chain and the Second Island Chain. See Anthony Cordesman and Steven Colley, *Chinese Military Modernization in 2015: A Comparative Analysis* (Washington, DC: Center for Strategic and International Studies, 2015), p. 134. For the origin and role of the First and Second Iland Chains, see US Department of Defense, Air Sea Battle: Service Collaboration to Address Anti-Access and Area Denial Challenges (Arlington, VA: US

How will China behave in the SCS down the road? It is impossible to predict China's future behavior because China has acted based on multiple motives at different times, and there could be many unpredictable events.[122] It is reasonable to infer that, for one thing, China's future strategy for the SCS may derive from the necessity that the world should remain safe from the Party's rule over China.[123] For another, the region's future depends on whether the Party and the Chinese people perceive the SCS as a core interest.[124] Certainly, regardless of its concrete intentions or goals, China will work harder to drive the US out of the Western Pacific, not to mention the SCS,[125] thereby inextricably undermining the foundation of the current regional and maritime order, from the US perspective.[126]

Department of Defense, 2013), p. 2; Jeremy Page, China's Submarines Add Nuclear-Strike Capability, Altering Strategic Balance, *Wall Street Journal*, October 24, 2014, at https://www.wsj.com/articles/chinas-submarine-fleet-adds-nuclear-strike-capability-altering-strategic-balance-undersea-1414164738 (predicting that China would strive to "establish naval dominance within the first chain by 2010, within the second chain by 2020 and become a global naval power by 2050").

122 Joseph S. Nye, "Is the American Century Over?" *Political Science Quarterly*, 130, no. 3 (2015), p. 400. See also Leszek Buszynski, "Southeast Asia in the Post-Cold War Era," *Asian Survey*, 32, no. 9 (September 1992), p. 835.

123 Samuel P. Huntinaon, *The Clash of Civilization and the Remaking of World Order* (New York: Simon and Schuster, 1996), p. 159; Aaron L. Friedberg (2011), p. 160.

124 Jinghan Zeng et al. (2015), p. 247 (noting that the malleable boundaries between core and non-core interests make it difficult to predict Chinese diplomatic behavior). A 2015 survey that identified 108 Chinese academic articles concerning China's core interests published between 2008 and 2013 from the China Academic Journals Full-text Database shows that only a few Chinese scholars perceive the SCS issues as constituting a Chinese core interest (3.7 percent of papers refer to the SCS islands as constituting a core interest). See *ibid.*, pp. 248, 259–61. Similarly, on July 1, 2021, at the CCP's 100th-anniversary ceremony, Xi Jinping emphasized Taiwan, Hong Kong, and Macao concerning China's sovereignty and security, but not the SCS. See Xi Jinping, Full text of Xi Jinping's speech on the CCP's 100th anniversary, *Nikkei Asia*, July 1, 2021, at https://asia.nikkei.com/Politics/Full-text-of-Xi-Jinping-s-speech-on-the-CCP-s-100th-anniversary. In contrast, according to a 2011 survey by the People's Daily, the majority of the Chinese people requested that the SCS be upgraded as a core interest. See Edward Wong, China Hedges over Whether South China Sea Is a "Core Interest" Worth War, *The New York Times*, March 30, 2011.

125 To this end, China strives to integrate naval power projection capabilities to become "blue water" designed for use in the open sea, overcoming "green water" bound for coastal defense. See Marc Lanteigne, *Chinese Foreign Policy: An Introduction* (Abingdon, Oxon; New York, NY: Routledge, 2016), p. 112.

126 Michael J. Mazarr et al. (2018), p. 71; Michael Tkacik (2018), p. 335; Rosemary Foot, Restraints on Conflict in the China-US Relationship: Contesting Power Transition Theory, in Asle Toje (2018), p. 81.

3 Realist Evaluation of the South China Sea Dispute

Realists assume that rising powers have been "troublemakers" throughout history, in the eyes of then-existing hegemonic powers.[127] The SCS dispute (as the leading edge of a full-brown conflict over the US-led global order) is predicted to either become more embroiled in a costly US-China strategic rivalry or to cause region-wide accommodation of Chinese power.[128] Almost all realist discussions on US-China relations are premised on the theory of power transition, which argues that power shifts will likely lead to war between a growing dissatisfied state and an existing hegemonic state.[129]

3.1 *Ominous Prediction of Balance-of-Power Politics*

"Balance of power" means the distribution of power (military and economic) among states, which inextricably affects states' foreign policy;[130] states aim to prevent any state from becoming so powerful to the extent that it poses a threat to others.[131] Realists view balance of power as shaping Asia's post-war regional relations, with America remaining as a chief regional balancer.[132] China's ascent and the future of East Asia, not to mention the SCS, are not an exception to realists' balance of power analysis. Realists are pessimistic about the likely geopolitical consequences of China's rise; a rising state with a large population and a rapidly expanding economy invariably becomes a military power. They closely monitor power distribution between China (the second

---

127 Aaron L. Friedberg (2005), p. 18.

128 Robert S. Ross, Balance of Power Politics and the Rise of China: Accommodation and Balancing in East Asia, *Security Studies,* 15, no. 3 (July–September 2006), p. 357; William C. Wohlforth, Not Quite the Same as It Ever Was: Power Shifts and Contestation over the American-Led World Order, in Asle Toje (2018), p. 58.

129 Rosemary Foot, Restraints on Conflict in the China-US Relationship: Contesting Power Transition Theory, in Asle Toje (2018), p. 80.

130 Joseph S. Nye (2015), pp. 394–5 (defining that "Power is the ability to affect others to get the outcomes one wants").

131 Anne-Marie Slaughter, International Relations, Principal Theories in Rüdiger Wolfrum (2012), Vol. VI, p. 129 (noting that [i]nternational stability is best maintained "where a roughly equal distribution of power amongst States ensures that none will risk attacking another").

132 Paul Dibb, Toward a New Balance of Power in Asia, Adelphi Paper 295 (London: International Institute for Strategic Studies, 1995); Michael Leifer, The ASEAN Regional Forum, Adelphi Paper 302 (London: International Institute for Strategic Studies, 1996).

most powerful state) and the US (the most powerful state) to see if whether there are sharp power asymmetries.[133]

Contemporary balance-of-power politics do not necessarily require the emergence of a global power; the emergence of a regional great power that challenges the vital security interests of a status quo power is enough to invoke this theory.[134] It means that China's rise as a regional great power may pose a threat to the security of the US. The SCS is one of the most dangerous flash-points in which China may have more militaristic options to support its claims inasmuch as China's power increases relative to that of the US.[135] Worse yet, both China and the US will have a "military with significant offensive capability and unknowable intentions."[136]

China has more than 1.4 billion people and a rapidly modernizing economy.[137] Realists interpret history to argue that a rising state wants more in proportion to its growing capabilities to set a new goal of achieving first place in the system; simply put, "China will do what all great powers do" in order to "shape that environment in ways that are conducive to its national interests."[138]

It is not that every realist ominously predicts the consequence of the rise of China. Realist optimists (a term borrowed from Friedberg) base their projection on some serious disruption caused by China's economic failure (the middle-income trap) or domestic social and political turbulence (e.g., unrest in Tibet and Xinjiang) that will cause China to remain weak, modest, and even

---

133 John Mearsheimer (2001), p. 44–46. Realists argue that China (a realist state for millennia) monitors how power is distributed in Asia in searching for maximizing its power. See *ibid.*, p. 34; Jack Snyder (2004), p. 55.

134 Robert S. Ross (2006), p. 361.

135 Michael Mastanduno, "Realism and Asia" in Saadia M. Pekkanen, John Ravenhill, and Rosemary Foot (2014), p. 33.

136 John J. Mearsheimer, "The Gathering Storm: China's Challenge to US Power in Asia," *The Chinese Journal of International Politics*, 3 (2010), p. 388.

137 China is the world's most populous country with a population estimated at 1,439.3 million in 2020 (18.5% of the world's population). It is the second largest economy in the world, and its share of the world economy has risen from 3.6% in 2000 to 17.8% in 2020. See CEBR, World Economic League Table: a world economic league table with forecasts for 193 countries to 2035, December 2020, 12th edition, p. 70, at https://cebr.com/wp-content/uploads/2020/12/WELT-2021-final-23.12.pdf.

138 Robert J. Art, The United States and the Rise of China: Implications for the Long Haul, in Robert S. Ross and Zhu Feng (2008), pp. 261–3. See also Samuel P. Huntington, "America's Changing Strategic Interests," *Survival*, 33, no. 1 (January/February 1991), p. 12 (noting that "[t]he external expansion of the UK and France, Germany and Japan, [USSR and US] coincided with phases of intense industrialization and economic development"); John Mearsheimer (2001), p. 144 (adducing the example of Germany that had a large population and a robust economy scared Europe's other great powers before World War I and II).

conservative.[139] Yet, more realists observe that China will grow inasmuch as the Party has improved its resilience in dealing with such problems, capable of knowing what it should do and must not do; in addition, if economic and domestic disasters beset China, it may apply force to external aggressions to direct attention away from those problems.[140] China is expected to surpass the US as the world's largest economy by 2028, even if its economy slows down.[141] If this occurs, China is likely to have a far more powerful military in 2028 than it has in 2021 because China's rapidly growing economy will bring expanding military capabilities backed by the technological competence that comes with economic growth.[142]

While reliable figures are elusive, China's military spending has increased annually by about 10% for more than two decades, shifting the regional and global distribution of capabilities.[143] According to the Stockholm International Peace Research Institute, China's military expenditure is US$ 261,082 million, which is much higher than all Western European countries ($205,770.6) and all East and Southeast Asian countries ($165,508.7, no data on Vietnam) combined, and about the same, if India and Russia were added.[144] Some writers

---

139 Aaron L. Friedberg (2005), pp. 24–5; Oriana Skylar Mastro, "In the shadow of the Thucydides Trap: International Relations Theory and the Prospects for Peace in U.S.-China Relations," *Journal of Chinese Political Science*, 24 (2019), p. 38; Rosemary Foot, Restraints on Conflict in the China-US Relationship: Contesting Power Transition Theory, in Asle Toje (2018), p. 93.

140 Oriana Skylar Mastro, "In the shadow of the Thucydides Trap: International Relations Theory and the Prospects for Peace in U.S.-China Relations," *Journal of Chinese Political Science*, 24 (2019), p. 38; Michael Tkacik (2018), p. 336; Robert S. Ross and Zhu Feng, Introduction, in Robert S. Ross and Zhu Feng (2008), p. 5 (noting that "prolonged economic decline can contribute to foreign policy belligerence").

141 CEBR, World Economic League Table: a world economic league table with forecase for 193 countries to 2035, December 2020, 12th edition, p. 71, at https://cebr.com/wp-content/uploads/2020/12/WELT-2021-final-23.12.pdf (expecting "the trend rate of growth for China to be 5.7% annually from 2021–25 and 4.5% annually from 2026–30 and 3.9% annually from 2031–35").

142 John J. Mearsheimer (2010), p. 394; Aaron L. Friedberg (2005), p. 18.

143 Øystein Tunsjø, US-China Relations: From Unipolar Hedging toward Bipolar Balancing, in Robert S. Ross and Øystein Tunsjø (eds.), *Strategic Adjustment and the Rise of China* (Ithaca and London: Cornell University Press, 2017), p. 41; Michael Tkacik (2018), p. 332. China's constant military buildup receives a great deal of attention by American strategists and neo-conservatives insofar as China modernizes its military as vital national interests, which potentially paralizes future Sino–US relations. See Yinhong Shi, Rising China: Political Leadership, Foreign Policy, and "Chineseness," in Vinod K. Aggarwal and Sara A. Newland (2015), pp. 108–9.

144 See https://www.sipri.org/databases/milex. Meanwhile, US military expenditure is US$ 731,751 million.

assess that China's growing military posture is defensive or reactive to the assertiveness of others in the region.[145]

However, again, most realists assert that a militarized China will keep trying to crowd the US out of East Asia and set boundaries of acceptable behavior to its neighbors, not allowing them to violate the points. In this view, China will seamlessly contrive to become a regional hegemon so as to effectively deal with its various conflicts (Taiwan, the East and South China Seas, and Senkakus/Diaoyudao) and retrieve its sphere of influence (status recalibration).[146]

Until the mid-2000s, China did not regard itself as a realistic challenger to the US and the existing order.[147] Yet, in the wake of the US 2008 economic and financial crisis, China arguably gained confidence in envisioning a future in which China becomes number one, expressing such ambition more assertively.[148] Many scholars note that the decrease in US supremacy and the increase in the US-China rivalry in East Asia have been observed since 2009, from unipolarity to bipolarity.[149]

---

145 Zhu Feng, China's Rise Will Be Peaceful How Unipolarity Matters, in Robert S. Ross and Zhu Feng (2008), p. 40; Edward Wong, Chinese Military Seeks to Extend its Naval Power, *New York Times*, April 23, 2010; Klaus Heinrich Raditio (2019), p. 87; Timothy Glogan, China's' Assertive' South China Sea Policy and Rhetoric: Proactive, Reactive or Myth, Pro Gradu Thesis (University of Turku, 2011), p. 73; Michael D. Swaine and M. Taylor Fravelı, "China's Assertive Behavior—Part Two: The Maritime Periphery," *China Leadership Monitor*, no. 35 (2011).

146 Aaron L. Friedberg (2011), p. 231; Stephen M. Walt, Rising Powers and the Risks of War: A Realist View of Sino-American Relations, in Asle Toje (2018), p. 21 (noting that "no great power wants its primary competitor to have close security alliances with many of its neighbors and to deploy powerful military forces on or near its borders").

147 One Chinese scholar observed in 2005 that "[i]t would be foolhardy ... for Beijing to challenge directly the international order and the institutions favored by the Western world [and] such a challenge is unlikely" mainly because of the lack of necessary economic and military power." See Wang Jisi, "China's Search for Stability with America," *Foreign Affairs*, 84, no. 5 (2005), p. 43. Similarly, Ross observed in 2006 that "China is not a rising power and it is not balancing U.S. power" in East Asia, concluding that "the distribution of power is stable, as China has yet to challenge US military supremacy." See Robert S. Ross, Balance of Power Politics and the Rise of China: Accommodation and Balancing in East Asia, *Security Studies*, 15, no. 3 (July–September 2006), pp 369. 372–3 (adding that "[US] possesses absolute military superiority in maritime East Asia ... Chinese surface vessels both at sea and in port are increasingly vulnerable to U.S. air and naval power").

148 Daniel W. Drezner, Perception, Misperception, and Sensitivity, in Robert S. Ross and Øystein Tunsjø (2017), p. 76; Klaus Heinrich Raditio (2019), p. 138.

149 Robert S. Ross (1999), pp. 81–118; Øystein Tunsjø, US-China Relations: From Unipolar Hedging toward Bipolar Balancing, in Robert S. Ross and Øystein Tunsjø (2017), pp. 60, 65–6 (explaining that China asserted its interests in the maritime domain in the incidents of USNS *Impeccable* (March 2009) and USS *Cowpens* (December 2013)); US Office of Naval Intelligence, *The PLA Navy: New Capabilities and Missions for the 21st Century* (Washington, DC: U.S. Office of Naval Intelligence, 2015), pp. 4, 37 (noting that "Since

Although it is not that all realists presuppose the US decline in East Asia,[150] many realists assume that the potential benefits of changing the US-led system outweigh the perceived costs of achieving that change for China.[151] Notably, Chinese elites begin complaining about the old distribution of power in East Asia, which reveals a harbinger of revisionist complaints. China gradually develops its dissatisfaction with territory distribution, hierarchies of prestige, and the norms and principles that were created when China was weak,[152] expecting more voices and roles in global affairs commensurate with its growing power.[153]

Supposedly, China expected US recognition of Chinese spheres of influence for the SCS and Taiwan in the early 2010s, but to no avail.[154] Again, China has

---

2009, however, friction between China and its neighbors in the South China and East China Seas has grown significantly").

150 For example, Ross argues that despite China's splendid military growth and resultant assertions in East Asian waters, the US sustains its predominance in the maritime domain. See Robert S. Ross, The United States and China in Northeast Asia: Third-Party Coercion and Alliance Relations, in Robert S. Ross and Øystein Tunsjø (2017), p. 261–284. Also, Raditio argues that "the US position as a global power [will be] unchallenged … [and] that China will take over the US position in the near future is unfounded." See Klaus Heinrich Raditio (2019), p. 164.

151 Øystein Tunsjø, Conclusion: East Asia at the Center: Power Shifts and Theory, in Robert S. Ross and Øystein Tunsjø (2017), p. 289; Robert Gilpin, *War and Change in World Politics* (Cambridge: Cambridge University Press, 1981), p. 187. In the meantime, China may challenge the US "when it believes it has sufficient strength" even before its GDP or military capabilities approaches those of the US. See Steven E. Lobell, How Should the US Respond to a Rising China?, in Asle Toje (2018), p. 360.

152 Aaron L. Friedberg (2005), p. 19; House of Commons Foreign Affairs Committee, China and the Rules-Based International System, Sixteenth Report of Session 2017–19, March 26, 2019, pp. 10–12; Oriana Skylar Mastro, "In the shadow of the Thucydides Trap: International Relations Theory and the Prospects for Peace in U.S.-China Relations," *Journal of Chinese Political Science*, 24 (2019), p. 32; Randall L. Schweller and Xiaoyu Pu (2011), p. 43; Robert Gilpin, *War and Change in World Politics* (Cambridge: Cambridge University Press, 1981), p. 187 (arguing that the rising state attempts to "change the rules governing the international system, the division of the spheres of influence, and, most important of all, the international distribution of territory").

153 Great powers invariably wish to retain their sphere of influence in discontent with their position in the international system falling far short of their expected share of power. See Denny Roy (2019), p. 55. See also Doug Bandow, Look Out, Asia: China's Peaceful Rise Is Over, *National Interest*, July 18, 2016, at https://nationalinterest.org/blog/the-skeptics/look-out-asia-chinas-peaceful-rise-over-17026 (noting that "China's emergence as an increasingly significant power has upended the regional status quo. The existing territorial and juridical order was established at a time of Chinese isolation and weakness … Beijing is dissatisfied with the results and … increasingly appears unwilling to live with the status quo").

154 Leszek Buszynski, "The South China Sea: Oil, Maritime Claims, and US–China Strategic Rivalry," *The Washington Quarterly*, 35, no. 2 (2013), pp. 147–8 (noting that "Chinese interest in separate spheres of influence was seen in the preparations for the Hanoi ASEAN

suggested the idea of a New Type of Great Power Relations (新型大国关系) to the US since 2012[155] on the premise that the "most revolutionary change in the international balance of power since modern times" is in full swing.[156] This is why many realism theorists label China as "revisionist," looking for opportunities to shift the balance of power, expelling the US from Asia using force, if necessary (China threat).[157] Of course, Chinese scholars complain about the "revisionist" label or "China threat."[158] To examine the propriety of the "China

Regional Forum in July 2010"). For an account of Taiwan as a Source of friction in US–China relations, see Scott L. Kastner, US–China Economic Integration and its Implications for US Policy in the Taiwan Strait, in Vinod K. Aggarwal and Sara A. Newland (2015), pp. 115–6.

155 Oriana Skylar Mastro, "In the shadow of the Thucydides Trap: International Relations Theory and the Prospects for Peace in U.S.-China Relations," *Journal of Chinese Political Science*, 24 (2019), p. 32.

156 Michael J. Mazarr et al. (2018), p. 72. China has explicitly expressed its goal of becoming a leading global power by 2049, the 100th anniversary of the establishment of the PRC. See Alexi Arbitov, *Engaging China in Nuclear Arms Control* (Carnegie Moscow Center, October 9, 2014).

157 John Mearsheimer (2001), pp. 2–3, 21, 402; Denny Roy (1994), pp. 159–160; James R. Holmes and Toshi Yoshihara, "China's 'Caribbean' in the South China Sea," *SAIS Review*, 26, no. 1 (2006); Michael Tkacik (2018), p. 335. For an account of "China threat," see, e.g., Robert Ross, "Balance of Power Politics and the Rise of China: Accommodation and Balancing in East Asia," *Security Studies*, 15, no. 3 (2006), pp. 355–95; Adam Ward, "China and America: Trouble Ahead?" *Survival*, 45, no. 3 (2003), pp. 35–5; Thomas J. Christensen, "Posing Problems Without Catching Up: China's Rise and the Challenges for US Security Policy," *International Security*, 25, no. 4 (2001), pp. 5–40; Thomas J. Christensen, "Fostering Stability or Creating a Monster? The Rise of China and U.S. Policy toward East Asia," *International Security*, 31, no. 1 (2006), pp. 81–126. In contrast, some scholars argue that China does not have revisionist intentions in its satisfaction with the status quo. See Alastair Iain Johnston, "Is China a Status Quo Power?" *International Security*, 27 (2003), pp. 5–56; David C. Kang, *China Rising: Power and Order in East Asia* (New York: Columbia University Press, 2007); Zhu Feng, China's Rise Will Be Peaceful How Unipolarity Matters, in Robert S. Ross and Zhu Feng (2008), p. 42.

158 Randall L. Schweller and Xiaoyu Pu (2011), pp. 44–7 (noting that "any state that openly espouses a desire to restore a balance of power will be targeted by the hegemon as a threat not only to its primacy but also to its established order and the interests of allies that support that order"). For an account of "US threat," see Zhu Feng, China's Rise Will Be Peaceful How Unipolarity Matters, in Robert S. Ross and Zhu Feng (2008), p. 39. Furthermore, China criticizes the US for labeling it as not a responsible stakeholder that "China can only be described as responsible if it works with [US] in maintaining the existing international order." See Wang Te-chen, "Zhong-Mei yuedi duihua zhuanjia cheng yiti guangfan" [China–US Dialogue Will Start Toward the End of This Month; Expert Says the SubjectsWill beWide-Ranging], Da Gong Bao (July 22, 2009), cited in Alison Adcock Kaufman, "The 'Century of Humiliation,' Then and Now: Chinese Perceptions of the International Order," *Pacific Focus*, 25, no. 1 (2010), p. 15, fn. 36.

threat," China's military posture, strategies, and doctrines are to be reviewed,[159] despite the lack of transparency of the Chinese military-related information.[160]

To sum up, realism concludes that China is destined to seek regional preponderance at any cost with its favorable land security environment[161] as the US achieved regional hegemony in the Western Hemisphere in the 19th century.[162] Chinese writers do not shy away from such a prediction. Men Honghua asserts that regional preponderance is vitally crucial for China, urging China to "gain global influence by becoming the dominant power in the Asia-Pacific region."[163] The SCS is a mere reflection of the Sino-US rivalry evolving around security dilemmas between the two sides; China will undermine the current regional maritime order, America will resist, and less stability and security will inevitably transpire.[164]

3.2 *Power Transition Theory and the Inevitability of War*

Power transitions are a common phenomenon in international relations. In most cases, realists peer into these episodes through the lens of the theory of power transition, which can provide the SCS region with a theoretical analysis. Power transition theory supposes that war is inevitable between China and

---

159 Shiping Tang (2010), p. 259.

160 Office of the Secretary of Defense, Military and Security Developments Involving the PRC 2020, Annual Report to Congress, pp. 15, 86–7 (noting, *inter alia*, that "China's lack of transparency regarding the scope and scale of its nuclear modernization program ... raises questions regarding its future intent as it fields larger, more capable nuclear forces"); Jihyun Kim (2016), p. 27. According to Kydd, states' beliefs about others depend on two variables: the information received and the likelihood of error in reports. See Andrew H. Kydd, *Trust and Mistrust in International Relations* (Princeton: Princeton University Press, 2007), p. 58.

161 Aaron L. Friedberg (2011), pp. 163–170 (noting that "[the condition] of 'land stable, sea changeable, land relaxed, sea tense' has persisted into the twenty-first century").

162 For an extreme version of challenging the military balance of power in the region, see Andrew F. Krepinevich Jr, "How to deter China: the case for archipelagic defense," *Foreign Affairs*, March/April 2015, pp. 78–86; John Mearsheimer (2001), pp. 37–8, 168, 213, 232–8, 371.

163 Men Honghua, "Zhongguo guoji zhanlue liyi de tuozhan (Expansion of China's national strategic interest]," Zhanlue Yu Guanli, No. 1 (March 2003), pp. 83–89, cited in Aaron L. Friedberg (2011), p. 165, fn. 20.

164 Klaus Heinrich Raditio (2019), p. 153; William C. Wohlforth, Not Quite the Same as It Ever Was: Power Shifts and Contestation over the American-Led World Order, in Asle Toje (2018), p. 57; Doug Bandow, Look Out, Asia: China's Peaceful Rise Is Over, *National Interest*, July 18, 2016, at https://nationalinterest.org/blog/the-skeptics/look-out-asia-chinas-peaceful-rise-over-17026.

the US in the SCS, owing to some conditions for war despite the presence of nuclear weapons.[165]

Organski advances power change as *causae belli* because a growing power challenges the creation of a new international order rather than simply wishing to take over the leadership of the existing system.[166] Also, Gilpin suggests that "the replacement of a declining dominant power by a rising dominant power" takes place all the time. In such a process, a rising power is ineluctably obliged to "change the rules governing the system, the division of the spheres of influence, and, most important of all, the international distribution of territory."[167]

Power transition theory postulates that states with enhanced power (a function of population, economic productivity, and political capacity) are non–status quo states,[168] and they demand redistributing power and goods in the system no matter the cost.[169] In this view, fundamental power shifts between the most dominant power and the second most dominant state often beget power transition wars, as with the Peloponnesian War and World War I and II.[170] This is because rapid changes bring about "windows of opportunities" for challengers and the "fear of aggression" for the status quo states.[171]

165 Jack S. Levy, Power Transition Theory and the Rise of China, in Robert S. Ross and Zhu Feng (2008), pp. 17–8.

166 A. F. K. Organski, *World Politics* (New York: Knopf, 1958), p. 441; A. F. K. Organski and Jacek Kugler, *The War Ledger* (Chicago: University of Chicago Press, 1980), p. 13.

167 Robert Gilpin, *War and Change in World Politics* (New York: Cambridge University Press, 1981), pp. 42–3, 187.

168 Jack S. Levy, Power Transition Theory and the Rise of China, in Robert S. Ross and Zhu Feng (2008), p. 18; Robert S. Ross and Zhu Feng, The Rise of China: Theoretical and Policy Perspectives, in Robert S. Ross and Zhu Feng (2008), p. 305.

169 Robert S. Ross and Zhu Feng, Introduction, in Robert S. Ross and Zhu Feng (2008), p. 1.

170 For example, Dale Copeland seems to abridge, by reviewing the literature, that the hegemon starts a preventive war against a rising challenger when it believes it has still more power, while Robert Gilpin claims that the hegemonic war occurs when a rising power is filled with discontent over the lack of benefits from the old system below the level it thinks it deserves. Further, according to Organski, power transition wars are caused by many factors such that a challenger achieves an approximate balance of power with the hegemon, or that a challenger initiates before such a balance is reached. See Dale C. Copeland, *The Origins of Major War* (Ithaca and London: Cornell University Press, 2001), pp. 35–55; Robert Gilpin (1981), pp. 186–210. A. F. K. Organski (1958), p. 333.

171 Stephen M. Walt, Rising Powers and the Risks of War: A Realist View of Sino-American Relations, in Asle Toje (2018), pp. 18–9 (adding that "diplomatic skill, shared political and cultural values, and adroit crisis management ... cannot eliminate the pressures for conflict that major power shifts invariably generate" *ibid.*, 14).

Some realists, such as Wohlforth, Schweller, and Foot, further articulate the utility of hegemonic wars as a practical means of resolving the contradiction and the hierarchy prestige. The nub of their claims is that war could positively resolve the gap (arising from significant power shifts) between a system's material base and its governance superstructure. War also would help heal the ill effects of political inertia, enable a new hegemon to emerge, clarify power relations, and entitle the new hegemon to enact new rules.[172]

The variables that can motivate China to start hegemonic war are the combination of "parity, overtaking, and dissatisfaction."[173] If "the power of a dissatisfied rising state reaches parity with a declining status quo lead state," war is highly likely.[174] Is China (dis)satisfied with the current regional and international system? The realist explanation is that, in an anarchical society, national interests are defined by capabilities. The more capabilities one has, the more state interests will ensue: "[a]mbition follows power."[175]

The Chinese understanding of the international legal and law of the sea system stands in stark contrast to that of the West; as a result, China's dissatisfaction with the current regional maritime legal order can substantially rise. Also, China's frustration with the regional (maritime) order will likely increase insofar as China perceives that the proper "respect" (in the form of, *inter alia,* access to territories and raw materials, or treaty interpretation amenable to China's interests) is not given to China, which is supposed to be accompanied by the narrowed Sino-American power disparities.[176]

---

172 William C. Wohlforth, Not Quite the Same as It Ever Was: Power Shifts and Contestation over the American-Led World Order, in Asle Toje (2018), pp. 59–60; Randall L. Schweller, *Maxwell's Demon and the Silver Hammer* (Baltimore: Johns Hopkins University Press, 2014), p. 107, 143; Rosemary Foot, Restraints on Conflict in the China-US Relationship: Contesting Power Transition Theory, in Asle Toje (2018), p. 81.

173 The relationship among these variables is unclear. See Jack S. Levy, Power Transition Theory and the Rise of China, in Robert S. Ross and Zhu Feng (2008), p. 14.

174 G. John Ikenberry, The Rise of China Power, Institutions, and the Western Order, in Robert S. Ross and Zhu Feng (2008), p. 93. See also Bill Hayton (2014), p. 223–224 (assessing that "China may have the ambition to drive the US away, but does not have the military capacity to do so–for now. Gradually, however, the gap between the two sides will narrow and the chances of conflict will grow"); Jack S. Levy, Power Transition Theory and the Rise of China, in Robert S. Ross and Zhu Feng (2008), pp. 13–14 (noting that "[t]he probability of war is quite low before the challenger achieves parity").

175 Robert S. Ross and Zhu Feng, The Rise of China: Theoretical and Policy Perspectives, in Robert S. Ross and Zhu Feng (2008), p. 305.

176 G. John Ikenberry, The Rise of China Power, Institutions, and the Western Order, in Robert S. Ross and Zhu Feng (2008), p. 94. See also Nico Krisch (2005), p. 374 (noting that a deep-rooted sentiment behind China's legal dissatisfaction pertains to the hegemonic nature

Furthermore, misperception, miscalculation, and the US alliance system may contribute to war between China and the US.[177] First, neither China nor the US could have been prepared for political, legal, and psychological tuning accompanying the shift; it is unprecedented that a poor country with over a 1.4 billion population breaks out of poverty and becomes a military power in human history.[178] Second, misperception and miscalculation arising from the lack of understanding can motivate China and America to wage war.[179] Third, deep American engagement in East Asia through an alliance can usher in war insofar as its allies react aggressively to China's assertiveness in the region.[180]

Power transition theory is premised on a global scale power change; however, as Lemke suggests, the regional hierarchies are seen as nested within the global hierarchy. It means that the same conditions of parity, overtaking, and dissatisfaction can account for variations in regional war.[181] In history, many hegemonic wars have been started over regional conflicts; a war in the SCS between China and the US is feasible.[182]

In *Destined for War,* Allison adduces twelve clues that have historically militated against war between a challenger and a dominant power, which can be abridgely categorized: (1) higher authorities that help resolve rivalry, (2) large economic, political, and security institutions that constrain war, (3) wise and wily leaders, (4) auspicious timing of actions, (5) cultural commonalities that help prevent war, (6) nuclear deterrence, (7) economic interdependence, (8) military alliance, and (9) rising powers' domestic performance.[183]

---

of international law, which has been "utilized by dominant powers to give a semblance of legitimacy to their hegemony").

177 Michael Mastanduno, Realism and Asia in Saadia M. Pekkanen et al. (2014), p. 31.

178 Hugh White (2012), p. 31 (stating that "We have no experience of what such a country will be like, what kind of power it will have, and how it will behave").

179 A. F. K. Organski and Jacek Kugler, *The War Ledger* (Chicago: University of Chicago Press, 1980), p. 21.

180 Jong Kun Choi and Yong-Soo Eun (2018), p. 148.

181 Douglas Lemke, *Regions of War and Peace* (Ann Arbor: University of Michigan Press, 2001). For a contrary view regarding the applicability of power transition theory to the regional level, see Jack S. Levy, Power Transition Theory and the Rise of China, in Robert S. Ross and Zhu Feng (2008), p. 24.

182 Robert S. Ross and Zhu Feng, The Rise of China: Theoretical and Policy Perspectives, in Robert S. Ross and Zhu Feng (2008), p. 298. See also Bill Hayton (2014), p. 201 (noting that As the SCS disputes and the global rivalry between China and the US become interlinked, the SCS is coming to the fore as a "potentially dangerous place").

183 Allison divides nuclear weapons and mutually assured destruction into four categories: "nuclear weapons," "mutually assured destruction," "how war between unclear superpowers is thus no longer a justifiable option," and "leaders of nuclear superpowers must nonetheless be prepared to risk a war they cannot win." See Graham Allison, *Destined for war:*

Given the anarchic nature of the international community and the right of veto by China and the US at the UN Security Council, there are neither higher authorities nor other institutions that help constrain war. The character of leaders and good timing of actions are hard to forecast, but leaders are prone to adopting assertive actions to elicit domestic support for nationalism. With regard to cultural commonalities, a negative assessment will command agreement. The existence of nuclear weapons and mutually assured destruction would seem the most plausible candidates of war avoidance.[184] However, many scholars contend that although the risk of an all-out war between these nuclear superpowers remains low, the risk of armed conflict in maritime East Asia today is markedly high.[185] Tunsjø argues the risk of conventional war in the East Asian Seas is high because regional decision-makers may think that "the possibility of a full-scale invasion or major war is less likely," which poses a direct existential threat to each other.[186] Also, nuclear weapons notwithstanding, the persistent asymmetry in vulnerability renders conventional conflict thinkable.[187]

Although liberalism credits the role of economic interdependence in war avoidance, realism denies the efficacy of economic interdependence. Mearsheimer asserts that political calculations trump economic considerations in the face of national security, as shown by Europe's efforts on the eve of World War I. Mearsheimer also emphasizes the treacherous role of nationalism: "nationalism is at the core of Chinese thinking on Taiwan and the South China Sea."[188] White also observes that "China's leaders will sometimes make

Can America and China escape Thucydides' Trap? (New York: Houghton Mifflin Harcourt, 2017), pp. 187–213.

184 Robert J. Art, The United States and the Rise of China: Implications for the Long Haul, in Robert S. Ross and Zhu Feng (2008), p. 273 (stating that "Nuclear deterrence should work to lower dramatically the possibility of war by either miscalculation or deliberate decision"). See also Jack S. Levy, Power Transition Theory and the Rise of China, in Robert S. Ross and Zhu Feng (2008), p. 25 (pointing out that "power transition theory minimizes the deterrent effects of nuclear weapons on the outbreak of war").

185 Yan Xuetong, China Can Thrive in the Trump Era, *New York Times*, January 25, 2017, at https://www.nytimes.com/2017/01/25/opinion/china-can-thrive-in-the-trump-era.html (noting that "[t]he nuclear deterrent should still prevent an all-out war, but confrontation will be the core of these two giants' relationship for the foreseeable future").

186 Øystein Tunsjø, Conclusion: East Asia at the Center: Power Shifts and Theory, in Robert S. Ross and Øystein Tunsjø (2017), p. 297–8.

187 The question of whether China possesses secure second strike capabilities is uncertain. See Oriana Skylar Mastro (2019), p. 37.

188 John J. Mearsheimer (2014), p. 408.

decisions that they believe enhance China's power and status at the expense of its economy."[189]

The above analysis would arguably conclude that Allison's war-restraining clues are hardly found in East Asia and the SCS, with the only exception being the existence of the American military alliance[190] and China's continuous domestic performance.[191]

An inevitability of war in the SCS pertains to the nature of territorial disputes. Fravel stresses that territorial disputes "have been the most common issue over which states collide and go to war," thereby diagnosing that Asia today is more vulnerable to war, due to many territorial disputes than other parts of the world.[192] Further, Vasquez notes that disputes over strategic territory are regarded as having a high risk of war.[193] Certainly, there is no territorial

---

189 Hugh White (2012), pp. 47–52 (noting further that "When a choice has to be made … in the glare of an international crisis, it is very hard to put economics first"). Moreover, according to some, interlinked economic ties sometimes empower Chinese to exert economic, political, and military heft in the region, diffusing tensions over the SCS territorial disputes. See Yukon Huang (2017), pp. 163–6 (assessing that in the Asian Infrastructure Investment Bank, China holds a nearly 30% voting share, alluding to China's disproportionate power over the patrons); Brahma Chellaney, China's Debt-Trap Diplomacy, *The Hill*, May 2, 2021, at https://thehill.com/opinion/international/551337-chinas-debt-trap-diplomacy (emphasizing that "The heavier the debt burden on the borrower, the greater China's own leverage becomes"); Larry Bell, China's Rare Earth Metals Monopoly Needn't Put an Electronics Stranglehold on America, *Forbes*, April 15, 2012, at https://www.forbes.com/sites/larrybell/2012/04/15/chinas-rare-earth-metals-monopoly-neednt-put-an-electronics-stranglehold-on-america/#251a089b2d6d.

190 Lobell claims that "[expensive] deep engagement encourages reckless behavior on the part of America's allies." See Steven E. Lobell, How Should the US Respond to a Rising China? in Asle Toje (2018), p. 356.

191 Despite some pessimistic projections, many economists see the potential for 5–7% growth of the Chinese economy well into the next decades, becoming the world's largest economy by around 2030. See Yukon Huang (2017), pp. 181–3; Justin Yifu Lin, *Demystifying the Chinese Economy* (New York: Cambridge University Press, 2012); CEBR, World Economic League Table: a world economic league table with forecasts for 193 countries to 2035, December 2020, 12th edition, p. 71, at https://cebr.com/wp-content/uploads/2020/12/WELT-2021-final-23.12.pdf.

192 M. Taylor Frave, "Territorial and Maritime Boundary Disputes in Asia" in Saadia M. Pekkanen et al. (2014), p. 525. See also P.R. Hensel, Territory: Theory and Evidence on Geography and Conflict in J.A. Vasquez (eds.), *What Do We Know About War* (Lanham, MD: Rowman and Littlefield, 2012), p, 57–84; D.B. Carter and H.E. Goesman, "The Making of the Territorial Order: New Borders and the Emergence of Interstate Conflict," *International Organization*, 65, no. 2 (2011), pp. 275–309; John A. Vasquez, *The War Puzzle Revisited* (New York: Cambridge University Press, 2009), pp. 343–362.

193 John A. Vasquez (2009), p. 373 (noting that disputes only involving economic resources can be peacefully settled).

dispute between China and the US in the SCS. However, China will have a territorial problem with the US with the issue of whether a low-tide elevation can be appropriated as territory. The Chinese Society of International Law asserts that the question of appropriation of a low-tide elevation is "in itself a issue of territorial sovereignty."[194] The 2016 SCS arbitration opines that all these low-tide elevations are submerged landmass, incapable of appropriation.[195] If China were to materialize its view by, e.g., proclaiming the outlying archipelago status in and around the Spratly Islands, the US could not accept that, thereby producing a seemingly territorial dispute between the two.

3.3 *A Possible Way out from the Realist Perspective*

If power transition theory is correct, a straightforward American realist policy would be containment or deterrence, as its effectiveness was proved during the Cold War.[196] Western scholars stress, however, that containment hurts US interests a great deal unless China makes a first strike or adopts a militarily aggressive foreign policy toward East Asia. This is because China may make the most of its holdings of Treasury securities, refusing to buy more of them, and the US may take the flak of unilateralism, blaming its premature containment or encirclement.[197] Further, the potential costs and dangers of a power transition war are severe and devastating.[198]

Balance-of-power logic argues that if the rivals can agree on existing balance of power realities beforehand, there would be no war because both sides can reasonably reach the same outcome through negotiation rather than war.[199] If the old order keeps prevailing over the system, war is bound to break out; in

194 Chinese Society of International Law (2018), pp. 265, 296 (arguing that "China has sovereignty over Nansha Qundao (the Spratlys) as a whole; Meiji Jiao, Ren'ai Jiao, Zhubi Jiao, Nanxun Jiao, and Dongmen Jiao are part of Nansha Qundao and, as such, are a part of Chinese territory").

195 The South China Sea Arbitration, Award of 12 July, para. 1203. B. (3)-(7).

196 Scholars assess that with maritime supremacy, the US can utilize its Command of the Global Common, and prevail over the East Asian Seas, maintaining freedom of navigation. See Barry R. Posen, "Command of the Commons: The Military Foundation of U.S. Hegemony," *International Security*, 28, no. 1 (Summer 2003), pp. 5–46; Robert J. Art, The United States and the Rise of China: Implications for the Long Haul, in Robert S. Ross and Zhu Feng (2008), p. 286.

197 Robert J. Art, The United States and the Rise of China: Implications for the Long Haul, in Robert S. Ross and Zhu Feng (2008), pp. 265–6, 284 (noting that premature containment may provide cause to Chinses heavy-handedness).

198 Aaron L. Friedberg (2011), p. 2.

199 John Mearsheimer (2001), pp. 57–58; T.V. Paul, The accommodation of rising powers in world politics, in T.V. Paul (2016), pp. 10–11; James D. Fearon, "Rationalist Explanations for War," *International Organization*, 49, no.3 (Summer 1995), pp. 379–414.

Gilpin's parlance, the current East Asian political situation is in a "state of disequilibrium" within which the existing regional order does not square with the underlying distribution of power and interests.[200] If this equilibrium persists, a rapidly-growing China will invariably seek to reflect the change to reach a new equilibrium in the system. Correcting disequilibrium improves the miscalculation situation (a cause of war) between the two powers.[201] The Chinese motive for challenging the US-led regional order is to "restore a balance of power."[202]

In this respect, international norms can reflect the underlying balance of power between China and the US one way or another. Also, legal institutions can reflect Chinese interests in proportion to its power. In fact, the existing legal status quo reflects the distribution of power immediately after WWII, mirroring the interests of the US and the West.[203] The UNCLOS regime and the East Asian maritime order also reflected Western interests in the 1970s.[204]

It is instructive to review the discussion on international status to understand Chinese assertiveness in the SCS. Political scientists adduce that states seek status as an important national objective.[205] Status theorists explain that status "refers to higher-order beliefs about a state's relative ranking – beliefs about what others believe"[206] and a "rising power needs to be sure that it is being granted privileges because it is a great power":[207] more significantly, "status deficits strongly predict the initiation of conflict."[208] China will derive

200 G. John Ikenberry, A New Order of Things?: China, America, and the Struggle over World Order, in Asle Toje (2018), p. 37.

201 Stephen M. Walt, Rising Powers and the Risks of War: A Realist View of Sino-American Relations, in Asle Toje (2018), p. 18.

202 Randall L. Schweller and Xiaoyu Pu (2011), p. 72.

203 Stephen M. Walt, Rising Powers and the Risks of War: A Realist View of Sino-American Relations, in Asle Toje (2018), p. 15.

204 Third World States often regarded UNCLOS as "the temporary victory of a contested position," not a permanent one. See Surabhi Ranganathan, "Decolonization and International Law: Putting the Ocean on the Map," *Journal of the History of International Law*, 2020, p. 19.

205 Jonathan Renshon, *Fighting for Status: Hierarchy and Conflict in World Politics* (Princeton, N.J.: Princeton University Press, 2017), p. 1 (arguing that "status is more even than the 'everyday currency of international relations,' because status is also the end goal for political leaders, many of whom are plainly obsessed with investing in, seizing, and defending it").

206 Deborah Welch Larson et al., Status and World Order, in T.V. Paul et al., (2014), p. 8.

207 Thodore McLauchlin, Great power accommodation and the processes of international politics, in T.V. Paul (2016), p. 308.

208 Jonathan Renshon (2017), pp. 21, 33, 258 (defining "status community" as a "hierarchy composed of the group of actors that a state perceives itself as being in competition with" p. 33).

status from its position in international law, including a leadership role in developing international norms.[209] In brief, war avoidance is possible "through status concessions before the escalation to violent conflict occurs" in the process of adjusting international law.[210]

It is argued that China's position (satisfied/dissatisfied) on the international order has been highly differentiated in each issue-area of the order.[211] China generally supports the existing order and participates in existing institutions, but it disagrees with some of them, demanding the reform of certain suborders ("selective revisionist").[212] In the case of a maritime legal order, Chinese elites request "reforming representation" within existing maritime institutions (e.g., military activities in foreign EEZs) to reflect the voices of China.[213] Accommodation is the key to peace.[214]

In general, accommodation of China means that China is given the status and perks associated with the rank of great power in the regional or global system, including recognition of its sphere of influence or the decision not to challenge it militarily.[215] It is difficult for the status quo power to decide "reasonable" concessions to aptly satisfy the rising power to the point that it restrains itself from demanding more.[216] In this respect, political scientists explain that a rising power's intention matters in deciding accommodation

209 *Ibid.*, p. 35.

210 *Ibid.*, p. 270.

211 Michael J. Mazarr et al. (2018), p. 4.

212 *Ibid.*, pp. 8, 33. See also Jack S. Levy, Power Transition Theory and the Rise of China, in Robert S. Ross and Zhu Feng (2008), pp. 21, 38 (assuming that China is "participating in international institutions but shaping them to better support China's interests and ambitions"). For a detailed analysis of selective revisionist in terms of international financial institutions, see Daniel McDowell, "New Order: China's Challenge to the Global Financial System," *World Politics Review*, April 14, 2015.

213 Michael J. Mazarr et al. (2018), p. 28.

214 As US power continued to rise, Britain gradually adopted an accommodation policy, came to terms with territorial and commercial disputes in North and South America, and invited American troops to Europe to fight in WWI. See Stephen M. Walt, Rising Powers and the Risks of War: A Realist View of Sino-American Relations, in Asle Toje (2018), p. 21. Accommodation involves "mutual adaptation and acceptance by established and rising powers, and the elimination or substantial reduction of hostility between them." See T.V. Paul, The accommodation of rising powers in world politics, in T.V. Paul (2016), p. 4.

215 T.V. Paul, The accommodation of rising powers in world politics, in T.V. Paul (2016), p. 5.

216 Aaron L. Friedberg (2005), p. 20 (explaining that "Successful policies of engagement/appeasement are certainly possible in theory, but in practice they have proven to be difficult to implement").

or containment.[217] Appeasement is necessary if a rising power is conservative (not harming the vital interests of the status quo power), while containment is best for a highly ambitious power.[218]

Chinese efforts to advance its interpretation of the law of the sea institutions come, for the most part, from its (legitimate) security concern on the oceanfront. Indeed, China had less voices in making the current maritime regimes; some adjustment of the maritime order will satisfy the security demands of China.[219] Further, scholars point out that China does not threaten US core interests, such as American security.[220] If the US does not accommodate Chinese legal interests, China could create different flatforms (alternative institutions) in the ocean system as it did in the international financial regime, thereby duplicating existing US-led institutions and delegitimizing the current order.[221] If America redraws interpretive boundaries of some legal institutions

---

217 Some worry that any reforms to American strategy will inevitably attract more Chinese demands, entailing the collapse the security structure, whereas others claim that if America does not accommodate China, it facilitate China's rise and elicit hard balancing on the part of the great powers. See Lyle J. Goldstein, *Meeting China Halfway: How to Defuse the Emerging US-China Rivalry* (Washington, D.C.: Georgetown University Press, 2015), p. 359; Zhu Feng, China's Rise Will Be Peaceful How Unipolarity Matters, in Robert S. Ross and Zhu Feng (2008), p. 52; Robert S. Ross and Zhu Feng, Introduction, in Robert S. Ross and Zhu Feng (2008), p. 6.

218 Robert S. Ross and Zhu Feng, The Rise of China: Theoretical and Policy Perspectives, in Robert S. Ross and Zhu Feng (2008), pp. 306–7 (emphasizing that "containment policies directed at a cooperative state can beget greater ambitions less amenable to management; appeasement directed toward an ambitious leadership can beget even greater ambition and greater likelihood of instability"). See also Jeffrey W. Legro, Purpose Transitions China's Rise and the American Response, in Robert S. Ross and Zhu Feng (2008), pp. 185–6 (noting that "[i]f a revisionist mindset is guiding China and the U.S. reinforces that with conciliatory policies that allow revisionist parties to claim success Chinese supporters of integration will be marginalized").

219 Chinese lawyers find China's role and influence in the creation and interpretation of UNCLOS insufficient, which is "undoubtedly extremely disproportionate to China's economic status and overall strength." See Zhipeng He and Lu Sun (2020), p. 142.

220 Robert J. Art, The United States and the Rise of China: Implications for the Long Haul, in Robert S. Ross and Zhu Feng (2008), p. 272. See also G. John Ikenberry, The Rise of China Power, Institutions, and the Western Order, in Robert S. Ross and Zhu Feng (2008), p. 110 (observing the benefit of nuclear weapons for the US in saying that "Even if the other major powers wanted to overturn the existing order … war is no longer available … the [US] was lucky enough to be on top when this happened").

221 Michael J. Mazarr et al. (2018), p. 81 (adding that Chinese elits debate whether to support the establishment of an alternative system or to support a stay within the system with specific reforms, ibid., p. 78); Jane Perlez, "China Creates a World Bank of Its Own, and the U.S. Balks," *New York Times*, December 4, 2015, at https://www.nytimes.com/2015/12/05/business/international/china-creates-an-asian-bank-as-the-us-stands-aloof.html

and accepts China as a regional maritime power, Chinese elites will be satisfied that America proactively embraces the new realities of shifting regional power dynamics.[222]

Of course, there is a bottom line for US accommodation.[223] If China prevents freedom of commercial navigation through the SCS, by any means, America will not tolerate it because free trade is at the core of American interests.[224] Unless the Chinese proposal of revision undermines American core interests, war is not inevitable; accommodation is possible.[225]

In short, China would arguably respect the (UN-based) multilateral maritime order embedded in UNCLOS while hoping to change some institutions in which the US has played a disproportionate role since 1945.[226] Realism advises that America and China behave proactively and bilaterally if they want to avoid war, instead of relying on "human wisdom, clever diplomacy, or weak and contested international institutions."[227] Accommodation is a slow and exceptionally complicated process, and balance-of-power considerations seem to call on America to assume a greater role in making adjustments in cooperation with China.[228] Otherwise, the international community and future generations will hold China and America accountable for hegemonic wars. Timing is crucial

(-noting that "resistance by Western officials in the IMF to Chinese demands for expanded voting rights ... reportedly fueled China's determination to set up the AIIB").

222 Robert S. Ross and Zhu Feng, The Rise of China: Theoretical and Policy Perspectives, in Robert S. Ross and Zhu Feng (2008), p. 289. For a similar view, see David Lampton, China and the US Must Get Their Strategic Relationship Right, South China Morning Post, June 8, 2015, at https://www.scmp.com/comment/insight-opinion/article/1818410/china-and-us-must-get-their-strategic-relationship-right (supporting accommodation of the Chinese legitimate aspirations to a greater voice in the region); Øystein Tunsjø, Conclusion: East Asia at the Center: Power Shifts and Theory, in Robert S. Ross and Øystein Tunsjø (2017), p. 289; Katherine Combes, "Between Revisionism and Status Quo: China in International Regimes," *Polis*, 6 (Winter 2011–2012), p. 32.

223 Aaron L. Friedberg (2005), p. 20 (noting that for the status quo power a rising state's ambitions are sometimes too extensive to satisfy).

224 Robert J. Art, The United States and the Rise of China: Implications for the Long Haul, in Robert S. Ross and Zhu Feng (2008), p. 281.

225 Stephen M. Walt, Rising Powers and the Risks of War: A Realist View of Sino-American Relations, in Asle Toje (2018), p. 16.

226 Michael J. Mazarr et al. (2018), p. 5.

227 Stephen M. Walt, Rising Powers and the Risks of War: A Realist View of Sino-American Relations, in Asle Toje (2018), p. 29.

228 Oriana Skylar Mastro (2019), p. 28; T.V. Paul, The accommodation of rising powers in world politics, in T.V. Paul (2016), pp. 16–19. Suppose that the US adjusts the law of sea regime to the extent to which Chinese voices are heard; such accommodation will be "symbolic accommodation" through which China can be satisfied with the progress, expecting further accommodation, and "regional-specific accommodation" in which the US does not

here: if the accommodation does not succeed at the early stage of the shift in power distribution, containment, deterrence, and a gloomy determinism of balance of power will take hold of the strategy.[229]

4 Liberalist Evaluation of the South China Sea Dispute

Liberalists see history as a "smoothly ascending curve" despite anarchy.[230] Liberalists understand that power transition theory entails limitations on understanding the Sino-American power transition in East Asia.[231] China's economic interdependence (with the US and the international community) is at the core of liberal optimism for the Sino-American rivalry in East Asia. Also, international regimes are perceived as helping the status quo power and the challenger alike to restrain from provoking abject conflicts.

4.1 *Optimistic Prediction of Economic Interdependence, International Institutions, and Globalization*

Liberalists are optimists in terms of the prospects for peace, cooperation, and understanding among nations. Economic interdependence, international regimes, and democratization (mix and match) are viewed to provide the pull of peace continually. Trade is viewed to promote democracy in China, thereby eroding security competition between China and the US;[232] in short, there are different types of power transitions, not generating security competition or war.[233]

That being said, liberalism does not entirely rule out the possibility of a Sino-American war. Also, liberalism opens the possibility of the remaking of global order under Chinese auspices as a result of the power shift underway

concede at the global level. See T.V. Paul, The accommodation of rising powers in world politics, in T.V. Paul (2016), p. 6.

229 T.V. Paul, The accommodation of rising powers in world politics, in T.V. Paul (2016), p. 16 (asserting that accommodation is in the self-interest of the US in the long-run).

230 Aaron L. Friedberg (2005), p. 17.

231 Jihyun Kim (2016), p. 29.

232 Aaron L. Friedberg (2005), pp. 12–6.

233 G. John Ikenberry, The Rise of China Power, Institutions, and the Western Order, in Robert S. Ross and Zhu Feng (2008), p. 90; G. John Ikenberry, A New Order of Things?: China, America, and the Struggle over World Order, in Asle Toje (2018), p. 34 (noting that "the future is never simply a reproduction of the past—not least when it comes to struggles over international order").

today.[234] However, again, a commonly held view among liberal theorists posits that China is a satisfied, cooperative, and peaceful country in the present liberal international order.[235] In other words, China is the "conservative great power" or "integrationist" inasmuch as China accepts the "basic principles of the existing international order" despite some sources of dissatisfaction.[236]

First, commercial liberalists argue that economic interdependence helps states shy away from waging war in consideration of its inexorable costs.[237] The economic consequences of war in the region (between China and its neighbors or the US) will influence the decision-making process within each government.[238] Russett argues that war is about two-and-a-half times less likely to break out between highly interdependent states than non-interdependent countries.[239] Liberalist has also adduced empirical data on the efficacy of economic interdependence in war avoidance: for instance, Gartzke et al. point out

---

234 G. John Ikenberry, The Rise of China Power, Institutions, and the Western Order, in Robert S. Ross and Zhu Feng (2008), p. 91 (foreseeing that "[i]f China's material interests truly are frustrated within the existing international order and if it grows into the world's dominant power, the international order will surely be transformed").

235 Zhu Feng, China's Rise Will Be Peaceful How Unipolarity Matters, in Robert S. Ross and Zhu Feng (2008), p. 54. For an overview of China's attitude as a status quo power, see Ann Kent, *Beyond Compliance: China, International Organizations, and Global Security* (Stanford: Stanford University Press, 2007).

236 Jeffrey W. Legro, Purpose Transitions China's Rise and the American Response, in Robert S. Ross and Zhu Feng (2008), pp. 167–8. Meanwhile, liberalism appraises the positive role that the US (as a benign hegemon) has played for the liberal international order since 1945. American has provided the collective goods (e.g., security, free trade backed by freedom of navigation, and free access to the US market by Asian countries), which has helped China and other East Asian countries develop their economy. See Ming Wan, Economic Interdependence and Economic Cooperation, in Muthiah Alagappa (ed.), *Asian Security Order: Normative and Instrumental Features* (Stanford, CA: Stanford University Press, 2003). For an account of public goods, common pool resources, inclusive club goods/patented goods, and private goods, see Vinod K. Aggarwal, Reconciling Multiple Institutions: Bargaining, Linkages, and Nesting, in Vinod K. Aggarwal (ed.), *Institutional Designs for a Complex World: Bargaining, Linkage, and Nesting* (Ithaca and London: Cornell University Press, 1998), pp. 8–13.

237 Stephan Haggard, The Liberal View of the International Relations of Asia, in Saadia M. Pekkanen et al. (2014), p. 56.

238 Rosemary Foot, Restraints on Conflict in the China-US Relationship: Contesting Power Transition Theory, in Asle Toje (2018), p. 93.

239 Bruce Russett, What Else Causes War?, *Boston Review*, at https://bostonreview.net/archives/BR22.5/russett.html#1 (noting that "[i]f we bomb the cities or factories of a close trading partner—where we also are likely to have heavy private investments—we are bombing our own markets, suppliers, and even the property of our own nationals"). In contrast, Potter contends that "[t]he preponderance of empirical findings indicates a negative relationship between economic exchange and conflict." See Philip B.K. Potter,

that states tend to constrain war because of the simple opportunity costs of relinquishing trade and the resolve to break the commercial tie of the other states.[240] Wong has summarized the correlation between economic interdependence and Chinese foreign policy on the SCS dispute over three periods (1950–1999, 2000–2008, and 2009–2015), showing that although during 2009–2015 the islands and reefs were militarized, there have been no documented uses of force due mainly to economic interdependence. Wong predicts that "the potential for conflict in the [SCS] is relatively low, and the use of force should remain constrained so long as economic interdependence and regional norms continue to be consistent."[241]

Sino-American economic relations is one of the most highly interconnected webs in the world. In 2020, China was the largest US goods trading partner (with total trade at $695.5 billion), the third-largest export market (at $120.3 billion), and the largest source of US imports (at $539.2 billion).[242] Similarly, China and its neighbors are also closely interdependent in terms of trade. The Association of Southeast Asian Nations (ASEAN) has replaced the EU to emerge as China's largest trading partner in 2020. Sino-ASEAN bilateral trade has soared from $8 billion in 1991 to $680 billion in 2020, and it is expected to keep growing with the China-ASEAN Free Trade Agreement (CAFTA).[243] A war

---

Globalization, interdependence, and major power accommodation, in T.V. Paul (2016), pp. 58–60.

240 Erik Gartzke, Quan Li, and Charles Boehmer, "Investing in the Peace: Economic Interdependence and International Conflict," *International Organization,* 55, no. 3 (2001), pp. 391–438.

241 Bailey Wong, "Understanding the Potential for Conflict in the South China Sea," Clocks and Clouds, 7, No. 1 (2016), at http://www.inquiriesjournal.com/a?id=1567.

242 In 2015, US exports to China were reported to support 1.8 million new jobs and $165 billion in GDP, and by 2030 US exports to China are expected to rise to more than $520 billion. See Congressional Research Service, US-China Trade Relations, *In Focus,* February 16, 2021, at https://fas.org/sgp/crs/row/IF11284.pdf; Oxford Economics for the US-China Business Council, Understanding the US-China Trade Relationship, January 2017, at www.uschina.org/reports/understanding-us-china-trade-relationship.

243 Wang Yaguang and Mao Pengfei, World Insights: China, ASEAN open new chapter in common development, prosperity, *Xinhua,* July 19, 2021, at http://www.xinhuanet.com/english/asiapacific/2021-07/19/c_1310070503.htm; ASEAN becomes China's leargest trading partner, *Global Times,* March 7, 2020, at https://www.globaltimes.cn/content/1181864.shtml. In addition, with the Regional Comprehensive Economic Partnership (RCEP), which was signed between China and 14 other countries in the Asia Pacific on November 15, 2020, China's economic interdependence with its East Asian neighbors will increase. See Kripa Anand, China-led RCEP to change global order? *Observer Research Foundation,* April 27, 2021; Min Gyo Koo (2009) p. 156 (noting that "the virtual absence of commercial ties between China and Vietnam provided little deterrence to the violent clash in 1988").

involving China, other disputants, and the US will have disastrous economic consequences for all sides. In particular, "[w]e have never before seen the escalation of strategic competition between two countries that are as deeply economically interdependent as America and China."[244]

As we have discussed above, realism refutes the efficacy of economic interdependence in war avoidance; when security is high, economic interdependence reinforces peaceful trends, but when security is low or believed to be low, war is more likely.[245] Moreover, Barbieri points out that under particular circumstances, trade even precipitates conflict.[246] In this regard, liberalists contend that the nature of economic interdependence has dramatically changed from a form of mere trade and exchange in the 19th century to the contemporary transnational production and supply chain, which has a "deeper and more durable impact on national political and security autonomy."[247] Notably, the Chinese regime has gained its legitimacy from an economic performance that is inextricably linked with regional stability.[248] Hence, liberalists predict that China will continue to manage its territorial and maritime disputes to not evolve to an extreme degree.[249]

244 Hugh White (2012), p. 116.

245 Robert J. Art, The United States and the Rise of China: Implications for the Long Haul, in Robert S. Ross and Zhu Feng (2008), p. 271. See also Barry Buzan, "Economic Structure and International Security: The Limits of the Liberal Case," *International Organization*, 38, no. 4 (Autumn 1984), pp. 597–624 (arguing that interdependence does not matter one way or the other in a world dominated by security concerns). Also, realists refute that World War I broke out despite the high level of interdependence, See Jeffrey W. Legro, Purpose Transitions China's Rise and the American Response, in Robert S. Ross and Zhu Feng (2008), pp. 169–171.

246 Katherine Barbieri, *The Liberal Illusion: Does Trade Promote Peace?* (Ann Arbor: University of Michigan Press, 2002).

247 Amitav Acharya, Thinking Theoretically about Asian IR, in David Shambaugh and Michael Yahunda (2014), p. 70. See also Rosemary Foot, Restraints on Conflict in the China-US Relationship: Contesting Power Transition Theory, in Asle Toje (2018), p. 92 (noting that "Interdependence in 2014 was not the same as interdependence in 1914").

248 Jihyun Kim (2016), p. 52; John Mearsheimer (2001), p. 407–408 (noting that "[p]ublics today expect their leaders to deliver economic growth; if they fail, they are likely to be thrown out of office ... In a world of economically interdependent states, leaders have a marked aversion to conflict, for fear it will put an end to prosperity as well as their political careers").

249 Meanwhile, Stephan Haggard points out that economic interdependence disproportionately provides China with the basis of political leverage, thereby engendering bandwagoning as dependent trading partners accommodate China's economic and strategic interests. See Stephan Haggard, "The Liberal View of the International Relations of Asia" in Saadia M. Pekkanen et al. (2014), p. 56.

Second, neoliberal institutionalists believe that proper international institutions can provide cooperation and collective security, enabling states to avoid armed conflict.[250] Empirical findings show that dense networks of membership in international institutions "make an independent contribution to the avoidance of serious militarized disputes."[251] Developing a multilateral mechanism has served to shore up "liberal peace" by constraining force in East Asia through engagement and soft balancing.[252] In this view, institutions are tools of states, by which the political formation reflecting the distribution of state power is processed.[253]

Complex interdependence theory further emphasizes the role of international institutions. When multiple channels (interstate, transgovernmental, and transnational) connect societies, multiple agendas are arranged in the absence of a clear hierarchy, and the role of military force is limited (a complex interdependence situation), and international institutions play important roles in providing agenda-setting and coalition-formation.[254] Indeed, multiple issues are mixed in the SCS, and the players often formulate coalitions per issue area.[255]

East Asia was a region without a sense of community during post-World War II.[256] However, Aggarwal and Koo assess that the "new institutional

---

250 T.V. Paul, The accommodation of rising powers in world politics, in T.V. Paul (2016), p. 13; Vinod K. Aggarwal, Reconciling Multiple Institutions: Bargaining, Linkages, and Nesting, in Vinod K. Aggarwal (1998), p. 11.

251 Bruce Russett, John R. Oneal, and David R. Davis, "The Third Leg of the Kantian Tripod for Peace: International Organizations and Militarized Disputes, 1950–85," *International Organization*, 52, no. 3 (Summer 1998), pp. 441–467.

252 Vinod Aggarwal, *Liberal Protectionism: The International Politics of Organized Textile Trade* (Berkeley: University of California Press, 1985), p. 28; T.V. Paul, The accommodation of rising powers in world politics, in T.V. Paul (2016), p. 23.

253 G. John Ikenberry, The Rise of China Power, Institutions, and the Western Order, in Robert S. Ross and Zhu Feng (2008), p. 92.

254 Robert O. Keohane and Joseph S. Nye (2012), pp. 20–1, 31.

255 *Ibid.*, pp. 29–30 (noting a positive role of institutions for small and weak states concerning political initiative and linkage). Regional institutions, such as ASEAN, ASEAN+3, AIIB, and the Shanghai Consensus are understood to play a great role in this political bargaining process. See Toru Takahashi, What Beijing really wants from South China Sea code of conduct, *Nikkei Asian*, August 12, 2019, at https://asia.nikkei.com/Spotlight/Comment/What-Beijing-really-wants-from-South-China-Sea-code-of-conduct.

256 Min Gyo Koo (2009) p. 38. The East Asian institutional peculiarity (consensus decision-making structures, nonbinding commitments, and a lack of delegation in scope) has been blamed for the cause of limited cooperation of the region. See Stephan Haggard, "The Liberal View of the International Relations of Asia" in Saadia M. Pekkanen et al. (2014), p. 54.

environment in Asia now revolves around the proliferation of FTAs, regional financial cooperation, and bilateral and minilateral security dialogues."[257] Also, as Oksenberg and Economy note, China's increasing participation in regional institutions is the stabilizing effects of regional politics.[258]

On this basis, liberalists expect that the SCS dispute and the Sino-American rivalry in East Asia will be contained by proliferative institutions that support the negotiation process, mutual policy adjustments, access to information, and dispute resolution.[259] In this view, regime building with narrow membership will be an effective expedient, enabling the conclusion of agreements and more high-level meetings.[260]

In short, liberalists view China as a satisfied power within economic interdependence, multilateral institutions, and globalization; as a corollary, China will not wage war or challenge the fundamental elements of international order, despite territorial and maritime dissatisfaction.[261] This liberalist prediction is further bolstered by the argument that domestic vulnerabilities (such as political reform or good governance), the lack of immediate American military threats, and domestic economic priorities will prevent China from taking a dangerous measure.[262]

---

257 Vinod K. Aggarwal and Min Gyo Koo (eds.), *Asia's new institutional architecture: Evolving structures for managing trade, financial, and security relations* (New York: Springer, 2008), pp. 290–291.

258 Michael Oksenberg and Elizabeth Economy, Introduction: China Joins the World, in Michael Oksenberg and Elizabeth Economy (eds.), *China Joins the World: Progress and Prospects* (New York: Council on Foreign Relations, 1999), pp. 1–41.

259 Stephan Haggard, "The Liberal View of the International Relations of Asia" in Saadia M. Pekkanen et al. (2014), pp. 45–6. A growing body of empirical evidence suggests that institutions not only facilitate functional cooperation, but also have the broader effect of moderating conflict. See Edward D. Mansfield and Jon C. Pevehouse, "Institutions, Interdependence, and International Conflict, in Gerald Schneider et al. (2003), pp. 233–50.

260 Regime theorists put forward several benefits of regime building, such as (1) lowering transactional costs (multilateral mechanism is cheaper than multiple bilateral contacts), (2) providing information (thereby reducing the fear of being lied and minimizing misunderstanding, and (3) developing reputations (thereby putting convince into other members that interaction will continue for the foreseeable future). See also Vinod Aggarwal (1985), p. 28; Robert O. Keohane (1985), pp. 89–96, 105; Stephan Haggard, "The Liberal View of the International Relations of Asia" in Saadia M. Pekkanen et al. (2014), pp. 54–55.

261 Jihyun Kim (2016), p. 54.

262 Tony Saich, *Governance and Politics of China,* 2d ed. (Houndmills: Palgrave Macmillan, 2004), p. 169; Avery Goldstein, "Great Expectations: Interpreting China's Arrival," *International Security*, 22 (Winter 1997–98), pp. 36–73; Zhu Feng, China's Rise Will Be Peaceful How Unipolarity Matters, in Robert S. Ross and Zhu Feng (2008), p. 47; Rosemary Foot, Restraints on Conflict in the China-US Relationship: Contesting Power Transition Theory, in Asle Toje (2018), p. 94.

4.2 *The South China Sea Dispute within the Current World Order*

Political liberalists assume that Chinese dissatisfaction with regional maritime order notwithstanding, the current international order post-1945 has reached a point at which "it is harder to overturn and easier to join."[263] What is the characteristic of the current international order? Liberalists assert that the current international order established by the US is "inclusive enough to accommodate China's rise and viable enough to survive China's challenge."[264]

First, the architecture of the current order (America) was isolated from the other powers as it grew powerful without conquest. Second, the current rules-governed multilateral order produces reciprocal, consensual, and institutionalized relations, which are more benevolent and less coercive. This means that governing power lies not in one hegemon but an array of great powers, middle and small powers, and stakeholders while economic gains are spread across the system.[265] Third, the existing liberal international order, upon which the East Asian maritime order has nested, is a "more stable, expansive, and deeply integrated order" in which the US yields institutionalized hegemonic leadership offering attractions and opportunities for participants, including China.[266] As a corollary, the existing international order (materialized in democracy, capitalism, openness, a system of the American alliance, the rule of law, and human rights) makes a Chinese effort to oppose and challenge all the more difficult; "China faces a very different type of status quo international order than past rising states."[267]

As a matter of fact, China has benefited most from the existing order.[268] Thus, liberalists anticipate that the current order will likely remain the same as

---

263 G. John Ikenberry, The Rise of China Power, Institutions, and the Western Order, in Robert S. Ross and Zhu Feng (2008), pp. 91, 106 (parsing that the nature of the current order influences "China's underlying interests, security dilemma dynamics, and the overall geopolitical balance of power between China and the West").

264 Congyan Cai (2019), p. 1.

265 G. John Ikenberry, A New Order of Things?: China, America, and the Struggle over World Order, in Asle Toje (2018), pp. 41–2, 46; G. John Ikenberry, The Rise of China Power, Institutions, and the Western Order, in Robert S. Ross and Zhu Feng (2008), p. 95.

266 G. John Ikenberry, The Rise of China Power, Institutions, and the Western Order, in Robert S. Ross and Zhu Feng (2008), p. 100 (noting that "The institutional underpinning of this order made America's power position both more durable and less threatening to other states"); G. John Ikenberry, A New Order of Things?: China, America, and the Struggle over World Order, in Asle Toje (2018), p. 41.

267 G. John Ikenberry, A New Order of Things?: China, America, and the Struggle over World Order, in Asle Toje (2018), pp. 34–6.

268 From this perspective, Ikenberry supposes China backing the WTO regime that "[t]he world order may be hierarchical but powerful states do abide by WTO rulings. A rising

the post-World War II international order regardless of the US decline. Again, the Chinese government derives its legitimacy from economic performance; performing under the existing order will guarantee the success of this goal.[269] Indeed, China supports the current UN-based international order, if not in its entirety.[270] From this perspective, China is viewed to remain within the regional order unless its survival is threatened[271] and perceived working within the current order as enhancing its sovereignty (territorial integrity and autonomy).[272]

Political scientists divide the attitude of a growing power respective of its intention for an international order. Legro divides it into (1) integration (accepting the dominant rules of the existing order; "status quo," "satisfied," or "conservative), (2) revision (seeking to revise the current system; "dissatisfied" or "revolutionary"), and (3) separation (attempting to separate from the dominant rules). Legro explains Chinese leaders today sticking to "integration."[273] On the other hand, Friedberg divides rising powers' intention into four gradations: separatist, integrationist, revisionist, and revolutionist. In this gradation, revisionists are defined as having more modest and limited aims, seeking marginal adjustments to the status quo, not seeking fundamental change.[274]

Meanwhile, Schweller and Pu adduce three possible Chinese visions of global order: (1) a new Chinese order by evincing a competing view on global governance (a spoiler), (2) a modified liberal order by working within the existing system (a supporter), and (3) a negotiated order by evading responsibilities

---

China will want these rule- based protections." See G. John Ikenberry, The Rise of China Power, Institutions, and the Western Order, in Robert S. Ross and Zhu Feng (2008), p. 107.

269 Jeffrey W. Legro, Purpose Transitions China's Rise and the American Response, in Robert S. Ross and Zhu Feng (2008), pp. 180–1 (noting that "economic prosperity has also emerged as a core responsibility of government").

270 Fu Ying, "Doubling Down? China and International Order(s)," China-US Focus, Munich Security Conference, February 13, 2016, at https://www.chinausfocus.com/foreign-policy/putting-the-orders-shift-in-perspective/.

271 Zhu Feng, China's Rise Will Be Peaceful How Unipolarity Matters, in Robert S. Ross and Zhu Feng (2008), p. 43.

272 Jeffrey W. Legro, Purpose Transitions China's Rise and the American Response, in Robert S. Ross and Zhu Feng (2008), p. 181.

273 Jeffrey W. Legro, "What China Will Want: The Future Intentions of a Rising Power," *Perspectives on Politics*, 5, no. 3 (September 2007), p. 516–8; Jeffrey W. Legro, Purpose Transitions China's Rise and the American Response, in Robert S. Ross and Zhu Feng (2008), pp. 164–9 (showing that the China's approach has shifted from revisionism to integration over time, such as (1) Qing, 1800–60 (separatist), 2) Republican, 1896–1939 (integrationist), (3) Mao, 1949–76 (revisionist), (4) Deng, 1978–96 (integrationist), (5) Post-Deng, 1997– (integrationist).

274 Aaron L. Friedberg (2005), pp. 26–7.

and selectively contributing to global governance, while seeking a gradual implementation of its vision (a shirker). Schweller and Pu predict the "modified liberal order" for a feasible order that China pursues, claiming that Chinese dissatisfaction with the existing order lies not in the "essential rules of the game" *per se* but in "representation and the application of the rules."[275] This analysis is shared by Mazarr et al. in that "China has not been an opponent of the postwar order—it is revisionist concerning US hegemony, not the concept of a rule-based order."[276]

Even if China were a revisionist (in Legro's definition) or revolutionist (in Friedberg's definition), this would not necessarily mean that China opposes all the system's existing principles and norms. Great powers can have different regional and global interests, thereby exercising their power in a heterogeneous manner.[277] China can seek reform in a specific issue-area, though respecting the existing broad outlines of order, to stabilize rules through reflecting new balance-of-power realities.[278] Taken together, I argue that China's attitude toward the law of the sea regime has been "revisionist" in Friedberg's terms since the 2016 SCS arbitration (Tables 3.1 and 3.2).

To sum up, liberalism predicts that China will not overthrow a rules-based multilateral order *per se* in East Asia,[279] rather primarily demanding "a voice within global institutions and manipulating the rules and regimes to suit their

---

275 Randall L. Schweller and Xiaoyu Pu (2011), pp. 50–51, 58.

276 Michael J. Mazarr et al. (2018), p. 66 (noting that China does not see itself as revisionist against the multilateral system). Mazarr et al. also put forward that China may take different approaches to different issues: supportive participant, free rider or spoiler. See *ibid.*, pp. 21–22, 92.

277 T.V. Paul, The accommodation of rising powers in world politics, in T.V. Paul (2016), p. 10. A similar observation, but with different implications, is adduced by realists. Walt assesses that China may have no intention to overturn the entire international order, aiming to challenge US dominance in Asia. See Stephen M. Walt, Rising Powers and the Risks of War: A Realist View of Sino-American Relations, in Asle Toje (2018), p. 26 (noting the possibility that a low-level rivalry over the SCS is easily turning into a "far more dangerous test of strength").

278 Theodore McLauchlin, Great power accommodation and the processes of international politics, in T.V. Paul (2016), p. 302.

279 For instance, Guide Jia, then Director-General for the Department of Treaty and Law of the Chinese Ministry of Foreign, in 2019 rather denounces the US as adopting "unilateralism, protectionism and bullying behavior rise" and laments multilateralism, international law and order are challenged and threatened by such US behaviors. See JIA Guide, New China and International Law: Practice and Contribution in 70 Years, *Chinese Journal of International Law*, 18, no. 4 (2019), p. 732.

TABLE 3.1 China's attitude toward the law of the Sea Regime

Period	Attitude	Evidence
1969–1971 (From the Foundation of PRC, through UNCLOS I (1958), to the Acquisition of the UN Membership (1971)	From Revolutionist to Separatist	Not being a member of the UN, opposed the imperialistic nature of the law of the sea Proclaimed the territorial sea up to 12 nm, not conferring innocent passage on foreign vessels
1971–1982 (From the Acquisition of the UN Membership to the Adoption of UNCLOS)	Integrationist	Identifying itself as the leader of the Third World Adopting the open-door policy in December 1978
1983–2016 (On the heels of UNCLOS III to the South China Sea Arbitration	Integrationist with Some Dissatisfaction	Making significant inroads in implementing UNCLOS in the domestic domain (see Table 3.2) Taking part in the exploration for polymetallic nodules of the international seabed area in 2001
2016–now (post the SCS Arbitration)	Revisionist (in Friedberg's term)	Having scaled up its legal campaign to aim at requiring marginal adjustments to regional maritime order in East Asia, to reassure the international community that its interpretation of UNCLOS is fairer for and palatable to the interest of coastal states[a]

a For example, see Chinese Society of International Law (2018).

interest."[280] The question that arises is what the Chinese-envisioned regional maritime order will be. Western writers grumble about the lack of a coherent or specific view of a Chinese-led regional order and the blurriness of how it

280 G. John Ikenberry, A New Order of Things?: China, America, and the Struggle over World Order, in Asle Toje (2018), p. 51 (abridging that the current discussion pertains to fairness and justice in the organization of the global order and the growing need for China's voice to be heard); Rosemary Foot, "Chinese Strategies in a US-Hegemonic Global Order: Accommodating and Hedging," *International Affairs*, 82, no. 1 (2006), p. 93.

TABLE 3.2 Participation in International Maritime Institutions—China and the US

	China	United States
UNCLOS	O	X
International Tribunal for the Law of the Sea	O	X
Commission on the Limits of the Continental Shelf	O	X
International Court of Justice	Δ (national judge O; acceding jurisdiction X)	Δ (national judge O; acceding jurisdiction X)
Antarctic Treaty System	O	O
Arctic Council	Δ (observer)	O (full membership)

achieves the goal.[281] However, as far as regional maritime order is concerned, China has evinced a new Chinese modified order.[282] As detailed in Chapter 2, the Chinese legal view on international law and the law of the sea is conspicuous enough, focusing on adjusting the post-1945 maritime legal system.[283]

4.3 *A Possible Way out from the Liberalist Perspective*

Liberalism evaluates that major Sino-American war is avoidable on the back of US, Chinese, and other claimants' enmeshment in the web of global and regional economy and institutions under globalization.[284] In this view, actors are encouraged to enhance their economic interdependence continually. Nevertheless, on the eve of World War I, observers in both Britain and Germany

281 Michael J. Mazarr et al. (2018), p. 104.

282 Randall L. Schweller and Xiaoyu Pu (2011), p. 59.

283 Chinese Journal of International Law extensively provides a venue of debate for Western scholars and their Chinese counterparts on the issues of human rights law, the law of the sea, international dispute settlement regime, and by doing so it evinces the Chinese interpretation of international law. Roberts points out that "the Chinese government has adopted policies aimed at encouraging the development of lawyers with knowledge of international law and experience gained in Western legal systems, but its goals are expressly nationalistic: 'the priority is to cultivate international law professionals who have knowledge of international laws and can participate in international affairs in order to protect national interests.'" See Anthea Roberts (2017), p. 44.

284 Robert S. Ross and Zhu Feng, The Rise of China: Theoretical and Policy Perspectives, in Robert S. Ross and Zhu Feng (2008), p. 314 (attributing mitigation of security dilemma to unipolarity, regional bipolarity, geography, and weapons systems).

had predicted peace rather than war, based on growing economic links and societal connections; clearly, interdependencies failed to avoid war.[285]

Liberalists acknowledge that war may break out in the East Asian Seas if the existing order fundamentally threatens China's economy and security interests.[286] In this respect, liberalists emphasize the importance of knowing Chinese concerns, democratizing the Chinese regime, and utilizing liberal institutions to avoid the "Thucydides' trap."[287]

First, understanding China's interests within the current order is essential. Liberalists argue that the US (and the international community) should pay considerable attention to China's claims and interests to realize "where the risks of confrontation and the necessity of accommodation lie."[288] As discussed above, accommodation is necessary because China shows general respect for the concept of international law and multilateral order, and Chinese regional security interests do not pose threats to the US and the East Asian order, despite the ideological and policy gaps between actors.[289]

Liberalism warns of a stark dichotomy of revisionist versus status quo (confrontation or support) that neglects China's complex foreign policy circumstance.[290] If the existing maritime order responds to China's voices flexibly out of regard for its core interests, China will not oppose or overturn the current order.[291] Further, some writers argue that if China pursues a new maritime order, it would not contain a distinctively different set of organizational principles.[292]

---

285 Aaron L. Friedberg (2005), p. 45.

286 G. John Ikenberry, The Rise of China Power, Institutions, and the Western Order, in Robert S. Ross and Zhu Feng (2008), p. 114.

287 Stephen M. Walt, Rising Powers and the Risks of War: A Realist View of Sino-American Relations, in Asle Toje (2018), p. 28. Also, wise statecraft, sophisticated diplomacy, and prudent and far-sighted foreign policies are understood as necessary.

288 Theodore McLauchlin, Great power accommodation and the processes of international politics, in T.V. Paul (2016), p. 295. See also Steven E. Lobell, Realism, balance of power, and power transitions, in T.V. Paul (2016), pp. 33–52 (calling on Western observers to investigate the origins of conflict in a specific way).

289 Terrence Kelly et al., *The U.S. Army in Asia, 2030–2040* (Santa Monica, Calif.: RAND Corporation, 2014), p. 135.

290 Michael J. Mazarr et al. (2018), p. 107; Theodore McLauchlin, Great power accommodation and the processes of international politics, in T.V. Paul (2016), pp. 305–6.

291 G. John Ikenberry, A New Order of Things?: China, America, and the Struggle over World Order, in Asle Toje (2018), p. 41; Robert S. Ross and Zhu Feng, The Rise of China: Theoretical and Policy Perspectives, in Robert S. Ross and Zhu Feng (2008), p. 309.

292 G. John Ikenberry, The Rise of China Power, Institutions, and the Western Order, in Robert S. Ross and Zhu Feng (2008), p. 108.

Second, democratic peace theory (democracies hardly wage war with each other) anticipates China becoming a democratic nation down the road. Democratic peace theorists examine that the current Chinese political culture, ensconced in economic development and increasing openness to trade, may engender a long-term transition to democracy; in the end, a democratized China enables a peaceful power transition.[293] Two aspects need to be noted: (1) a China that is in transition from authoritarianism toward democracy is more prone to war, at least in its early stages of political developments,[294] and (2) China's ruling elites have no interest in democracy; they assert that China is "too complex and turbulent to be governable by a truly open, competitive form of democracy."[295]

Third, liberalism suggests regime building for the resolution of the SCS dispute. Regime theorists expect regimes to work in East Asia, facilitating cooperation among disputants despite anarchy because the disputants' interests are not necessarily conflictual.[296] The more China engages in regional and international regimes, the less China will consider waging war.[297] How much can international institutions reduce the Sino-American rivalry in East Asia? Scholarship has yet to clarify the relationship between regimes and the (re) distribution of power;[298] however, it is clear that "current power shifts in the international system have created stresses for a variety of institutions."[299]

One may argue that we do not need a new regime for the SCS because the ASEAN regime and relevant documents therein (such as the Declaration on

293 Robert S. Ross and Zhu Feng, The Rise of China: Theoretical and Policy Perspectives, in Robert S. Ross and Zhu Feng (2008), p. 304; Aaron L. Friedberg (2005), p. 15; Kai He, Chna's bargaining strategies for a peaceful accommodation after the Cold War, in T.V. Paul (2016), p. 220 (explaining that in 2006, 121 of the 194 countries are some type of democracy, and thus, China may want to become a democratic regime as well).

294 Aaron L. Friedberg (2005), pp. 30–1.

295 Andrew J. Nathan and Bruce Gilley, *China's New Rulers: The Secret Files* (New York: New York Review of Books, 2003), p. 263 (stating further that China's elites "see themselves as a qualified managerial elite, uniquely able to manage their society's modernization," out of conviction that the Communist Party should stay in power).

296 Anu Bradford, Regime Theory, in Rudiger Wolfrum (ed.), *Max Planck Encyclopedias of International Law* (Oxford: Oxford University Press, 2012), Vol. VIII, pp. 737–8.

297 Ronald L. Tammen and Jacek Kugler (2006), p. 54.

298 Theodore McLauchlin, Great power accommodation and the processes of international politics, in T.V. Paul (2016), p. 304.

299 Vinod K. Aggarwal, Reconciling Multiple Institutions: Bargaining, Linkages, and Nesting, in Vinod K. Aggarwal (eds), *Institutional Designs for a Complex World: Bargaining, Linkages, and Nesting* (Cornell University Press, 1998), pp. 1–2 (explaining that "changing power relationship in the international security system ... have challenged the post-World War II consensus among western powers").

Conduct or a future Code of Conduct) will function as workable regimes. However, the SCS region is closer to a "non-regime situation" due to the lack of agreed norms and procedures or exceptions to the rules.[300]

Scholars point out that ASEAN lacks the capacity to deal with the SCS dispute with China.[301] To begin with, only four of the ten states in ASEAN are involved in territorial and maritime disputes with China, rendering the majority of ASEAN members to have little interest in the dispute. Next, six non-SCS ASEAN members want neither to sacrifice their ties with China nor compromise because of the perceived high stakes, focusing on the benefits of Chinese investment and largess. As a corollary, ASEAN is internally divided and pulled in different directions as an "easy-to-manipulate regional entity."[302] The disqualification of ASEAN for the SCS dispute is best exemplified by the 2012 ASEAN Summit in which Cambodia (chair) contrived to keep the SCS subject off the agenda, ending up with a failure to issue a joint statement for the first time in ASEAN history.[303] China may also find ASEAN unsuitable for attending to the regional problems or integration to establish an East Asian Community that "would develop a sense of 'we-ness' that excludes the West," and will be ingrained in China's traditional cultural influence.[304]

The efficacy of a soon-to-be Code of Conduct is suspect as well.[305] This is simply because a settlement of the territorial and maritime dispute is not a

300 Robert O. Keohane and Joshep S. Nye, Jr. (2012), p. 17.

301 For a contrary view regarding the growing capacity of ASEAN, see Jihyun Kim (2016), p. 56 (arguing that "[a]s a more cohesive regional entity ASEAN would be able to influence the rising China's emergence ... [taking] part in more tangible multilateral conflict management in the [SCS]").

302 Bill Hayton (2014), p. 192; Jihyun Kim (2016), p. 34; M. Taylor Fravel, "Territorial and Maritime Boundary Disputes in Asia" in Saadia M. Pekkanen et al. (2014), pp. 539–540; Mark J. Valencia, "A South China Sea Code of Conduct? Don't Get Your Hopes Up," *The Diplomat*, May 30, 2017, at https://thediplomat.com/2017/05/a-south-china-sea-code-of-conduct-dont-get-your-hopes-up/.

303 Jihyun Kim (2016), p. 41.

304 Michael Tkacik (2018), p. 330; Mark Beeson and Fujian Li, "Charmed or Alarmed? Reading China's Regional Relations," *Journal of Contemporary China*, 21, no. 73 (November 2011), p. 41.

305 In August 2017, the parties adopted a bare-bones framework for the COC, and on August 2, 2018, Singapore's Foreign Minister Vivian Balakrishnan announced that the sides had reached agreement on a single draft negotiating text for the COC. Leaked details of the text show that significant hurdles remain, especially over the most sensitive issues like the agreement's geographic scope, potential dispute settlement mechanisms, and details of resource exploration and development. See Defusing the South China Sea Disputes: A Regional Blueprint – A Report of the CSIS Expert Working Group on the South China Sea, Center for Strategic & International Studies, October 2018, p. 2.

feasible goal of the Code of Conduct which will merely purport to head off the tension of regional conflict. Again the non-claimant ASEAN members have no direct stakes.[306] As a matter of law, a final resolution of sovereignty and maritime claims should be resolved by applying international law. It is unfeasible for a Code of Conduct to deal with all the essential issues, such as fisheries management, joint development of oil and gas, and environmental protection, let alone territorial sovereignty and delimitation.[307]

Other difficulties place hope in a Code of Conduct and include the way it is negotiated and the conditions that China imposes. Ten ASEAN members negotiate bilaterally with China (not as a group against China), and China allegedly demands that a Code of Conduct reflect its positions that: (1) UNCLOS has no bearing on the SCS, (2) joint military exercises with foreign states, other than China and the claimants, should receive the prior consent of all the signatories, and (3) resource development should be conducted only by signatories.[308] Obviously, UNCLOS should prevail over any other documents that fall far short of hard law. Thus, the US will hold military exercises (jointly or unilaterally) in the SCS based on its UNCLOS interpretation no matter how the Code of Conduct is stipulated.[309]

Another legal aspect to note is that the SCS may have the high seas area depending on methods that decide the legal status of maritime features (rocks or islands or submerged features) in the Spratly or Paracel Islands.[310] In case

306 Furthermore, Nehginpao Kipgen argues that it remains unclear whether a future COC is legally binding or not, and if it were to take the form of a legally binding, no enforcement measures will be available in case of China's infringement. See Nehginpao Kipgen, *The Politics of South China Sea Disputes* (London & New York: Routledge, 2020), p. 106.

307 Defusing the South China Sea Disputes: A Regional Blueprint–A Report of the CSIS Expert Working Group on the South China Sea, *Center for Strategic & International Studies*, October 2018, p. 2. See also Gregory B Poling, "South China Sea Code of Conduct Still a Speck on the Horizon," *East Asia Forum*, September 6, 2018, at https://www.eastasiaforum.org/2018/09/06/south-china-sea-code-of-conduct-still-a-speck-on-the-horizon/.

308 Toru Takahashi, What Beijing really wants from South China Sea code of conduct, *Nikkei Asia,* August 12, 2019, at https://asia.nikkei.com/Spotlight/Comment/What-Beijing-really-wants-from-South-China-Sea-code-of-conduct; Jim Gomez, "Philippines: China Wanted to Restrict Foreign Forces at Sea," *AP News*, September 11, 2019, at https://apnews.com/article/72416e1ced064a7290c6687c206a92a0.

309 In November 2018, John Bolton, then US national security adviser, made the point that the US would oppose any agreements between China and other claimants if they hamstring freedom of navigation. See Jake Maxwell Watts, Bolton Warns China Against Limiting Free Passage in South China Sea, *Wall Street Journal*, November 13, 2018, at https://www.wsj.com/articles/bolton-warns-china-against-limiting-free-passage-in-south-china-sea-1542110191.

310 The South China Sea Arbitration (The Republic of Philippines v. The Republic of China), Award of 12 July 2016, paras. 539–551.

that the high seas and the Area (the seabed and subsoil underneath the high seas) exist, the relevant UNCLOS provisions should also prevail.[311]

5 Constructivist Evaluation of the South China Sea Dispute

The theoretical tools of constructivism are "useful and valid in the examination of East Asia's international relations," which involves the SCS dispute and the Sino-American rivalry.[312] Constructivism focuses on the role of ideational forces (culture, norms, identity, epistemic communities, etc.) instead of a purely materialistic perspective. The birth of ASEAN in 1967 and regionalism in Southeast Asia are inadequately explained through the lens of realism or liberalism; rather, a shared identity and ideational forces are attributable to regionalism.[313] Moreover, some regional aspects, such as colonial history or the century of humiliation, bode well for constructivist theoretical claims.[314]

5.1 *Beliefs, Ideas, Identities, and the South China Sea Dispute*

Constructivists believe in the potential malleability of social relationships.[315] Compared to realism and liberalism, the filtration of domestic politics in understanding international relations is the strong point of constructivism.[316] Yet, the lack of theory on power transition is the weak point of constructivism as a theoretical tool for the SCS dispute. Nevertheless, constructivist ideas on change can suggest the expedient of peaceful power transition and the accommodation of rising powers.[317]

In this view, the development of the SCS dispute and the Sino-American rivalry are subject to change in accordance with how people think: beliefs

311 The high seas are "open to all States," and the Area and its resources are "common heritage of mankind" which development should be subject to Part XI of UNCLOS. See Part VII (High Seas) and Part XI (The Area) of UNCLOS.

312 David Leheny, "Constructivism and International Relations in Asia" in Saadia M. Pekkanen et al. (2014), p. 71.

313 Amitav Acharya, "Thinking Theoretically about Asian IR," in David Shambaugh and Michael Yahunda (2014), pp. 74–5.

314 David Leheny, "Constructivism and International Relations in Asia" in Saadia M. Pekkanen et al. (2014), at 67.

315 Aaron L. Friedberg (2005), p. 35.

316 Jeffrey W. Legro, Purpose Transitions China's Rise and the American Response, in Robert S. Ross and Zhu Feng (2008), p. 172.

317 T.V. Paul, The accommodation of rising powers in world politics, in T.V. Paul (2016), p. 14 (pointing out that constructivists have not developed a theoretical situation that the non-Western norms or non-liberal norms prevails as a rising power's idea).

shape foreign relations.[318] In fact, constructivists often test the role of ideas against East Asian institutionalism because regional institutionalism is at the core of constructivism's understanding of Asia's post-1945 foreign relations.[319] Further, diplomatic relations in East Asia are perceived as germane to collective identities and socially constructed and subjectively shaped ideational objects;[320] from this perspective, the identities of the disputants form their (collective) interests and behaviors.[321] Also, constructivism is the preferable international relations theory in China.[322]

Constructivism adduces, by implication, that Chinese people have a collective conscience and cultural heritage through which they see themselves tied up with their territories and the SCS.[323] Nonetheless, it is important to note that China has not conquered all the disputed maritime features because it perceives other claimants (*inter alia,* Vietnam and the Philippines) as friends, despite their disparities; put simply, "power is not the issue" in the SCS.[324]

In the SCS, constructivism argues that China tries to establish the identity of a sea power to protect its regional interests; China's ongoing SCS project is part of "identity construction."[325] Put another way, "China's more assertive

318 Aaron L. Friedberg (2005), p. 35.

319 Amitav Acharya, "Ideas, Identity and Institution-Building: From the 'ASEAN Way' to the 'Asia-Pacific Way'?" *Pacific Review,* 10, no. 3 (1997), pp. 319–46. Amitav Acharya, "How Ideas Spread: Whose Norms Matter? Norm Localization and Institutional Change in Asian Regionalism," *International Organization,* 58, no. 2 (Spring 2004), pp. 239–75.

320 Amitav Acharya, "Thinking Theoretically about Asian IR," in David Shambaugh and Michael Yahunda (2014), p. 73; Aaron L. Friedberg, 2005), p. 34 (defining identities as the "collective self-perceptions of political actors and their shared perceptions of others, norms as "beliefs not only about what is efficacious but also about what is right or appropriate in the international realm," and strategic cultures as "sets of beliefs about the fundamental character of international politics and about the best ways of coping with it").

321 Ted Hopf, "The Promise of Constructivism in International Relations Theory," *International Security,* 23, no. 1 (1998), pp. 171–200.

322 Amitav Acharya, "Thinking Theoretically about Asian IR," in David Shambaugh and Michael Yahunda (2014), p. 75.

323 See, e.g., G. Brown and M. Baer, "Protecting the Turf: The Effect of Territorial Marking on Others' Creativity," *Journal of Applied Psychology,* 100, no. 6 (2015), pp. 1785–1797.

324 Alexander Wendt (1992), p. 415.

325 Rex Li, "China's Sea Power Aspirations and Strategic Behavior in the South China Sea from the Theoretical Perspective of Identity Construction" in Enrico Fels and Truong-Minh Vu (eds.), *Power Politics in Asia's Contested Waters: Territorial Disputes in the South China Sea* (Cham: Springer International Publishing: 2016), pp. 117–137 (explaining that "how the development of Chinese maritime capabilities is inextricably linked to Beijing's efforts to construct the identity of a global power that has full command of the sea in East Asia and beyond").

posture on the [SCS] disputes evidently reflects its changing identity discourse and the resultant re-evaluation of its strategic interests."[326] At the same time, Chinese elites may be confused regarding, "what their country will want" in the SCS, meaning that Chinese policy on regional maritime order can fluctuate between revisionism and integration.[327] Again, the dominant ideas within the claimants are the key to evaluating regional politics regarding the SCS.[328] Seen in this way, at any time, conflicts can arise depending on the "peculiar construction of national identity or interest."[329]

What ideas (images) does China or the US hold on the other side? In most cases, Americans regard China as "illegitimate and potentially dangerous" while seeing themselves as the "defenders of freedom in Asia."[330] In contrast, China is convinced that America seeks to isolate, contain, diminish, internally divide China, and sabotage China's leadership.[331] As a corollary, China's (defensive) military policy is interpreted by the US as offensive in the context of the "China threat,"[332] whereas China interprets American alliances as part of a plan to contain China.[333]

Nonetheless, Chinese elites understand that if the US loses its leadership role, the world may become less effective on many fronts, while the possibility of a "collective leadership" by non-US powers is quite low.[334] Moreover, regional actors suspect Chinese leadership supplementing a US declining capacity to maintain regional maritime order. If such regional suspicion gradually grows, China is perceived as not being able to maintain a peaceful regional

326 *Ibid.*, p. 133.

327 Jeffrey W. Legro, "What China Will Want: The Future Intentions of a Rising Power," *Perspectives on Politics*, 5, no. 3 (September 2007), pp. 515, 519.

328 *Ibid*, p. 516 (arguing that "it behooves the international community to be proactive (not just reactive to behavior) by nurturing groups and ideas in China that offer more benign replacements to the less desirable alternatives.").

329 Thomas Berger, "Set for Stability? Prospects for Conflict and Cooperation in East Asia," *Review of International Studies*, 26, No. 3 (July 2000), p. 420.

330 Aaron L. Friedberg (2005), p. 37.

331 Yukon Huang (2017), p. 174. See also Yukon Huang, *Cracking the China Conundrum: Why Conventional Economic Wisdom Is Wrong* (New York: Oxford University Press, 2017), p. 174; Steven E. Lobell, How Should the US Respond to a Rising China? in Asle Toje (2018), p. 353.

332 John Mearsheimer (2001), p. 382.

333 Michael J. Mazarr et al. (2018), p. 29. Furthermore, China may perceive that big ideas, such as capitalism or democracy, have been shaped by America, and thus, it is possible to shift them or at least try alternatives.

334 Yang Shilong, The Tsinghua University Report on Global Security Forum Stresses Need to Build a Sustained, Stable International System, Outlook (了望), No. 49 (December 5, 2011), pp. 58–59, cited in Michael J. Mazarr et al. (2018), p. 75.

order alone.[335] Suppose that the US reduces or (temporarily) suspends freedom of navigation operations in the SCS as China wishes. If trade through the SCS were disrupted due to the lack of US protection, regional actors (including Japan and Korea) would seek a more vital role of the US in maintaining *mare liberum*, the prerequisite for the region's economic performance.[336]

Constructivism expects China to offer alternative ideas for the region's benefit that could replace American ideational force. Insofar as such alternative ideas only benefit Chinese interests ignoring others, regional actors will turn their back on China. If Chinese overtures help enhance regional peace and actors' interests, collective beliefs or ideas will gradually take sides with China. If this happens, most regional states will follow the Chinese ideas (e.g., the Chinese version of the interpretation and application of the law of the sea), despite US opposition.

Similarly, suppose the traditional Chinese world order (a hierarchical regional system) that purports to acknowledge the "subordination of all local authorities to the central and awe-inspiring power of the emperor" is perceived by regional actors as contributing to peace. In that case, this idea will also retain considerable purchase in the region.[337] In this regard, a *tanxia* concept

335 For an account of US decline and China's inability to maintain the order, see Michael J. Mazarr et al. (2018), p. 71.

336 Xi Jinping also obliquely mentioned this possibility at the 19th Party Congress that "changes in the global governance system and the international order are speeding up" and thus "we face growing uncertainties and destabilizing factors." See Full Text of Xi Jinping's Report to the 19th Party Congress," 2017.

337 David C. Kang, China, Hegemony, and Leadership in East Asia, in Vinod K. Aggarwal and Sara A. Newland (eds.), *Responding to China's Rise: US and EU Strategies* (Cham: Springer: 2015), pp. 27–50; David C. Kang, "Getting Asia Wrong: The Need for New Analytical Frameworks," *International Security*, 27, no. 4 (Spring 2003), pp. 57–85 (asserting that "[w]hen China has been strong and stable, order has been preserved. East Asian regional relations have historically been hierarchic, more peaceful, and more stable than those in the West" esp. p. 66). See also Yan Xuetong, *Ancient Chinese Thought, Modern Chinese Power* (Princeton and Oxford: Princeton University Press, 2011), pp. 105–6 (claiming that "hierarchy is a pejorative term, implying inequality. Objectively, however, not all states are alike in power, and therefore hierarchical norms are the only way to ensure equity. The norm of equality cannot maintain equity"). In contrast, Wang argues that t traditional regional hegemony of Ming China was secured with military might, instead of mere acceptance of neighbors. Wang also claims that "military strength was the foundation of the Ming tribute system." See Yuan-kang Wang, The Myth of Chinese Exceptionalism: A Historical Perspective on China's Rise, in Vinod K. Aggarwal and Sara A. Newland (2015), pp. 51–76, esp. p. 67.

(a hierarchical system) may contribute to dealing with territorial and maritime disputes with China's neighbors.[338]

In short, the current lack of US-Chinese cooperation stems from "mismatched interests, values, and capabilities"—not from ignoring each other's importance.[339] What constitutes the backbone of constructivist thinking on a way out of the SCS dispute is bound up with enhancing matched interests, identities, and values among China, the US, and other disputants, which is the subject of the following Subsection.

5.2 *A Possible Way out from the Constructivist Perspective*

Constructivists adduce that changes in identities, ideas, interests, and norms are the key to war avoidance between the status quo power and the rising power; changes enable them to seek alternative routes or integrate into normative orders.[340] For such changes to occur, organized discourse and social interactions among actors are critical: "discourse among states is a key ingredient in the formation of a particular identity and norm within a community in which those states interact."[341] The importance of discourse in avoiding war is supported by the empirical evidence of the pursuit of a trans-European project among European nations. The modern history of Europe until 1945 is a story of nationalist-inspired conflicts. However, in the process of discourse within the regional institutions of the European Union, nationalist sentiment dissipated; instead, the idea of Europe (supra nationalist sentiment) grew.[342]

---

338 Allen Carlson, "Moving Beyond Sovereignty? A brief consideration of recent changes in China's approach to international order and the emergence of the tianxia concept," *Journal of Contemporary China*, 20, no. 68 (2011), pp. 101–2. For an account of the contemporary meaning of tianxia, see David A. Bell, Realizing Tianxia: Traditional Values and China's Foreign Policy, in Ban Wang (ed.), *Chinese Visions of World Order: Tianxia, Culture, and World Politics* (Durham and London: Duke University Press, 2017), p. 132 (noting that "[i]n contemporary times, tianxia was famously revived by the philosopher Zhao Tingyang, who gave it a normative definition … [T]ianxia has three meanings: a geographical meaning referring to the whole world; a psychological meaning that the hearts of all the world's peoples are unified, like a big family; and an institutional meaning of a world government with the power to ensure universal order").

339 Elizabeth C. Economy and Adam Segal, "The G-2 Mirage," *Foreign Affairs*, 88, no. 3 (May/June 2009), p. 15.

340 T.V. Paul, The accommodation of rising powers in world politics, in T.V. Paul (2016), p. 15.

341 Jong Kun Choi and Yong-Soo Eun (2018), pp. 141–159, esp. p. 153 (emphasizing that discourse will help members of a regional community to reshape their behaviors based on shared identity and interest); Aaron L. Friedberg (2005), p. 35 (stating constructivist ideas that through discourse the underlying beliefs or mental categories of national leaders will shift from competition and violence to community and cooperation).

342 Michael Mastanduno, "Realism and Asia" in Saadia M. Pekkanen et al. (2014), p. 37.

The first constructivist way out pertains to a top-down discourse-boosting approach through institution-building. Regional institutions are essential to the development of norms in East Asia, which in turn constrains the use of force in the region.[343] In this view, regional institutions encourage a dialog, explain the change of events, and cause vivid interaction on the back of regional commonalities in "historical, political, cultural, social, and other such realities."[344] That is, institutions are understood to have real influence over the behavior of states not only by regulating state behavior but also by constituting state identities.[345]

Unlike liberalism, that stresses the narrow cost-benefit calculations of regimes' advantage, constructivism stresses the actual efficacy of changing beliefs and interests of the participants in the process of discourse. That is, regional actors' future stance on regional maritime order will be set by each government leader's subjective perception of (national or collective) interests and their beliefs about the ways of achieving them.[346]

To the extent this analysis is correct, building a regional institution attending to the SCS dispute will considerably help resolve this politico-legal problem. Above all, regional peace will be significantly enhanced by engaging China in the web of regional institutions in which Chinese elites can entertain beliefs and expectations consistent with the emerging community consensus.[347] As detailed in Chapter 4, if China and the US take part in an SCS regime, the emerging rivalry would be managed so as to avoid major conflict and open the potential for cooperation.

The second constructivist way out is a bottom-up approach aimed at developing discourse through the epistemic community. Constructivist theory emphasizes the role of expert consensus and the interplay of experts and politicians.[348] In this view, regimes change in accordance with shifts in the supply of

343 David C. Kang (2003), pp. 57–85 (arguing that Southeast Asia shows a bandwagoning environment, which is at variance with realist presuppositions esp. p. 68).

344 Nehginpao Kipgen (2020), p. 9.

345 Amitav Acharya, "Thinking Theoretically about Asian IR," in David Shambaugh and Michael Yahunda (2014), p. 73. See also Aaron L. Friedberg (2005), pp. 34–36 (explaining the efficacy of interactions with the example of [USSR] and the West on the issue of arms control experts).

346 Michael J. Mazarr et al. (2018), p. 13.

347 Aaron L. Friedberg (2005), p. 35–36.

348 Ernst B. Haas, "Is there a hole in the whole? Knowledge, technology, interdependence, and the construction of international regimes," *International Organization*, 29, no. 3 (Summer 1975), p. 872 (noting that "[o]ur notion of the public interest stressed the role of the expert as the producer of the knowledge which can influence the perceptions of interdependence and the formulation of purposes").

consensual knowledge and interest group pressures on the politician; the role of norm entrepreneurs and "epistemic communities" is essential to establishing and managing regimes.[349] East Asian "invisible colleges" of international lawyers would agree that a final resolution of the SCS dispute is predicated upon territorial sovereignty of maritime features and maritime delimitation of overlapping sea areas; until such moment comes, the necessity of cooperation across the region (e.g., joint development) inevitably stands out.[350]

Specifically, the whereabouts of a Chinese epistemic community will get increasing attention from other claimants. Many Chinese international lawyers and diplomats that compose the epistemic community have received an American (or Western) legal education, thereby being equipped with robust knowledge of stylized international law.[351] Despite divergent legal positions between Chinese and American lawyers, epistemic communities composed of international lawyers or political scientists in both states may agree that peaceful change is possible, and the prevention of major war is in the interest of all. In this sense, the Chinese epistemic community may play a decisive role in establishing a regional institution for the SCS.

Further, Chinese elites and "new thinkers" may find the "efficacy" (the source of Chinese policy change) of institution-building a less zero-sum approach against the US.[352] Johnston states that "there is considerable, if subtle, evidence of the socialization of Chinese diplomats, strategists and analysts in certain counter-realpolitik norms and practices as a result of participation

349 Peter M. Haas, Introduction: epistemic communities and international policy coordination, in Peter M. Haas (ed.), Knowledge, Power and International Policy Coordination, *International Organization*, 46, no. 1 (Special Issue, 1992), pp. 31–32. According to Haas, an epistemic community may have: (1) a shared set of normative and principled beliefs, which provide a value-based rationale for the social action of community members; (2) shared causal beliefs, which are derived from their analysis of practices leading or contributing to a central set of problems in their domain and which then serve as the basis for elucidating the multiple linkages between possible policy actions and desired outcomes; (3) shared notions of validity—that is, intersubjective, internally defined criteria for weighing and validating knowledge in the domain of their expertise; and (4) a common policy enterprise—that is, a set of common practices associated with a set of problems to which their professional competence is directed, presumably out of the conviction that human welfare will be enhanced as a consequence. *Ibid.*, p. 3, fn. 5).

350 Mark J. Valencia, *A Maritime Regime: For North-East Asia* (Oxford University Press, 1996), p. 24.

351 Kenneth W. Abbot, "International Law and International Relations Theory: Building Bridges," *ASIL Proceedings*, 1992, p. 171.

352 Robert S. Ross and Zhu Feng, The Rise of China: Theoretical and Policy Perspectives, in Robert S. Ross and Zhu Feng (2008), p. 308; Aaron L. Friedberg (2005), p. 43.

in these institutions."[353] In the end, China may embrace internationalization within institution-building because of the high efficacy of doing so, despite China's hitherto opposition.[354]

Constructivists view that, in the long term, a growing influence of its epistemic community will benefit China. In the life of regimes, "definition of issues" and "agenda-setting" is crucial. Also, all norm promoters at the international level need some organizational platform to promote their norms. If China provides ontological support to regime-building and leads the agenda-setting within an established institution, it can play a decisive role in the norm-making discussion; eventually, the regime may independently promote norms favoring China.[355]

In short, epistemic communities in the SCS region will grow, and the voices of experts that value principles of international law will become louder. If circumstances become more intense, each epistemic community can persuade each government to avoid war and initiate a dialog for regime-building in the SCS;[356] each government should heed their (individual or collective) voices.

6 Conclusion

Theories of international relations provide insight into legal response to the SCS dispute. Table 3.3 adumbrates political scientist analyses of the SCS dispute.

Realist evaluation is ominous; a peaceful process of redistributing power is not feasible.[357] War is inevitable unless some unlikely situations transpire,

353 Alastair Iain Johnston, *Social States: China in International Institutions, 1980–2000* (Princeton, N.J.: Princeton University Press, 2008), p. XXII. See also Ann Kent, "China's International Socialization: The Role of International Organizations," *Global Governance*, 8, no. 3 (July–September 2002), p. 350 (analysing that China's engagement in the order has reshaped its conception of interests and supported China's "readiness to shoulder the costs" of a multilateral order).

354 Klaus Heinrich Raditio (2019), p. 106 (noting that "[t]he idea of involving only 'states directly concerned' is also odd, since the SCS is a regional issue").

355 Martha Finnemore and Kathryn Sikkink, "International Norm Dynamics and Political Change," *International Organization*, 52, no. 4 (Autumn 1998), p. 899.

356 Yuwa Wei suggests "a constructive China" by taking four steps; a final step would be that China "assumes an active role in international cooperation and partnerships. See Yuwa Wei, *Issues Decisive for China's Rise or Fall: An International Law Perspective* (Springer, 2019), p. 182.

357 Robert S. Ross and Zhu Feng, The Rise of China: Theoretical and Policy Perspectives, in Robert S. Ross and Zhu Feng (2008), p. 295. One extreme view expects that China will

TABLE 3.3 IR Theories' Analyses and Predictions of the SCS Dispute

	Realism	Liberalism	Constructivism
Basic arguments	States (main actor) pursue national interest; power maximization (offensive); survival, and security (defensive)	States, multinational corporations, and international organizations aim to cooperate and coordinate to achieve collective goals	States, epistemic communities, and norm entrepreneurs aim to build community by interactions and shared normative frameworks
Preferred International Order	A balance of power system underpinned by self-help and alliances to maintain international order	A collective security system underpinned by free trade, liberal democracy, and institutions	Global and regional security communities forged through shared norms and collective identity
Who we are and what we value	Rational actors in anarchy pursuing power	Rational actors caring about benefits of cooperation	We consist of identities that form our interests, which fashioning foreign policies
Regional order in East Asia and regional institutions' role	Regional order rests on bilateralism No capacity as a force for peace: adjuncts to balance of power (offensive); instruments of the Chinese sphere of influence (defensive)	Regional order rests on multilateralism/ institutions Regimes promote free trade arising from growing interdependence and manage South China Sea disputes	Regional order rests on multilateralism Norm-setting and community building through discourse and dialog in institutions constitute state identities; the development of ideas and the "norm entrepreneurs" who made the spread possible are important

(*continued.*)

TABLE 3.3 IR Theories' Analyses and Predictions of the SCS Dispute (*cont.*)

	Realism	Liberalism	Constructivism
Asia's future will resemble	Unstable (ripe for rivalry); Europe's past (Friedberg); America's past (Mearsheimer)	None yet, brighter: peace by expanding interdependence and the web of institutions	Asia's past; hierarchical peace (Kang)
Causes of the South China Sea Dispute	Sino-American strategic competition/rivalry and nationalism	Lack of institutional support	Lack of institutions and collective identity/consensus for peace in the region
Prediction of the South China Sea Dispute	US-Chinese war (at sea); Security dilemma; War avoidance is (scarcely) possible if balance of power reflects the reality through accommodation	Cooperation is possible due to economic interdependence that makes war costly; Regional regime-building enables war avoidance; American-built liberal order in Asia will persist with adjustment to China's voices	War is avoidable if disputants (including the US) develop "collective identity" through interaction and socialization within institutions; Traditional Chinese hierarchical order will help resolve or manage the SCS dispute peaceably

such as sudden economic collapse, the democratization of China, the advent of supranational institutions that could control China and the US, or peace-loving leaders governing both states.[358] Liberalists and constructivists present a more optimistic proposition based on economic interdependence or regimes, or discourse and dialog leading to (peaceful) collective identities or epistemic communities, both of which do not preclude the possibility of war.

Regardless of which theory one employs, the first step is to build mutual understanding and accept mutual influence to prevent an apocalyptic World War III between China and the US.[359] Indeed, "socialization is not a one-way street": reciprocal adjustment should be premised. Only then, all the regional players will acknowledge the legitimacy of the regional maritime order.[360] During tectonic change, political scientists demand a more active role for the status quo power.[361] That is, peaceful change in the distribution of power is inextricably linked with "whether established powers pursue a strategy of gradual accommodation prior to, and at each stage of, a structural competition and whether they succeed in convincing the rising power to join ranks in maintaining a peaceful order."[362]

The Future of the SCS region and East Asia is in the hands of the consortium of China, the US, and other claimants. China's bargaining with the US and other claimants will influence American and other claimants' reactions.[363] One certainty is that China will continue to rise, like it or not: "denying the new reality and refusing to negotiate with China cannot stop China's rise."[364] As a fertilizer for a peaceful resolution, international law can contribute to the process of accommodation that is commensurate with a shift in power

make no compromise, no concession, no treaty; yet the Chinese military can assemble as soon as summoned, fight any battle and win. See Helene Cooper, During Hagel visit, China showed its military might, and its frustrations, *The New York Times*, April 10, 2014, at https://www.nytimes.com/2014/04/11/world/asia/during-hagel-visitchina-showed-its-military-might-and-its-frustrations.html.

358 Oriana Skylar Mastro (2019), p. 39.

359 Theodore McLauchlin, Great power accommodation and the processes of international politics, in T.V. Paul (2016), p. 310.

360 *Ibid.*

361 Lyle J. Goldstein, *Meeting China Halfway: How to Defuse the Emerging US-China Rivalry* (Washington, D.C.: Georgetown University Press, 2015), pp. 360–1.

362 T.V. Paul, The accommodation of rising powers in world politics, in T.V. Paul (2016), p. 16.

363 Kai He, Chna's bargaining strategies for a peaceful accommodation after the Cold War, in T.V. Paul (2016), p. 201.

364 *Ibid.*, p. 220. See also Graham Allison (2017), p. 215 (asserting that "There is no 'solution' for the dramatic resurgence of [China] ... Constructing a strategy proportionate to this challenge will require a multiyear, multiminded effort").

distribution. By this legal process, the Sino-American rivalry in East Asia will pan out peacefully, enabling the SCS dispute to be managed and resolved at the end of the day. Despite disparities in legal interpretation and ideas for regional order, rivals throughout history have found ways to accept intolerable circumstances for other benefits.[365] The next Chapter switches gears and looks at how international law should react to changes in international relations, bearing very much in mind the resolution of the SCS dispute.

365 Graham Allison (2017), p. 225.

CHAPTER 4

What Should International Law Do for the South China Sea Dispute?

This Chapter discusses the desirable role of international law in resolving the South China Sea (SCS) dispute with reference to the analyses of international relations theories.[1] In international society, power lies in almost any of the elements at any given time.[2] The law cannot exist without politics, and likewise, politics cannot exist without the law.[3] Politics provides law with its "rough content" and a certain level of a "driving force," upon which law develops its final form in a specific normative manner. In this Chapter, realism offers the starting point of debate, inasmuch as realism remains the most compelling general framework for understanding international politics.[4] No theory is perfect; that is why this Chapter bases its arguments on eclecticism.[5]

Three caveats should be noted before starting this Chapter. First, states are subjects and rule-makers of international law, holding the right to develop international custom.[6] Second, although many aspects of legal solutions should comport with great power politics, legal suggestions must be welcomed

1 Political scientists criticize that international law cannot proactively resolve the SCS disputes. Scott critically elaborates that "[i]nternational law fails to offer a clear solution to this [SCS] problem," and Rahmen and Tsamenyi observe that "[UNCLOS] is an inadequate basis for the establishment of [a] stable maritime regime." See David Scott, "Conflict Irresolution in the South China Sea," *Asian Survey*, 52, no. 6 (2012), pp. 1019–1042; Chris Rahman and Martin Tsamenyi, "A Strategic Perspective on Security and Naval Issues in the South China Sea," *Ocean Development & International Law*, 41 (2010), pp. 315–6.

2 Michael Byers (2003), p. 220.

3 Miro Cerar, "The Relationship Between Law and Politics," *Annual Survey of International & Comparative Law*, 15, Issue 1 (2009), pp. 21–3 (noting that in politics' view "the legal system can be viewed as part of the political system, which means that the legislatures and courts are political institutions, the rule of law is a political ideal, and adjudication and legal reasoning are practices and techniques which are part of the political culture of the society in which they flourish" esp. p. 22).

4 Stephen M. Walt (1998), p. 43.

5 William C. Wohlforth, Not Quite the Same as It Ever Was: Power Shifts and Contestation over the American-Led World Order, in Asle Toje (2018), p. 58 (noting that theoretical pessimism overestimates the "scale and significance of change," whereas optimism underestimates the "levels of dissatisfaction and the challenge of accommodation").

6 SU Jinyuan, "The East China Sea Air Defense Identification Zone and International Law," *Chinese Journal of International Law*, 2015, p. 295.

 | DOI: 10.1163/9789004696358_005

and supported by regional countries to fortify the foundation of peace and stability in Asia.[7] Third, in regards to searching for a resolution: the earlier, the better. The politico-legal pendulum appears to swing in favor of China.[8]

1 The Role of International Law in Times of Power Shift

The effectiveness of international law is inextricably tied up with power—normative, cognitive, or physical.[9] International law effectively operates when balance of power is sustained, regarding itself as the bulwark against damage to balance of power by labeling actions that undermine the balance as international wrongs.[10] Law is less adaptable than politics, even when change is desirable for the benefit of the international community. However, once international law is adapted to power distribution, peace and stability are fortified by the predictability and reliability of the law.[11]

---

7 Hugh White (2012), p. 82 (emphasizing that regional players, including other claimants, "will not sacrifice their interests in peace and stability, and good relations with China, to support US primacy unless that is the only way to avoid Chinese domination"); Congyan Cai (2019), p. 25 (noting that "great powers may find that they are more and more unable to unilaterally exert their power and thereby have to make compromises with less powerful states").

8 Chinese leaders may have "strong incentives to delay the settlements of these offshore island disputes, while slowly but steadily reinforcing their physical and symbolic footholds in the area." See Min Gyo Koo, Island Disputes and Maritime Regime Building in East Asia: Between a Rock and a Hard Place (Springer, 2009) p. 139. Upon investigation into scenarios in which China fails to rise—(a) China collapses internally such as the USSR; (b) China decentralizes and the provinces withhold revenues from the central government; (c) China self-destructs economically or faces a severe economic downturn that could disrupt its current growth trajectory; and (d) China becomes a practicing democracy and falls victim to the democratic peace proposition—Fravel concludes that all of the above are less likely, and instead, China "would become the leading nation in the international system by 2075." See M. Taylor Fravel (2010), p. 507.

9 Miro Cerar (2009), p. 28.

10 Alfred Vagts and Detlev F. Vagts (1979), p. 555. Nico Krisch emphasizes this aspect of international law as "stabilization"—preserving an "order that reflects the hegemon's preferences." See Nico Krisch (2005), p. 373 (presenting "regulation," "pacification," and "stabilization" as three primary functions of multilateral institutions in situations of hegemony).

11 Miro Cerar (2009), p. 33.

1.1 *Power in International Law*

In political parlance, power can be defined as the "capacity to do things and in social situations to affect others to get the outcomes we want."[12] From this definition, one may reasonably infer that more powerful states apply power to have some effect on the development, maintenance, and change of rules of international law; or "great" powers may have more opportunities to efficiently "behave in ways which will significantly influence [customary rules]" than do weak states.[13]

International lawyers worry that acknowledging inequalities of power in law may result in a denial of the equality of states. That is, the proposition that hegemons largely contribute to and disproportionately take part in the life of international law than less powerful states is viewed at variance with the principle of sovereign equality—the backbone of the international legal system as provided for in Article 2(1) of the UN Charter.[14] Also, international lawyers suppose, on the basis of sovereign equality, that (objective) international law has nothing to do with power.[15]

Powerful states, however, have looked down on the concept of sovereign equality and disliked principles arising from this concept, such as the one-state-one-vote rule.[16] History suggests that the hegemons, in varying degrees, have conveniently utilized international law when it is suitably adapted.[17] In *The Epochs of International Law*, Grewe argues that successive hegemons—through the periods of the predominance of Spain (1494–1648), France (1648–1815), and Britain (1815–1919)—have shaped the foundations of the international legal system.[18] If we assume that power is the overriding

12 Joseph S. Nye, Jr., *The Future of Power* (New York: Punlic Affaris, 2011), pp. 5–6 (also parsing that relational power has three different aspects: "commanding change, controlling agendas, and establishing preferences" esp. p. 11). Another definition of power is the "capacity to impose one's will on others by reliance on effective sanctions in case of non-compliance." See Georg Schwarzenberger, *Power Politics*, 3rd ed. (London: Stevens, 1964), p. 14.

13 Michael Byers (2003), pp. 35, 37.

14 Article 2(1) proclaims that "[UN] is based on the principle of the sovereign equality of all its Members."

15 Detlev F. Vagts (2001), p. 845; Michael Byers (2003), p. 35.

16 Nico Krisch, More equal than the rest? Hierarchy, equality and US predominance in international law, in Michael Byers and Georg Nolte (2003), p 136; Nico Krisch (2005), p. 388

17 Detlev F. Vagts (2001), pp. 845, 848.

18 Wilhelm G. Grewe, *The Epochs of International Law*, trans. and rev. Michael Byers (Berlin: de Gruyter, 2000).

consideration in international society, the primary function of law is to be understood as assisting "in maintaining the supremacy of force and the hierarchies established on the basis of power."[19]

Most international legal scholars understand that balance of power provided the foothold in the Peace of Westphalia in 1648.[20] Grote parses that balance of power was a "necessary and indispensable corollary to the functioning of the international system inaugurated by the Westphalian system."[21] In 1713, "equilibrium of power" was inscribed in the Peace of Utrecht, which terminated the War of Spanish Succession, stipulating its aim as "establishing and stabilizing the peace and tranquility of the Christian world by a just equilibrium of power."[22]

The first legal scholar to note power in relation to international law was Alberico Gentili (1550–1608): "the balance of power should be maintained among the princes of Italy."[23] Although some early international lawyers, including Hugo Grotius (1583–1645), appear to criticize or negatively approach the inclusion of the concept of balance of power on a legal consideration,[24] a theory that balance of power constitutes a core concept or a determinant of international law was widely shared among early international scholars, such as Christian Wolff (1679–1754) and Emmerich de Vattel (1714–1767).[25] As such,

---

19 Georg Schwarzenberger, *Power Politics*, 3rd ed. (London: Stevens, 1964), p. 199. Echoing this understanding, Scheuerman asserts that "[i]nternational law remains one of the least developed areas of modern law" and "employment [of law] ... subject to the opportunistic whims of great powers." See William E. Scheuerman, *The End of Law: Carl Schmitt in the Twenty-First Century* (London and New York: Rowman & Littlefield, 2020), p. 165.

20 The Peace of Westphalia opened the rule-based balance of power period. See Alfred Vagts and Detlev F. Vagts (1979), p. 560.

21 Rainer Grote, Westphalian System, in Rüdiger Wolfrum (2012), Vol. X, p. 871. Many Chinese scholars belittle the rules symbolized under Westphalian system as devoid of civilization and cultural discrimination. See, e.g., Xue Hanqin (2012), p. 34.

22 Alfred Vagts and Detlev F. Vagts (1979), p. 560.

23 *Ibid.*, p. 559.

24 Hugo Grotius negatively assesses a contemporary argument that "according to the law of nations it is right to take up arms in order to weaken a growing power which, if it becomes too great, may be a source of danger." In addition, Johann Ludwig Klueber (1762–1837) observes balance as "a mere idea of diplomats or politicians, very vague, simply founded upon a feeling of convenience which consequently lacks the essential character of a source of international law." See *ibid.*, pp. 566–7.

25 Wolff acknowledges a special role of balance of power for international society and notes that "equilibrium is especially useful to protect the common security." Wolff also claims that in the face of manifest attacks of other state, nations "have the right for the purpose of preserving the equilibrium, to overthrow the growing power by armed force." Vattel perceived equilibrium as crucial to Europe's order and liberty. Nicolaus Hieronymus Gundling (1673–1731) suggests that a ruler is entitled to draw his sword provided that other

natural law scholars kept the balance of power concept inside the universe of law by blending power relations with other views in the interest of a better world community.[26] Leonce Donnadieu perceived balance, by extension, as having the legal character: "the political equilibrium ... is the expression of a law in the life of nations."[27]

With the advent of legal positivism, the above legal tradition underwent a sea change. John Austin (1790–1859), the founding father of legal positivism,[28] divides laws into three groups: "positive law," "natural law," and "international law." First, "positive law" or "law existing by position" is laws set by men (often political superiors) for men (political inferiors) with sanctions or enforcement of obedience applied if a duty is broken. Second, "natural law" (the law of nature, the Divine law, or the law of God) is laws established by God for humans. Divine laws are also called "religious duties," and thus, violations of these duties are called "sins," entailing religious sanctions. Third, "international law" (the law of honor, positive morality, positive international morality, or practical international law) is laws set and enforced by "mere opinion" as morals. Austin explains that "[t]he name morality severs them from positive law, while the epithet positive disjoins them from the law of God."[29] In this view, international law cannot be called "law" because of the lack of sanction by political superiors.[30]

With the rise of positivism's disparagement of international law, international lawyers have tried to conceptualize international law as something different from morality or mere opinion.[31] Hans Kelsen developed the pure

---

party "is on the increase or stepping out of the balance." Karl von Rotteck (1775–1840) regards the idea of the balance of power an essential support of international law. See *ibid.*, , pp. 561–2, 566.

26 *Ibid.*, p. 579.

27 *Ibid.*, pp. 572–3.

28 Johann Jacob Moser (1701–1785) is also mentioned as a founder of modern positivism in international law. See *ibid.*, pp. 562–3. For an overview of positivism in international law, see Roberto Ago, Positivism, in Rudolf Bernhardt (ed.), *Encyclopedia of Public International Law* (Amsterdam: North-Holland, 1984), Vol. 7, p. 385.

29 John Austin, *The Province of Jurisprudence Determined* (Cambridge University Press: Cambridge, 1995; reprinted in 2001), pp. 18–22, 38, 112–3, 181.

30 Rosalyn Higgins, *Problems and Process: International Law and How We Use It* (Oxford: Oxford University Press, 1994), p. 13.

31 Similar to the influence of positivism on international law but from a different perspective, "Classical legal thought" contends that international law is a neutral and apolitical venue. Classical legal thought (legal orthodoxy) dominated the thinking of American lawyers from roughly 1880 to 1973 and assumed that "only law that was objective ... could be legitimate in a democratic republic." See Classical Legal Theory, *The Oxford International Encyclopedia of Legal History*, online version: 2009; Richard H. Steinberg and Jonathan M.

theory of law to answer the questions of "what (international) law is" and "how it ought to be" as a science of law, not political exposition.[32] Withana assesses that "[t]he main project of positivist thinkers in international law has been to determine a body of legal rules that are truly juridic in nature and not tainted by non-legal considerations such as morality or ethics."[33]

Admittedly, positivism is the most pervasive legal philosophy among international lawyers. This paradigm predicates that legal issues or positions are distinct from non-legal issues or positions. Also, positivist international lawyers perceive that "law exists prior to policy and that the process of legal analysis should be undertaken prior to the determination of policy." By extension, positivists argue that international law *sua sponte* is enough to determine state behavior yet negate the relationship between international law and state behavior or power relations.[34]

However, positivist international law brushes aside the reality of world society, thereby obstructing an evolution of international rules.[35] More concretely, positivism utterly ignores the role of "shared understanding" in international society; certainly, shared understanding of legal relevance counts for much in transforming state practice into customary international rules.[36] Higgins points out that the assumption that law is concerned not with power but only with the concept of authority is a fantasy because "authority cannot exist in the total absence of control."[37]

Zasloff, "Power and International Law," *American Journal of International Law*, 100, no. 64 (2006), p. 67.

32 Hans Kelsen, *Pure Theory of Law* (Berkeley: University of California Press, 1967 trans. by Max Knight), p. 1; Hans Kelsen, *General Theory of Law and State* (Cambridge: Harvard University Press, 1949, trans. by Anders Wedberg), p. 113 (proposing the existence of some higher norm that has authorities: "Norm creating power is delegated from one authority to another authority; the former is the higher, the latter the lower authority. The basic norm of a dynamic system is the fundamental rule according to which the norms of the system are to be created").

33 Radhika Withana, *Power, Politics, Law: International Law and State Behavior During International Crises* (Leiden and Boston: Martinus Nijhoff Publishers, 2008), p. 21.

34 *Ibid.*, pp. 19–27.

35 Monica Garcia-Salmones Rovira, "The Project of Positivism in International Law," *European Journal of International Law*, 25 (2014), p. 603; Anlei Zuo (2018), p. 50 (citing a Chinese scholar's argument that "The seemingly productive, systematization of international law and enhanced legitimacy of the Western-dominated international law reinforces international law to be a tool for international exploitation and dominance by some countries").

36 Michael Byers (2003), p. 205.

37 Rosalyn Higgins (1994), pp. 3–4.

The pendulum of legal philosophy has swung back again in favor of acknowledging the role of power in legal consideration. This is due in good part to the development of the New Haven School and Critical Legal Studies. First, the New Haven School, promoted by Harold Lasswell, M.S. McDougal, amongst others, adopted a purely sociological approach to legal scholarship (a "policy science"), giving consideration to the authority and control exercised by decision-makers. From this viewpoint, law is a product of the decision-making process, during which authority and control are made,[38] and power is regarded as an essential part of international law in its entirety.[39]

Next, Critical Legal Studies, promoted by, *inter alia*, David Kennedy and Martti Koskenniemi, holds that there is no clear distinction between law and politics, and thus, the international legal system is neither self-contained nor apolitical.[40] Scholars of this school of thought affirm that "political considerations influencing the development of a legal rule should be acknowledged to expose bias and show how law is not living up to its image of political neutrality."[41]

Both the New Haven School and Critical Legal Studies investigate law with the involvement of social theory, place legal process in a social context, and make values primary. As is widely advocated by lawyers, international law embodies values, not a mere system of order.[42] It is not that international law only keeps its legitimacy or lawfulness by ignoring everything that is not "rules." Instead, considering common values and community interests in the

38 Michael Byers (2003), p. 207.

39 Oscar Schachter, "The Role of Power in International Law," *Proceedings of the Annual Meeting*, American Society of International Law, 93 (March 24–27, 1999), p. 201. Hoof fulminates against the New Haven School's approach to international law in that this approach "can lead to international law being used by states as a device for post facto justifying decisions without really taking international law into account." On this criticism, Higgins contends that there is no a real international law that all men of good faith can recognize regardless of circumstance and context. See Rosalyn Higgins (1994), p. 7.

40 David Kennedy, "A New Stream of International Law Scholarship," *Wisconsin International Law Journal*, 7, 1988, pp. 1–49; Michael Byers (2003), pp. 45, 210 (adding that Critical Legal Studies try to "expose the myths of objectivity, of value-freedom and of determinacy in law and law creation by deconstructing legal texts").

41 Radhika Withana (2008), p. 54. Koskkenniemi argues that political components of international law are concerned with the dependence of law on political power and with the utopian political aspirations. See Martti Koskenniemi, "The Politics of International Law," *European Journal of International Law*, 1 (1990), p. 9.

42 Morton A. Kaplan and Nicholas deB. Katzenbach, *The Political Foundations of International Law* (New York and London: John Wiley & Sons, Inc., 1961), p. 17.

making of international law would provide additional support for making international law "legal."[43]

It would seem incongruous to assume that power relations play no role in the process of international law as if an international legal process were the completely neutral and procedurally objective mechanism. In reality, international rules result from an interactive and evolving social process that encompasses states with varying degrees of power. Acknowledging a social process in the life of international law comports more with a world society in which international law should exist.[44]

Indeed, looking at state practice in the making of customary international law, powerful states can extensively contribute to the formation of custom with their capacity to act, respond, or publicize reports containing legal analyses supporting their practice.[45] Dominant players wield more latitude in interpreting and applying mostly customary and vague rules. Such a power advantage over the weak still remains significant in the making of customary rules inasmuch as the process of the identification of custom invariably includes a weighing of supporting and opposing state practice.[46] In other words, hegemons' behaviors and remarks on particular issues are more likely to be considered, and thus, expansively measured in the making of customary rules due to the frequency and heaviness of their engagement in the international legal system.[47] Charles De Visscher observes that "[e]very international custom is the work of power ... Many customs owe their origin wholly to decisions or acts of great Powers."[48] Schachter also points out that "[a]s a historical fact,

---

43 Rosalyn Higgins (1994), p. 9. However, this is not to argue that balance of power or the principle of equilibrium is a judicial rule. See Alfred Vagts and Detlev F. Vagts (1979), pp. 574–5 (citing a Dupuis' distinction that a judicial rule is to "supply clear, precise and identical solutions in all identical cases," while balance of power is "vague, uncertain and changeable").

44 Michael Byers (2003), p. 216.

45 Stephen Toope, Powerful but unpersuasive? The role of the United States in the evolution of customary international law, in Michael Byers and Georg Nolte (2003), p. 316; Anthony D'Amato, *The Concept of Custom* (Ithaca: Cornell University Press, 1971), pp. 96–7; Michael Byers (2003), pp. 35–40 (emphasizing that powerful states' military, economic, and political strength has a bearing on enforcing jurisdiction claims, imposing sections, and diverting criticism).

46 No formal customary international law-making procedures exist. See Michael Byers (2003), pp. 5, 151–7; Nico Krisch (2005), p. 387.

47 Michael Byers (2003), p. 19.

48 Charles De Visscher, *Theory and Reality in Public International Law* (Princeton: Princeton University Press, 1957, translated by P.E. Corbett), pp. 149–150.

[customary rules were] made by remarkably few States … [Powerful states'] views and positions are noticed and usually respected."[49]

Indeed, it is argued that custom cannot develop customary international law without hegemonic participation, due to such custom's disqualification in satisfying the requirement of "general practice" (hegemons are regarded as "specially affected states"), as required for customary international law under Article 38 of the ICJ Statute.[50] Nevertheless, nothing stated thus far invites the conclusion that all the bodies of international law are entirely dependent on the will of great powers.[51]

1.2 *Power Shift Entailing Law Shift*

One observation that flows from the previous Section is that changes in the distribution of power do influence, in varying degrees, the process and substance of international law.[52] Indeed, political power is generally expressed and conserved in the form of law. The exiting (or changed) distribution of power inevitably influences the contents of international law; in return, law contributes to sustaining the balance, as holding values and needs.[53]

The 1951 San Francisco Peace Treaty is a noteworthy example, demonstrating how balance of power has laid the foundation for international law development, maintenance, and change. This Treaty is viewed as a product of the Cold War. The power aspect of this Treaty is ascertained by a dramatic change of a US position on Japan, from isolationism in the prewar era to the conclusion of the 1951 US-Japan Security Treaty, which was signed along with this

---

49 Oscar Schachter, New Custom: Power, Opinio Juris and Contrary Practice, in Jerzy Makarczyk (ed.), *Theory of International Law at the Threshold of the 21st Century: Essays in Honour of Krzysztof Skubiszewsk* (The Hague: Kluwer, 1996), pp. 536–7.

50 Detlev F. Vagts (2001), p. 847. For a criticism on this suggestion, see Gennady Danilenko, *Law-Making in the International Community* (Dordrecht: Martinus Nijhoff, 1993), p. 96 (criticizing that "[i]n the absence of a clear definition, the notion of 'specially affected' states may be used as a respectable disguise for 'important' or 'powerful' states which are always supposed to be 'specially affected' by all or almost all political-legal developments within the international community").

51 For example, new institutions, such as EEZ up to 200 nautical miles and 12 nautical miles of territorial seas, found their positions in the law of the sea, despite great powers' aversion to accept. See Oscar Schachter, "The Role of Power in International Law," *Proceedings of the Annual Meeting*, American Society of International Law, 93 (March 24–27, 1999), p. 203.

52 William W. Burke-White, "Power Shifts in International Law: Structural Realignment and Substantive Pluralism," *Harvard International Law Journal*, 56 (2015), p. 3; Morton A. Kaplan and Nicholas deB. Katzenbach (1961), p. 3.

53 Niklas Luhmann, *Trust and Power* (Chichester: John Wiley & Sons, 1979), p. 170; Oscar Schachter (1999), p. 205.

Treaty.[54] Simply put, the 1951 Peace Treaty is "nothing but a byproduct of the regional Cold War in the Asia-Pacific."[55]

UNCLOS is not an exception. The Cold War rivalry existed right behind the negotiation for the negotiations in the 1970s.[56] For example, China participated in UNCLOS III, but it did not have enough power compared to the great powers at that time (US, the Soviet Union, Japan, and UK) to insert a maritime order conducive to its interests into the system.[57]

Changes in power relations heavily influence bilateral agreements than multilateral ones.[58] States may conclude a treaty agreeing on particular agendas; if relative power advantage between the parties dramatically changes, the shift

---

54 Thomas Schwartz and John Yoo, "Asian Territorial Disputes and the 1951 San Francisco Peace Treaty: The Case of Dokdo," *Chinese Journal of International Law,* 18 (2019), p. 511.

55 Kimie Hara, *Cold War Frontiers in the Asia-Pacific: Divided Territories in the San Francisco System* (London and New York: Routledge, 2007), p. 69. In the Yalta Blueprint—US, the British, and Soviet Union leaders met at Yalta, Crimea in February 1945 to design the port-war international order—the post-war settlement with Japan was planned in a harsh and severe manner. In the course of the Cold War, however, American policy toward Japan did an about face; furthermore, the advent of communism in China in 1949, and North Korea's invasion of South Korea in 1950 caused the US to strive to secure Japan for the Western bloc. As a result, the final product became far too lenient with Japan to avoid a situation that benefits a communist-dominated China for territorial disposition. *Ibid.,* pp. 49, 140, 157.

56 Donald Rothwell et al., Charting the Future for the Law of the Sea, in Donald Rothwell et al. (eds.), *The Oxford Handbook of the Law of the Sea* (Oxford: Oxford University Press, 2015), pp. 899–900 (noting that "the text was negotiated and concluded against the backdrop of the Cold War").

57 Anisa Heritage and Pak K. Lee, "The Sino-American confrontation in the South China Sea: insights from an international order perspective," *Cambridge Review of International Affairs*, 33, no. 1 (2020), p. 142; Bill Hayton (2014), p. 112. Also, UNCLOS was not designed to address the "severity of contemporary realities"; in other words, the need for adapting the law of the sea system to a circumstance has been suggested ever since. See Katherine Morton, "China's ambition in the South China Sea: is a legitimate maritime order possible?" *International Affairs*, 92, no. 4 (2016), p. 913.

58 One example of a bilateral treaty being more vulnerable to changes in balance of power is the Sino-British Joint Declaration in 1997 concerning a handover of the exercise of sovereignty over Hong Kong. This treaty acknowledges "one country, two systems" as the governing framework codified in the Basic Law of the Hong Kong Special Administrative Region. Hong Kong was granted a "high degree of autonomy" for 50 years following the handover. In recent years, however, China has changed its legal position arguing that "the Joint Declaration expired in 1997 with the handover and the adoption of the Basic Law." One commentator examines that the Chinese proposition finds no basis in the international law applicable to treaties. See Robert D. Williams, International Law with Chinese Characteristics: Beijing and the "Rules-Based" Global Order, Brookings, October 2020, at https://www.brookings.edu/wp-content/uploads/2020/10/FP_20201012_international_law_china_williams.pdf. Meanwhile, North Korea's withdrawal from the Nuclear

may lead to a break-up of the treaty.[59] Further, if states perceive a treaty as inconsistent with their interests or harming them, they often deny or attack the treaty contents.[60] That is, when a growing state advances as a dominant player in the system, the state will not passively follow the old (multilateral or bilateral) rules at variance with its national interests.[61]

Also, balance of power has a decisive effect on the establishment of international organizations. An attempt to create the Permanent Court of Arbitral Justice was unsuccessful because the firm insistence of Latin American countries on the formal equality of all members was refused by the great powers; the court never came into being. In contrast, some power disparity was widely agreed upon, in tacit consent, not only for creating the League of Nations in 1919 but also for establishing the United Nations in 1945 (especially in the role of the Security Council).[62]

The question is how that power shift is transmitted to law shift. To examine this question, one unique characteristic of international law that domestic law cannot share needs to be noted: violation of law can lead to the formation of new law. If a body of norms undergoes substantial non-compliance over some time, a societal expectation that behavior is required as legal obligation fades out, and subsequently, the normative character of the norm loses.[63]

From the opposite perspective, a new rule will be observed as long as societal members find it legitimate. Legitimation brings about authority, and in the end, states will perceive that the new law should be complied with as law.[64] Put differently, when a rising state want to challenge rules advocated by the dominant power, the challenger will pursue delegitimizing the existing rules while promoting legitimacy of new rules.[65] Legitimacy is the key to eliciting

Nonproliferation Treaty demonstrates that states go through hardship when they try to change their multilateral treaty obligations. See Frederic L. Kirgis, "North Korea's Withdrawal from the Nuclear Nonproliferation Treaty," American Society of International Law insights, 8, Issue 2 (January 24, 2003), at https://www.asil.org/insights/volume/8/issue/2/north-koreas-withdrawal-nuclear-nonproliferation-treaty.

59 John Yoo, "Embracing the Machines: Rationalist War and New Weapons Technologies," *California Law Review*, 105 (2017), p. 129.

60 Mico A Galang (2016), p. 1.

61 Stephen M. Walt, Rising Powers and the Risks of War: A Realist View of Sino-American Relations, in Asle Toje (2018), p. 15

62 Nico Krisch (2005), pp. 397–8.

63 Rosalyn Higgins (1994), p. 19.

64 Nico Krisch (2005), p. 374.

65 Until the challenger reaches the point in which it could execute delegitimizing current rules, the challenger "partially and temporarily accept the legitimacy of the hegemon" taking advantage of "opportunities and authorized channels within the order to

TABLE 4.1 The effectiveness of Hegemonic International Law (HIL)

How HIL Changes and Works		
Stable	Unstable (Legal Order)	Stable
Old Rules → Delegitimizing (old) Rules → Legitimizing New Rules → Authority → Convicted Dominance		
Gaining Dominance	Simple Dominance	
Why States Comply with HIL		
By internalization of norms	By Calculus	By internalization of norms
HIL Enforcement Cost		
Low	High	Low

SOURCE: AUTHOR WITH REFERENCE TO NICO KRISCH, "INTERNATIONAL LAW IN TIMES OF HEGEMONY: UNEQUAL POWER AND THE SHAPING OF THE INTERNATIONAL LEGAL ORDER," *EUROPEAN JOURNAL OF INTERNATIONAL LAW*, 16, NO.3 (2005), P. 374.

authority in society: the new hegemon will pay little for enforcement of the legitimized rules. If the challenger relies only on power, illegitimacy may hound the new legal system of the new hegemon (Table 4.1).[66]

More specifically, over time, delegitimizing the legal authority of a particular rule will cause other states to face a complicated calculation process. If new (interpretation of) rules satisfy states' diverse interests, their conviction of the legality or legitimacy of old (interpretation of) rules may be blurred and eroded.[67] A "revisionist counterhegemonic coalition" can be formed among those whose legal interests are more aligned with the challenger's positions, which provides the foundation of a demand for a new international legal system.[68] This delegitimizing phase may accelerate with the challenger seizing a commanding share of the global market.[69]

make relative gains and to contest particular behaviors of the hegemon." Of course, the challenger may overcome the order when such an option becomes viable. See Randall L. Schweller and Xiaoyu Pu (2011), p. 50.

66 Congyan Cai, The Rise of China and International Law: Taking Chinese Exceptionalism Seriously (New York, NY: Oxford University Press, 2019), p. 19; Nico Krisch (2005), p. 373.

67 Aaron L. Friedberg (2011), p. 175.

68 For an account of a cyclical pattern of political order change, see George Modelski, "The Long Cycle of Global Politics and the Nation-State," *Comparative Studies in Society and History*, 20, no. 2 (April 1978), pp. 214–235 (expounding that "The long cycle of global politics is the product of two conditions: the urge to make a global order; and the special properties and the necessary weak-nesses of the global systems the world has experienced to date," esp. p. 224).

69 Michael J. Mazarr et al. (2018), p. 118.

TABLE 4.2 Mechanism of changes in normative structure caused by the challenger

Disagreements over the Meaning of the Rules → Actions → Reactions → Lawfare with Competing analysis → A. (If others agree with the challenger's analysis) Modification of the Rules [Changed Normative Structure] → B. (If others disagree with the challenger's analysis) Continuance of the Rules [Unchanged Normative Structure]

SOURCE: AUTHOR WITH REFERENCE TO WAYNE SANDHOLTZ AND ALEC STONE SWEET, LAW, POLITICS, AND INTERNATIONAL GOVERNANCE, IN CHRISTIAN REUS-SMIT (ED.), *THE POLITICS OF INTERNATIONAL LAW* (CAMBRIDGE: CAMBRIDGE UNIVERSITY PRESS, 2004), PP. 257–8.

The above process is unfolded in the hegemonic normative structure in which "lawfare" between the hegemon and a potential hegemon happens. Once the challenger has the upper hand, the existing rules undergo modification; and in the end, the altered norms set the new framework for subsequent actions, discourses, and disputes.[70] Table 4.2 schematizes such a mechanism of changes in hegemonic normative structure.

Through the above mechanism, applications of power and state practice are legitimately transformed into a legal obligation and customary rules, which is called as "legalized hegemony" or "legislative inequality."[71] One item to note is that weak states usually follow hegemons' legal positions; the weak do not have enough power to challenge the universality of hegemonic international law, or to receive hegemonic rewards for following that rules and, on some occasions, they are simply forced to accept such rules.[72]

In principle, international law has dual functions: "social stability" and "social adaptation."[73] It is true that the law tends to suspiciously perceive

70 Wayne Sandholtz and Alec Stone Sweet, Law, politics, and international governance, in Christian Reus-Smit (ed.), *The Politics of International Law* (Cambridge: Cambridge University Press, 2004), pp. 257–8.

71 Michael Byers (2003), p. 6; Gerry Simpson (2004), p. 73; Nico Krisch (2005), p. 378 (stating that hegemonic international law offers hegemons "an excellent tool for international regulation and for the pacification and stabilization of their dominance, especially because of the high degree of legitimacy that action through legal forms and procedures enjoys").

72 Congyan Cai (2019), p. 19; Nico Krisch (2005), p. 373.

73 The law in general has these two functions. See Newton Edwards, "Stability and Change in Basic Concepts of Law Governing American Education," *The School Review*, 65, no. 2 (Summer 1957), pp. 161–2.

change, demanding "stares decisis special justification for departure from the past."[74] The proclivity for stability, if not a standstill, lies at the core of international law.[75] However, if international law continues to refuse to adapt to other societal elements (such as balance of power), the international legal system will face malfunction, incapable of contributing to a changing political world.[76] By sticking to past rules, international law will lose the ability to deal with today's problems, and subsequently, decay and suffer substantial incompliance and disobedience.[77] To address this issue, international law should strike a balance between the conflicting demands of stability and adaptation.[78]

With this in mind, the existing dominant power ought to perceive that it has more duties than does the challenger to maintain global or regional stability.[79] Krisch puts the danger of legal anachronism as the following:

> By focusing on the past, international law allows previous generations to rule over present ones, and this makes it difficult for powerful actors to remake the international legal order according to their own vision. In international law, this problem is especially acute because changes in international law require widespread consent and are usually slow and incremental.[80]

---

74 Robert B. McKay, "Stability and Change in Constitutional Law," *Vanderbilt Law Review*, 17 (1963), p. 203. In common law systems, legal stability and predictability are bolstered by judicial adherence to precedent and the informal norm of stare decisis. See Stefanie A. Lindquist and Frank C. Cross, Stability, Predictability and the Rule Of Law: Stare Decisis As Reciprocity Norm, at https://law.utexas.edu/conferences/measuring/The%20Papers/Rule%20of%20Law%20Conference.crosslindquist.pdf.

75 Pound, Interpretation of Legal History (1923), p. 1, cited in Robert B. McKay, "Stability and Change in Constitutional Law," *Vanderbilt Law Review*, 17 (1963), p. 203, fn. 1 (explaining that "Law must be stable, and yet it cannot stand still"); Jutta Brunnée and Stephen J Toope, INTERNATIONAL LAW AND THE PRACTICE OF LEGALITY: STABILITY AND CHANGE, Victoria University of Wellington Law Review (Special Symposium Issue 'The Dynamic Evolution of International Law'), pp. 429–450.

76 Rosalyn Higgins (1994), p. 3.

77 *Ibid.*

78 Mr. Justice Cardozo emphasizes that "some path of compromise" will offer promise of growth. See Robert B. McKay (1963), p. 203.

79 Michael Mastanduno, "Realism and Asia" in Saadia M. Pekkanen et al. (2014), p. 41 (emphasizing that East Asian regional security is subject to how the US reacts to the rise of China).

80 Nico Krisch (2005), p. 377.

Certainly, it is difficult for the dominant power to draw the line between enforcing current rules and negotiating new agreements.[81] Therefore, decision-makers of the relatively declining power cautiously approach the request for a legal shift of a rising challenger not to regard it as an enemy's camouflage.[82] Indeed, "different understandings of international law ... are to be seen as normal or expected."[83] In this respect, Cerar affirms that "each era must write its legal science anew" to maintain equilibrium between the static and dynamic aspects of the law, understanding that "the fiction of a 'correct law' is only temporary in nature."[84]

More importantly, war or peace is a function of the social stability and social adaptation aspects of law. Yoo points out that peace or war can occur on the basis of how the parties approach the situation (by amending treaties or refuting overtures) of allocating the resources or territory when balance of power has shifted between them.[85] That being said, it is true that international law is vulnerable to sudden shifts in power relationships.[86] Therefore, changes in international law are to be a gradual process in line with the whole legal system adapting to the political realities of a new age.[87] With this qualification,

---

81 Theodore McLauchlin, Great power accommodation and the processes of international politics, in T.V. Paul (2016), p. 312.

82 *Ibid.*, p. 305.

83 Lu Zhu, Anthea Roberts' Is International Law International? (Book Review), *Chinese Journal of International Law*, 18, Issue 4 (2019), pp. 1009–1012 (adding that "it is a natural outgrowth for non-Western States, such as China, to have greater ability to promote their normative agendas as global power shifts").

84 Miro Cerar (2009), p. 30.

85 John Yoo (2011), pp. 23–24. Yoo further illustrates that in a hypothetical world of two states (one weak and one strong) that divides the benefits of cooperation commensurate with their relative power, law governing the exploitation of resources will divide the resources in proportion to relative power strength between the two. If power changes, the previously weak state that has gained relative power will demand law shift to get more control over the resources than exists in the status quo; the previously predominant state must decide between conceding or going to war. See Eric A. Posner and John Yoo (2006), p. 8.

86 Robert Keohane (1984), pp. 85–109.

87 Michael Byers, The complexities of foundational change, in Michael Byers and Georg Nolte (2003), pp. 1–2; Katherine Morton (2016), p. 913. See also Morton A. Kaplan and Nicholas deB. Katzenbach (1961), p. 8 (noting that "[i]n the absence of developed supranational legislative institutions, rules are prescribed, amended, adjusted, and applied by a time-consuming process of agreement ... [International rules] are often quite fluid until formalized in treaties, [subjecting to] political strain in their interpretation and application."

the rising state should have patience with seeking gradual normative adjustments.[88] And the existing power should consider that a rational settlement should mirror the balance of power out of regard for their objective chances of prevailing in a conflict on the other.[89] Otherwise, the international legal system will ineluctably fall into a state of disequilibrium, thereby causing severe international crises, not to mention security dilemmas.[90]

1.3 *The Condition and Process of the Law of the Sea Shift*

International lawyers in different regions interpret rules and principles differently according to their own (local) perspectives. The same generally holds true for UNCLOS. Many UNCLOS principles and institutions (e.g., freedom of navigation) are often subject to a wide range of interpretations insofar as "international lawyers are not ... uprooted from the local context they inhabit."[91] Further, "radical indeterminacy" or the "semantically ambiguous, open-ended legal standards" (terms borrowed from Schmitt) of some UNCLOS institutions complicate the Sino-American lawfare.[92]

For a long time, Western or American interpretations of the law of the sea institutions have primarily influenced the views of the majority of the actors in the international community.[93] With greater military, economic, and political strength, the US—posing as a champion of universal (Western) interpretation of the law of the sea—has enforced its "jurisdictional claims" over others by imposing sanctions.[94] In other words, the large, well-financed American lawyering and diplomatic corps have prevailed over the "interpretative lawfare" against China.[95]

88 T.V. Paul, The accommodation of rising powers in world politics, in T.V. Paul (2016), p. 20.

89 John Yoo (2017), p. 149.

90 Nazli Choucri and Robert C. North, *Nations in Conflict: National Growth and International Violence* (San Francisco, Calif.: W.H. Freeman, 1975), p. 28; Randall L. Schweller and Xiaoyu Pu (2011), p. 43.

91 Arnulf Becker Lorca (2014), p. 26.

92 William E. Scheuerman, *The End of Law: Carl Schmitt in the Twenty-First Century* (London and New York: Rowman & Littlefield, 2020), p. 171 (noting that "All forms of liberal law are necessarily plagued by the problem of radical indeterminacy").

93 Paulus argues that even the concept of the "international community" would not be constructed without regard to US views on it. See Andreas Paulus, The influence of the United States on the concept of the "International Community," in Michael Byers and Georg Nolte (2003), p. 89.

94 Michael Byers (2003), p. 37.

95 In this lawfare, contrary views on the law of the sea have been successfully suppressed. See *ibid.*

From a Chinese viewpoint, Western-centric legal views fail to recognize the existence of "indeterminacy" in the current law of the sea system while just adhering to the concept of the "one and universal" law of the sea.[96] China criticizes Western lawyers for assuming that their legal experience in the regional context is the embodiment of the universality of the law of the sea without thinking "interaction between the international and the local [viewpoints] as a relevant dimension of their professional practice."[97]

In the shadow of US hegemonic influence, states on the periphery have led a seemingly tranquil international life in the eyes of Western states; yet most of that stability was due to the size and reach of the broader intellectual, legal, and cultural environment that the US made.[98] However, peripheral states, such as a China previously, did entertain different visions for and perspectives on legitimate interpretations of the law of the sea according to their historical and local context.[99]

Having gained more power, China—posing as a champion of non-Western interpretation of UNCLOS—puts forward its interpretation of the maritime institutions to address "long-standing injustice of international law," which is (in China's view) full of "development deficit" and "democracy deficit."[100] China claims that the legal situations of the majority of states will be improved if the maritime legal system accepts more proposals for interpreting UNCLOS from developing states.[101] As discussed in Chapter 2, the Chinese legal view stands in sharp contrast to that of the US, meaning that controversy over the interpretation and implementation of UNCLOS will likely continue as to whether a particular act is lawful.[102]

Questions are thus posed to legal scholarship: until what point can the current Western-centric maritime legal arrangements (and its leading interpretation) survive as politically tolerable? And in case of institutional changes

---

96 Arnulf Becker Lorca (2014), p. 26.

97 *Ibid.*, p. 29.

98 Wayne Sandholtz and Alec Stone Sweet, Law, politics, and international governance, in Christian Reus-Smit (ed.), *The Politics of International Law* (Cambridge: Cambridge University Press, 2004), p. 270.

99 Arnulf Becker Lorca (2014), pp. 27–8 (stating that "international law and international legal profession are actually embedded in concrete contexts"). See also Kai He, Chna's bargaining strategies for a peaceful accommodation after the Cold War, in T.V. Paul (2016), p. 206.

100 Congyan Cai (2019), p. 24. See also Wayne Sandholtz and Alec Stone Sweet, Law, politics, and international governance, in Christian Reus-Smit (2004), p. 245.

101 Congyan Cai (2013), pp. 775–783.

102 Morton A. Kaplan and Nicholas deB. Katzenbach (1961), p. 7 (noting that controversy will continue because of the absence of authority for judicial resolution).

of maritime institutions, which means (orderly adaptation through interpretation or amendment or less orderly means like use of force) will prevail?[103] For one thing, China rejects US ideological hegemony over the privilege in UNCLOS interpretation, in which America has maintained maritime stability, despite the indeterminacy of UNCLOS.[104] Also, in East Asia, "ideological control by [US] virtual monopoly on the production of social, cultural, and symbolic capital" over defining the meanings of maritime institutions seems to have dramatically decreased, which negatively impacts political tolerability for maritime institutions.[105]

For another, states have been compelled to explain and justify their action in legal terms, which has implications for the mode of maritime institutional change.[106] States make use of international law in arguing about, bolstering and contending particular decisions against concrete settings.[107] Material power alone cannot support legal authority over maritime governance in East Asia.[108] If the US ignores a reasonable demand for institutional change, despite a growing number of states calling for adaptation of the law of the sea system, the American authority to interpret UNCLOS will significantly recede. In addition, if China or the US relies on a less orderly means in lieu of consultation and accommodation, instability and escalation will ensue; in such a case, the regional community will not regard such an interpretation as "legal" or "legitimate."[109]

---

103 *Ibid.*, pp. 16–7.

104 Peter-Tobias Stoll, Compliance: multilateral achievements and predominant powers, in Michael Byers and Georg Nolte (2003), p. 476.

105 Randall L. Schweller and Xiaoyu Pu (2011), p. 49–50 (mentioning that non-unipolar (bipolar or multipolar) order in East Asia precipitates the change).

106 Heath Pickering, "Why Do States Mostly Obey International Law?" E-International Relatios, February 2014, at https://www.e-ir.info/2014/02/04/why-do-states-mostly-obey-international-law/; Andrew Hurrell, International Society and the Study of Regimes: A Reflective Approach, in Volker Rittberger and Peter Mayer (eds.), *Regime Theory and International Relations* (Oxford: Clarendon Press, 1993), p. 59.

107 Monica Hakimi, "Why Should We Care About International Law?" *Michigan Law Review*, 118 (2020), p. 1306; James R. Crawford, Brounlie's Principles of Public International Law 15 (2012) (noting that "[a]ll normal governments employ experts to provide routine and other advice on matters of international law and constantly define their relations with other States in terms of international law").

108 Monica Hakimi, "Why Should We Care About International Law?" *Michigan Law Review*, 118 (2020), p. 1299 (arguing that law fosters "the expectation that governance decisions must be rooted in authority").

109 Stephen Toope, Powerful but unpersuasive? The role of the United States in the evolution of customary international law, in Michael Byers and Georg Nolte (2003), p. 316; Michael Byers (2003), p. 6.

So far, both China and the US have adopted an orderly means for the lawfare to obtain other players' appraisal of "legitimate interpretation" within the UNCLOS normative structures.[110] Since China adduces alternative interpretative concepts in the eyes of East Asia, its propositions should offer better legal situations for the region;[111] otherwise, "the result could be a return to the old thinking."[112]

Theoretically, the most dominant state does not always prevail in this normative debate because the law of the sea is not a "mere static body of rules" but a "whole decision-making process"[113] or, in the perception of the New Haven School, "[a] process of continuous interaction, of continuous demand and response, [in which] other decision-makers ... weigh and appraise these competing claims."[114] China and the US clarify how the "interests and values of a broader group" have been reflected in their interpretation,[115] and then, regional decision-makers (audience) will take part in an "argumentative practice," making use of public normative references.[116] In the end, regional players will take

110 Jeffrey W. Legro, Purpose Transitions China's Rise and the American Response, in Robert S. Ross and Zhu Feng (2008), p. 173; Wayne Sandholtz and Alec Stone Sweet, Law, politics, and international governance, in Christian Reus-Smit (2004), pp. 256–7. Weak players internalize certain interpretations of powerful states as "legitimate" through socialization. See Nico Krisch (2005), p. 374.

111 Yinhong Shi, Rising China: Political Leadership, Foreign Policy, and "Chineseness," in Vinod K. Aggarwal and Sara A. Newland (2015), p. 109 (insisting that "[China] must do its utmost to keep old friends and win new ones along its geographical periphery, mitigating old resentments, avoiding new antagonisms, and creating strategic partners or even allies over the longer term").

112 Jeffrey W. Legro, Purpose Transitions China's Rise and the American Response, in Robert S. Ross and Zhu Feng (2008), p. 173.

113 Wayne Sandholtz and Alec Stone Sweet, Law, politics, and international governance, in Christian Reus-Smit (2004), p. 258; McDougal, Myres, "The Hydrogen Bomb Tests and the International Law of the Sea," *American Journal of International Law*, 49 (1955), pp. 356–7.

114 McDougal, Myres (1955), pp. 356–7. See also Rosalyn Higgins, "Policy Considerations and the International Judicial Process," *International & Comparative Law Quarterly*, 17 (1968), pp. 58–9 (noting that "[i]nternational law is the whole process of competent persons making authoritative decisions in response to claims which various parties are pressing upon them, in respect of various views and interests").

115 Monica Hakimi (2020), pp. 1300, 1305 (noting that such justification and clarification are subject to "external scrutiny and debate"). On the proponent of an argumentative practice structured in the international law system, see Martti Koskenniemi, *From Apology To Utopia: The Structure of International Legal Argument* (Cambridge: Cambridge University Press, 2005).

116 Monica Hakimi (2020), pp. 1300–2.

sides with a particular interpretation that is, in their view, consistent with their regional or global preferences for maritime order.[117]

In maritime institutional change, East Asian countries may be compelled by the US to support traditional Western views on UNCLOS.[118] The US assesses the Chinese interpretation of UNCLOS and the accompanying campaign to attract states to its position to be "noncompliance" and an "incitement" to noncompliance. However, according to Byers, "[s]ometimes noncompliance actually led to improved compliance; [resulting] in the development of new multilateral instruments or the clarification of particular points of law."[119] In fact, when China perceives some UNCLOS regimes as squarely hampering Chinese core interests (e.g., security) it attempts to "justify this in terms of other norms or by a reinterpretation of the old norm" ("legislating change").[120]

The law of the sea system is under pressure to align itself more closely with the shifting (and shifted) balance of power in the region for the benefit of peaceful international life. Purportedly, China will continue to resist the American-led interpretation of UNCLOS ("everyday resistance"), thereby shifting epistemic patterns of the international community.[121] Since a concert of power and adaptation does not happen naturally, measures to deal with power shift must be carefully built and maintained.[122] To this end, we need more than political dialogues.[123] The law of the sea can ease the pressure of the Sino-American rivalry in the SCS by reflecting the mutually acceptable

117 *Ibid.*, p. 1305 (explaining that the "argumentative practice thus gives external actors an important say on whether particular conduct is acceptable"). If the US or China disengages from this argumentative practice, the outcome will become "independent wrongs." *Ibid.*, p. 1303.

118 Robert S. Ross, "Balance of Power Politics and the Rise of China: Accommodation and Balancing in East Asia," *Security Studies*, 15, no. 3 (July–September 2006), pp. 366–7.

119 Michael Byers, The complexities of foundational change, in Michael Byers and Georg Nolte (2003), p. 17.

120 Morton A. Kaplan and Nicholas deB. Katzenbach (1961), p. 343. Along the same line, Michael J. Mazarr et al. argue, citing Schweller and Pu, that if rightful resistance produces reforms, the perceived injustices of a system will be reduced, thereby rendering the system more legitimate and sustainable. See Michael J. Mazarr et al. (2018), p. 66.

121 Michael Byers, The complexities of foundational change, in Michael Byers and Georg Nolte (2003), p. 2; Randall L. Schweller and Xiaoyu Pu (2011), p. 49–50.

122 Hugh White (2012), p. 133.

123 Dialogues often end up "never-ending dialogues" to establish "more empty frameworks for dialogues." See Elizabeth C. Economy and Adam Segal, "The G-2 Mirage," *Foreign Affairs*, 88, no. 3 (May/June 2009), p. 23. See also Lyle J. Goldstein (2015), p. 339.

limits between them.[124] Both sides must acknowledge the necessity of mutual accommodation between *mare liberum* and *mare clausum*. Whose interpretative campaign will prevail will hinge on how much each side legitimizes their envisioned maritime legal order, reflecting local, regional, and international interests.[125]

2 The Mode of Power Shift Reflection in the Law of the Sea

This Section discusses the mode of adaptation available under the law of the sea system. A legal injunction regarding a treaty may shift in accordance with changes in prevailing interpretations of the treaty text.[126] UNCLOS (as a multilateral treaty) inevitably undergoes "continuous evolution" arising from its absolute mutable character.[127] In theory, the SCS dispute can be, in large part, resolved when the law of the sea system works appropriately.[128] To that end, the law of the sea needs to adapt proactively by concluding US-Chinese declarations or using the in-built UNCLOS mechanism.

2.1 *US-Chinese Joint Declarations or Agreements*

A bilateral deal between China and the US is an effective way of achieving adaptation in the law of the sea regime. UNCLOS contains many indeterminable provisions that (un)willingly allow considerable latitude for states in their implementation. Joint declarations or agreements can significantly reduce differences arising from interpretation.[129]

124 James Manicom (2014), p. 366 (emphasizing that the first step for American and China should be cooperation and avoiding war, even though neither party seems prepared to accommodate the preferences of the other); Hugh White (2012), p. 127.

125 In general terms, Charles Kupchan lists three conditions that characterize peaceful transition. See Charles A. Kupchan, Introduction: Explaining Peaceful Power Transition, in Charles A. Kupchan et al. (2001), pp. 8–9.

126 Andreas Laursen, *Changing International Law to Meet New Challenges: Interpretation, Modification and the Use of Force* (Copenhagen: Djøf Publishing, 2006), p. 27.

127 *Barcelona Traction, Light and Power Company, Limited, Second Phase*, Judgment, *ICJ Reports* 1970, p. 33. See also *South West Africa, Second Phase*, Judgment, *ICJ Reports* 1966, Dissenting Opinion of Judge Jessup, p. 439 (opining, in his dissenting opinion, that "the law can never be oblivious to the changes in life, circumstance and community standards in which it functions. Treaties—especially multipartite treaties of a constitutional or legislative character—cannot have an absolute immutable character").

128 Rosalyn Higgins (1994), p. 1 (explaining that if a legal system operates well, legal disputes are mostly avoided).

129 Morton A. Kaplan and Nicholas deB. Katzenbach (1961), p. 24.

It is not new for the law of the sea system to attend to interpretative differences by joint declarations or agreements. For instance, in 1989, the US and the Soviet Union (USSR) concluded a bilateral declaration, after two naval conflicts, intending to ascertain the right of warships to innocent passage in the territorial seas of coastal states:[130] the "Joint Statement on Uniform Interpretation of Rules of International Law Governing Innocent Passage."[131] Also, the US and Canada concluded the 1988 Canada-US Arctic Cooperation Agreement to resolve the type of access right that navigating states have to the Northwest Passage in the Arctic Ocean.[132]

The Sino-American "lawfare" can be managed by an "agree to disagree" joint agreement. Indeed, China is a more reliable partner than the USSR, which sought its political legitimacy from the provocation of perpetual American antagonism. As long as China's stability and economic performance remain robust, China will find vast room to maneuver to make a deal with the US.[133] By extension, China's growing interests in developing a globally mobile navy to primarily protect its lines of commerce may lead China to arrive at some kind of common understanding with America on some contentious issues, such as military activities in foreign EEZs.[134]

Indeed, the "legitimacy deficit" problem urges both China and the US to make a deal to improve the legal situation in East Asia. For the US, the more it enforces its legal position in the SCS (e.g., FON operations), the more instability

130 J. Ashley Roach and Robert W. Smith (2012), pp. 232–239.

131 Article 2 of the 1989 USA-USSR Joint Statement on the Uniform Interpretation of Rules of International Law Governing Innocent Passage: All ships, including warships, regardless of cargo, armament or means of propulsion, enjoy the right of innocent passage through the territorial sea in accordance with international law, for which neither prior notification nor authorization is required. Visit at https://cil.nus.edu.sg/wp-content/uploads/formidable/18/1989-USA-USSR-Joint-Statement-with-Attached-Uniform-Interpretation-of-Rues-of-International-Law-Governing-Innocent-Passage.doc.

132 The US argues that the Northwest Passage (NWP) meets the geographical criteria of an international strait and contends its right to transit the passage on this basis. In contrast, Canada argues that the NWP is internal waters and therefore all transits need Canadian permission. An agree-to-disagree formula emerged in 1985 when a US Coast Guard vessel announced it would transit the NWP. See James Manicom (2014), p. 361.

133 Hugh White (2012), pp. 160–1.

134 James Manicom (2014), p. 358 (adding that reaching an accommodation may reduce the probability of conflict). See also Robert J. Art, The United States and the Rise of China: Implications for the Long Haul, in Robert S. Ross and Zhu Feng (2008), p. 288; Anthea Roberts (2017), p. 319 (noting that even if China and the US cannot agree on how to approach military activities in foreign EEZs, they can understand each other's perspectives by seeing how the same actions might be viewed through another's eyes).

the region suffers.[135] On the flip side, Chinese unilateral actions (e.g., excessive law enforcement or adhering to the "nine-dash line") are perceived as an attempt to "gain advantage in changing the status quo while ignoring the legitimate concerns of other regional states."[136] China and the US can address "legitimacy deficit" by coming up with a new regional maritime order because Asian countries will support American resistance to Chinese hegemony, but not the denial of a larger Chinese role in Asian affairs.[137]

China and the US have already agreed upon some non-binding agreements within the UNCLOS system. In April 2014, for instance, both navies led the adoption of a Code for Unplanned Encounters at Sea (CUES), which was signed by 21 Pacific nations at the Western Pacific Naval Symposium hosted by China. Shortly thereafter, at a US-China Summit in Beijing in November 2014, both leaders announced two memoranda of understanding (MOUs) as military-to-military confidence-building measures.[138] This "agree to disagree" formula does not prejudice either side's perspective on military activities permissible in EEZs, but effectively shows a mutual interest in avoiding unplanned, dangerous encounters at sea and in the air.[139]

Within this "agree to disagree" formula, the US purportedly conducts a less frequent intelligence-gathering program, signaling its benign intentions. When the US provides notification of its operations taking place in the Chinese EEZ, China could regard it as "asking permission" required under its domestic law.[140] In return, China seemingly follows internationally accepted

135 James Manicom (2014), p. 358 (emphasizing that "US forces are now seen as an unwelcome, highly-mobile foreign military presence in the Chinese sphere of influence").

136 Katherine Morton (2016), p. 930.

137 Hugh White (2012), p. 81. See also Yukon Huang (2017), p. 171 (noting that most of regional states, including disputants, are eager for having both states in the region as a "positive force" in the interest of maintaining peace through balance that provides more options in the region).

138 The first MOU is Memorandum of Understanding Between the United States of America Department of Defense and the People's Republic of China Ministry of National Defense on Notification of Major Military Activities Confidence-Building Measures Mechanism, which was signed in Washington and Beijing, October 31 and November 4, 2014, at https://dod.defense.gov/Portals/1/Documents/pubs/141112_MemorandumOfUnderstandingOnNotification.pdf. The next MOU is Memorandum of Understanding Between the Department of Defense of the United States of America and the Ministry of National Defense of the People's Republic of China Regarding the Rules of Behavior for Safety of Air and Maritime Encounters, which was signed in Washington and Beijing, November 9–10, 2014, at https://digital.library.unt.edu/ark:/67531/metadc949788/.

139 Ian E. Rinehart and Bart Elias, China's Air Defense Identification Zone (ADIZ), Congressional Research Service, 7–5700, p. 32.

140 James Manicom (2014), pp. 361–3.

patterns of behaviors at sea when intercepting, in order to reduce the risk of misunderstanding.[141] That is, the MOUS neither harm America's legal position on navigational freedoms nor ignore Chinese domestic restrictions by law.[142]

There are some advantages to taking this approach. First, an "agree to disagree" formula will satisfy China and practically soften the primary source of China's dissatisfaction with American-centric maritime order while helping safer navigations for US vessels.[143] Second, China and the US can choose one issue at a time for consultation (not as a one-size-fits-all formula). Multiple declarations, if any, can be accumulated at some point for the benefit of clarification. Third, the geographical boundary of application can also be decided to not hamper US interests in navigational freedoms for other parts of the world by limiting the scope to only the East Asian Seas.[144] Fourth, no third party can claim any additional rights based on the Sino-American declaration.[145] Fifth, the domestic implementation process will be easier than treaty ratification.[146]

Focusing on the fact that restraint will be reciprocated by the other will help the start of dialog on interpretative disputes over international rules, which is a zero-sum game.[147] Also understanding another's existence and preference for

141 *Ibid.*

142 *Ibid.*

143 *Ibid.*, p. 360.

144 Some worry that if the US reaches a compromise with China in the SCS, such practice could have a global impact regardless of whether China intends so or not. See Peter Dutton, Cracks in the Global Foundation: International Law and Instability in the South China Sea, in Patrick Cronin (2012), p. 74.

145 This advantage of a non-binding formula is also relevant to the previous point. It is possible that other states request the US for special treatments as it has done to China. See, e.g., Anisa Heritage and Pak K. Lee (2020), pp. 145–146. However, these concerns are misplaced. The shift in power distribution, in particular in East Asia, is at the core of the discussion of accommodation between a dominant power and a challenger. The challenge of other small and middle powers may fall far short of the extent to which the US is expected to respond.

146 Meanwhile, Manicom claims that the Sino-American agreement should remain "informal and secret" so as to "eliminate any concern of it building a precedent for the exercise of American seapower in parts of the globe." See James Manicom (2014), p. 361. However, these concerns are misplaced. There will be more negative effects than positive ones for the agreements remaining informal and secret. Some in China and America can give a plausible pretext of not observing the agreement or terminating it. Notwithstanding its non-binding character, making it public will enhance compliance for China and the US, and respect for maritime regime from the regional states.

147 David C. Gompert and Philip C. Saunders, *The Paradox of Power: Sino-American Strategic Restraint in an Age of Vulnerability* (Washington DC: National Defense University Press, 2011), esp. pp. 3, 13, 19–37; James Manicom (2014), p. 358.

the East Asian Seas facilitates the negotiation process,[148] such that "China will need to live with US seapower" in the SCS, and reciprocally, the US "may need to live with a less intrusive maritime operation."[149]

Similar to the US interpreting UNCLOS institutions in the context of its security interests,[150] China also interprets them in light of its security interests, which is at the core of Chinese discomfort with, and concerns about, the law of the sea system.[151] In approaching the issue of security concerns within the UNCLOS regime, the legitimate application of Article 59[152] and the development of military technology that increasingly blurs a point of reference need to be taken into account.[153] On this basis, scholars urge the US to consider negotiating new regional maritime order with China to reflect its security concerns or voluntarily develop guidelines regarding military activities in the East Asian Seas.[154] Time is not on the American side:[155] China is a leading member and interpreter of UNCLOS, whereas the US is not a formal party to it.[156]

---

148 Robert Axelrod, and Robert O. Keohane, Achieving Cooperation under Anarchy: Strategies and Institutions, in Kenneth A. Oye (ed.), *Cooperation under Anarchy* (Princeton University Press, 1986), pp. 226–54.

149 James Manicom (2014), p. 364.

150 Charles Pirtle, "Military Uses of Ocean Space and the Law of the Sea in the New Millennium," *Ocean Development and International Law*, 31 (2000), pp. 8–9.

151 Michael J. Mazarr et al. (2018), p. 93.

152 Article 59 of UNCLOS reads: In cases where this Convention does not attribute rights or jurisdiction to the coastal State or to other States within the exclusive economic zone, and a conflict arises between the interests of the coastal State and any other State or States, the conflict should be resolved on the basis of equity and in the light of all the relevant circumstances, taking into account the respective importance of the interests involved to the parties as well as to the international community as a whole.

153 Sienho Yee (2010), pp. 3–4. See also Sam Bateman, "Security and the Law of the Sea in East Asia: Navigational Regimes and Exclusive Economic Zones" in David Freestone et al. (2006), p. 383 (emphasizing that coastal States may view that it gains some security by restricting the availability of knowledge on its coastal environment that is conducted by high-tech military assets).

154 James Manicom (2014), p 359. The US may consider a scheme in which it refrains "active intelligence-gathering operations or interference with coastal state electronic systems" from conducting if China acquiesces certain US military activities in and over its EEZ. Ibid.

155 Hugh White (2012), pp. 153–4 (noting that "[i]t is ... in America's interests to negotiate a new relationship with China as soon as possible ... That means America should take the initiative to offer China as much as it reasonably can to bring it to the table").

156 Michael J. Mazarr et al. (2018), p. 93.

2.2 *Modification under the Built-in* UNCLOS *Mechanism*

No multilateral treaties last forever; every treaty inevitably becomes outdated. What is more, compliance and implementation are hard to measure if a treaty partakes of (deliberate) vagueness and ambiguity.[157] Certainly, UNCLOS is neither everlasting nor self-evident. Since the adoption of UNCLOS, power distribution has changed and subsequent state practice has varied.

UNCLOS takes a flexible stance on amendments. The minimum period necessary for amendments has already passed (Article 312)[158] as UNCLOS entered into force on November 16, 1994. Besides, a simplified amendment procedure is available (Article 313).[159] Be that as it may, despite considerable differences in power distribution and subsequent practice since 1982, the amendment of UNCLOS or the development of another instrument to replace it is neither conceivable nor called for by state parties.[160] However, this is not the end of the story.

UNCLOS is an "open framework agreement" as a "living treaty."[161] As a living treaty, UNCLOS is designed to be responsive to contemporaneous cries from the seas. It therefore stands to reason that duties and obligations under UNCLOS ought to be read in a sustainable fashion.[162] In other words, the international community should endeavor to interpret UNCLOS to address the evolving challenges of today's world.[163]

---

157 Paul C. Yuan (984), pp. 432–3.

158 Article 312(1): After the expiry of a period of 10 years from the date of entry into force of this Convention, a State Party may … propose specific amendments to this Convention … and request the convening of a conference to consider such proposed amendments.

159 Article 313(3): If, 12 months from the date of the circulation of the communication, no State Party has objected … the proposed amendment shall be considered adopted.

160 Donald Rothwell et al., Charting the Future for the Law of the Sea, in Donald Rothwell et al. (2015), pp. 905–6; Robin Churchill, The 1982 United Nations Convention on the Law of the Sea, in Donald Rothwell et al. (2015), p. 45.

161 A Boyle, Further Development of the 1982 Convention on Law of the Sea: Mechanisms for Change, in David Freestone et al. (2006), p. 46; Victor Alencar Mayer Feitosa Ventura, *Environmental Jurisdiction in the Law of the Sea: The Brazilian Blue Amazon* (Cham: Springer, 2020), p. 214.

162 Richard Barnes, The Law of the Sea Convention and the Integrated Regulation of the Oceans, in David Freestone et al. (2013), p. 190.

163 Maria Gavouneli, Protection Standards for the Marine Environment: Updating Part XII of the Law of the Sea Convention?, in Stephen Minas and H. Jordan Diamond (eds.), *Stress Testing the Law of the Sea: Dispute Resolution, Disasters & Emerging Challenges* (Leiden: Brill, 2018), p. 254; Michael Wood, Reflections on the United Nations Convention on the

One may worry that the sophisticated and complex nature of the UNCLOS system is not suitable for modification. In reality, however, despite complex treaty regimes, UNCLOS is "amenable to subsequent development through a range of mechanisms that go beyond formal amendment."[164] UNCLOS can be modified and supplemented through treaty interpretation and subsequent rules of customary law of the sea. Moreover, the ambiguous nature of many UNCLOS provisions that have granted states some leeway in interpreting and implementing can militate in favor of modification by subsequent practice, reducing normative conflict.[165] Rothwell et al. explains it that under the current UNCLOS framework, "piecemeal adaptation" occurs through institutionalized cooperation.[166]

There are several built-in adaptation mechanisms for UNCLOS.[167] First, an implementation agreement is a good option: for example, the 1994 Agreement relating to the Implementation of Part XI of UNCLOS functions as a treaty modification.[168] Second, in-built UNCLOS fora can operate in a way that supports interpretation for adaptation, which include the Meeting of the States Parties (SPLOS),[169] United Nations Open-ended Informal Consultative Process

---

Law of the Sea: A living instrument, in Jill Barrett & Richard Barnes (eds), *Law of the Sea. UNCLOS as a living treaty* (BIICL, London 2016), LXXVII–LXXXII.

164 Irina Buga, Between Stability and Change in the Law of the Sea Convention: Subsequent Practice, Treaty Modification, and Regime Interaction, in Donald Rothwell et al. (2015), p. 47.

165 *Ibid.*, p. 65.

166 Donald Rothwell et al., Charting the Future for the Law of the Sea, in Donald Rothwell et al. (2015), pp. 905–6.

167 The reflection of state practice, UNCLOS-relevant international institutions, and international judicial bodies are understood as contributing to the UNCLOS mechanism. See Keyuan Zou, Certain Controversial Issues in the Development of the International Law of the Sea, in Stephen Minas and H. Jordan Diamond (2018), pp. 188–9.

168 Irina Buga, Between Stability and Change in the Law of the Sea Convention: Subsequent Practice, Treaty Modification, and Regime Interaction, in Donald Rothwell et al. (2015), pp. 52–3 (explaining that "by participating in ISA activities, non-parties to the Agreement can be deemed to have consented to the Agreement as a result of their subsequent practice").

169 SPLOS is convened in accordance with Article 319(2)(e) of UNCLOS, which states that the Secretary-General "shall convene necessary meetings of States Parties in accordance with this Convention." General Assembly resolution 37/66 approved "the assumption by the Secretary-General of the responsibilities entrusted to him under the Convention and the related resolutions." And, resolutions 49/28 and 52/26 requested that the Secretary-General should continue "preparing for and convening the Meetings of States Parties to the Convention and providing the necessary services for such meetings, in accordance with the Convention."

on Oceans and the Law of the Sea (the Consultative Process),[170] Regular Process[171] amongst others.[172] Although discussions in SPLOS are currently limited to informational and administrative matters,[173] most state parties may adopt a more forward-looking approach to discussing substantive matters on UNCLOS institutions in SPLOS. If this happens, SPLOS, not to mention the Consultative Process and the Regular Process, can investigate state practice to suggest optimal interpretation for the benefit of piecemeal adaptation.[174]

Third, the International Law Commission (ILC) is also a helpful tool for the adaptation process for UNCLOS. In fact, ILC met for seven years to prepare 1958 UNCLOS I, thereby elaborating seventy-three draft articles; and again, ILC

170 In 1999, the General Assembly (GA) established the Consultative Process in order to facilitate the annual review by the GA of developments in ocean affairs and the law of the sea by considering the report of the Secretary-General on oceans and the law of the sea and by suggesting particular issues to be considered by it, with an emphasis on identifying areas where coordination and cooperation at the intergovernmental and inter-agency levels should be enhanced (resolution 54/33). See https://www.un.org/depts/los/consultative_process/consultative_process.htm.

171 The Regular Process for Global Reporting and Assessment of the State of the Marine Environment, including Socioeconomic Aspects (Regular Process) is a global mechanism established after the 2002 World Summit on Sustainable Development to regularly review the environmental, economic and social aspects of the world's oceans, both current and foreseeable. It is accountable to the United Nations General Assembly, and its purpose is to contribute to the strengthening of the regular scientific assessment of the state of the marine environment in order to enhance the scientific basis for policymaking. See https://www.un.org/regularprocess/.

172 The clearest illustration of this adaptation is the debate on marine genetic resources ("MGR"). With the discovery of MGR on the ocean floor of the Seabed Area, the international community began to negotiate what legal regime would govern this new issue. In 2004, an Open-ended Informal Working Group was established to study the issue, and later in 2007, it was discussed in the Consultative Process. As a result, in December 2017, the General Assembly, by resolution 72/249, established the "Intergovernmental Conference on an international legally binding instrument under the United Nations Convention on the Law of the Sea on the conservation and sustainable use of marine biological diversity of areas beyond national jurisdiction" ("BBNJ Conference"). At long last, the BBNJ Conference, at the resumed fifth session from February 20 to March 3, 2023, adopted the draft agreement under UNCLOS on the conservation and sustainable use of marine biological diversity of areas beyond national jurisdiction. The agreement was adopted on June 19, 2023. See Joanna Mossop, Marine Bioprospecting, in Donald Rothwell et al. (eds.), The Oxford Handbook of the Law of the Sea (Oxford: Oxford University Press, 2015), p. 837; Visit at https://www.un.org/bbnj/.

173 There are on-going debates about whether SPLOS is authorized by UNCLOS the function of a discussion over substantive issues. See, Article 2 of Annex II, Articles 4, 6, 18, and 19 of Annex VI, and Article 319(2)(e).

174 Irina Buga, Between Stability and Change in the Law of the Sea Convention: Subsequent Practice, Treaty Modification, and Regime Interaction, in Donald Rothwell et al. (2015), p. 49 (arguing that SPLOS can be of "significant law-making effects").

submitted draft texts and commentary to UNCLOS II in 1960.[175] The main object of ILC is the "promotion of the progressive development of international law and its codification."[176] Given that the ILC's work usually involves both aspects of the progressive development and the codification of international law on a particular topic,[177] ILC can elaborate reports on the interpretation or draft an implementation agreement UNCLOS.

Fourth, a competent international body may seek an advisory opinion from a judicial organ (ICJ or ITLOS).[178] Suppose that China, through a competent body, seeks an advisory opinion about a disputing interpretative issue; the judicial organ has to contemplate such an issue to hand down clarified contents of obligations.[179]

Procedurally, the international community can task ILC with the study of contentious topics of UNCLOS; once ILC submits its reports, states can let SPLOS or the Consultative Process can review the reports before starting a review conference in accordance with Article 312.[180] A mix-and-match approach can be available, in which one or two procedures can be omitted or replaced with another (e.g., advisory opinion instead of ILC's reports).

175 Myron H. Nordquist and William G. Phalen, Interpretation of UNCLOS Article 121 and Itu Aba (Taiping) in the South China Sea Arbitration Award, in Myron H. Nordquist et al. (2017), pp. 10, 50.

176 ILC was established by the General Assembly, in 1947, to undertake the mandate of the Assembly, under article 13(1)(a) of the UN Charter to "initiate studies and make recommendations for the purpose of ... encouraging the progressive development of international law and its codification." See https://legal.un.org/ilc/.

177 See https://legal.un.org/ilc/.

178 Advisory opinions are given to public international organizations. See Articles 65–6 of the Statute of the ICJ; The International Court of Justice: Handbook, p, 82, at https://www.icj-cij.org/public/files/publications/handbook-of-the-court-en.pdf. See also the Rules of ITLOS, Articles 130–138, at https://www.itlos.org/fileadmin/itlos/documents/basic_texts/ITLOS_8_25.03.21.pdf.

179 Yoshifumi Tanaka, "The Legal Consequences of Obligations *Erga Omnes* in International Law," *Netherlands International Law Review* (published online: March 2021), pp. 27–8 (noting, on the provisions of the marine environment protection, that If the issue of marine degradation is reasoned within advisory proceedings, such an opinion may serve to clarify the contents of obligations (*erga omnes*) under Part XII of UNCLOS). Philippe Gautier, who served as Registrar of ITLOS from 2001 to 2019, bespeaks that in advisory proceedings, non-governmental organizations (NGOs) may play a role, despite the lack of provisions on the status of NGOs before ICJ or ITLOS. See Philippe Gautier, "The role of international courts and tribunals in the development of environmental law," Proceedings of the Annual Meeting, the American Society of International Law, 109 (2015), pp. 192–3.

180 Keyuan Zou also mentions the need for the review conference mechanism provided for by UNCLOS. See Keyuan Zou, Certain Controversial Issues in the Development of the International Law of the Sea, in Stephen Minas and H. Jordan Diamond (2018), p. 189.

Obviously, this modification process through the built-in UNCLOS mechanism is compatible with the formal amendment process in UNCLOS.[181]

No matter what procedure states may take, the importance lies in the identification of subsequent practice.[182] In 2009 *Dispute Regarding Navigational and Related Rights* (Costa Rica v. Nicaragua) ICJ opines that "there are situations in which the parties' intent upon conclusion of the treaty was … a meaning or content capable of evolving, not one fixed once and for all, so as to make allowance for … developments in international law."[183] ICJ further confirms that "where the parties have used generic terms in a treaty, the parties necessarily having been aware that the meaning of the terms was likely to evolve over time."[184] This ICJ's confirmation seems to support the argument that declarations or statements can constitute a modification of UNCLOS (despite Article 310)[185] if "there [are] a sufficiently large number of declarations expressing the same view of the meaning of [UNCLOS] so that they constitute subsequent practice in the application of a treaty."[186] From this perspective, it is possible for most UNCLOS members, including BRICS, to express the same view on particular UNCLOS institutions in a declaration with a view to engendering a modification effect.

In fact, the subsequent practice of coastal states has been developed in conjunction with national security concerns under the EEZ regime. On the adoption of UNCLOS, Yuan assessed that every state cannot be satisfied with

181 Irina Buga, Between Stability and Change in the Law of the Sea Convention: Subsequent Practice, Treaty Modification, and Regime Interaction, in Donald Rothwell et al. (2015), p. 48 (noting that even a tacit modification by subsequent practice is compatible with the amendment mechanism of UNCLOS).

182 Donald Rothwell et al., Charting the Future for the Law of the Sea, in Donald Rothwell et al. (2015), p. 894 (explaining that UNCLOS has been developed by heavily relying on state practice).

183 *Dispute Regarding Navigational and Related Rights* (Costa Rica v. Nicaragua), *ICJ Reports* 2009, p. 242, para. 64.

184 *Ibid.*, p. 242, para. 66 (adding that "where the treaty has been entered into for a very long period … the parties must be presumed … to have intended those terms to have an evolving meaning").

185 Article 310: Article 309 (reservations are not allowed) does not preclude a State … from making declarations or statements … provided that such declarations or statements do not purport to exclude or to modify the legal effect of the provisions of this Convention in their application to that State.

186 Robin Churchill, The 1982 United Nations Convention on the Law of the Sea, in Donald Rothwell et al. (2015), p. 34. Article 31(3)(b) of the Vienna Convention on the Law of the Treaties (VCLT) sets out that "[t]here shall be taken into account, together with the context: … (b) any subsequent practice in the application of the treaty which establishes the agreement of the parties regarding its interpretation."

all of the UNCLOS institutions; however, one question that has to be asked is "whether the point in disagreement is substantial and of such dimension as to threaten the national interests of the country concerned in a fundamental way."[187] At the risk of oversimplifying, the US-Chinese "lawfare" is all about national security concerns.[188]

In East Asia, there has been effort to clarify the legal nature of the EEZ regime. For instance, about 14 ocean law and policy scholars from Japan, Australia, Indonesia, the Philippines, China, South Korea, Vietnam, India, and a judge from ITLOS (the so-called "EEZ Group 21") held a series of meetings from 2003 to 2005 and adopted "Guidelines for Navigation and Overflight in the Exclusive Economic Zone A Commentary."[189] Despite non-binding character of the guidelines, the Guidelines can contribute to balancing and clarifying the rights and duties of maritime powers and coastal states as "works of reference."[190] However, the US is reported to have repudiated the guidelines, leaving no room for adaptation. The US simply sticks to the position that it enjoys high seas freedoms of navigation and overflight and all other internationally lawful uses of the sea related to these freedoms in EEZs.[191]

Rothwell et al. point out that "contemporary maritime security concerns have taken on new and complex dimensions."[192] Although excessive claims will continue to be challenged by the international community, legitimate security concerns of coastal states will increasingly command agreement. In other words, the reference to maritime security to some degree is necessitated in animating many aspects of the UNCLOS regime in terms of balancing maritime powers' interests in naval navigation and coastal states' worry.[193]

187 Paul C. Yuan (1984), pp. 432–3.

188 Donald Rothwell et al., Charting the Future for the Law of the Sea, in Donald Rothwell et al. (2015), p. 891.

189 Guidelines for Navigation and Overflight in the Exclusive Economic Zone A Commentary, The Nippon Foundation, at https://nippon.zaidan.info/seikabutsu/2005/00817/mokuji.htm.

190 Mark J. Valencia and Kazumine Akimoto, "Guidelines for navigation and overflight in the exclusive economic zone," *Marine Policy*, 30 (2006), p. 707.

191 Yann-huei Song, Possibility of US Accession to the LOS Convention and its Potential Impact on State Practices and Maritime Claims in the South China Sea, in Yann-huei Song and Keyuan Zou (2014), p. 112.

192 Donald Rothwell et al., Charting the Future for the Law of the Sea, in Donald Rothwell et al. (2015), pp. 899–900.

193 Donald Rothwell et al., Charting the Future for the Law of the Sea, in Donald Rothwell et al. (2015), pp. 892, 899 (noting that the phenomenon of "creeping jurisdiction" is particularly worrisome, 892). American values are more aligned with great powers; therefore, small and middle powers that have supported the US interpretation on UNCLOS can change their positions insofar as they find more values and interests in the Chinese

Now, we turn to review the effect of US non-ratification of UNCLOS concerning a multilateral way of reflecting power shift. The US government and many scholars hold that ratifying UNCLOS is beneficial to the US and the global order. The advantage includes legitimizing its FON operations, eliminating hypocrisy,[194] legitimately checking Chinese behaviors,[195] enhancing its credibility,[196] and exercising leadership.[197] Ratification would also permit the US to formally, more effectively participate in the interpretation and development of UNCLOS when the "rights that are vital to [American] interests are debated and interpreted."[198]

Regardless of ratification, the US will continue to challenge (by, e.g., FON) the coastal states that behave, in the eyes of America, at variance with the law of the sea.[199] In addition, the US can take part, indirectly, in the UNCLOS law-making or law-interpreting process through its allies (such as EU, Australia,

---

version of interpretation, centered on security. See Peter-Tobias Stoll, Compliance: multilateral achievements and predominant powers, in Michael Byers and Georg Nolte (2003), p. 476 (explaining that many states will decide whether they continue to rely on a powerful ally by agreeing on US values and interests "in spite of its sometimes doubtful methods").

194 Michael J. Mazarr et al. (2018), pp. 130–1; Klaus Heinrich Raditio (2019), p. 166.

195 Michael J. Kelly, "United States Ratification of the Law of the Sea Convention: Securing our Navigational Future While Managing China's Blue Water Ambitions," *Case Western Reserve Journal of International Law*, 45 (2012), pp. 463–464, at: https://scholarlycommons.law.case.edu/jil/.

196 James Manicom (2014), p. 366; Hillary Rodham Clinton, Secretary of State, San Francisco Marriott Marquis, San Francisco, CA, Remarks on Innovation and American Leadership to the Commonwealth Club, October 15, 2010, at https://2009-2017.state.gov/secretary/20092013clinton/rm/2010/10/149542.htm.

197 Yann-huei Song, Possibility of US Accession to the LOS Convention and its Potential Impact on State Practices and Maritime Claims in the South China Sea, in Yann-huei Song and Keyuan Zou (2014), p. 77; Aaron M. Riggion, "Giving Teeth to the Tiger: How the South China Sea Crisis Demonstrates the Need for Revision to the Law of the Sea," *Military Law Review*, 224, no. 3 (2016), p. 636, fn. 228.

198 David D. Caron & Harry N. Scheiber, The United States and the 1982 Law of the Sea Treaty, *ASIL Insights*, 11, Issue 16 (June 11, 2007), at https://www.asil.org/insights/volume/11/issue/16/united-states-and-1982-law-sea-treaty. See also The White House Council on Environmental Quality, Final Recommendations of the Interagency Ocean Policy Task Force, July 19, 2010, pp. 8–9, at https://obamawhitehouse.archives.gov/files/documents/OPTF_FinalRecs.pdf; Aaron M. Riggion, "Giving Teeth to the Tiger: How the South China Sea Crisis Demonstrates the Need for Revision to the Law of the Sea," *Military Law Review*, 224, no. 3 (2016), p. 634.

199 Yann-huei Song, Possibility of US Accession to the LOS Convention and its Potential Impact on State Practices and Maritime Claims in the South China Sea, in Yann-huei Song and Keyuan Zou (2014), p. 117.

and Japan). More to the point, a non-party status will guarantee the US freedom of maneuvering without treaty constraint.[200]

Nonetheless, such freedom does not come without harm to American interests and maritime legal order. Non-ratification will make the US remain devoid of a necessary voice in the interpretation and development of UNCLOS.[201] Being an observer or off-shore balancer will increasingly reduce US influence over the law of the sea discussion in the system. Illustrative of this is the discussion on the conservation and sustainable use of marine biodiversity in areas beyond national jurisdiction (BBNJ).[202] The US maintained that the high seas regime should be applied to BBNJ during negotiations. Despite this effort, in 2017, the international community, led by China and the G77 group of nations, established the "Intergovernmental Conference" to develop a legally binding instrument for BBNJ under UNCLOS.[203]

Also, US non-ratification may has a negative effect on its "lawfare" against China: (1) China can invoke US hypocrisy regularly; (2) China can formulate new customary rules, blocking the challenge of non-parties' oppositions;[204] (3) other states may suspect that a weak US legal position in challenging the denial of rights of third states by coastal states may prevent it from joining UNCLOS;[205] (4) gradually, the lawfulness of US enforcement activities (e.g.,

200 Robert S. Ross and Zhu Feng, The Rise of China: Theoretical and Policy Perspectives, in Robert S. Ross and Zhu Feng (2008), p. 301 (noting that collective rule-making within institutions can constrain the behavior of status quo powers).

201 Yann-huei Song, Possibility of US Accession to the LOS Convention and its Potential Impact on State Practices and Maritime Claims in the South China Sea, in Yann-huei Song and Keyuan Zou (2014), pp. 78–86.

202 With the discovery of marine genetic resources (MGR) on the ocean floor of, particularly, the Seabed Area, the international community, centered on UNCLOS, started negotiating to figure out which legal regime would regulate MGR in areas beyond national jurisdiction (ABNJ. Since Part XI of UNCLOS only deals with "mineral extraction," the legal regime that applies to the Area is hard to regulate MGR. See Joanna Mossop, Marine Bioprospecting, in Donald Rothwell et al. (2015), p. 836.

203 Joanna Mossop, Marine Bioprospecting, in Donald Rothwell et al. (2015), pp. 837–8; https://www.un.org/bbnj/.

204 Xuexia Liao, "The LOSC as a Package Deal and Its Implications for Determination of Customary International Law," *International Journal of Marine and Coastal Law*, 35 (2020), p. 21 (arguing that "[t]he limited number of non-Parties should not be an obstacle to establishing the content of the customary rule").

205 Manjula R. Shyam, "The U.N. Convention on the Law of the Sea and Military Interests in the Indian Ocean," *Ocean Development & International Law*, 15, No 2 (1985), pp. 167–8 (suspecting that "American claims that military freedoms incorporated within the Convention are part of customary law are questionable, and it is doubtful if they can be sustained in an international legal forum").

FON) falls under challenges by, *inter alia*, countries bordering the SCS;[206] and (5) the US will be blamed for undermining the generality of international maritime order, not to mention multilateral institutional machinery.[207]

Of course, the US can remain the predominant power in the law of sea area for a long time. Yet, even in such a case, UNCLOS will inevitably lose its effectiveness due to the absence of a hegemon's participation in it. Eventually, the institutional design that UNCLOS contains—such as the package deal, the zonal approach to the oceans, and institutions that help enforce the deal—may collapse, which entails a functional disorder and instability of ocean commons.[208] Under this scenario, the SCS neighboring countries will likely blame America for such regional instability, looking to Chinese leadership in recovering stable regional maritime order.[209]

3 Regime Creation for the South China Sea Dispute

This Section reviews the possibility of a reflecting shift in power distribution in East Asia by creating a soft-law maritime regime. Power shift gives rise to changes in international regimes.[210] As discussed in Chapter 3, the SCS is a non-regime situation, and thus, regime-building for the SCS dispute is a

206 Peter-Tobias Stoll, Compliance: multilateral achievements and predominant powers, in Michael Byers and Georg Nolte (2003), p. 476; Yann-huei Song, Possibility of US Accession to the LOS Convention and its Potential Impact on State Practices and Maritime Claims in the South China Sea, in Yann-huei Song and Keyuan Zou (2014), p. 118.

207 Catherine Redgwell, US reservations to human rights treaties: all for one and one for all?, in Michael Byers and Georg Nolte (2003), p. 413 (explaining such an effect with regard to US non-participation in human rights instruments).

208 David D. Caron & Harry N. Scheiber, The United States and the 1982 Law of the Sea Treaty, *ASIL Insights*, 11, Issue 16 (June 11, 2007), at https://www.asil.org/insights/volume/11/issue/16/united-states-and-1982-law-sea-treaty; Edward Kwakwa, The international community, international law, and the United States: three in one, two against one, or one and the same?, in Michael Byers and Georg Nolte (2003), p. 56.

209 US non-ratification and its reliance upon power than the legal system will be criticized for legitimate or, in some cases, unlawful because legal author is an integral element of being lawful. See Rosalyn Higgins (1994), p. 4.

210 Robert Keohane, The Theory of Hegemonic Stability and Changes in International Economic Regimes, 1967–1977, in Robert Keohane (ed.), *International Institutions and State Power* (Boulder: Westview, 1989), p. 75. See also Oran Young, *International Cooperation* (Ithaca: Cornell University Press, 1989), p. 205 (arguing that "[i]nstitutions change in response to an array of political, economic, technological, sociocultural, and even moral developments").

conceivable option as a part of the SCS dispute resolution.[211] The politico-legal milieu in the SCS region is ripe for the "South China Sea Council."

3.1 *The Propriety of Regime Creation in the South China Sea*

The SCS is in need of regimes not only because of the management of maritime and territorial disputes but also because of the complex nature of the ecosystem and resources distribution, albeit future maritime boundaries and settled territorial titles.[212] International institutions are rarely created in a vacuum or from chaos.[213] Regimes are more likely to arise under conditions or the existence of shared interests in complex interdependence.[214]

Rapid economic integration sets the backdrop for the liberal peace debate about whether economic interdependence fosters peaceful relations by giving states an economic incentive to avoid costly disputes.[215] Neoliberal institutionalists would argue that the salience of territorial disputes in East Asia has steadily declined due to increasing economic interdependence.[216] A regional maritime regime with a specific mandate and limited membership will offer more effective ocean governance.[217]

Indeed, the lack of institutionalized cooperative structures to attend to the SCS dispute is a major problem, which entails weak bilateral and multilateral consultations.[218] Yet, ironically, the SCS is assumed to be in a good situation for regime-creation inasmuch as "issue density is high and such interdependence

211 Sam Bateman, Maritime Boundary Delimitation, Excessive Claims and Effective Regime Building in the South China Sea, in Yann-huei Song and Keyuan Zou (2014), p. 131 (explaining that no effective regime exists in the SCS).

212 Jonathan I. Charney, "Central East Asian Maritime Boundaries and the Law of the Sea," *American Journal of International Law*, 89, Issue 4 (1995), p. 748.

213 Vinod K. Aggarwal, Reconciling Multiple Institutions: Bargaining, Linkages, and Nesting, in Vinod K. Aggarwal (1998), p. 1.

214 Robert O. Keohane (1985), p. 79.

215 From the late 1960s, substantial efforts for regional cooperation have been made in East Asia. Along the way, many regional groups emerged to help advance economic and political security. See Frank Frost, Australia's proposal for an "Asia Pacific Community": Issues and prospects, Research Paper, Parliamentary of Australia, no. 13 (December 2009), pp. 1–2.

216 Min Gyo Koo (2009) p. 29.

217 Since 1945, specific sets of rules and procedures have been developed to guide states and transnational actors in a wide variety of areas. See Robert O. Keohane and Joshep S. Nye, Jr. (2012), p. 17, fn. 21.

218 James D. Bindenagel, "Pacific Community for Peace and Governance: Toward a Framework for Peace and Security in the Pacific" in Enrico Fels and Truong-Minh Vu (eds.),

of issues can increase the demand for international regimes."[219] The cost of regime building in the region is also viewed as relatively low, owing to active formal and informal communication among the disputants under complex interdependence.[220] More important, security concerns of the disputants (e.g., Vietnam and the Philippines) associated with the rise of China, can be alleviated by regime creation, despite competing territorial claims.[221]

In the past, East Asia was perceived as very poor soil for implanting a sense of community and regional institutions.[222] However, as scholars point out, in recent years, East Asia has seen dramatic changes in perceptions about and responses to regional order, which have revolved around the new institutional environment, such as the proliferation of FTAS, regional financial cooperation, and bilateral and minilateral security dialogues.[223]

From the UNCLOS perspective, particular cooperation is called for under Articles 122 and 123, specifically that the semi-enclosed SCS[224] should be managed "directly or through an appropriate regional organization."[225] Actually, at

---

Power Politics in Asia's Contested Waters: Territorial Disputes in the South China Sea (Cham: Springer International Publishing: 2016), p. 511.

219 Mark J. Valencia (1996), p. 25.

220 Stephen D. Krasner (1982), p. 196.

221 States that border directly on China or have territorial disputes with China fear China's rising power. See Stephen M. Walt, Rising Powers and the Risks of War: A Realist View of Sino-American Relations, in Asle Toje (2018), p. 24. In fact, Asia has had more armed conflicts over disputed territories than other regions between 1945 and 2000. See M. Taylor Fravel, "Territorial and Maritime Boundary Disputes in Asia" in Saadia M. Pekkanen et al. (2014), pp. 527–9.

222 Min Gyo Koo (2009) p. 38.

223 Vinod K. Aggarwal and Min Gyo Koo, The Past, Present, and Future of Asia's Institutional Architecture, in Vinod K. Aggarwal and Min Gyo Koo (2008), pp. 290–291.

224 International law scholars generally agree on the semi-enclosed character of the SCS. See, e.g., Zou Keyuan (2009), p. 130; Nien-Tsu Alfred Hu, "South China Sea: Troubled Waters or a Sea of Opportunity?" *Ocean Development & International Law,* 41, no. 3, 2010, pp. 203–213.

225 Article 123: States bordering an enclosed or semi-enclosed sea should cooperate with each other in the exercise of their rights and in the performance of their duties under this Convention. To this end they shall endeavour, directly or through an appropriate regional organization: (a) to coordinate the management, conservation, exploration and exploitation of the living resources of the sea; (b) to coordinate the implementation of their rights and duties with respect to the protection and preservation of the marine environment; (c) to coordinate their scientific research policies and undertake where appropriate joint programmes of scientific research in the area; (d) to invite, as appropriate, other interested States or international organizations to cooperate.

the final meeting of UNCLOS III in 1982, Vietnam proposed that "large-scale international cooperation among bordering States for rational utilization of the SCS for the benefit of all countries concerned in conformity with Article 123 of the Convention."[226]

Here, the propriety of regime creation for the SCS will be examined in accordance with Krasner's five causal variables in the development of regimes: egoistic self-interest, political power, norms and principles, habit and custom, and knowledge.[227] First, egoistic self-interest should be assessed since self-interests, in most cases, prevail in international politics. In calculating interest, the most intractable issue is by far territorial title. However, most of the disputants may consider shelving the territorial issue for the sake of maintaining complex interdependence. Empirical data shows that regional states exercise considerable restraint in territorial claims for the benefit of economic interdependence.[228] Charney suggests that the East Asian Seas can be multilaterally used without prejudice to the underlying territorial and maritime boundary issues by deferring these "more politically charged issues to the indefinite future."[229] Ba also forecasts that the other claimants might compromise sovereignty over the Spratlys by freezing their claims to induce China to cooperate.[230]

Second, political power is necessary for regime building. In other words, the political will of all parties is paramount to the success of establishing a cooperative regime.[231] Political power is materialized by providing the common good and by enhancing particular interests of actors within the system.[232]

226 Speech by Vietnamese Ambassador Le Kim Chung, Head of Vietnamese Delegation, Jamaica, December 1982, Vietnamese Foreign Ministry's Doc., Vol. 12, 1982, quoted in Pham Hao, An Overview of the Law of the Sea Implications in Vietnam 3 (paper written by a legal officer in the Dept. of International Law and Treaties of the Vietnam Foreign Ministry, 1993).

227 Stephen D. Krasner (1982), pp. 195–204. Min Gyo Koo also analizes the feasibility of regime building in the region by using Krasner's theory. See Min Gyo Koo (2017), pp. 59–64.

228 For a general description of interdependence between China and ASEAN, see Stephen V. Marks and Cheryl Jia Min Yau, China and the ASEAN Economies: Interdependence and Rivalry, in Roderick Macdonald (eds), *Southeast Asia and the ASEAN Economic Community* (Palgrave Macmillan, 2019), pp. 381–419. For the effect of interdependence for avoiding war between China and Vietnam, see Min Gyo Koo (2009) p. 141.

229 Jonathan I. Charney (1995), pp. 747–8.

230 Mark J. Valencia et al. (1997), p. 186, fn. 151.

231 Shih-Ming Kao et al., "Regional Cooperation in the South China Sea: Analysis of Existing Practices and Prospects," *Ocean Development & International Law*, 43 (2012), p. 292.

232 Stephen D. Krasner (1982), pp. 917–8.

The claimants can show their political power, borrowing Kindleberger's lists, in (1) protecting actors from force by eradicating piracy and setting an effective search and rescue mechanism; (2) establishing maritime standards for, *inter alia*, safe navigation, marine scientific research, and cooperative fisheries; (3) constructing public works through projects, such as the Belt and Road Initiative (BRI);[233] and (4) compensating for ocean imperfections by, e.g., providing scientific data for climate change.[234]

Notably, China has provided certain functions of the above to show off its political power to the SCS.[235] It seems that political power will be increasingly furnished in the region with the Sino-American rivalry underway today. Hegemonic stability theory offers that hegemon can facilitate a particular type of cooperation.[236] If this theory is correct, China—as a returning regional hegemon—may facilitate a regional regime that is conducive to China-led maritime order.[237]

Third, norms and principles endogenously influence the creation, persistence, and dissipation of regime, while having no bearing on the issue area of the regime. Diffuse principles and norms, such as sovereignty and reciprocity in international relations, condition state behavior.[238] Above all, basic principles of international law and UNCLOS (e.g., peaceful dispute settlement or free trade through the SCS) work as norms of the region.[239] Additionally, the

233 Over the first five years of the initiative, more than $500 billion in BRI-related capital has flowed into Cambodia, Indonesia, Malaysia, Singapore, and Vietnam alone. Much of this capital comes from Chinese sources for developing transportation links. See Carla P. Freeman and Mie Ōba, Bridging the Belt and Road Divide, Carnegie Endowment for International Peace (Alliance Policy Coordination Brief), October 2019, P. 1. A recent survey shows that many Asian opinion leaders in 26 Asian nations perceive that the BRI is a positive development, facilitating international economic cooperation and development. See Pradumna b. Rana, Chia Wai-Mun and ji Xianbai, *China's Belt and Road Initiative: A perception survey of Asian Opinion Leaders,* S. Rajaratnam School of International Studies Singapore, The RSIS Working Paper series, November 25 2019, NO. 325.

234 Stephen D. Krasner (1982), p. 918.

235 Koo regards the freedom of the high seas, security and safety of sea lanes, maintenance of orderly use of the sea, and protection of ocean environment as political power. See Min Gyo Koo (2017), p. 60.

236 Robert O. Keohane (1985), p. 31.

237 *Ibid.*

238 Stephen D. Krasner (1982), pp. 200–1.

239 In its recent white paper on "China's Policies on Asia-Pacific Security Cooperation," China reaffirmed its commitment to UNCLOS, while reiterating that "for disputes over territories and maritime rights and interests, the sovereign states directly involved should … seek a peaceful solution through negotiation and consultation." See Ministry of Foreign Affairs of PRC, China's Policies on Asia-Pacific Security Cooperation, January 11, 2017, at https://www.fmprc.gov.cn/mfa_eng/zxxx_662805/t1429771.shtml.

"Five Principles of Peaceful Coexistence" that China has incorporated into its diplomatic documents with over 160 countries can play as an underlying ethos of the region.[240] Further, the concept of *tianxia*—a hierarchical system—may develop into regional norms provided that "a tianxia order [paves] the way for the novel solution of [territorial disputes], and [leads] to greater stability within the region."[241] In theory, a dominant state prefers a "softer and more hierarchical international law";[242] as such, many Chinese scholars promote the value of hierarchical international norms for contributing to international peace.[243] In brief, a tianxia order may boost the idea of regime creation.

Fourth, usage and custom—as a supplementing pressure for interest, power, and values—are "regular patterns of behavior" that lead to "shared expectations."[244] Max Weber defines usage as a typically uniform activity kept on the beaten track simply because men are "accustomed" to it and persist in it by unreflective imitation.[245] The uniformity of mere usages can be of importance in the formation of groups of social intercourse: giving a certain impetus toward the formation of feelings of "ethnic" identification and, in that way, contribute to the creation of community.[246]

Although the SCS was noted for significant military clashes,[247] the region has been witnessed several multilateral cooperative activities since the establishment of ASEAN in 1967[248] that include: (1) the adoption of the Declaration

240 JIA Guide, New China and International Law: Practice and Contribution in 70 Years, *Chinese Journal of International Law*, 18, no. 4 (2019), p. 731. Legro assures that China's dogged promotion of the Five Principles will produce "no real commitment to major revision of the system." See Jeffrey W. Legro, Purpose Transitions China's Rise and the American Response, in Robert S. Ross and Zhu Feng (2008), pp. 167–8.

241 Allen Carlson, "Moving Beyond Sovereignty? A brief consideration of recent changes in China's approach to international order and the emergence of the tianxia concept," *Journal of Contemporary China*, 20, no. 68 (2011), pp. 101–2. See also John K. Fairbank, A Preliminary Framework, in John K. Fairbank (1968), p. 2.

242 Nico Krisch (2005), pp. 390–2.

243 Yan Xuetong (2011), p. 105 (arguing that during the Cold War, within each block (NATO and Warsaw Pact) no military conflict was observed because of America's and USSR's special status inside of the system).

244 Stephen D. Krasner (1982), pp. 202–3.

245 Max Rheinstein, *Max Weber on Law in Economy and Society* (Cambridge-Massachusetts: Harvard University Press, 1966), p. 20.

246 *Ibid.*, p. 21.

247 Between 1974 and 1999, there were 13 military clashes among the claimants: 4 between China and Vietnam, 5 between China and the Philippines, 2 between Vietnam and the Philippines, 1 between Taiwan and Vietnam, and 1 between Malaysia and the Philippines. See Sulan Chen, Instrument and Induced Cooperation: Environmental Politics in the South China Sea, Ph.D. Dissertation at the University of Maryland, 2005, p. 8.

248 Michael Leifer, "The ASEAN States: No Common Outlook," *International Affairs*, 49, 1973, pp. 600–607.

on the Conduct of Parties in the SCS (DOC) in 2002; (2) the ongoing consultation between ASEAN and China on a Code of Conduct (COC) since 1996;[249] (3) the East Asian Seas Action Plan (1981-present) and the United Nations Environmental Programme (UNEP)/Global Environmental Facility (GEF) SCS Project entitled "Reversing Environmental Degradation in the SCS and Gulf of Thailand (2002–2008)" (the UNEP/GEF SCS Project);[250] (4) the Workshops on Managing Potential Conflicts in the SCS (1990-present),[251] and; (5) Multilateral Mechanisms in the Asia-Pacific Region.[252] In short, regional cooperation has continued in the SCS since the 1980s centered on the marine environmental protection. The UNEP/GEF SCS Project was officially transferred to the Coordinating Body on the Seas of East Asia (COBSEA) in 2009,[253] which gives further support for regime creation that covers the environmental protection.[254]

249 The first draft of guidelines to implement the COC was drawn up in 2005, although they are still in limbo. See Defusing the South China Sea Disputes: A Regional Blueprint—A Report of the CSIS Expert Working Group on the South China Sea, Center for Strategic & International Studies, October 2018, P. 2. In November 2018, Chinese Premier Li Keqiang demanded that COC should be concluded in 3 years, which deadline is already passed. See Lee Chyen Yee, "Chinese Premier Li says talks on South China Sea code should end in three years," *Reuters*, November 12, 2018.

250 "The East Asian Sea Action Plan" was part of UNEP's globally managed Regional Seas Programme and the "UNEP/GEF SCS Project" was developed under the auspices of, and approved by, the Coordinating Body on the Seas of East Asia (COBSEA), the intergovernmental decision-making body of the "East Asian Seas Action Plan" (the Action Plan). These two projects are closely linked and their mandate is partly overlapping. See Sulan Chen, Instrument and Induced Cooperation: Environmental Politics in the South China Sea, Ph.D. Dissertation at the University of Maryland, 2005, pp. 15–17.

251 One example is the "Workshop on Managing Potential Conflict in the South China Sea" which is jointly organized by the Indonesian Foreign Ministry and the Center for Southeast Asian Studies. The 29th Workshop was held in Batam, Riau Islands, on September 10–12, 2019, attended by 54 experts (in their personal capacities) from Indonesia, China, Lao PDR, Malaysia, the Philippines, Taiwan, and Vietnam. See Indonesian Foreign Ministry, "Batam Hosts Workshop on Managing Potential Conflict in the South China Sea," at https://kemlu.go.id/portal/en/read/587/berita/batam-hosts-workshop-on-managing-potential-conflict-in-the-south-china-sea.

252 These include, *inter alia*: (1) ASEAN-China Cooperation; (2) ASEAN+3; (3) China-Japan-Korea Cooperation; (4) East Asia Summit; (5) ASEAN Regional Forum; (6) ASEAN Defense Ministers' Meeting Plus; (7) Lancang-Mekong Cooperation; and (8) Shanghai Cooperation Organization.

253 COBSEA oversees the implementation of the East Asian Seas Action Plan. See UNEP, New Strategic Direction for COBSEA (2008–2012), UNEP EAS/RCU, Coordinating Body for the Seas of E. Asia Secretariat, at https://www.unep.org/cobsea/resources/policy-and-strategy/new-strategic-direction-cobsea-2008-2012.

254 Shih-Ming Kao et al., "Regional Cooperation in the South China Sea: Analysis of Existing Practices and Prospects," *Ocean Development & International Law*, 43 (2012), pp. 287–8;

Moreover, there have been some significant attempts at joint development between the disputants. For example, in March 2005, the state-owned oil companies of China, Vietnam, and the Philippines agreed on joint seismic exploration in a designated area (143,000 km2) of the SCS, although the envisaged cooperation did not materialize.[255] Also, in October 2011, Vietnam and China agreed to cooperate in issue areas, such as search and rescue, marine environmental protection, and scientific research, in several "less sensitive" areas.[256]

Fifth, the last variable is the shared knowledge of the benefit and utility of a regime as a tool to combat maritime challenges.[257] Policymakers can wield influence on domestic debate over regime creation for the SCS if such knowledge is embedded in them. The notion of shift in power distribution in East Asia is understood by actors as "new knowledge" that can usher in "revolutionary change."[258]

In summary, "power and interest" (the decisive variables that directly lead to the creation of regimes)[259] are furnished by China, putting aside the question of sovereignty.[260] When a regime creation option is under consideration, the SCS disputants should make allowance for the factors that hinder institutionalized cooperation (such as a lack of interest, mission uncertainty, shortage

Sam Bateman, Maritime Boundary Delimitation, Excessive Claims and Effective Regime Building in the South China Sea, in Yann-huei Song and Keyuan Zou (2014), p. 131.

255 The three parties affirm that the signing of the Tripartite Agreement will not undermine the basic positions held by their respective Governments on the SCS issue. See Embassy of the People's Republic of China in the Republic of the Philippines, Oil Companies of China, the Philippines and Vietnam signed Agreement on South China Sea Cooperation, March 15, 2005, at http://ph.china-embassy.org/eng/zt/nhwt/t187333.htm; Keyuan Zou, Bringing the South Pole to the South China Sea: Toward the Establishment of an International Regime for Peace and Security, in Yann-huei Song and Keyuan Zou (2014), p. 156.

256 Stein Tønnesson, The Tonkin Gulf Agreements: a model of conflict resolution? in C.J. Jenner and Tran Troung Thuy (ed.), *The South China Sea: A Crucible of Regional Cooperation or Conflict-Making Sovereignty Claims?* (Cambridge: Cambridge University Press, 2016), p. 164.

257 Knowledge can be defined as "the sum of technical information and of theories about that information which commands sufficient consensus at a given time among some social goal." See Ernst Haas, "Why Collaborate? Issue-Linkage and International Regimes," *World Politics*, 32, no. 3 (April 1980), pp. 367–368.

258 Stephen D. Krasner (1982), p. 204.

259 *Ibid.*, p. 205.

260 On August 13, 1990, Li Peng, then Chinese Premier, announced that China was ready to join efforts with ASEAN countries to develop the Spratlys; however, other disputants were not willing to put aside the territorial title and worried that China would define and dictate the terms. See Mark J. Valencia et al., (1997), p. 78; Bill Hayton (2014), pp. 130, 258. China suggested joint development for the East China Sea with Japan in 1978 and in the SCS with the Philippines in 1986 and 1988. See *ibid.*, p. 121.

of funds, trained personnel and equipment, and different perceptions of the costs of surrendering national autonomy) in its regime design.[261] The issue of regime design will be discussed in Section 3.3. Before that, the following Sections will switch gears and look at how regime creation benefits China as the most important player in the regime approach.

3.2 *Why Does Regime Creation Benefit China?*

Why will China agree on regime building for the SCS dispute? It is commonly understood that China opposes multilateral dialog—which it calls "internationalization"—for the SCS issues. China may believe that a bilateral setting will give more than a multilateral dealing in fear of isolation in an internationalized forum.[262] Further, China may find strong incentives to delay the settlement of the SCS dispute for a more powerful China to attend to later.[263] As Valencia et al. examine, regime creation in the SCS cannot be conceivable if it takes no account of recognizing the vital role of China on one level and the interests of other claimants on another.[264]

Keohane and Nye's theoretical models for regime change are used to examine how regimes can reflect China's vital role and interests. The "overall power structure model" explains that the rules for international regimes will change in accordance with power change.[265] From this perspective, a growing China can enact rules for regimes within the system since the distribution of military power determines the power structure.[266] In theory, if China were to establish regional rules within a regime, international courts would make reference to such rules in search of customary international law, which would provide another long-term benefit to China.[267] Secondly, the "issue area

261 Jon M. Van Dyke and Sherry P. Broder, Regional Maritime Cooperation in the South China Sea: COBSEA and PEMSEA, in Yann-huei Song and Keyuan Zou (2014), p. 18; Mark J. Valencia (1996), p. 303.

262 Craig A. Snyder, "Building Multilateral Security Cooperation in the South China Sea," *Asian Perspective*, 21, no. 1 (Spring-Summer 1997), p. 6.

263 Min Gyo Koo (2009) p. 139.

264 Mark J. Valencia et al. (1997), p. 171.

265 Robert O. Keohane and Joshep S. Nye, Jr. (2012), p. 36 (adding that this overall structure approach does not differentiate significantly among issue areas in world politics).

266 For the same reason, Japan was considered a hegemon in the fisheries and marine science regimes in Northeast Asia, and such regimes were viewed to militate in favor of Japanese interests. See Mark J. Valencia (1996), p. 20.

267 Robert T. Kline, "The Pen and the Sword: The People's Republic of China's Effort to Redefine the Exclusive Economic Zone through Maritime Lawfare and Military Enforcement," *Military Law Review*, 216 (2013), pp. 126.

power structure model" (issue structuralism) suggests that state power can be wielded per issue area—analysis of politics has to be conducted by issue area, and the strong state in the issue area will make the rules.[268] China is the strongest player vis-à-vis other claimants in terms of fisheries, military activities, law enforcement, marine scientific research, and resource exploitation in the SCS. Under issue structuralism, China will strongly influence each issue area in the operation of a regime.

According to regime theorists, Chinese influence will be doubled through linking issues. By linking issues and side payments, issue A (e.g., territorial title) can affect issue B (e.g., fisheries) within the same regime.[269] Through issue-linkage, a regime will provide China with wide latitude in discussion and decision-making. Put another way, "[w]ithout international regimes linking clusters of issues to one another, side-payments and linkages would be challenging to arrange in world politics."[270]

Furthermore, by initiating a regime and creating rules therein, China can ascertain its peaceful development intention and its willingness of self-restraint.[271] In fact, China's neighbors bordering the SCS have the deepest concerns about China's use of force in resolving territorial and maritime disputes. Despite the 2003 Treaty of Amity and Cooperation between China and ASEAN, other claimants are concerned about the likelihood of China using force against them.[272] By building a regime, China can soothe its neighbors' concerns. In addition, America grumbles about the Chinese denial of global leader burden; yet regime creation may settle US dissatisfaction with China.[273]

---

268 Robert O. Keohane and Joshep S. Nye, Jr. (2012), pp. 42–3. "Issue areas" are sets of issues that are dealt with in common negotiations and handled by the same or closely associated bureaucracies, such as those responsible for fisheries, delimitation, or environmental protection. See Robert O. Keohane (1985), p. 61.

269 Mark J. Valencia (1996), p. 24.

270 Robert O. Keohane (1985), p. 91. A SCS regime structure may help China in dealing with other regimes, such as ASEAN, ASEAN plus three, etc. See *ibid*, p. 244.

271 Kai He, Chna's bargaining strategies for a peaceful accommodation after the Cold War, in T.V. Paul (2016), p. 204; Klaus Heinrich Raditio (2019), p. 109 (noting that "self-restraint in offensive realism is a strategy, while in defensive realism it is a mindset or paradigm").

272 Kai He, Chna's bargaining strategies for a peaceful accommodation after the Cold War, in T.V. Paul (2016), pp. 210–211; Stephen M. Walt, Rising Powers and the Risks of War: A Realist View of Sino-American Relations, in Asle Toje (2018), p. 23; Michael J. Mazarr et al. (2018), p. XIII (explaining that distrusful Asian countries of Chinese power will adopt countervailing reactions against China); Jihyun Kim (2016), p. 51.

273 Randall L. Schweller and Xiaoyu Pu (2011), pp. 68–9 (stating that "most rising powers throughout history have been less than eager to assume the responsibilities associated with system management").

Regime-building is also in line with China's official confirmation that China upholds multilateralism through international cooperation and supports a peaceful settlement of international disputes through equal and uniform international law.[274] Gradually, multilateralism is gaining in popularity among Chinese elites as a means of promoting China's ambition for status and socializing within regional society.[275] China has historically favored multilateral approaches in finding fairer and more inclusive solutions for complex issues. Similarly, China today still seeks to increase its political influence (including soft power) by actively participating in multilateralism, creating new international and regional organizations, and setting the agenda therein.[276]

In fact, China has experience in building regimes that are amenable to its interests. China created (due to its discontent with the governance system of the IMF and World Bank) the Asian Infrastructure Investment Bank in 2016, a multilateral financial institution with 102 approved member states. Also, China's experience of working within other regimes may have a spill-over effect on the SCS; more specifically, China supports the principles underlying the Antarctic Treaty System.[277]

If China initiates regime-building in the SCS, how should the US respond to such a Chinese regional hegemonic initiative? The short answer is: support.[278] It is the US that has encouraged China to engage the region through multilateral institutions. Huang argues that it is in the interest of the US that China become more integrated into the multilateral politico-economic system

274 For instance, in 2019, JIA Guide (then Director-General for the Department of Treaty and Law at the Chinese Ministry of Foreign Affairs) evinces four characteristics of China's foreign policy: (1) the respect for State sovereignty; (2) preferring peace to war; (3) upholding fairness and justice, and maintaining international law; and (4) upholding multilateralism. See JIA Guide (2019), pp. 749–50.

275 Mark Beeson and Fujian Li, "Charmed or Alarmed? Reading China's Regional Relations," *Journal of Contemporary China*, 21, no. 73 (November 2011), pp. 40, 42 (noting that regional integration is understood to allow China to pursue "its interests" and consolidate "its historical position at the center of regional affairs"); Guo Shuyong, Daguo Chengzhang de Luoji: Xifang Daguo Jueqi de Guojizhengzhi Shehuixue fenxi [The logic of the great power growth: A study of the rise of Western powers from the perspective of international political sociologyl (Beijing: Peking University Press, 2006), cited in Randall L. Schweller and Xiaoyu Pu (2011), p. 56, fn. 59.

276 Yukon Huang (2017), p. 179; Randall L. Schweller and Xiaoyu Pu (2011), p. 53.

277 Mark J. Valencia et al. (1997), p. 180.

278 For a contrary view that establishing a regional institution for the SCS may be harmful to the US, see Aaron L. Friedberg (2011), p. 167 (noting that "China has begun to build new regional institutions that are designed to exclude the United States, thereby enhancing its own leverage").

insofar as China is integrated on acceptable terms.[279] A RAND report urges America to encourage China to participate with a multilateral spirit, despite some degree of geopolitical risk.[280] Similarly, Art exhorts America to accept a China-led regional regime unless overarching American interests in East Asia are seriously influenced.[281] Suppose the US does not accept China-led regime-building in the SCS, though the regime does not limit American interests; China will take more aggressive approaches, and others, in all likelihood, will follow such a Chinese leadership.[282]

3.3 *Soft-Law Regime Building: the South China Sea Council*

The SCS and the Polar Regions have a lot of politico-legal characteristics in common. First, territorial and maritime disputes exist in the SCS, Antarctica and the Southern Ocean, and the Arctic. The territorial claims of seven countries to the Antarctic have been a significant obstacle to international cooperation.[283] The Arctic region is at the core of geopolitical tension among the Arctic states due to overlapping claims to the center of the Arctic Ocean. Coastal states, especially Russia, increasingly assert their sovereignty in the region.[284] As is the case with the SCS, there are the 1.1 million square miles of open water (the high seas and outside national jurisdictions) lying north of the five Arctic EEZs (the so-called Arctic Ocean "donut hole").[285]

---

279 Yukon Huang (2017), p. 175.

280 Michael J. Mazarr et al. (2018), pp. 120, 124.

281 See Robert J. Art, The United States and the Rise of China: Implications for the Long Haul, in Robert S. Ross and Zhu Feng (2008), pp. 273–282 (arguing that if regime-building does not disrupt the "peaceful settlement of the SCS dispute," the "preservation of freedom of commercial navigation in the [SCS]," and the "preservation of economic openness in East Asia," the US will accommodate such China's initiative).

282 Michael J. Mazarr et al. (2018), p. 93.

283 The first claim was made by Britain in 1908. Since then, six other countries have also made their claims to Antarctica: New Zealand in 1923, France in 1924, Australia in 1933, Norway in 1939, Chile in 1940 and Argentina in 1942. See Keyuan Zou, Bringing the South Pole to the South China Sea: Toward the Establishment of an International Regime for Peace and Security, in Yann-huei Song and Keyuan Zou (2014), p. 141.

284 Shiloh Rainwater, International Law and the "Globalization" of the Arctic: Assessing the Rights of Non-Arctic States in the High North," *Emory International Law Review*, 30 (2015), pp. 123–4. In particular, the so-called Lomonosov Ridge, a massive underwater range splitting the central Arctic Ocean, is at the center of the dispute, to which Denmark, Russia, and Canada all claim as a "natural prolongation" of their landmass. *Ibid.*, p. 135.

285 Council on Foreign Relations, The Emerging Arctic, at https://www.cfr.org/emerging-arctic/#!/.

Second, each region involves great powers: China in the SCS, the former Soviet Union, Russia in the Arctic and Antarctic, and America in all three regions. As such, balance of power appears to influence the development of legal situations in each area invariably. For example, soft-law cooperation in the Arctic was only able in the wake of the end of the Cold War.[286]

Third, natural resources in the SCS and the Arctic are subject to the sovereign jurisdictions of the littoral states, provided that there are neither the high seas nor continental shelf depending on certain methods of measurement.[287]

Fourth, great powers adopt obscure legal positions with a view to expanding their legal claims at the future negotiation table.[288] For instance, China relies on the "nine-dash line" in the SCS, and the USSR relied on the drawing of lines at sea (the so-called "sector lines") in the Arctic based on the 1926 Soviet Decree.[289]

Fifth, territorial and maritime disputes in the SCS, Antarctica, and the Arctic will be hard to resolve in the foreseeable future, thereby entailing the need for regional actors to focus, for the time being, on shared interests and cooperation.[290]

Sixth, the issues of the SCS, the Antarctic, and the Arctic are no longer regarded as "strictly regional" matters. Climate change and its impact on the wider oceans is one reason, and the shift in global and regional power distribution associated with the US-Chinese rivalry, which inevitably influences more expansive issue areas, is another.[291]

Although there are more commonalities than differences between the SCS and the Polar Regions, the polar approaches to the management and resolution of the dispute stand in sharp contrast to those of the SCS. A hard-law regime has covered Antarctica (the Antarctic Treaty System) since 1959 to attend to states' opposite claims.[292] On the other hand, the Arctic region is managed

286 Evan T. Bloom, "Establishment of the Arctic Council," *American Journal of International Law*, 93, no. 3 (1999), p. 713.

287 Shiloh Rainwater (2015), p. 116 (noting that Arctic resources belong to the five littoral Arctic states—Russia, Canada, Norway, Denmark, and the US).

288 Erik Franckx, Bringing the North Pole to the South China Sea: Dots and Lines on Maps and their Explanation, in Yann-huei Song and Keyuan Zou (2014), p. 172.

289 *Ibid.*, pp. 164–6.

290 Sam Bateman, Maritime Boundary Delimitation, Excessive Claims and Effective Regime Building in the South China Sea, in Yann-huei Song and Keyuan Zou (2014), p. 134.

291 Shiloh Rainwater (2015), p. 116.

292 December 1, 2020 marked the 61st anniversary of the Antarctic Treaty, which was signed on 1 December 1959 by the twelve countries whose scientists had been active in and around Antarctica during the International Geophysical Year (IGY) of 1957–58. As of 2021, 54 state parties meet regularly, exchange information, consult on matters of common interest,

under a soft-law regime, which began with a mere Finnish Government's proposal to address Arctic-wide environmental issues. In 1991, eight Arctic states adopted the Arctic Environmental Protection Strategy; afterward, on September 19, 1996, a soft-law regime (the Arctic Council) came into being based on the Declaration on the Establishment of the Arctic Council, signed in Ottawa, Canada.[293]

Before the Arctic Council came along, scholars had suspected the Soviet's participation in the regional regime; surprisingly, Russia joined the Arctic Council.[294] After that, many geopolitical analysts again supposed that the Arctic regime would not operate well because the region would be haunted by "great-power rivalry reminiscent of the Cold War"; despite conventional thinking, participants committed to settling conflicts peaceably within this soft-law regime.[295]

On the whole, the lack of a regime in the SCS will damage the national interests of the disputants in the long term, from resource management to safety and security.[296] However, the Polar Regions have different institutional

---

and adopt measures regarding the peaceful use, scientific and conservatory, of Antarctica for peaceful purposes. See Secretariat of the Antarctic Treaty, 61st Anniversary of the Antarctic Treaty General Information, Nov 26, 2020, at https://www.ats.aq/devph/en/news/185. Scholars assess that this System has adapted to changing circumstances by holding consultative meetings without being bureaucratically rigid. See Mark J. Valencia (1996), p. 33.

293 The Arctic Council was established based on the Declaration on the Establishment of the Arctic Council, signed in Ottawa, Canada. Originally, the Arctic Council was expected to serve as a forum for states bordering the Arctic to discuss environmental issues along with sustainability. Meanwhile, the role of the Arctic Council was requested to accommodate changes in the region in 2015. See Evan T. Bloom (1999), p. 712; The Arctic Council: A Backgrounder, Arctic Council, at https://oaarchive.arctic-council.org/server/api/core/bitstreams/39ab0339-4d74-4475-8534-458e35b0a98f/content.

294 Gail Osherenko, "Environmental Cooperation in the Arctic: Will the Soviets Participate?" *Current Research on Peace and Violence*, 12, no. 3 (1989), p. 144 (noting that "Westerners clung to the view that the Soviets would obstruct multilateral regime formation for the region because they regard the Arctic … as too sensitive to be an appropriate focus for international cooperation"). See also Oran R. Young and Osherenko, "International Cooperation in the Arctic: Soviet Attitudes and Actions," in Lawson Brigham (ed.), *The Soviet Maritime Arctic* (London: Belhaven, 1991), pp. 258–283, 321–327.

295 Council on Foreign Relations, The Emerging Arctic, at https://www.cfr.org/emerging-arctic/#!/.

296 Sam Bateman, Maritime Boundary Delimitation, Excessive Claims and Effective Regime Building in the South China Sea, in Yann-huei Song and Keyuan Zou (2014), p. 136; Yann-huei Song and Keyuan Zou, Conclusions and Further Reflections, in Yann-huei Song and Keyuan Zou (2014), p. 298 (warning that a future binding Code of Conduct notwithstanding, "unilateral activities will continue in the [SCS], which would become a

settings. The success of a regime for an international dispute may depend on regime design.[297] As suggested later in this Section, I argue that a soft-law-based regime is well-suited to the region considering the nature of the dispute and the politico-legal milieu thereof.

Of course, hard law is legally binding, provides a strong framework, reduces the post-agreement costs of managing and enforcing commitments, and resolves problems of incomplete contracting; yet, agreeing on hard law is difficult and slow with significant contracting costs.[298] The success story of soft law has bocame the "talk of the town"—the utility and advantage of soft law (regimes) have received a great deal of attention.

First of all, albeit lacking binding force, soft law generates significant legal effects—soft-law regimes are generally successful.[299] Second, soft law provides a "more flexible and expedient way to address urgent issues," facilitating compromise between actors with different interests and values, and different degrees of power.[300] Third, soft law produces low levels of delegation; thus, states do not worry about diminution of sovereignty.[301] Fourth, soft law offers states an "opportunity to learn about the consequences of their agreement," thereby lowering the perceived costs of subsequent moves to harder legalization.[302] Fifth, the domestic process of joining a soft law regime is, in most cases, easier and simpler in terms of no need for new legislation or big fund.[303]

---

barrier to regional cooperation and a disturbing factor to regional peace and stability as well").

297 Robert O. Keohane et al., The effectiveness of international environmental institutions, in Peter M Haas, Robert O. Keohane and Marc A. Levy (1993), p. 18 (noting that "sometimes institutions will play meager roles not due to unfortunate circumstance, but by design").

298 Kenneth Abbott and Duncan Snidal, "Hard and soft law in international governance," *International Organization*, 54, no. 3 (2000), p. 434; Shih-Ming Kao et al. (2012), p. 285. For legal positivism, non-binding soft law is not law because legal obligations distinguish law from mere norms. See Ida Folkestad Soltvedt, "Soft Law, Solid Implementation? The Influence of Precision, Monitoring and Stakeholder Involvement on Norwegian Implementation of Arctic Council Recommendations," *Arctic Review on Law and Politics*, 8 (2017), p. 75.

299 Daniel Thürer, Soft Law, in Rüdiger Wolfrum (2012), Vol. IX, p. 277; Oran Young, *International Cooperation* (Ithaca: Cornell University Press, 1989), p. 24.

300 Shih-Ming Kao et al. (2012), p. 285; Kenneth Abbott and Duncan Snidal, "Hard and soft law in international governance," *International Organization*, 54, no. 3 (2000), pp. 447–8 (noting that soft law provides the "crucial basis for cooperation between the weak and the strong").

301 Kenneth Abbott and Duncan Snidal (2000), p. 437.

302 *Ibid.*, p. 435.

303 Evan T. Bloom (1999), pp. 721–2.

Sixth, in case of non-compliance, less condemnation ensues; in other words, states will enjoy flexibility ("a large degree of freedom of action") in soft law implementation.[304]

Soft law scholars uphold that soft law *per se* is of excellent value, not just as a "steppingstone to hard law," in creating normative "covenants" and providing a basis for efficient international contracts.[305] Unlike conventional wisdom, Puchala and Hopkins point out that the effectiveness of regimes measured in terms of the probabilities of participants' compliance does not differ between hard law and soft law regimes.[306] Each soft-law and hard-law regime has its own utility and benefit, meaning that a soft law regime is not necessarily inefficient and weak. Rather, soft law is sometimes better complied with than hard law that is "precisely stated and complicated obligation."[307]

All in all, the SCS dispute can be effectively managed and gradually resolved through a soft-law regime, not to mention the convenience and affordability of initiating and agreeing on regime creation. I suggest the establishment of the "South China Sea Council" should be based on the experience of the international community in the Arctic Council. By design, the Arctic Council is an informal cooperative forum (not an intergovernmental organization) rooted in a ministerial declaration (not a binding treaty).[308] Since the norms created by the Arctic Council are not binding, in theory, the Arctic Council members do not have to abide by suggestions from the Council or its working groups.[309] Despite limitations of a soft-law character, the regime is designed to shrewdly deal with political change in no need of a new institution or treaty.[310]

---

304 Daniel Thürer, Soft Law, in Rüdiger Wolfrum (2012), Vol. IX, p. 270.

305 Kenneth Abbott and Duncan Snidal (2000), p. 456.

306 Donald J. Puchala and Raymond F. Hopkins, "International Regimes: Lessons from Inductive Analysis," International Organization, 36, no. 2, *International Regimes* (Spring 1982), p. 272.

307 Edith Brown Weiss, Conclusion: Understanding Compliance with Soft Law, in Dinah Shelton (ed.), *Commitment and Compliance: The Role of Non-Binding Norms in the International Legal System* (Oxford University Press, 2000), pp. 535–553, esp. p. 548. See also Donald Rothwell et al., Charting the Future for the Law of the Sea, in Donald Rothwell et al. (2015), p. 902 (noting that "there is no one on one relationship between institutional set-up and regime effectiveness").

308 Evan T. Bloom (1999), p. 712; Shiloh Rainwater (2015), p. 139.

309 Members can decide to either comply with or ignore such rules based on national interests and political motivations. See Evan T. Bloom (1999), p. 718.

310 Alison Ronson, "Political Climate Change: The Evolving Role of the Arctic Council," *Northern Review*, 33 (2011), p. 100.

The Arctic Council is comprised of members,[311] permanent participants (representing Arctic indigenous peoples),[312] observers,[313] the Council chair, the secretariat,[314] and six working groups.[315] The question that arises is who will get membership in the SCS Council.

For regional regimes, there is a clear trade-off between "widening" (the breadth of interests) and "deepening" (their ability to forge substantive agreements).[316] It is often argued that a small number of states with more congruent interests are suitable for a regional regime so as to have a "better chance of achieving more specific objectives, with more strongly binding requirements."[317] Echoing this logic, Kao argues that operational decision-making ought to be bestowed upon fewer states that are the direct disputants.[318] Also, Keohane and Nye explain that "specific international regimes often have important effects on interdependent relationships that involve a few

311 The "Arctic Eight" includes Canada, Russia, Norway, Denmark, the U.S., Finland, Sweden, and Iceland.

312 Permanent participants was given to six organizations representing Arctic indigenous peoples, which include the Aleut International Association, the Arctic Athabaskan Council, Gwich'in Council International, the Inuit Circumpolar Council, Russian Association of Indigenous Peoples of the North, and the Saami Council. See The Arctic Council: A Backgrounder, Arctic Council, at https://oaarchive.arctic-council.org/server/api/core/bitstreams/39ab0339-4d74-4475-8534-458e35b0a98f/content.

313 The category of observer status was created for non-Arctic states, along with intergovernmental, inter-parliamentary, global, regional, and non-government organizations for the ability to contribute to the Arctic Council. Ibid. As of November 2021, thirteen non-Arctic observer states include France (since 2000), Germany (1998), Italy (2013), Japan (2013), The Netherlands (1998), People's Republic of China (2013), Poland (1998), India (2013), Republic of Korea (2013), Singapore (2013), Spain (2006), Switzerland (2017), and United Kingdom (1998).

314 It was only 2011 that the Arctic Council established a permanent secretariat in Tromso, Norway. Yet, the Arctic Council still does not have international legal personality, let alone the secretariat. See Shiloh Rainwater, International Law and the "Globalization" of the Arctic: Assessing the Rights of Non-Arctic States in the High North," *Emory International Law Review*, 30 (2015), p. 140.

315 Ministerial meeting (the highest level of interaction) is held every two years, and the work of the Council is directed by the Senior Arctic Officials between ministerial meetings. Decisions in the Arctic Council are made by consensus of all the Arctic Eight, and the Council's revenue is derived from individual Arctic states on a voluntary basis. See Evan T. Bloom 3 (1999), p. 718 (adding that the consensus method does not impose participants' domestic policies, *ibid.*, p. 722).

316 Stephan Haggard, "The Liberal View of the International Relations of Asia" in Saadia M. Pekkanen et al (2014), p. 53.

317 Shih-Ming Kao et al. (2012), p. 285.

318 *Ibid.*, p. 290.

countries."[319] Indeed, the small number of states with similar preferences (as Haggard assesses) can more effectively cooperate and establish institutions "without having to move policies far from their stand-alone ideals"[320] and can (as Keohane parses) overcome dilemmas of collective actions.[321]

Taken together, membership of a likely SCS Council should be limited to states directly bordering the SCS. This regime design is consistent with China's long-standing position; for instance, despite its aversion to the internationalization of the SCS, China joined the UNEP's East Asian Sea Action Plan program in 2001 but with one condition of setting up a "Project Coordinating Unit" to manage the project. This is because China allegedly opposed the participation of states that do not border the SCS in the program management.[322] China will likely object to the involvement of non-SCS bordering states as members in regional initiatives.

Then what about observers? As for the Arctic Council, granting the observer status to non-Arctic states is mostly symbolic (as a secondary role) without voting rights.[323] Nevertheless, the existence of observers signals international consensus as to the "legitimacy of the 'patchwork' legal regime administering the Arctic region."[324] More significantly, by accepting non-regional observers, Arctic Eight's sovereignty, sovereign rights, and jurisdiction in the Arctic are resultantly consolidated because observer candidates should recognize such rights of the Arctic Eight. Observers should also demonstrate a political willingness and financial ability to the work of the Arctic Council.[325] In short,

319 Robert O. Keohane and Joshep S. Nye, Jr. (2012), p. 17 (emphsizing that "[s]ince World War II ... specific sets of rules and procedures have been developed to guide states and transnational actors in a wide variety of areas").

320 Stephan Haggard, The Liberal View of the International Relations of Asia, in Saadia M. Pekkanen et al. (2014), p. 48 (explaining the politics of regional regimes involving the conflict between "high-demanders" and "low-demanders" from the regime).

321 Robert O. Keohane (1985), p. 77.

322 PCU consisted of Cambodia, China, Indonesia, Malaysia, Philippines, Thailand and Vietnam. See Sulan Chen (2005), p. 17.

323 Observers shall be invited to the meetings of the Arctic Council and may submit written statements at ministerial meetings. They may propose projects through members or permanent participant, but financial contributions from observers to any given project may not exceed the financing from Arctic States, unless otherwise decided by the the Senior Arctic Officials. In the Council's subsidiary boudies, observers may make statements, present written statements, submit relevant documents, and provide views on the issues under discussion. See Arctic Council, Senior Arctic Officials (SAO) Report to Ministers, Nuuk, Greenland (May 2011), pp. 50–51.

324 Shiloh Rainwater (2015), p. 147.

325 See Arctic Council, Senior Arctic Officials (SAO) Report to Ministers, Nuuk, Greenland (May 2011), pp. 50–51.

granting the observer status to non-SCS states will enhance the legitimacy of the claimants and regional exclusiveness of the issues.

Further, the success of the SCS Council has some bearing on granting observer status to the US. China may think that US involvement induces rapid "internationalization"; however, as indicated above, it will boost the consolidation of the claimants' rights and the enhancement of the "regional profile." Suppose China rejects granting the observer status to the US, the SCS issues and regime building thereon will elicit a more negative response, which entails real internationalization.

In fact, other disputants want a US presence in the SCS for maritime safety in the first place. America will continue to be a hegemonic player in the East Asia Seas, and will for a considerable period of time.[326] On the other hand, it will be a challenge for the US to welcome and encourage China-led regional multilateral initiatives. Nevertheless, "what the US should do is not military action or building military coalitions but rather support a multilateral diplomatic channel to find some solution."[327]

Parenthetically, by design, neutrality and authority are important to the legitimacy and stabilization of the regime in its operation.[328] If the SCS Council is established, its scope of agendas may include marine environmental protection, marine scientific research, the safety of navigation and communication at sea, search and rescue operations, and combating transnational crime, all of which have been highlighted in the 2002 DOC.[329] Furthermore, the management and development of living and non-living resources, along with eco-systems and marine biodiversity, can be discussed within the regime.[330] Certainly, the SCS Council, as the Arctic Council has done, will be able to produce hard law treaties, despite its soft-law foundation.[331] On the whole, such

326 Shih-Ming Kao et al. (2012), p. 291; Jihyun Kim (2016), p. 56.

327 Nehginpao Kipgen (2020), p. 102; Michael J. Mazarr, et al. (2018), p. 127.

328 Nico Krisch (2005), p. 375 (explaining that independence of the institutions will inevitably produce constraints on the participants, including the hegemon); Edith Brown Weiss, Conclusion: Understanding Compliance with Soft Law, in Dinah Shelton (2000), p. 547.

329 Shih-Ming Kao et al. (2012), p. 290.

330 Sam Bateman, Maritime Boundary Delimitation, Excessive Claims and Effective Regime Building in the South China Sea, in Yann-huei Song and Keyuan Zou (2014), p. 132.

331 In 2011, the Arctic Council adopted a search-and-rescue treaty, and in 2013, a second binding agreement concerning oil spill preparation and response was signed at the Kiruna Ministerial Meeting. See "Agreement on Cooperation on Aeronautical and Maritime Search and Rescue in the Arctic," May 12, 2011, at https://oaarchive.arctic-council.org/handle/11374/531 and "Agreement on Cooperation on Marine Oil Pollution Preparedness and Response in the Arctic," May 15, 2013, at https://oaarchive.arctic-council.org/handle/11374/529.

cooperation supported by the SCS Council will function as a "necessary first step to resolving sovereignty disputes."[332]

4 Conclusion

One of the purposes of international law of the sea is to control both present and future state behavior at sea.[333] To this end, the law of the sea is urged to reflect both "the demands of the powerful and the ideals of justice held by international society at a given moment."[334] In other words, the role and rules of international law should be constructed and adapted out of regard for the balance of power on one side, and the interests of the region on the other.[335]

If China or the US, not to mention other regional players, sticks to one particular way of interpreting UNCLOS as a "moral mandate" (not "as the product of international negotiation"), gradual and peaceful adaptation will be hard to establish: "for institutions to be effective, they need to be treated not with veneration, but as a tool for resolving disputes, useful in the short run and adaptable to change."[336] Suppose the disputants, especially China as a regional hegemon, ignore the necessity of establishing a regional maritime regime without regard to other successful institutions (e.g., the Arctic Council), which have been successful in a similar politico-legal milieu as the SCS; such a non-regime situation will inflict unacceptable damage on each player's national interests, let alone regional stability.

As Yoo points out, today's war—in comparison with the purpose of war in the past (occupation or annexation or colonies)—pertains to removing threats to stable international order.[337] If taken without limit, if the US inexorably perceives the Chinese interpretation of UNCLOS in the SCS as a threat to a stable

332 Shih-Ming Kao et al. (2012), p. 292.
333 Michael Byers (2003), p. 49.
334 Nico Krisch (2005), p. 408.
335 Alfred Vagts and Detlev F. Vagts (1979), p. 556.
336 Theodore McLauchlin, Great power accommodation and the processes of international politics, in T.V. Paul (2016), p. 307.
337 John Yoo, *The Powers of War and Peace: the Constitution and Foreign Affairs after 9/11* (Chicago and London: The University of Chicago Press, 2005), pp. 161–163 (noting that "[US] went to war not to gain territory or a colony, nor to defeat an enemy ideology, but to remove a threat to the international order posed by a tyrannical dictator" p. 163). Political scholars suggest, concerning law and war, that "norms don't constrain states at all" or "norms matter, but states will violate them when they can." See Jonathan Renshon, *Fighting for Status: Hierarchy and Conflict in World Politics* (Princeton, N.J.: Princeton University Press, 2017), p. 176.

regional maritime order, war may break out between China and the US in the region. In this sense, how to reflect a power shift in the law of the sea system is the right question to ask when avoiding war because the ultimate measure for adaptation should influence not only the utility and effectiveness of the law of the sea but also peace and stability of the region. The same holds true for the lack of cooperative institutions in attending to territorial and maritime disputes in the SCS; the dispute can be managed within a regional maritime regime so that a less orderly means will not be considered by the stakeholders, especially China and the US.

For international lawyers and diplomats, these important tasks are on the table. If the law of the sea regime produces gradual adaptations each year, this should be viewed as a success;[338] yet, if international lawyers are unwilling to seize the initiative, and therefore, no role international law adduces for the SCS dispute, then realpolitik and soldiers may intervene in full scale to lead the SCS issues.[339] We should remember that international law and politics must "evolve to confront the threats of this century, not those of the last, without encouraging conflicts that cause more harm than good."[340]

338 Michael J. Mazarr et al. (2018), p. 125.

339 Frank Chink, Dark side of the Great Renewal: Chinese nationalism, *The Globe and Mail*, December 5, 2012, at https://www.theglobeandmail.com/opinion/dark-side-of-the-great-renewal-chinese-nationalism/article5973783/.

340 John Yoo, *Point of Attack: Preventive War, International Law, and Global Warfare* (New York: Oxford University Press, 2014), p. 3.

Bibliography

International Agreements

Convention on the Territorial Sea and the Contiguous Zone, Geneva, April 29, 1958.

Memorandum of Understanding Between the Department of Defense of the United States of America and the Ministry of National Defense of the People's Republic of China Regarding the Rules of Behavior for Safety of Air and Maritime Encounters, which was signed in Washington and Beijing, November 9–10, 2014.

Memorandum of Understanding Between the United States of America Department of Defense and the People's Republic of China Ministry of National Defense on Notification of Major Military Activities Confidence-Building Measures Mechanism, which was signed in Washington and Beijing, October 31 and November 4, 2014.

United Nations Convention on the Law of the Sea, Montego Bay, opened for signature December 10, 1982, entered into force November 16, 1994, 1833 UNTS 397.

USA-USSR Joint Statement on the Uniform Interpretation of Rules of International Law Governing Innocent Passage, Adopted in Wyoming, USA on September 23, 1989.

Cases of International Courts and Tribunals

Case Concerning Sovereignty over Pedra Branca/Pulau Batu Puteh, Middle Rocks and South Ledge (Malaysia/Singapoer), Judgment, *ICJ Reports 2008.*

Case concerning the Barcelona Traction, Light and Power Company, Limited (Belgium v. Spain), Second Phase, Judgment, *ICJ Reports 1970.*

Case Concerning the Land, Island and Maritime Frontier Dispute (El Salvador/Honduras, Nicaragua intervening), *ICJ Reports 1992.*

Continental Shelf Case (Tunisia/Libyan Arab Jamahiriya), Judgment, *ICJ Reports 1982.*

Corfu Channel (UK v. Albania), *ICJ Reports 1949.*

Dispute Regarding Navigational and Related Rights (Costa Rica v. Nicaragua), *ICJ Reports 2009.*

Eritrea/Yemen – Sovereignty and Maritime Delimitation in the Red Sea, Award of the Arbitral Tribunal in the First Stage – Territorial Sovereignty and Scope of the Dispute, Judgment, October 9, 1998, PCA.

Fisheries Case (U.K. v. Norway), *ICJ Reports 1951.*

Fisheries Jurisdiction Case (Federal Republic of Germany v. Iceland), Judgment, *ICJ Report 1973.*

Frontier Dispute (Burkina Faso v. Mali), Judgment, *ICJ Reports 1986.*

Honduras Borders (Guatemala v. Honduras), 2 R.I.A.A. (1933).
Island of Palmas (1928) 2 RIAA.
Legal Status of Eastern Greenland (Denmark v. Norway), PCIJ, Series A/B, No. 53, April 5, 1933.
Legality of the Threat or Use of Nuclear Weapons, Advisory Opinion, *ICJ Report 1996*.
Maritime Delimitation and Territorial Questions between Qatar and Bahrain (Qatar v. Bahrain), Judgment, *ICJ Reports 2001*.
North Sea Continental Shelf (Federal Republic of Germany/Denmark; Federal Republic of Germany/Netherlands), Judgment, *ICJ Reports 1969*.
S.S. Lotus (France v. Turkey), PCIJ, Series A, No. 10, September 7, 1927.
South West Africa (Liberia v. South Africa), Second Phase, Judgment, *ICJ Reports* 1966.
Sovereignty over Pedra Brance/Pulau Batu Phteh, Middle Rocks and South Ledge (Malaysia/Singapore), *ICJ Reports 2008*.
Sovereignty over Pulau Ligitan and Pulau Sipadan (IndonesialMalaysia), Judgment, *ICJ Reports 2002*.
Temple of Preah Vihear (Cambodia/Thailand), *ICJ Reports 1962*.
Territorial and Maritime Dispute (Nicaragua v. Colombia), *ICJ Reports 2012*.
Territorial and Maritime Dispute between Nicaragua and Honduras in the Caribbean Sea (Nicaragua v. Honduras), Judgment, *ICJ Reports 2007*.
The *Minquiers and Ecrehos* Case (France v. the U.K.), Judgment, *ICJ Report 1953*.
The South China Sea Arbitration (The Republic of Philippines v. The Republic of China), Award of 12 July 2016.

Documents and Reports

A Free and Open Indo-Pacific, Advancing a Shared Vision, November 4, 2019.
A/AC.138/SC.II/L.34
A/CONF.13/L.58, 1958, UNCLOS, Off. Rec. vol. 2.
Accession to the 1982 Law of the Sea Convention and Ratification of the 1994 Agreement Amending Part XI of the Law of the Sea Convention: Hearing Before the S. Comm. On Foreign Relations, 112th Cong. (2012).
Arctic Council, Senior Arctic Officials (SAO) Report to Ministers, Nuuk, Greenland (May 2011).
Bureau of Intelligence & Research, US Department of State, Limits in the Seas No. 33, Straight Baselines: the Philippines (1973).
Bureau of Oceans and International Environmental and Scientific Affairs, US Department of State, Limits in the Seas, China: Maritime Claims in the South China Sea, No. 143.
Burke, Edmund J., Astrid Stuth Cevallos, *In Line or Out of Order? China's Approach to ADIZ in Theory and Practice* (RAND Corporation, 2017).

Campbell, Caitlin, et al., *China's "Core Interest" and the East China Sea*, US-China Economic and Security Review Commission Self Research Backgrounder, May 10, 2013.

Cheng, Dean, Winning Without Fighting: Chinese Legal Warfare, Heritage Foundation, Backgrounder, No. 2692 (May 18, 2012).

Congressional Research Service, US-China Trade Relations, *In Focus*, February 16, 2021, at https://fas.org/sgp/crs/row/IF11284.pdf.

Cordesman, Anthony, and Steven Colley, *Chinese Military Modernization in 2015: A Comparative Analysis* (Washington, DC: Center for Strategic and International Studies, 2015).

Council on Foreign Relations, The Emerging Arctic, at https://www.cfr.org/emerging-arctic/#!/.

Defusing the South China Sea Disputes: A Regional Blueprint – A Report of the CSIS Expert Working Group on the South China Sea, *Center for Strategic & International Studies*, October 2018.

Department of Defense, Annual Report to Congress [on] Military and Security Developments Involving the People's Republic of China 2017, May 15, 2017.

Department of the Navy, Office of the Chief of Operations, OPNAVINST 3128.9F, July 1, 2014.

Dibb, Paul, Toward a New Balance of Power in Asia, Adelphi Paper 295 (London: International Institute for Strategic Studies, 1995).

Dunlap, Charles J. Jr., Law and Military Interventions: Preserving Humanitarian Values in 21st Century Conflicts, Harvard University Kennedy School of Government, Carr Center for Human Rights Working Paper, November 29, 2001.

Ezra, Dvir Aviam, China's Perspective of International Courts and Tribunals, Student Paper of Hebrew University.

Fravel, M. Taylor, Policy Report: U.S. Policy Toward the Disputes in the South China Sea Since 1995, S. Rajaratnam School of International Studies (RSIS), March 2014.

Frost, Frank, Australia's proposal for an "Asia Pacific Community": Issues and prospects, Research Paper, Parliamentary of Australia, No. 13 (December 2009).

Galang, Mico A, "Power Shifts and International Law: The Geopolitics of the South China Sea Dispute and Its Implications for the United Nations Convention on the Law of the Sea," *A Publication Series on National Security Issues by the National Defense College of the Philippines*, NDCP Policy Brief (December 2016, No. 3).

House of Commons Foreign Affairs Committee, China and the Rules-Based International System, Sixteenth Report of Session 2017–19, March 26, 2019.

Hsu, Kimverly, and Craig Murray, *China's Expanding Military operations in Foreign Exclusive Economic Zones*, US-China Economic and Security Review Commission Staff Research Backgrounder, June 19, 2013, at https://www.uscc.gov/sites/default/files/Research/Staff%20Backgrounder_China%20in%20Foreign%20EEZs.pdf.

International Hydrographic Organization, The Need for a Hydrographic Service, IHO Publication M2 (June 2018).

Ji, Guoxing, The Spratlys Disputes and Prospects for Settlement, ISIS, Malaysia, 1992.

Juridical regime of historic waters, including historic bays – Study Prepared by the Secretariat, A/CN.4/143 (1962), originally printed in Yearbook of the International Law Commission, Vol. II (1962).

Leifer, Michael, The ASEAN Regional Forum, Adelphi Paper 302 (London: International Institute for Strategic Studies, 1996).

Letter from the Ambassador of the People's Republic of China to the Kingdom of the Netherlands to the individual members of the Tribunal, February 6, 2015.

Marine Scientific Research: A revised guide to the implementation of the relevant provisions of the United Nations Convention on the Law of the Sea, Division for Ocean Affairs and the Law of the Sea, Office of Legal Affairs, United Nations, UN Publication Sales No. E.10.V.12, 2010.

Moynihan, Harriet, *China's Evolving Approach to International Dispute Settlement*, March 2017, Chatham House the Royal Institute of International Affairs.

O'Rourke, Ronald, "Maritime Territorial and Exclusive Economic Zone (EEZ) Disputes Involving China: Issues for Congress," Congressional Research Service (R42784), May 24, 2018.

Office of the Secretary of Defense, Military and Security Developments Involving the People's Republic of China 2020, Annual Report to Congress.

Office of the Secretary of Defense, Military and Security Developments Involving the PRC 2020, Annual Report to Congress.

PRC Ministry of Foreign Affairs, Veil of the Arbitral Tribunal Must be Tore Down – Vice Foreign Minister Liu Zhenmin Answers Journalists' Questions on the So-called Binding Force of the Award Rendered by the Arbitral Tribunal of the South China Sea Arbitration Case, July 16, 2016, at http://www.fmprc.gov.cn/mfa_eng/wjbxw/t1381879.shtml.

Rana, Pradumna b., Chia Wai-Mun and ji Xianbai, *China's Belt and Road Initiative: A perception survey of Asian Opinion Leaders*, S. Rajaratnam School of International Studies Singapore, The RSIS Working Paper series, November 25 2019, No. 325.

Remarks by Chinese Foreign Minister Wang Yi on the Award of the So-called Arbitral Tribunal in the South China Sea Arbitration, July 12, 2016, at http://www.fmprc.gov.cn/mfa_eng/zxxx_662805/t1380003.shtml.

Report of the International Law Commission to the General Assembly," in Yearbook of the International Law Commission, vol. 2 (New York, 1956).

Report of the Secretary General, U.N. Doc., A/51/645, November 1, 1996.

Rinehart, Ian E., and Bart Elias, China's Air Defense Identification Zone (ADIZ), Congressional Research Service, 7–5700.

Sixth Meeting of the Second Committee on Territorial Waters of the Conference for the Codification of International Law, League of Nations Doc.C.351(b).1930.V (L.N. Pub. No.1930.V.16).

The Congressional Research Service, U.S.-China Strategic Competition in South and East China Seas: Background and Issues for Congress, R42784, September 24, 2019.

The Government of the Philippines, "Government States Position," New Philippines (July 10, 1971).

The Ministry of Foreign Affairs, *The Hoang Sa and Truong Sa Archipelagoes and International Law* (Hanoi, 1988).

The White House Council on Environmental Quality, Final Recommendations of the Interagency Ocean Policy Task Force, July 19, 2010, at https://obamawhitehouse.archives.gov/files/documents/OPTF_FinalRecs.pdf.

The White House, the National Security Strategy of the United States, August 1991, at https://nssarchive.us/wp-content/uploads/2020/04/1991.pdf.

UN Doc A/AC.138/SC.II/L.34.

UN Doc A/AC.138/SC.II/SR.55 (1973).

UN, Marine Scientific Research A revised guide to the implementation of the relevant provisions of the United Nations Convention on the Law of the Sea, Division for Ocean Affairs and the Law of the Sea Office of Legal Affairs, 2010.

UN, Office for Ocean Affairs and the Law of the Sea, The Law of the Sea: National Legislation, Regulations and Supplementary Documents on Marine Scientific Research in Areas under National Jurisdiction (New York: UN, 1989).

UNEP, New Strategic Direction for COBSEA (2008–2012), UNEP EAS/RCU, Coordinating Body for the Seas of E. Asia Secretariat, at https://www.unep.org/cobsea/resources/policy-and-strategy/new-strategic-direction-cobsea-2008-2012.

United Nations, Division for Ocean Affairs and the Law of the Sea, Office of Legal Affairs, *The Law of the Sea: National Legislation on the Exclusive Economic Zone* (New York: UN, 1993).

United States Oceans Policy, Statement of the President (10 March 1983), 19 Weekly Compilation of Presidential Documents, No. 10 (March 14, 1984).

United States Trade Representative, 2017 Report to Congress on China's WTO Compliance, January 2018.

US Department of Defense, Air Sea Battle: Service Collaboration to Address Anti-Access and Area Denial Challenges (Arlington, VA: US Department of Defense, 2013).

US Office of Naval Intelligence, *The PLA Navy: New Capabilities and Missions for the 21st Century* (Washington, DC: U.S. Office of Naval Intelligence, 2015).

Working paper co-sponsored by Canada, Chile, Iceland, India, Indonesia, Mauritius, Mexico, New Zealand and Norway, A/CONF.62/L.4, UNCLOS III Official Records, Vol. III, pp. 82–83.

Books

Aggarwal, Vinod K, *Liberal Protectionism: The International Politics of Organized Textile Trade* (Berkeley: University of California Press, 1985).

Aggarwal, Vinod K (ed.), *Institutional Designs for a Complex World: Bargaining, Linkage, and Nesting* (Ithaca and London: Cornell University Press, 1998).

Aggarwal, Vinod K., and Min Gyo Koo (eds.), *Asia's new institutional architecture: Evolving structures for managing trade, financial, and security relations* (New York: Springer, 2008).

Aggarwal, Vinod K., and Sara A. Newland (eds.), *Responding to China's Rise: US and EU Strategies* (Cham: Springer, 2015).

Alagappa, Muthiah (ed.), *Asian Security Order: Normative and Instrumental Features* (Stanford, CA: Stanford University Press, 2003).

Allison, Graham, *Destined for war: Can America and China escape Thucydides' Trap?* (New York: Houghton Mifflin Harcourt, 2017).

Aust, Anthony, *Handbook of International Law* (Cambridge University Press, 2010).

Austin, John, *The Province of Jurisprudence Determined* (Cambridge University Press: Cambridge, 1995; reprinted in 2001).

Barbieri, Katherine, *The Liberal Illusion: Does Trade Promote Peace?* (Ann Arbor: University of Michigan Press, 2002).

Barrett, Jill, and Richard Barnes (eds), *Law of the Sea. UNCLOS as a living treaty* (BIICL, London 2016).

Batemen, Sam, and Ralf Emmers (eds), *Security and International Politics in the South China Sea* (2009).

Baylis, J., and S. Smith (eds.), *The Globalization of World Politics* (Oxford: Oxford University Press, 2001).

Bekkevold, Jo Inge, and Geoffrey Till (eds.), *International Order at Sea: How it is challenged. How it is maintained* (Palgrave, London, 2016).

Bernhardt, Rudolf (ed.), *Encyclopedia of Public International Law* (Amsterdam: North-Holland, 1984), Vol. 7.

Brigham, Lawson (ed.), *The Soviet Maritime Arctic* (London: Belhaven, 1991).

Brown, E.D., *International Law of the Sea* (Dartmouth: Aldershot, 1994), Vol. I.

Byers, Michael, and Georg Nolte, *United States Hegemony and the Foundations of International Law* (New York: Cambridge University Press, 2003).

Byers, Michael, *Custom, Power and the Power of Rules: International Relations and Customary International Law* (New York: Cambridge University Press, 2003).

Cai, Congyan, *The Rise of China and International Law: Taking Chinese Exceptionalism Seriously* (New York: Oxford University Press, 2019).

Chen, Sulan, Instrument and Induced Cooperation: Environmental Politics in the South China Sea, Ph.D. Dissertation at the University of Maryland, 2005.

Choucri, Nazli, and Robert C. North, *Nations in Conflict: National Growth and International Violence* (San Francisco, Calif.: W.H. Freeman, 1975).

Churchill, Robin R., and Alan V. Lowe, *The International Law of the Sea,* 3rd edition (Manchester: Manchester University Press, 1999).

Clingan, Thomas A. (Jr.) (ed.), *Law of the Sea: State practice in zones of special jurisdiction* (Law of the Sea Institute, 1982).

Copeland, Dale C., *The Origins of Major War* (Ithaca and London: Cornell University Press, 2001).

Crawford, James, *Brownlie's Principles of Public international law*, 8th ed. (Oxford: Oxford University Press, 2012).

Cronin, Patrick (ed.), *Cooperation from Strength: The United States, China and the South China Sea* (Washington DC: Center for a New American Security 2012).

D'Amato, Anthony, *The Concept of Custom* (Ithaca: Cornell University Press, 1971).

Danilenko, Gennady, *Law-Making in the International Community* (Dordrecht: Martinus Nijhoff, 1993).

Dixon, Martin, *Textbook on International Law* (Oxford University Press, 2017).

Dunne, Tim, Milja Kurki and Steve Smith (eds.), *International Relations Theories: Discipline and Diversity* (Oxford: Oxford University Press, 2013).

Dunoff, Jeffrey L., and Joel P. Trachtman (eds.), *Ruling the World?: Constitutionalism, International Law, and Global Governance* (Cambridge: Cambridge University Press, 2009).

Dupuy, R.J., and D. Vignes (eds.), *A Handbook on the New Law of the Sea* (Dordrecht: M. Nijhoff, 1991).

Epstein, Richard A., *Simple Rules for a Complex World* (Harvard University Press, 1995).

Evera, Stephen Van, *Causes of War: Power and the Roots of Conflict* (Ithaca, NY: Cornell University Press, 1999).

Fairbank, John K. (ed.), *The Chinese World Order* (Cambridge: Harvard University Press, 1968).

Fels, Enrico, and Truong-Minh Vu (eds.), *Power Politics in Asia's Contested Waters: Territorial Disputes in the South China Sea* (Cham: Springer International Publishing: 2016).

Fietta, Stephen, and Robin Cleverly, *A Practitioner's Guide to Maritime Boundary Delimitation* (Oxford University Press 2016).

Finnemore, Martha, *National Interests in International Society* (Ithaca and London: Cornell University Press, 1996).

Franck, TM, Recourse to Force: State Action Against Threats and Armed Attacks (Cambridge, Cambridge University Press, 2002).

Freestone, David (ed.), *The 1982 Law of the Sea Convention at 30: Successes, Challenges and New Agendas* (Leiden and Boston: Nijhoff, 2013).

Freestone, David, Richard Barnes and David M. Ong (eds.), *The Law of the Sea: Progress and Prospects* (Oxford: Oxford University Press, 2006).

Friedberg, Aaron L., *A Contest for Supremacy: China, America, and the Struggle for Mastery in Asia* (New York: Norton, 2011).

Gavouneli, Maria, *Functional Jurisdiction in the Law of the Sea* (Leiden: Brill, 2007).

Gilpin, Robert, *War and Change in World Politics* (Cambridge: Cambridge University Press, 1981).

Glogan, Timothy, China's' Assertive' South China Sea Policy and Rhetoric: Proactive, Reactive or Myth, Pro Gradu Thesis (University of Turku, 2011).

Goldstein, Lyle J., *Meeting China Halfway: How to Defuse the Emerging US-China Rivalry* (Washington, D.C.: Georgetown University Press, 2015).

Gompert, David C., and Philip C. Saunders, *The Paradox of Power: Sino-American Strategic Restraint in an Age of Vulnerability* (Washington DC: National Defense University Press, 2011).

Grewe, Wilhelm G., *The Epochs of International Law*, trans. and rev. Michael Byers (Berlin: de Gruyter, 2000).

Guzman, Andrew T., *How International Law Works: A Rational Choice Theory* (Oxford: Oxford University Press, 2008).

Hara, Kimie, *Cold War Frontiers in the Asia-Pacific: Divided Territories in the San Francisco System* (London and New York: Routledge, 2007).

Harrison, James, *Making the Law of the Sea* (Cambridge: Cambridge University Press, 2011).

Haas, Peter M, Robert O. Keohane and Marc A. Levy (eds.), *Institutions for the Earth: Sources of Effective International Environmental Protection* (Cambridge: The MIT Press, 1993).

Hayton, Bill, *The South China Sea: The Struggle for Power in Asia* (Yale University Press, 2014).

He, Zhipeng, and Lu Sun, *A Chinese Theory of International Law* (Law Press China and Springer, 2020).

Heizing, Dieter, *Disputed Islands in the South China Sea: Paracels-Spratlys-Pratas -Macclesfield Bank* (Wiesbaden: O. Harrasowitz, 1976).

Henkin, Louis, *How Nations Behave*, 2nd ed. (New York: Columbia University Press, 1979).

Higgins, Rosalyn, *Problems and Process: International Law and How We Use It* (Oxford: Oxford University Press, 1994).

Holsti, Ole R., Randolph M. Siverson and Alexander L. George (eds.), *Change in the International System* (Boulder, CO: Westview Press, 1980).

Hong, Nong, *UNCLOS and Ocean Dispute Settlement: Law and Politics in the South China Sea* (Abingtdon: Routledge, 2012).

Hsü, Immanuel C. Y., *China's Entrance into the Family of Nations: The Diplomatic Phase, 1858–1880* (Cambridge: Harvard University Press, 1960).

Huang, Yukon, *Cracking the China Conundrum: Why Conventional Economic Wisdom Is Wrong* (New York: Oxford University Press, 2017).

Huntinaon, Samuel P., *The Clash of Civilization and the Remaking of World Order* (New York: Simon and Schuster, 1996).

Ikenberry, G. John, and Michael Mastanduno (eds.), *Interactional Relations Theory and the Asia-Pacific* (New York: Columbia University Press, 2003).

Jenner, C.J., and Tran Troung Thuy (ed.), *The South China Sea: A Crucible of Regional Cooperation or Conflict-Making Sovereignty Claims?* (Cambridge: Cambridge University Press, 2016).

Jepperson, Ronald L. et al., Norms, Identity, and Culture in National Security, in Peter J. Katzenstein (ed.), *The Culture of National Security* (New York: Columbia University Press, 1996).

Jessup, Philip C., *A Modern Law of Nations: An Introduction* (New York: Macmillan, 1948).

Johnston, Alastain Iain, and Robert S. Ross (eds.), *Engaging China: The Management of an Emerging Power* (London: Routledge, 1999).

Johnston, Alastair Iain, *Social States: China in International Institutions, 1980–2000* (Princeton, N.J.: Princeton University Press, 2008).

Kang, David C., *China Rising: Power and Order in East Asia* (New York: Columbia University Press, 2007).

Kant, Immanuel, "Perpetual Peace: A Philosophical Sketch" In Hans Reiss, *Kant's Political Writings* (Cambridge: Cambridge University Press, 1970).

Kaplan, Morton A., and Nicholas deB. Katzenbach, *The Political Foundations of International Law* (New York and London: John Wiley & Sons, Inc., 1961).

Kaplan, R.D., *Asia's cauldron: the South China Sea and the end of a stable Pacific* (New York: Random House, 2014).

Katzenstein, Peter J., and Takashi Shiraishi (eds.), *Network Power: Japan and Asia* (Ithaca, NY: Cornell University Press, 1997).

Keller, Helen, and Daniela Thurnherr, *Taking International Law Seriously* (Berne: Staempfli Publishers Ltd., 2005).

Keller, Perry (ed.), *Chinese Law and Legal Theory* (Aldershot, Hampshire: Ashgate Publishing Limited, 2001).

Kelly, Terrence K. et al., Employing Land-Based Anti-Ship Missiles in the Western Pacific (Santa Monica, CA: RAND, 2013).

Kelly, Terrence, et al., The U.S. Army in Asia, 2030–2040 (Santa Monica, Calif.: RAND Corporation, 2014).

Kelsen, Hans, *General Theory of Law and State* (Cambridge: Harvard University Press, 1949, trans. by Anders Wedberg).

Kelsen, Hans, *Pure Theory of Law* (Berkeley: University of California Press, 1967 trans. by Max Knight).

Kent, Ann, *Beyond Compliance: China, International Organizations, and Global Security* (Stanford: Stanford University Press, 2007).

Keohane, Robert O. (ed.), *International Institutions and State Power* (Boulder: Westview, 1989).

Keohane, Robert O., *After Hegemony: Cooperation and Discord in the World Political Economy* (Princeton University Press, 1984).

Keohane, Robert O., and Joshep S. Nye, Jr., *Power and Interdependece,* 4th ed. (Glenview, IL: Pearson, 2012).

Kim, Samuel S., *China, the United Nations and World Order* (New Jersey: Princeton University Press, 1979).

Kipgen, Nehginpao, *The Politics of South China Sea Disputes* (London & New York: Routledge, 2020).

Klein, Natalie (eds), *Litigating International Law Disputes* (Cambridge: Cambridge University Press, 2014).

Klein, Natalie, *Maritime Security and the Law of the Sea* (Oxford: Oxford University Press, 2011).

Koo, Min Gyo, *Island Disputes and Maritime Regime Building in East Asia: Between a Rock and a Hard Place* (Springer, 2009).

Kopela, Sophia, *Dependent Archipelagos in the Law of the Sea* (Leiden: Martinus Nijhoff Publishers, 2013).

Koskenniemi, Martti, *From Apology To Utopia: The Structure of International Legal Argument* (Cambridge: Cambridge University Press, 2005).

Kupchan, Charles A., Emanuel Adler, Jean-Marc Coicaud, and Yuen Foong Khong Power (eds.), *Transition: The Peaceful Change of International Order* (Tokyo: United Nations University Press, 2001).

Kwiatkowska, Barbara, *The 200 Mile Exclusive Economic Zone in the New Law of the Sea* (Dordrecht: Martinus Nijhoff, 1989).

Kydd, Andrew H., *Trust and Mistrust in International Relations* (Princeton: Princeton University Press, 2007).

Langenbacher, Eric, and Yossi Shain (eds.), *Power and the Past: Collective Memory and International Relations* (Washington DC: Georgetown University Press, 2010).

Lanteigne, Marc, *Chinese Foreign Policy: An Introduction* (Abingdon, Oxon; New York, NY: Routledge, 2016).

Laursen, Andreas, *Changing International Law to Meet New Challenges: Interpretation, Modification and the Use of Force* (Copenhagen: Djøf Publishing, 2006).

Lemke, Douglas, *Regions of War and Peace* (Ann Arbor: University of Michigan Press, 2001).

Lin, Justin Yifu, *Demystifying the Chinese Economy* (New York: Cambridge University Press, 2012).

Lorca, Arnulf Becker, *Mestizo International Law A Global Intellectual History 1842–1933* (Cambridge: Cambridge University Press, 2014).

Luhmann, Niklas, *Trust and Power* (Chichester: John Wiley & Sons, 1979).

Macdonald, Roderick (ed.), *Southeast Asia and the ASEAN Economic Community* (Palgrave Macmillan, 2019).

Macdonald, Ronald St. John (ed.), *Essays in Honour of Wang Tieya* (Dordrecht: Martinus Nijhoff Publishers, 1994).

Makarczyk, Jerzy (ed.), *Theory of International Law at the Threshold of the 21st Century: Essays in Honour of Krzysztof Skubiszewsk* (The Hague: Kluwer, 1996).

Mazarr, Michael J., Timothy R. Heath, and Astrid Stuth Cevallos, *China and the International Order* (Santa Monica, California: RAND Corporation, 2018).

Mearsheimer, John J., *The Tragedy of Great Power Politics* (Norton, 2014).

Merrills, J. G., *International Dispute Settlement*, 5th ed. (Cambridge University Press, 2011).

Minas, Stephen, and H. Jordan Diamond (eds.), *Stress Testing the Law of the Sea: Dispute Resolution, Disasters & Emerging Challenges* (Leiden: Brill, 2018).

Moir, Lindsay, *Reappraising the Resort to Force* (Oxford: Hart Publishing, 2010).

Morgenthau, Hans, *Politics Among Nations: The Struggle for Power and Peace*, 5th ed. (New Work: Knopf, 1973).

Müller, Jan-Werner (ed.), *Memory and Power in Post-War Europe: Studies in the Presence of the Past* (Cambridge: Cambridge University Press, 2002).

Nandan, S.R., and S. Rosenne (eds), *United Nations Convention on the Law of the Sea –A Commentary* (Dordrecht: Martinus Nijhoff, 1993).

Nathan, Andrew J., and Bruce Gilley, *China's New Rulers: The Secret Files* (New York: New York Review of Books, 2003).

Nolte, Georg (eds.), *Treaties and Subsequent Practice* (Oxford: Oxford University Press, 2013).

Nordquist, M. (eds.), *United Nations Convention on the Law of the Sea 1982: A Commentary* (The Hague/London/Boston: M. Nijhoff, 1995).

Nordquist, M. H., J. N. Moore, R. Beckman, and R. Long (eds.), *Freedom of Navigation and Globalization* (Leiden and Boston: Brill, 2015).

Nordquist, Myron H., John Norton Moore and Kuen-chen Fu (eds), *Recent Developments in the Law of the Sea and China* (Leiden: Martinus Nijhoff, 2006).

Nordquist, Myron H., John Norton Moore, and Ronán Long, *International Marine Economy: Law and Policy* (Brill Nijoff, 2017).

Nordquist, Myron H., Tommy K.B. Koh & John Norton Moore (eds), *Freedom of Seas, Passage Rights and the 1982 Law of the Sea Convention* (Leiden and Boston: Martinus Nijhoff, 2009).

Nye, Joseph S. Jr., *The Future of Power* (New York: Punlic Affaris, 2011).

Odgaard, Liselotte, *Maritime security between China and Southeast Asia: conflict and cooperation in the making of regional order* (Abingdon and New York: Routledge, 2016).

Oksenberg, Michael, and Elizabeth Economy (eds.), *China Joins the World: Progress and Prospects* (New York: Council on Foreign Relations, 1999).

Oppenheim, Lassa, *International Law: A Treaties* (London: Longmans, Green and Company, 1912), Vol. 1.

Orakhelashvili, Alexander (ed.), *Research Handbook on the Theory and History of International Law* (Edward Elgar Publishing Limited, 2011).

Organski, A. F. K., and Jacek Kugler, *The War Ledger* (Chicago: University of Chicago Press, 1980).

Organski, A. F. K., *World Politics* (New York: Knopf, 1958).

Organski, A. F. K., *World Politics,* 2nd ed. (New York: Knopf, 1968).

Oye, Kenneth A. (ed.), *Cooperation under Anarchy* (Princeton University Press, 1986).

Park, Choon-Ho, *East Asia and the Law of the Sea* (Seoul: Seoul National University Press, 1983).

Paul, T.V. (ed.), *Accommodating Rising Powers: Past, Present, and Future* (Cambridge: Cambridge University Press, 2016).

Paul, T.V., Deborah Welch Larson, and William C. Wohlforth (eds.), *Status in World Politics* (Cambridge: Cambridge University Press, 2014).

Pekkanen, Saadia M., John Ravenhill, and Rosemary Foot (eds.), *Oxford Handbook of the International Relations of Asia* (Oxford: Oxford University Press, 2014).

Proelss, Alexander (ed.), *The United Nations Convention on the Law of the Sea: A Commentary* (Oxford: Hart Publishing, 2017).

Raditio, Klaus Heinrich, *Understanding China's Behavior in the South China Sea: A Defensive Realist Perspective* (Singapore: Palgrave Macmillan, 2019).

Renshon, Jonathan, *Fighting for Status: Hierarchy and Conflict in World Politics* (Princeton, N.J.: Princeton University Press, 2017).

Reus-Smit, Christian (ed.), *The Politics of International Law* (Cambridge: Cambridge University Press, 2004).

Rheinstein, Max, *Max Weber on Law in Economy and Society* (Cambridge-Massachusetts: Harvard University Press, 1966).

Rittberger, Volker, and Peter Mayer (eds.), *Regime Theory and International Relations* (Oxford: Clarendon Press, 1993).

Roach, J. Ashley, and Robert W. Smith, *Excessive Maritime Claims*, 3rd ed. (Leiden: Brill, 2012).

Roberts, Anthea, *Is International Law International?* (Oxford University Press, 2017).

Ross, Robert S., and Øystein Tunsjø (eds.), *Strategic Adjustment and the Rise of China* (Ithaca and London: Cornell University Press, 2017).

Ross, Robert S., and Zhu Feng (eds.), *China's Ascent Power, Security, and the Future of International Politics* (Ithaca and London: Cornell University Press, 2008).

Rothwell, Donald et al. (eds.), *The Oxford Handbook of the Law of the Sea* (Oxford: Oxford University Press, 2015).

Saich, Tony, *Governance and Politics of China,* 2d ed. (Houndmills: Palgrave Macmillan, 2004).

Samuels, Marwyn S., *Contest for the South China Sea* (Methuen: New York and London, 1982).

Scheuerman, William E., *The End of Law: Carl Schmitt in the Twenty-First Century* (London and New York: Rowman & Littlefield, 2020).

Schneider, Gerald, Katherine Barbieri, and Nils Petter Gleditsch (eds.), *Globalization and Armed Conflict* (Lanham, MD: Rowman & Littlefield, 2003).

Schwarzenberger, Georg, *Power Politics*, 3rd ed. (London: Stevens, 1964).

Schweller, Randall L., *Maxwell's Demon and the Silver Hammer* (Baltimore: Johns Hopkins University Press, 2014).

Scovazzi, T., *The evolution of international law of the sea: new issues, new challenges* (Hague Academy Recueil des Cours, Vol. 286, 2000).

Shambaugh, David, and Michael Yahunda (eds.), *International Relations of Asia*, 2nd ed. (Lanham: Rowman & Lifflefield Publisher, 2014).

Shelton, Dinah (ed.), *Commitment and Compliance: The Role of Non-Binding Norms in the International Legal System* (Oxford University Press, 2000).

Shih, Hu, The Natural Law in the Chinese Tradition, Natural Law Institute Proceedings.

Simpson, Gerry, *Great Powers and Outlaw States* (Cambridge: Cambridge University Press, 2004).

Snyder, Jack L., *Myths of Empire: Domestic Politics and International Ambition* (Ithaca, NY: Cornell University Press, 1991).

Snyder, Jack, and Stephen Van Evera, Myths of Empire: *Domestic Politics and International Ambition* (Ithaca, NY: Cornell University Press, 1991).

Song, Yann-huei, and Keyuan Zou (eds.), *Major Law and Policy Issues in the South China Sea: European and American Perspectives* (London and New York: Routledge, 2014).

Soons, Alfred, *Marine Scientific Research and the Law of the Sea* (Springer, 1982).

Tanaka, Yoshifumi, *The international law of the sea* (Cambridge: Cambridge University Press, 2015).

Tang, Shiping, *A Theory of Security Strategies for Our Time: Defensive Realism* (New York: Palgrave Macmillan, 2010).

Tillman, Seth P., *Anglo-American Relations at the Paris Peace Conference of 1919* (Princeton and New Jersey: Princeton University Press, 2015).

Toje, Asle (ed.), *Will China's Rise Be Peaceful? Security, Stability, and Legitimacy* (New York: Oxford University Press, 2018).

Valencia, Mark J., *A Maritime Regime: For North-East Asia* (Oxford University Press, 1996).

Valencia, Mark J., John M. Van Dyke, and Noel Ludwig, *Sharing the Resources of the South China Sea* (The Hague: Kluwer Law International, 1997).

Van Dyke, Jon M., Consensus and Confrontation: The United States and the Law of the Sea Convention: a Workshop of the Law of the Sea Institute, January 9–13, 1984, Honolulu, Hawaii, Law of the Sea Institute, University of Hawaii, 1985.

Vasquez, J.A. (ed.), *What Do We Know About War* (Lanham, MD: Rowman and Littlefield, 2012).

Vasquez, John A., *The War Puzzle Revisited* (New York: Cambridge University Press, 2009).

Ventura, Victor Alencar Mayer Feitosa, *Environmental Jurisdiction in the Law of the Sea: The Brazilian Blue Amazon* (Cham: Springer, 2020).

Visscher, Charles De, *Theory and Reality in Public International Law* (Princeton: Princeton University Press, 1957, translated by P.E. Corbett).

Waltz, Kenneth, *Theory of International Politics* (Reading, MA: Addison-Wesley, 1979).

Wang, Ban (ed.), *Chinese Visions of World Order: Tianxia, Culture, and World Politics* (Durham and London: Duke University Press, 2017).

Wegelein, Florian H.Th., *Marine Scientific Research: the Operation and Status of Research Vessels and other Platforms in International Law* (Leiden: Brill, 2005).

Wei, Yuwa, *Issues Decisive for China's Rise or Fall: An International Law Perspective* (Springer, 2019).

Wendt, Alexander, *Social Theory of International Politics* (Cambridge: Cambridge University Press, 1999).

White, Hugh, *The China Choice: Why We Should Share Power* (Oxford: Oxford University Press, 2012).

Withana, Radhika, *Power, Politics, Law: International Law and State Behavior During International Crises* (Leiden and Boston: Martinus Nijhoff Publishers, 2008).

Wolfrum, Rüdiger (eds.), *Max Planck Encyclopedia of Public International Law* (Oxford: Oxford University Press, 2012).

WU, Shicun, and Keyuan Zou (eds.), *Arbitration Concerning the South China Sea: Philippines versus China* (Abingdon and New York: Routledge, 2016).

Wu, Shicun, *Solving Disputes for Regional Cooperation and Development in the South China: A Chinese Perspective* (Chandos Publishing, 2013).

Xue, Hanqin, *Chinese Contemporary Perspectives on International Law: History, Culture, and International Law* (Maubeuge: All-Pocket, 2012).

Yan, Xuetong, *Ancient Chinese Thought, Modern Chinese Power* (Princeton and Oxford: Princeton University Press, 2011).

Yoo, John, *Point of Attack: Preventive War, International Law, and Global Warfare* (New York: Oxford University Press, 2014).

Yoo, John, *The Powers of War and Peace: the Constitution and Foreign Affairs after 9/11* (Chicago and London: The University of Chicago Press, 2005).

Young, Oran R., and Gail Osherenko (eds), *Polar Politics: Creating International Environmental Regimes* (Ithaca: Cornell University Press, 1993).

Young, Oran, *International Cooperation* (Ithaca: Cornell University Press, 1989).

Zou, Keyuan, *China's Marine Legal System and the Law of the Sea* (Leiden/Boston: Martinus Nijhoff, 2005).

Zou, Keyuan, *China-ASEAN Relations and International Law* (Chandos Publishing, 2009).

Articles and Research Papers

Abbott, Kenneth W., "International Law and International Relations Theory: Building Bridges," *ASIL Proceedings*, 1992.

Abbott, Kenneth W., and Duncan Snidal, "Hard and soft law in international governance," *International Organization*, 54, no. 3 (2000).

Abraham, Garth, "Paradise Claimed: Disputed Sovereignty over the Chagos Archipelago," *South African Law Journal*, 128, no. 1 (2011).

Acharya, Amitav, "How Ideas Spread: Whose Norms Matter? Norm Localization and Institutional Change in Asian Regionalism," *International Organization*, 58, no. 2 (Spring 2004).

Acharya, Amitav, "Ideas, Identity and Institution-Building: From the 'ASEAN Way' to the 'Asia-Pacific Way'?" *Pacific Review*, 10, no. 3 (1997).

Adler, Emanuel, "Seizing the Middle Ground: Constructivism in World Politics," *European Journal of International Relations*, 3, no. 3 (1997).

Aggarwal, Vinod K., "Building International Institutions in Asia-Pacific," *Asian Survey*, 33, no. 11 (November, 1993).

Amador, F.V. García, The Latin American contribution to the development of the law of the sea, *American Journal of International Law*, 68 (1974).

Anand, R. P., "Sovereign equality of States in International Law," *Recueil des cours*, 197 (1986).

Antonov, Mikhail, Theoretical Issues of Sovereignty in Russia and Russian Law, *Review of Central and East European Law*, 37, no. 1 (2012).

Arbitov, Alexi, Engaging China in Nuclear Arms Control (Carnegie Moscow Center, October 9, 2014).

Astley III, John, and Michael N. Schmitt, "The Law of the Sea and Naval Operations," *Air Force Law Review*, 42 (1997).

Bateman, Sam, "Hydrographic Surveying in Exclusive Economic Zones: Jurisdictional Issues," *International Hydrographic Review*, 5 (2004).

Bateman, Sam, "Hydrographic Surveying in the EEZ: Differences and Overlaps with Marine Scientific Research," *Marine Policy*, 29 (2005).

Beckman, Robert, "The UN Convention on the Law of the Sea," *American Journal of International Law*, 107 (2013).

Beckman, Robert, and Clive Schofield, "Defining EEZ claims from islands: A potential South China Sea change," *International Journal of Marine and Coastal Law*, 29 (2014).

Beeson, Mark, and Fujian Li, "Charmed or Alarmed? Reading China's Regional Relations," *Journal of Contemporary China*, 21, no. 73 (November 2011).

Beller, Richard D., "Analyzing the Relationship between International Law and International Politics in China's and Vietnam's Territorial Dispute Over the Spratly Islands," *Texas International Law Journal*, 29, no. 2 (Spring 1994).

Berger, Thomas, "Set for Stability? Prospects for Conflict and Cooperation in East Asia," *Review of International Studies*, 26, no. 3 (July 2000).

Biddle, Stephen, and Ivan Oelrich, "Future Warfare in the Western Pacific: Chinese Antiaccess/Area Denial, U.S. Air Sea Battle, and Command of the Commons in East Asia," *International Security*, 41, no. 1 (Summer 2016).

Bloom, Evan T., "Establishment of the Arctic Council," *American Journal of International Law*, 93, no. 3 (1999).

Boczek, B., "Peaceful purposes provisions of the United Nations Convention on the Law of the Sea," *Ocean Development and International Law*, 20 (1989).

Boczek, B., "The peaceful purposes clauses: a reappraisal after the entry into effect of the Law of the Sea Convention," *Ocean Yearbook*, 13 (1998).

Boczek, Boleslaw A., "Peaceful Purposes Provisions of the United Nations Convention of the Law of the Sea," *Ocean Development and International Law*, 20 (1989).

Boon, Kirsten E., "International arbitration in highly political situations: the South China Sea dispute and international law," *Washington University Global Studies Law Review*, 13 (2014).

Brown G., and M. Baer, "Protecting the Turf: The Effect of Territorial Marking on Others' Creativity," *Journal of Applied Psychology*, 100, no. 6 (2015).

Burke-White, William W., "Power Shifts in International Law: Structural Realignment and Substantive Pluralism," *Harvard International Law Journal*, 56, no. 1 (2015).

Buszynski, Leszek, "Southeast Asia in the Post-Cold War Era," *Asian Survey*, 32, no. 9 (September 1992).

Buszynski, Leszek, "The South China Sea: Oil, Maritime Claims, and US–China Strategic Rivalry," *The Washington Quarterly*, 35, no. 2 (2013).

Buzan, Barry, "China in International Society: Is 'Peaceful Rise' Possible?" *The Chinese Journal of International Politics*, 3 (2010).

Buzan, Barry, "Economic Structure and International Security: The Limits of the Liberal Case," *International Organization*, 38, no. 4 (Autumn 1984).

Cai, Congyan, "New Great Powers and International Law in the 21st Century," *European Journal of International Law*, 24 (2013).

Carlson, Allen, "Moving Beyond Sovereignty? A brief consideration of recent changes in China's approach to international order and the emergence of the tianxia concept," *Journal of Contemporary China*, 20, no. 68 (2011).

Caron, David D., and Harry N. Scheiber, The United States and the 1982 Law of the Sea Treaty, *ASIL Insights*, 11, no. 16 (June 11, 2007).

Carr, Michael, "China and the Law of the Sea Convention," *Australian Journal of Chinese Affairs*, 9 (1983).

Carter, D.B., and H.E. Goesman, "The Making of the Territorial Order: New Borders and the Emergence of Interstate Conflict," *International Organization*, 65, no. 2 (2011).

Cerar, Miro, "The Relationship Between Law and Politics," *Annual Survey of International & Comparative Law*, 15, no. 1 (2009).

Chan, Phil C. W., "China's Approaches to International Law since the Opium War," *Leiden Journal of International Law*, 27 (2014).

Chang, Teh-Kuang, "China's Claim of Sovereignty Over Spratly and Paracel Islands: A Historical and Legal Perspective," *Case Western Journal of International Law*, 23 (1991).

Chao, "South China Sea: Boundary Problems Relating to the Nansha and Hsisha Islands," *Chinese Yearbook of International Law and Affairs*, 9 (1989).

Charney, Jonathan I., "Central East Asian Maritime Boundaries and the Law of the Sea," *American Journal of International Law*, 89, no. 4 (1995).

Chen, Tiqiang, "The People's Republic of China and Public International Law," *Dalhousie Law Journal*, 8 (1984).

Chinese Society of International Law, "The South China Sea Arbitration Awards: A Critical Study," *Chinese Journal of International Law*, 17 (2018).

Chiu, Hungdah, "Communist China's Attitude toward International Law," *American Journal of International Law*, 60, no. 2 (1986).

Chiu, Hungdah, and Choon-ho Park, "Legal Status of the Paracel and Spratly Islands," *Ocean Development and International Law*, 3 (1975).

Choi, Jong Kun, and Yong-Soo Eun, "What does international relations theory tell us about territorial disputes and their resolution?" *International Politics*, 55 (2018).

Christensen, Thomas J., "Fostering Stability or Creating a Monster? The Rise of China and U.S. Policy toward East Asia," *International Security*, 31, no. 1 (2006).

Christensen, Thomas J., "Posing Problems Without Catching Up: China's Rise and the Challenges for US Security Policy," *International Security*, 25, no. 4 (2001).

Combes, Katherine, "Between Revisionism and Status Quo: China in International Regimes," *Polis*, 6 (Winter 2011–2012).

Cronin, Bruce, "The Paradox of Hegemony: America's Ambiguous Relationship with the United Nations," *European Journal of International Relations*, 7, no. 1 (2001).

deLisle, Jacques, "China's Approach to International Law: A Historical Perspective," *American Society of International Law Proceedings*, 2000.

Diver, Colin S., "The Optimal Precision of Administrative Rules," *Yale Law Journal*, 93 (1983).

Djalal, Hasjim, "Indonesia and the SCS Initiative," *Ocean Development and International Law*, 32, no, 2 (2001).

Doyle, Michael, "Liberalism and World Politics," *American Political Science Review*, 80, no. 4 (December 1986).

Drifte, Reinhard, "Territorial conflicts in the East China Sea – From Missed Opportunities to Negotiation Stalemate," *The Asia-Pacific Journal*, 22, no. 3 (2009).

Duan, Jielong, "Statement on the Rule of Law at the National and International Levels," *Chinese Journal of International Law*, 6 (2007).

Dutton, Peter, "Three disputes and three objectives: China and the South China Sea," *Naval War College Review*, 64, no. 4 (2011).

Dzurk, D. J., "Boundary and Resources Disputes in the South China Sea," *Ocean Yearbook*, 5 (1985).

Economy, Elizabeth C., and Adam Segal, "The G-2 Mirage," *Foreign Affairs*, 88, no. 3 (May/June 2009).

Edwards, Newton, "Stability and Change in Basic Concepts of Law Governing American Education," *The School Review*, 65, no. 2 (Summer 1957).

Farer, TJ, "The Prospect for International Law and Order in the Wake of Iraq," *American Journal of International Law*, 97 (2003).

Fearon, James D., "Rationalist Explanations for War," *International Organization*, 49, no.3 (Summer 1995).

Finnemore, Martha, and Kathryn Sikkink, "International Norm Dynamics and Political Change," *International Organization*, 52, no. 4 (Autumn 1998).

Foot, Rosemary, "Chinese Strategies in a US-Hegemonic Global Order: Accommodating and Hedging," *International Affairs*, 82, no. 1 (2006).

Franckx, Erik, "American and Chinese views on navigational rights of warships," *Chinese Journal of International Law*, 10, no. 1 (2011).

Franckx, Erik, "Innocent Passage of Warships: Recent Developments in US-Soviet Relations," *Marine Policy*, 14 (1990).

Fravel, M. Taylor, "International Relations Theory and China's Rise: Assessing China's Potential for Territorial Expansion," *International Studies Review*, 12 (2010).

Friedberg, Aaron L., "The Future of U.S.-China Relations Is Conflict Inevitable?" *International Security*, 30, no. 2 (Fall 2005).

Galdorisi, George V., and Alan V. Kaufman, "Military Activities in the Exclusive Economic Zone: Preventing Uncertainty and Defusing Conflict," *California Western International Law Journal*, 32 (2002).

Gao, Zhiguo, and Bingbing Jia, "The Nine-Dash Line in the South China Sea: History, Status, and Implications," *American Journal of International Law*, 107, no. 1 (2013).

Gartzke, Erik, Quan Li, and Charles Boehmer, "Investing in the Peace: Economic Interdependence and International Conflict," *International Organization*, 55, no. 3 (2001).

Gau, M. Sheng-Ti, "The U-Shaped Line and a Categorization of the Ocean Disputes in the South China Sea," *Ocean Development & International Law*, 43, no. 1 (2012).

Gautier, Philippe, "The role of international courts and tribunals in the development of environmental law," Proceedings of the Annual Meeting, *the American Society of International Law*, 109 (2015).

Glaser, Charles, "Will China's Rise Lead to War?' *Foreign Affairs*, 90, no. 2 (March/April 2011).

Goldstein, Avery, "Great Expectations: Interpreting China's Arrival," *International Security*, 22 (Winter 1997–98).

Goswami, Namrata, Power Shifts in East Asia: Balance of Power vs. Liberal Institutionalism, *Perceptions*, 18, no. 1 (Spring 2013).

Gregory, Eugene, Ronald Alcala, and Shane Reeves, "Chinese Fazhi and the International Order," *Harvard International Review*, 39 (Fall 2018).

Haas, Ernst B., "Is there a hole in the whole? Knowledge, technology, interdependence, and the construction of international regimes," *International Organization*, 29, no. 3 (Summer 1975).

Haas, Ernst B., "Why Collaborate? Issue-Linkage and International Regimes," *World Politics*, 32, no. 3 (April 1980).

Haiwen, Zhang, "Is It Safeguarding the Freedom of Navigation or Maritime Hegemony of the United States? Comments on Raul (Pete) Pedrozo's Article on Military Activities in the EEZ," *Chinese Journal of International Law*, 9 (2010).

Hakimi, Monica, "Why Should We Care About International Law?" *Michigan Law Review*, 118 (2020).

Hamilton, Eric J., and Brian C. Rathbun, "Scarce Differences: Toward a Material and Systemic Foundation for Offensive and Defensive Realism," *Security Studies*, 22, no. 3 (2013).

Hara, Kimie, "The San Francisco Peace Treaty and Frontier Problems in the Regional Order in East Asia: A Sixty Year Perspective," *The Asia-Pacific Journal*, 10, no. 17 (2012).

Haas, Peter M., (ed.), Knowledge, Power and International Policy Coordination, *International Organization*, 46 (Special Issue, 1992).

Hayashi, Moritaka, "Military and Intelligence Gathering Activities in the EEZ: Definition of Key Terms," *Marine Policy*, 29 (2005).

Hayton, Bill, "When Good Lawyers Write Bad History: Unreliable Evidence and the South China Sea Territorial Dispute," *Ocean Development & International Law*, 48, no. 1 (2017).

Heritage, Anisa, and Pak K. Lee, "The Sino-American confrontation in the South China Sea: insights from an international order perspective," *Cambridge Review of International Affairs*, 33, no. 1 (2020).

Herz, John H., "Idealist Internationalism and the Security Dilemma," *World Politics*, 2, no. 2 (January 1950).

Higgins, Rosalyn, "Policy Considerations and the International Judicial Process," *International & Comparative Law Quarterly*, 17 (1968).

Hoffheimer, Daniel J., "China and the International Legal Order: An Historical Introduction," *Case Western Journal of International Law*, 11 (1979).

Holmes, James R., and Toshi Yoshihara, "China's 'Caribbean' in the South China Sea," *SAIS Review*, 26, no. 1 (2006).

Hong, Nong, Jianwei Li, and Pingping Chen, "The Concept of Archipelagic State and the South China Sea: UNCLOS, State Practice and Implication," *China Oceans Law Review*, 2013, no. 1.

Hopf, Ted, "The Promise of Constructivism in International Relations Theory," *International Security*, 23, no. 1 (1998).

Houck, James W., and Nicole M. Anderson, "The United States, China, and Freedom of Navigation in the South China Sea," *Washington University Global Studies Law Review*, 13 (2014).

Hu, Nien-Tsu Alfred, "South China Sea: Troubled Waters or a Sea of Opportunity?" *Ocean Development & International Law*, 41, no. 3 (2010).

Huntington, Samuel P., "America's Changing Strategic Interests," *Survival*, 33, no. 1 (January/February 1991).

Irish, Adam et al., "Bridging the International Law-International Relations Divide: Talking Stock of Progress," *Georgia Journal of International and Comparative Law*, 41 (2013).

Jervis, Robert, "Unipolarity: A Structural Perspective." *World Politics*, 61, no. 1 (2009).

JIA, Guide, New China and International Law: Practice and Contribution in 70 Years, *Chinese Journal of International Law*, 18, no. 4 (2019).

Jie, Chen, "China's Spratly Policy: With Special Reference to the Philippines and Malaysia," *Asian Survey*, 34, no. 10 (October 1994).

Jin, Shao, "The question of innocent passage of warships after UNCLOS III," *Marine Policy*, 13, no 1 (January 1989).

Jisi, Wang, "China's Search for Stability with America," *Foreign Affairs*, 84, no. 5 (2005).

Johnston, Alastair Iain, "Is China a Status Quo Power?" *International Security*, 27 (2003).

Kang, David C., "Getting Asia Wrong: The Need for New Analytical Frameworks," *International Security*, 27, no. 4 (Spring 2003).

Kao, Shih-Ming, Nathaniel Sifford Pearre, and Jeremy Firestone, "Regional Cooperation in the South China Sea: Analysis of Existing Practices and Prospects," *Ocean Development & International Law*, 43 (2012).

Kaplow, Louis, "Rules versus Standards: An Economic Analysis," *Duke Law Journal,* 42 (1992).

Kaufman, Alison Adcock, "The 'Century of Humiliation,' Then and Now: Chinese Perceptions of the International Order," *Pacific Focus*, 25, no. 1 (2010).

Kelly, Michael J., "United States Ratification of the Law of the Sea Convention: Securing our Navigational Future While Managing China's Blue Water Ambitions," *Case Western Reserve Journal of International Law,* 45 (2012).

Kennedy, David, "A New Stream of International Law Scholarship," *Wisconsin International Law Journal*, 7 (1988).

Kent, Ann, "China's International Socialization: The Role of International Organizations," *Global Governance*, 8, no. 3 (July–September 2002).

Khong, Yuen Foong, "Primacy or world order? The United States and China's rise: a review essay," *International Security*, 38, no. 3 (Winter 2013–14).

Kim, Jihyun, "Possible Future of the Contest in the South China Sea," *The Chinese Journal of International Politics*, 9, no. 1 (2016).

Kim, Samuel S., "The People's Republic of China and the Charter-Based International Legal Order," *American Journal of International Law,* 72 (1978).

Kinzelbach, Katrin, "Will China's Rise Lead to a New Normative Order? An Analysis of China's Statements on Human Rights at the United Nations (2000–2010)," *Netherlands Quarterly of Human Rights*, 30 (2012).

Kline, Robert T., "The Pen and the Sword: the People's Republic of China's Effort to Redefine the Exclusive Economic Zone through Maritime Lawfare and Military Enforcement," *Military Law Review*, 216 (2013).

Koo, Min Gyo, "Belling the Chinese Dragon: Western Theories and Asian Realities," *Ocean Development & International Law,* 48, no. 1 (2017).

Koskenniemi, Martti, "The Politics of International Law," *European Journal of International Law*, 1 (1990).

Krasner, Stephen D., "Realist Views of International Law," *Proceedings of the Annual Meeting*, American Society of International Law, 96 (March 13–16, 2002).

Krasner, Stephen D., "Structural Causes and Regime Consequences: Regimes as Intervening Variables," *International Organization*, 36, no. 2, International Regimes (Spring 1982).

Krepinevich Jr., Andrew F., "How to deter China: the case for archipelagic defense," *Foreign Affairs*, March/April 2015.

Krisch, Nico, "International Law in Times of Hegemony: Unequal Power and the Shaping of the International Legal Order," *The European Journal of International Law*, 16, no. 3 (2005).

Legro, Jeffrey W., "What China Will Want: The Future Intentions of a Rising Power," *Perspectives on Politics*, 5, no. 3 (September 2007).

Leifer, Michael, "The ASEAN States: No Common Outlook," *International Affairs*, 49 (1973).

Li, Chen, Universalism and Equal Sovereignty as Contested Myths of International Law in the Sino-Western Encounter, *Journal of the History of International Law*, 13 (2011).

Li, Jinming, and Dexia Li, "The dotted line on the Chinese map of the South China Sea: a note," *Ocean Development & International Law*, 34, no. 3–4 (2003).

Li, Weng, "Philosophical Influences on Contemporary Chinese Law," *Indiana International & Comparative Law Review*, 6 (1996).

Liao, Xuexia, "The LOSC as a Package Deal and Its Implications for Determination of Customary International Law," *The International Journal of Marine and Coastal Law*, 35 (2020).

Lilienthal, Gary, and Nehaluddin Ahmad, "The South China Sea Islands Arbitration: Making China's Position Visible in Hostile Waters," *Asian-Pacific Law & Policy Journal*, 18, no. 2 (2017).

Linos, Katerina, and Tom Pegram, "What Works in Human Rights Institutions?" *American Journal of International Law*, 111, no. 3 (2017).

Liu, Zhenmin, "Following the Five Principles of Peaceful Coexistence and Jointly Building a Community of Common Destiny," *Chinese Journal of International Law*, 13 (2014).

Logue, John, "The Revenge of John Selden: The Draft Convention on the Law of the Sea in Light of Hugo Grotius's Mare Liberum," *Grotiana*, 3 (1982).

Lynn-Jones, Sean M., "Offense-Defense Theory and Its Critics," *Security Studies*, 4, no. 4 (1995).

Manicom, James, "China and American Seapower in East Asia: Is Accommodation Possible?" *Journal of Strategic Studies*, 37, no. 3 (2014).

Mastro, Oriana Skylar, "In the shadow of the Thucydides Trap: International Relations Theory and the Prospects for Peace in U.S.-China Relations," *Journal of Chinese Political Science*, 24 (2019).

Mayali, Laurent, and John Yoo, "Resolution of Territorial Disputes in East Asia: The Case of Dokdo," *Berkeley Journal of International Law*, 36, no. 3 (2018).

McDougal, Myres, "The Hydrogen Bomb Tests and the International Law of the Sea," *American Journal of International Law*, 49 (1955).

McDowell, Daniel, "New Order: China's Challenge to the Global Financial System," *World Politics Review*, April 14, 2015.

McKay, Robert B., "Stability and Change in Constitutional Law," *Vanderbilt Law Review*, Vol. 17 (1963).

Mearsheimer, John J., "The Gathering Storm: China's Challenge to US Power in Asia," *The Chinese Journal of International Politics*, 3 (2010).

Milner, Helen, "International Theories of Cooperation among Nations: Strengths and Weaknesses," *World Politics*, Vol. 44 (1992).

Milner, Helen, "The Assumption of Anarchy in International Relations Theory: A Critique," *Review of International Studies*, 17, no. 1 (January 1991).

Modelski, George, "The Long Cycle of Global Politics and the Nation-State," *Comparative Studies in Society and History*, 20, no. 2 (April 1978).

Morton, Katherine, "China's ambition in the South China Sea: is a legitimate maritime order possible?" *International Affairs*, 92, no. 4 (2016).

Nguyen, Hoang-Anh, and Hong-Van Tran, "A Neoliberal Institutionalist Approach to the Modern Vietnam-China Maritime Dispute," *Yonsei Journal of International Studies*, 6, no. 2 (Fall/Winter 2014).

Nye, Joseph S., "Is the American Century Over?" *Political Science Quarterly*, 130, no. 3 (2015).

O'Keefe, Roger, "Legal Title versus Effectivités: Prescription and the Promise and Problems of Private Law Analogies," *International Community Law Review*, 13 (2011).

Odom, Jonathan G., "A China in the Bull Shop? Comparing the Rhetoric of A Rising China with the Reality of the International Law of the Sea," *Ocean and Coastal Law Journal*, 17 (2012).

Odom, Jonathan G., "The true 'lies' of the Impeccable Incident: What Really Happened, Who Disregarded International Law, and Why Every Nation (outside of China) Should be Concerned," *Michigan State Journal of International Law*, 18, no. 3 (2010).

Oegroseno, Arif Havas, "State Practices in Southeast Asia: Possible Collaboration amongst Claimants in the South China Sea Dispute," *The International Journal of Marine and Coastal Law*, 32 (2017).

Ogden, Suzanne, "Sovereignty and International Law: the Perspective of the People's Republic of China," *New York University Journal of International Law and Politics*, 7, no. 1 (1974).

Onea, Tudor, "Putting the 'Classical' in Neoclassical Realism: Neoclassical Realist Theories and US Expansion in the Post–Cold War." *International Relations*, 26, no. 2 (2012).

Osherenko, Gail, "Environmental Cooperation in the Arctic: Will the Soviets Participate?" *Current Research on Peace and Violence*, 12, no. 3 (1989).

Owena, Nick A., and Clive H. Schofield, "Disputed South China Sea hydrocarbons in perspective," *Marine Policy*, 36 (2012).

Oxman, Bernard H., "The Regime of Warships under the United Nations Convention on the Law of the Sea," *Virginia Journal of International Law*, 24 (1984).

Oxman, Bernard H., "The South China Sea Arbitration Award," *University of Miami International and Comparative Law Review*, 24 (2017).

Oxman, Bernard H., "The Territorial Temptation: a Siren Song at Sea," *American Journal of International Law*, 100, no. 4 (2006).

Oxman, Bernard H., "The Third United Nations Conference on the Law of the Sea: The Ninth Session," *American Journal of International Law*, 75, (1981).

Pan, Junwu, "Chinese Philosophy and International Law," *Asian Journal of International Law*, 1 (2011).

Pedrozo, Raul, "Close Encounters at Sea, The USNS Impeccable Incident," *Naval War College Review*, Summer 2009.

Pemmaraju, Sreenivasa Rao, "The South China Sea Arbitration (The Philippines v. China): Assessment of the Award on Jurisdiction and Admissibility," *Chinese Journal of International Law*, 15 (2016).

Pirtle, Charles E., "Military Uses of Ocean Space and the Law of the Sea in the New Millennium," *Ocean Development and International Law*, 31 (2000).

Posen, Barry R., "Command of the Commons: The Military Foundation of U.S. Hegemony," *International Security*, 28, no. 1 (Summer 2003).

Posner, Eric A., and John C. Yoo, "Judicial Independence in International Tribunals," *California Law Review*, 93, no. 1 (2005).

Posner, Eric A., and John C. Yoo, "International Law and the Rise of China," *Chicago Journal of International Law*, 7 (2006).

Puchala, Donald J., and Raymond F. Hopkins, "International Regimes: Lessons from Inductive Analysis," International Organization, 36, no. 2, *International Regimes* (Spring 1982).

Rahman, Chris, and Martin Tsamenyi, "A Strategic Perspective on Security and Naval Issues in the South China Sea," *Ocean Development & International Law*, 41 (2010).

Rainwater, Shiloh, International Law and the "Globalization" of the Arctic: Assessing the Rights of Non-Arctic States in the High North," *Emory International Law Review*, 30 (2015).

Ranganathan, Surabhi, "Decolonization and International Law: Putting the Ocean on the Map," *Journal of the History of International Law*, 2020.

Riggion, Aaron M., "Giving Teeth to the Tiger: How the South China Sea Crisis Demonstrates the Need for Revision to the Law of the Sea," *Military Law Review*, 224, no. 3 (2016).

Roach, J. Ashley, "Offshore Archipelagos Enclosed by Straight Baselines: An Excessive Claim?" *Ocean Development & International Law*, 49, no. 2 (2018).

Ronson, Alison, "Political Climate Change: The Evolving Role of the Arctic Council," *Northern Review*, 33 (2011).

Rose, Gideon, "Review: Neoclassical Realism and Theories of Foreign Policy," *World Politics*, 51, no. 1 (1998).

Ross, Robert S., "The Geography of Peace: East Asia in the Twenty-First Century," *International Security*, 23, no. 4 (1999).

Ross, Robert S., Balance of Power Politics and the Rise of China: Accommodation and Balancing in East Asia, *Security Studies*, 15, no. 3 (July–September 2006).

Rovira, Monica Garcia-Salmones, "The Project of Positivism in International Law," *European Journal of International Law*, Vol. 25 (2014).

Roy, Denny, "Assertive China: Irredentism or Expansionism?" *Survival*, 61, no. 1 (2019).

Roy, Denny, "Hegemon on the horizon? China's threat to East Asian security," *International Security*, 19, no. 1 (1994).

Ruggie, John Gerard, "International Response to Technology: Concepts and Trends," *International Organization* 29 (Summer 1975).

Russett, Bruce, John R. Oneal, and David R. Davis, "The Third Leg of the Kantian Tripod for Peace: International Organizations and Militarized Disputes, 1950–85," *International Organization*, 52, no. 3 (Summer 1998).

Schachter, Oscar, "International Law in Theory and Practice: General Course in Public International Law," *Recueil des cours*, 178 (1982).

Schachter, Oscar, "The Role of Power in International Law," *Proceedings of the Annual Meeting*, American Society of International Law, 93 (March 24–27, 1999).

Schwartz, Thomas, and John Yoo, "Asian Territorial Disputes and the 1951 San Francisco Peace Treaty: The Case of Dokdo," *Chinese Journal of International Law*, 18 (2019).

Schweller, Randall L., and Xiaoyu Pu, After Unipolarity: China's Visions of International Order in an Era of US Decline, *International Security*, 36, no. 1 (Summer 2011).

Scott, David, "Conflict Irresolution in the South China Sea," *Asian Survey*, 52, no. 6 (2012).

Sellars, Kirsten, "Rocking the Boat: The Paracels, The Spratlys, and the South China Sea Arbitration," *Columbia Journal of Asian Law*, 30 (2017).

Seo, Youngmin, "The Marine Environmental Turn in the Law of the Sea and Fukushima Wastewater," *Fordham International Law Journal*, 45, no. 1 (2021).

Shearer, Ivan, "Military Activities in the Exclusive Economic Zone: The Case of Aerial Surveillance," *Ocean Yearbook*, 17, 2003.

Shyam, Manjula R., "The U.N. Convention on the Law of the Sea and Military Interests in the Indian Ocean," *Ocean Development & International Law*, 15, no. 2 (1985).

Simmons, Beth A., "Capacity, Commitment, and Compliance: International Institutions and Territorial Disputes," *Journal of Conflict Resolution*, 46, no. 6 (2002).

Sison III, Maximo Paulino T., "Universalizing the Law of the Sea in the South China Sea Dispute," *Ocean Development and International Law*, 49, no. 2 (2018).

Slaughter, Anne-Marie, "International Law and International Relations Theory: A Dual Agenda," *American Journal of International Law*, 87 (1993).

Snyder, Craig A., "Building Multilateral Security Cooperation in the South China Sea," *Asian Perspective*, 21, no. 1 (Spring-Summer 1997).

Snyder, Jack, "One World, Rival Theories," *Foreign Policy*, no. 145 (November/December 2004).

Soltvedt, Ida Folkestad, "Soft Law, Solid Implementation? The Influence of Precision, Monitoring and Stakeholder Involvement on Norwegian Implementation of Arctic Council Recommendations," *Arctic Review on Law and Politics*, 8 (2017).

Song, Yann-huei, "Declarations and Statements with Respect to the 1982 UNCLOS: Potential Legal Disputes between the United States and China after U.S. Accession to the Convention," *Ocean Development & International Law,* 36 (2005).

Song, Yann-huei, "The PRC's Peacetime Military Activities in Taiwan's EEZ—A Question of Legality," *International Journal of Marine and Coastal Law*, 16 (2001).

Song, Yann-Huei, and Zou Keyuan, Maritime Legislation of Mainland China and Taiwan: Developments, Comparison, Implications, and Potential Challenges for the United States, *Ocean Development and International Law*, 31 (2000).

Steinberg, Richard H., and Jonathan M. Zasloff, "Power and International Law," *American Journal of International Law*, 100, no. 64 (2006).

SU, Jinyuan, "The East China Sea Air Defense Identification Zone and International Law," *Chinese Journal of International Law*, 2015.

Sun, Kuan-Ming, Policy of the Republic of China Toward the South China Sea, *Marine Policy*, Vol. 19 (1995).

Swaine, Michael D., "Chinese Views on the South China Sea Arbitration Case between the People's Republic of China and the Philippines," *China Leadership Monitor*, no. 51.

Swaine, Michael D., and M. Taylor Fraveh, "China's Assertive Behavior—Part Two: The Maritime Periphery," *China Leadership Monitor*, no. 35 (2011).

Tammen, Ronald L., and Jacek Kugler, "Power Transition and China–US Conflicts," *Chinese Journal of International Politics*, 1, (2006).

Tanaka, Yoshifumi, "The Legal Consequences of Obligations *Erga Omnes* in International Law," *Netherlands International Law Review* (published online: March 2021).

Tang, Shiping, "Offence-Defence Theory: Toward a Definitive Understanding," *Chinese Journal of International Politics,* 3, no. 2 (2010).

Tiqiang, Chen, "The People's Republic of China and Public International Law," *Dalhousie Law journal,* 8 (1984).

Tkacik, Michael, "Understanding China's goals and strategy in the South China Sea: bringing context to a revisionist systemic challenge-intentions and impact," *Defense & Security Analysis*, 34, no. 4 (2018).

Ton, Anh Duc, "Innocent Passage of Warships International Law and the Practice of East Asian Littoral States," *Asia-Pacific Journal of Ocean Law and Policy*, 1 (2016).

Vagts, Alfred, and Detlev F. Vagts, "The Balance of Power in International Law: A History of an Idea," *The American Journal of International Law,* 73 (1979).

Vagts, Detlev F., "Hegemonic International Law," *American Journal of International Law*, 95 (2001).

Valencia, Mark J., and Kazumine Akimoto, "Guidelines for navigation and overflight in the exclusive economic zone," *Marine Policy*, 30 (2006).

Van Dyke, Jon M., "Military Ships and Planes Operating in the Exclusive Economic Zone of Another Country," *Marine Policy*, 28 (2004).

Walt, Stephen M., "International Relations: One World, Many Theories," *Foreign Policy*, no. 110 (Spring 1998).

Wang, Jiangyu, "Legitimacy, Jurisdiction and Merits in the South China Sea Arbitration: Chinese Perspectives and International Law," *Journal of Chinese Political Science*, 22, no. 2 (2017).

Wang, Kuan-Hsiung, "The ROC's Maritime Claims and Practices with Special Reference to the South China Sea," *Ocean Development & International Law*, 41, no. 3 (2010).

Wang, Kuan-Hsiung, Peaceful Settlement of Disputes in the South China Sea through Fisheries Resources Cooperation and Management, *Maryland Series in Contemporary Asian Studies*, 2015, no. 3 (2015).

Wang, Tieya, "International Law in China: Historical and Contemporary Perspectives," *Recueil des Cours* (1990–II).

Wang, Yi, "China: a Staunch Defender and Builder of the International Rule of Law," *Chinese Journal of International Law*, 13 (2014).

Ward, Adam, "China and America: Trouble Ahead?" *Survival*, 45, no. 3 (2003).

Weil, P., "Toward Relative Normativity in International Law?" *American Journal of International Law*, 76 (1983).

Wendt, Alexander, "Anarchy is what states make of it: the social construction of power politics," *International Organization*, 46, no. 2 (Spring 1992).

Wendt, Alexander, "Constructing international Politics," *International Security*, 20, no. 1 (Summer 1995).

Wong, Bailey, "Understanding the Potential for Conflict in the South China Sea," *Clocks and Clouds*, 7, no. 1 (2016).

Wu, Hsin, "A Criticism of Bourgeois International Law on the Question of State Territory," *People's China and International Law*, 1 (1974).

Xiaofeng, Ren, and Cheng Xizhong, "A Chinese Perspective," *Marine Policy*, 29 (2005).

Yee, Sienho, "Agora: Military Activities in the EEZ," *Chinese Journal of International Law*, 9 (2010).

Yoo, John, "Embracing the Machines: Rationalist War and New Weapons Technologies," *California Law Review*, 105 (2017).

Yoo, John, "Rational Treaties: Article II, Congressional-Executive Agreements, and International Bargaining," *Cornell Law Review*, 97 (2011).

Yoroc, Haydee B., "The Philippine Claim to the Spratly Islands Group," *Philippine Law Journal*, 58, no. 2 (1983).

Yu, Mincai, "China Being a Maritime Power under the UNCLOS: Issues and Way Ahead," *Journal of East Asia and International Law*, 7 (2014).

Yu, Steven K. T., "Who Owns the Paracels and Spratlys? – An Evaluation of the Nature and Legal Basis of the Conflicting Territorial Claims," *Chinese Yearbook of International Law and Affairs*, 9 (1989).

Yuan, Paul C., "China's Challenge to Traditional International Law: An Exposition and Analysis of Chinese Views and Behavior in International Law and Politics," *Dalhousie Law Journal*, 10, no. 3 (1987).

Yuan, Paul C., "The United Nations Convention on the Law of the Sea from a Chinese Perspective," *Texas International Law Journal*, 19, no. 2 (Spring 1984).

Yue, Zhao, A Preliminary Criticism of Bourgeois International Law, *Journal of International Studies*, 3 (1959).

Zangl, Bernhard, Achim Helmedach, Aletta Mondré, Alexander Kocks, Gerald Neubauer and Kerstin Blome, "Between Law and Politics: Explaining International Dispute Settlement Behavior" *European Journal of International Relations*, 18, no. 2 (2011).

Zeng, Jinghan, Yuefan Xiao, and Shaun Breslin, "Securing China's core interests: the state of the debate in China," *International Affairs*, 91, no. 2 (2015).

Zhang, Haiwen, "Is it safeguading the freedom of navigation or maritime hegemony of the United States? – Comments on Raul (Pete) Pedrozo's article on military acitivities in the EEZ," *Chinese Journal of International Law*, 9, no. 1 (2010).

Zhang, Wenmu, "Sea Power and China's Strategic Choices," *China Security*, 2, no. 2 (2006).

Zhao, Tingyang, "A Political World Philosophy in Terms of All-under-heaven (Tianxia)," *Sage Journal*, 56, no. 5 (2009).

Zhu, Lu, Anthea Roberts' Is International Law International? (Book Review), *Chinese Journal of International Law*, 18, no. 4 (2019).

Zou, Keyuan, "Historic rights in international law and in China's practice," *Ocean Development & International Law*, 32, no. 2 (2001).

Zou, Keyuan, "Law of the Sea Issues Between the United States and East Asian States," *Ocean Development & International Law*, 39, no. 1 (2008).

Asian States, "Peaceful Use of the Sea and Military Intelligence Gathering in the EEZ," *Asian Yearbook of International Law*, 22 (2016).

Asian States, "Sino-Vietnamese Agreement on the Maritime Boundary Delimitation in the Gulf of Tonkin," *Ocean Development of International Law*, 36 (2005).

Zuo, Anlei, "China's Approaches to the Western-dominated International Law: A Historical Perspective from the Opium War to the South China Sea Arbitration Case," *University of Baltimore Journal of International Law*, 6, no. 1 (2018).

Other Electronic Sources

Ali, Idrees, and Matt Spetalnick, "U.S. Warship Challenges China's Claims in South China Sea," Reuters, October 21, 2016, at https://www.reuters.com/article/us-southchinasea-usa-exclusive/u-s-warship-challenges-chinas-claims-in-south-china-sea-idUSKCN12L1O9.

Anand, Kripa, China-led RCEP to change global order?, *Observer Research Foundation*, April 27, 2021, at https://www.orfonline.org/expert-speak/china-led-rcep-to-change-global-order/.

ASEAN becomes China's leargest trading partner, *Global Times*, March 7, 2020, at https://www.globaltimes.cn/content/1181864.shtml.

Asia Maritime Transparency Initiative, Center for Strategic and International Studies, at http://amti.csis.org/category/south-china-sea/.

Asia Maritime Transparency Initiative, China's New Spratly Island Defenses, December 15, 2016, at https://amti.csis.org/chinas-new-spratly-island-defenses/.

Asia Maritime Transparency Initiative, Reading Between the Lines: the Next Spratly Legal Dispute, March 21, 2019, at https://amti.csis.org/reading-between-lines-next-spratly-dispute/.

Asian Maritime Transparency Initiative, A Constructive Year for Chinese Base Building, December 14, 2017, at https://amti.csis.org/constructive-year-chinese-building/.

Australian Department of Foreign Affairs and Trade, Australia Supports Peaceful Dispute Resolution in the South China Sea, July 12, 2016, at https://www.dfat.gov.au/news/news/Pages/australia-supports-peaceful-dispute-resolution-in-the-south-china-sea.

Bandow, Doug Look Out, Asia: China's Peaceful Rise Is Over, *National Interest*, 18 July 2016, at https://nationalinterest.org/blog/the-skeptics/look-out-asia-chinas-peaceful-rise-over-17026.

Beech, Hannah, "U.S. Warships Enter Disputed Waters of South China Sea as Tensions With China Escalate," *New York Times*, April 21, 2020, at https://www.nytimes.com/2020/04/21/world/asia/coronavirus-south-china-sea-warships.html.

Bell, Larry, China's Rare Earth Metals Monopoly Needn't Put an Electronics Stranglehold on America, *Forbes*, April 15, 2012, at https://www.forbes.com/sites/larrybell/2012/04/15/chinas-rare-earth-metals-monopoly-neednt-put-an-electronics-stranglehold-on-america/#251a089b2d6d.

Bonnet, Francois-Xavier, "Geopolitics of Scarborough Shoal," Research Institute on Contemporary Southeast Asia, (IRASEC) Discussion Paper No. 14 (November 2012), at www.irasec.com/ouvrage34.

Carlson, Allen R., "Why Chinese Nationalism Could Impact the East and South China Seas VERY Differently," *The National Interest*, September 24, 2015, at https://nationalinterest.org/feature/why-chinese-nationalism-could-impact-the-east-south-china-13922.

Carpio, Antonio, *The South China Sea Dispute: Philippine Sovereign Rights and Jurisdiction in the West Philippine Sea* (2017), at https://www.imoa.ph/downloads/.

CCTV, China calls arbitral court "mouthpiece" for certain groups, July 5, 2016 at http://english.cctv.com/2016/07/05/VIDEVHUV2clDFs3O5QGWRmad160705.shtml.

CEBR, World Economic League Table: a world economic league table with forecase for 193 countries to 2035, December 2020, 12th edition, at https://cebr.com/wp-content/uploads/2020/12/WELT-2021-final-23.12.pdf.

Central Intelligence Agency, The World Factbook, at https://www.cia.gov/library/publications/the-world-factbook/geos/ch.html.

Chellaney, Brahma, China's Debt-Trap Diplomacy, *The Hill*, May 2, 2021, at https://thehill.com/opinion/international/551337-chinas-debt-trap-diplomacy.

Cheng, Dean, China's War against International law in the South China Sea, *National Interest*, May 19, 2015, at http://nationalinterest.org/feature/chinas-war-against-international-law-the-south-china-sea-12913?page=show.

China Increasingly Reliant on Oil Imports—IEA, *China Daily*, November 19, 2008, at http://www.china.org.cn/environment/news/2008-11/19/content_16790574.htm.

China, "Statement of the Ministry of Foreign Affairs of the People's Republic of China on the Award of 12 July 2016 of the Arbitral Tribunal in the South China Sea Arbitration Established at the Request of the Republic of the Philippines," at https://www.fmprc.gov.cn/nanhai/eng/snhwtlcwj_1/t1379492.htm.

China, Note Verbale No. CML/17/2009, May 7, 2009), at www.un.org/depts/los/clcs_new/submissions_files/mysvnm33_09/chn_2009re_mys_vnm_e.pdf.

China's declaration of August 25, 2006, made after its ratification of UNCLOS, at http://www.un.org/Depts/los/convention_agreements/convention_declarations.htm#China%20after%20ratification.

China's Position Paper, paras.20–21 (emphasis added). http://www.fmprc.gov.cn/mfa_eng/zxxx_662805/t1217147.shtml.

Chink, Frank, Dark side of the Great Renewal: Chinese nationalism, *The Globe and Mail*, December 5, 2012, at https://www.theglobeandmail.com/opinion/dark-side-of-the-great-renewal-chinese-nationalism/article5973783/.

Classical Legal Theory, *The Oxford International Encyclopedia of Legal History*, online version: 2009.

Clinton, Hillary Rodham, Secretary of State, San Francisco Marriott Marquis, San Francisco, CA, Remarks on Innovation and American Leadership to the Commonwealth Club, October 15, 2010, at https://2009-2017.state.gov/secretary/20092013clinton/rm/2010/10/149542.htm.

Clinton, Hillary, "Speech of Hillary Rodham Clinton at National Convention Center, Hanoi, Vietnam," US Department of State, July 23, 2010, at https://2009-2017.state.gov/secretary/20092013clinton/rm/2010/07/145095.htm.

Cole, Bernard D., *China's quest for great power: ships, oil, and foreign policy* (Naval Institute Press, 2016).

Cooper, Helene, During Hagel Visit, China Showed its Military Might, and Its Frustrations, *The New York Times*, April 10, 2014.

CSIS, Defusing the South China Sea Disputes: A Regional Blueprint, A Report of the CSIS Expert Working Group on the South China Sea, CSIS, October 2018.

CSIS, How Much Trade Transits the South China Sea?, *China Power*, at https://chinapower.csis.org/much-trade-transits-south-china-sea/.

CSIS's Asia Maritime Transparency Initiative: Fiery Cross Reef, at https://amti.csis.org/fiery-cross-reef/.

Department of Foreign Affairs, Philippine Position on Bajo de Masinloc (Scarborough Shoal) and the Waters Within Its Vicinity, Official Gazette of the Republic of the Philippines, Apr. 28, 2012, available at http://www.gov.ph/2012/04/18/philippine-position-on-bajo-de-masinloc-and-the-waters-within-its-vicinity.

Embassy of the People's Republic of China in the Republic of the Philippines, Oil Companies of China, the Philippines and Vietnam signed Agreement on South China Sea Cooperation, March 15, 2005, at http://ph.china-embassy.org/eng/zt/nhwt/t187333.htm.

Eno, R, Legalism and Huang-Lao Thought, Indiana University, Early Chinese Thought [B/E/P374] (2010), at http://www.indiana.edu/~p374/Legalism.pdf.

Experts Call For Vietnam to Sue China in International Court Over South China Sea Incursions, October 9, 2019, *Radio Free Asia*, at https://www.rfa.org/english/news/vietnam/lawsuit-10092019152725.html/.

Find Out Which Countries are Taking Sides in the South China Sea, Asia Maritime Transparency Initiative (2016), at https://amti.csis.org/sides-in-south-china-sea/.

Fravel, M. Taylor, et. al., What Is the Future of the South China Sea? *Foreign Policy*, July 12, 2016, athttps://foreignpolicy.com/2016/07/12/what-is-the-future-of-the-south-china-sea/.

G7 Foreign Ministers' Meeting Joint Communiqué, Lucca, April 10–11, 2017, at www.esteri.it/mae/resource/doc/2017/04/g7_-_joint_communiqu_final.pdf.

Gomez, Jim, "Philippines: China Wanted to Restrict Foreign Forces at Sea," *AP News*, September 11, 2019, at https://apnews.com/article/72416e1ced064a7290c6687c206a92a0.

Guidelines for Navigation and Overflight in the Exclusive Economic Zone A Commentary, The Nippon Foundation, at https://nippon.zaidan.info/seikabutsu/2005/00817/mokuji.htm.

Hayton, Bill, "Beijing shifts strategy in South China Sea," *Nikkei Asian Review*, July 12, 2017, at https://asia.nikkei.com/Politics/Beijing-shifts-strategy-in-South-China-Sea2.

Heydarian, R. J., Asia: All Eyes on the Obama–Xi Summit, *Asia Maritime Transparency Initiative*, September 25, 2015, at https://amti.csis.org/asia-all-eyes-on-the-obama-xi-summit.

Heydarian, Richard Javad, "The Importance of Being China," January 12, 2020, *The National Interest*, at https://nationalinterest.org/feature/importance-being-china-112951.

Holland, Steve, and Mai Nguyen, "Trump offers to mediate on South China Sea," *Reuters*, November 12, 2017, at https://www.reuters.com/article/us-trump-asia-vietnam

/trump-offers-to-mediate-on-south-china-sea-idUSKBN1DC04H. https://www.mdbg.net/chindict/chindict.php?page=cedict; https://dictionary.cambridge.org/dictionary/english-chinese-simplified/sovereignty. https://www.un.org/Depts/los/LEGISLATIONANDTREATIES/PDFFILES/chn_1998_eez_act.pdf . https://www.un.org/Depts/los/LEGISLATIONANDTREATIES/PDFFILES/PHL_1978_Decree.pdf.

Indonesian Foreign Ministry, "Batam Hosts Workshop on Managing Potential Conflict in the South China Sea," at https://kemlu.go.id/portal/en/read/587/berita/batam-hosts-workshop-on-managing-potential-conflict-in-the-south-china-sea.

Johnson, Jesse, "In First, China Permanently Stations Search-and-Rescue Vessel in South China Sea's Spratly Chain," *Japan Times*, July 29, 2018.

Kai, Jin, Is China's 'Assertiveness' in the South China Sea All About Nationalism? The narrative of a nationalistic China obscures the real dynamics in the South China Sea, *The Diplomat*, April 11, 2016, at https://thediplomat.com/2016/04/is-chinas-assertiveness-in-the-south-china-sea-all-about-nationalism/.

Kirgis, Frederic L., "North Korea's Withdrawal from the Nuclear Nonproliferation Treaty," *American Society of International Law insights*, 8, no. 2 (January 24, 2003), at https://www.asil.org/insights/volume/8/issue/2/north-koreas-withdrawal-nuclear-nonproliferation-treaty.

Koh, Tommy T.B., President, Third U.N. Conference on the Law of the Sea, A Constitution for the Oceans (December 1982), at http://www.un.org/depts/los/convention_agreements/texts/koh_english.pdf.

Lampton, David, China and the US Must Get Their Strategic Relationship Right, *South China Morning Post*, June 8, 2015, at https://www.scmp.com/comment/insight-opinion/article/1818410/china-and-us-must-get-their-strategic-relationship-right.

Liu, Zhihua, Report: China's oil consumption to peak by 2025, *China Daily*, October 17, 2019, at https://www.chinadaily.com.cn/a/201910/17/WS5da81492a310cf3e35571149.html).

Macias, Amanda, China Is Quietly Conducting Electronic Warfare Tests in the South China Sea, *CNBC*, July 5, 2018.

Ministry of Foreign Affairs of PRC, China's Policies on Asia-Pacific Security Cooperation, January 11, 2017, at https://www.fmprc.gov.cn/mfa_eng/zxxx_662805/t1429771.shtml.

Ministry of Foreign Affairs of the People's Republic of China, "Historical Evidence To Support China's Sovereignty over Nansha Islands," November 17, 2000, at https://www.fmprc.gov.cn/mfa_eng/topics_665678/3754_666060/t19231.shtml).

Ministry of Foreign Affairs of the People's Republic of China, "Its Origin," November 17, 2000, at https://www.fmprc.gov.cn/mfa_eng/topics_665678/3754_666060/t19233.shtml.

Ministry of Foreign Affairs of the PRC, The Five Principles of Peaceful Coexistence - The time-tested guideline of China's policy with neighbors, July 30, 2014.

Ministry of Foreign Affairs of the PRC, Veil of the Arbitral Tribunal Must Be Tore Down: Vice Foreign Minister Liu Zhenmin Answers Journalists' Questions on the So-called Binding Force of the Award Rendered by the Arbitral Tribunal of the South China Sea Arbitration Case, July 13, 2016, at https://www.fmprc.gov.cn/mfa_eng/wjbxw/t1381879.shtml.

Ministry of Foreign Affairs of the Russian Federation (2016), The Declaration of the Russian Federation and the People's Republic of China on the Promotion of International Law, June 25, 2016, at http://www.mid.ru/en/foreign_policy/position_word_order/-/asset_publisher/6S4RuXfeYlKr/content/id/2331698.19.

Ministry of Foreign Affairs, China, "Position Paper of the Government of the People's Republic of China on the Matter of Jurisdiction in the South China Sea Arbitration Initiated by the Republic of the Philippines," December 7, 2014, at http://www.fmprc.gov.cn/mfa_eng/zxxx_662805/t1217147.shtml.

Ministry of Foreign Affairs, PRC, Statement of the Government of the People's Republic of China on China's territorial sovereignty and maritime rights and interests in the South China Sea, July 12, 2016, at https://www.fmprc.gov.cn/nanhai/eng/snhwtlcwj_1/t1379493.htm.

Noh, K. J., Making a Mockery of International Law: the Arbitral Tribunal on the South China Sea Prepares the Way for War, (July 19, 2016), at http://www.counterpunch.org/2016/07/19/making-a-mockery-of-international-law-the-arbitral-tribunalon-the-south-china-sea-prepares-the-way-for-war/.

Oxford Economics for the US-China Business Council, Understanding the US-China Trade Relationship, January 2017, at www.uschina.org/reports/understanding-us-china-trade-relationship.

Page, Jeremy, China's Submarines Add Nuclear-Strike Capability, Altering Strategic Balance, *Wall Street Journal*, October 24, 2014, at https://www.wsj.com/articles/chinas-submarine-fleet-adds-nuclear-strike-capability-altering-strategic-balance-undersea-1414164738.

People's Daily, OP-ED: South China Sea Arbitration Abuses International Law, Threatens World Order, June 29, 2016, at http://en.people.cn/n3/2016/0629/c90000-9078797.html.

Perlez, Jane, and Steven Lee Myers, 'A Game of Chicken': U.S. and China Are Risking a Clash at Sea, *New York Times*, November 8, 2018, at https://www.nytimes.com/2018/11/08/world/asia/south-china-sea-risks.html.

Perlez, Jane, China Creates a World Bank of Its Own, and the U.S. Balks, *New York Times*, December 4, 2015, at https://www.nytimes.com/2015/12/05/business/international/china-creates-an-asian-bank-as-the-us-stands-aloof.html.

Perlez, Jane, Xi Jinping Extends Power, China Braces for a New Cold War, *New York Times*, February 27, 2018, at https://www.nytimes.com/2018/02/27/world/asia/xi-jinping-china-new-cold-war.html.

Pickering, Heath, "Why Do States Mostly Obey International Law?" E-International Relatios, February 2014, at https://www.e-ir.info/2014/02/04/why-do-states-mostly-obey-international-law/.

Poling, Gregory B, "South China Sea Code of Conduct Still a Speck on the Horizon," *East Asia Forum*, September 6, 2018, at https://www.eastasiaforum.org/2018/09/06/south-china-sea-code-of-conduct-still-a-speck-on-the-horizon/.

Pompeo, Michael R., US Position on Maritime Claims in the South China Sea, Press Statement, July 13, 2020, at https://2017-2021.state.gov/u-s-position-on-maritime-claims-in-the-south-china-sea/index.html.

Position Paper of the Government of the People's Republic of China on the Matter of Jurisdiction in the South China Sea Arbitration Initiated by the Republic of the Philippines, December 7, 2014, at https://www.fmprc.gov.cn/nanhai/eng/snhwtlcwj_1/t1368895.htm.

Power, John, and Catherine Wong, "Exclusive Details and Footage Emerge of Near Collision Between Warships in South China Sea," *South China Morning Post*, November 4, 2018, at https://www.scmp.com/week-asia/geopolitics/article/2171596/exclusive-details-and-footage-emerge-near-collision-between.

Radio Free Asia, U.S. Sends Note to UN Rebuking China's Claims in South China Sea, June 3, 2020.

Rajagopalan, Megha, and Nick Macfie, China Says More Than 40 Countries Support Its Stance on South China Sea, *Reuters*, May 20, 2016, at https://www.reuters.com/article/us-southchinasea-china-idUSKCN0YB1EO.

Reuters, US Destroyer Sails in Disputed South China Sea Amid Trade Talks, January 7, 2019, at https://www.reuters.com/article/us-usa-trade-china-southchinasea/u-s-navyship-sails-in-disputed-south-china-sea-amid-trade-talks-with-beijing-idUSKCN1P10DS.

Russett, Bruce, What Else Causes War?, *Boston Review*, at https://bostonreview.net/archives/BR22.5/russett.html#1.

Schmidt, Michael S., "Chinese Aircraft Fly Within 50 Feet of U.S. Plane Over South China Sea, Pentagon Says," *New York Times*, May 18, 2016.

Statement of the Chinese Foreign Ministry on the Award of 12 July 2016 of the SCS Tribunal established at the Request of the Republic of the Philippines, July 12, 2016, at http://www.fmprc.gov.cn/mfa_eng/zxxx_662805/t1379492.shtml.

Stefanie A. Lindquist and Frank C. Cross, Stability, Predictability and the Rule of Law: Stare Decisis As Reciprocity Norm, at https://law.utexas.edu/conferences/measuring/The%20Papers/Rule%20of%20Law%20Conference.crosslindquist.pdf.

Takahashi, Toru, What Beijing really wants from South China Sea code of conduct, *Nikkei Asian*, August 12, 2019, at https://asia.nikkei.com/Spotlight/Comment/What-Beijing-really-wants-from-South-China-Sea-code-of-conduct.

The Arctic Council: A Backgrounder, Arctic Council, at https://www.arctic-council.org/images/PDF_attachments/2015-07-03_Arctic_Council_Backgrounder_PRINT_VERSION_NO_LINKS.pdf.

The Regime of Exclusive Economic Zone: Issues and Responses, A Report of the Tokyo Meeting, 19–20 February 2003, Ship and Ocean Foundation and the East-West Center, 2003, p. 31, at https://www.eastwestcenter.org/system/tdf/private/EEZTokyoMeeting.pdf?file=1&type=node&id=31954.

Transcript of remarks by DOD Press Secretary Rear Admiral John Kirby at August 22, 2014, press briefing, at http://www.defense.gov/Transcripts/Transcript.aspx?TranscriptID=5493.

U.S. Department of Defense, "Freedom of Navigation Program Fact Sheet" (March 2015), at https://policy.defense.gov/Portals/11/Documents/gsa/cwmd/DoD%20FON%20Program%20--%20Fact%20Sheet% 20(March%202015).pdf.

U.S. Energy Information Administration, South China Sea, at https://www.eia.gov/international/analysis/regions-of-interest/South_China_Sea.

U.S. Navy, The Navy Unmanned Surface Vehicle (USV) Master Plan (2007), at http://www.navy.mil/navydata/technology/usvmppr.pdf.

US Department of State, Decision in the Philippines-China Arbitration, Press Statement, July 12, 2016, at https://2009-2017.state.gov/r/pa/prs/ps/2016/07/259587.htm

US Department of State, Limits in the Seas No. 127, Taiwan's Maritime Claims, November 15, 2005, at https://2009-2017.state.gov/documents/organization/57674.pdf.

US Suspicious of Beijing's Motive in South China Sea 'Code of Conduct,' *Radio Free Asia*, April 26, 2019, at https://www.rfa.org/english/news/china/malaysia-southchinasea-04262019163855.html.

Valencia, Mark J., "A South China Sea Code of Conduct? Don't Get Your Hopes Up," *The Diplomat*, May 30, 2017, at https://thediplomat.com/2017/05/a-south-china-sea-code-of-conduct-dont-get-your-hopes-up/.

Valencia, Mark J., "The South China Sea Brouhaha: Separating Substance from Atmospherics," *Policy Forum* 10–044, August 10, 2010.

Valencia, Mark J., "The US-China Maritime Surveillance Debate," *The Diplomat*, August 4, 2017.

VOA News, China Navy Chief Takes Dig at US Freedom of Navigation Patrols, April 23, 2019, at https://www.voanews.com/east-asia-pacific/china-navy-chief-takes-dig-us-freedom-navigation-patrols#:~:text=QINGDAO%2C%20CHINA%20%2D%20Freedom%20of%20navigation,disputed%20South%20China%20Sea%20islets.

Wang, Yaguang, and Mao Pengfei, World Insights: China, ASEAN open new chapter in common development, prosperity, *Xinhua*, July 19, 2021, at http://www.xinhuanet.com/english/asiapacific/2021-07/19/c_1310070503.htm.

Watts, Jake Maxwell, Bolton Warns China Against Limiting Free Passage in South China Sea, *Wall Street Journal*, November 13, 2018, at https://www.wsj.com/articles/bolton-warns-china-against-limiting-free-passage-in-south-china-sea-1542110191.

Williams, Robert D., International Law with Chinese Characteristics: Beijing and the "Rules-Based" Global Order, Brookings, October 2020, at https://www.brookings.edu/wp-content/uploads/2020/10/FP_20201012_international_law_china_williams.pdf.

Wong, Edward, China Hedges over Whether South China Sea Is a "Core Interest" Worth War, *The New York Times*, March 30, 2011.

Wong, Edward, Chinese Military Seeks to Extend its Naval Power, *New York Times*, April 23, 2010.

WU, Shicun, South China Sea: expect more instability in 2021 as the US encourages 'lawfare' and conflict, January 25, 2021, National Institute for South China Sea Studies, China, at http://en.nanhai.org.cn/index/research/paper_c/id/419.html.

Xi, Jinping, Full text of Xi Jinping's speech on the CCP's 100th anniversary, *Nikkei Asia*, July 1, 2021, at https://asia.nikkei.com/Politics/Full-text-of-Xi-Jinping-s-speech-on-the-CCP-s-100th-anniversary.

Xinhua News Agency, Law-abusing Tribunal Issues Ill-founded Award on South China Sea Arbitration, July 12, 2016, at http://news.xinhuanet.com/english/2016-07/12/c_135507651.htm.

Yan, Xuetong, China Can Thrive in the Trump Era, *New York Times*, January 25, 2017, at https://www.nytimes.com/2017/01/25/opinion/china-can-thrive-in-the-trump-era.html.

Yee, Lee Chyen, "Chinese Premier Li says talks on South China Sea code should end in three years," *Reuters*, November 12, 2018.

Ying, Fu, "Doubling Down? China and International Order(s)," China-US Focus, Munich Security Conference, February 13, 2016, at https://www.chinausfocus.com/foreign-policy/putting-the-orders-shift-in-perspective/.

Index